THE EVOLUTION OF A PROFESSION

THE EVOLUTION OF A PROFESSION

A Study of the Contribution
of Teachers' Associations
to the Development of School
Teaching as a Professional
Occupation

P. H. J. H. GOSDEN

BASIL BLACKWELL · OXFORD

© Basil Blackwell 1972

All Rights Reserved. No part of this publication may be reproduced, stored in a retrieval system, or transmitted, in any form or by any means, electronic, mechanical, photocopying, recording or otherwise, without the prior permission of Basil Blackwell & Mott Limited.

0 631 14050 6

Printed in Great Britain by
The Camelot Press Ltd., London and Southampton

Any professional occupation is generally held to possess certain attributes including a reasonable level of salaries, pensions, security of tenure, sound training and qualifications and some recognition by the community of the profession's right to influence the way in which the service it offers is administered.

The object of this book is to examine the contribution made by the teachers' associations towards the attainment of these characteristics.

SCHOOL BOARD OFFICES,

Victoria Street,

NOTTINGHAM, _Novr. 16th 1897,_

Dear Madam,

  I have pleasure in sending you below a Copy of the Terms of your Appointment. Kindly acknowledge receipt.

      Yours faithfully,

        W. J. ABEL,

          Clerk.

Miss M. Spray,
 (130 Radford Boulevard) 75 St. Annie's Road,
         Rotherham

Copy—Terms of Appointment by the NOTTINGHAM SCHOOL BOARD.

That the following Teacher be and is hereby appointed for the undermentioned School, at the Salary and from the date respectively stated below, and subject to the undermentioned Special Conditions :—

Name of School.	Name of Teacher.	Grade.	*Salary per Annum. £	Engagement to Date from.
Coventry Rd, Infants' Bulwell.	Minnie Spray	Senior	(To be open for consideration as usual annual revision of Salaries) £70 + 50/- per annum so long as engaged at Bulwell	When required.

*The Board's Salary Scale provides that Teachers shall not as a rule be eligible for an increase of Salary until they have completed at least 12 months' service, dating from 1st July.

Special Conditions.

1. This Engagement may be terminated by Two Months' Notice on either side, to expire at any time.

2. In the case of an Uncertificated Assistant, this engagement shall be subject to regular attendance at the Teachers' Certificate or Scholarship Classes, unless such attendance is specially excused by the School Management Committee.

3. Other Special Conditions as to payment of Bonuses to Assistant Teachers, Salary during absences, &c., will be found in the Code of Regulations, a copy of which is supplied to all Departments of the Board Schools.

200—9—97. W.

Teacher's letter of appointment from Nottingham School Board, 1897

EDUCATION  DEPARTMENT.

TEACHER'S CERTIFICATE.

THE LORDS OF THE COMMITTEE OF THE PRIVY COUNCIL ON EDUCATION

Hereby Certify That in the month of *June*, 1895 *Martha Fisher* having been a Student during two years in the *Darlington Training College* was examined for a Certificate and placed in the First Division of Candidates of the Second Year.

Also that the above-named Candidate served the required period of probation in the *Bradford, Whetley Lane Board* School.

This Certificate *qualifies* the Teacher to Superintend Pupil Teachers.

John Gorst
Vice-President.

Teacher's Certificate issued by the Committee of Council on Education, 1895

Acknowledgements

The preparation of this study has left me indebted to many. My thanks are due to officers of teachers' associations including the N.U.T., the N.A.S., the I.A.A.M., the A.A.M., the I.A.H.M., and the A.H.M. for help in answering queries and in tracing material. I would also like to thank the staffs of the Brotherton and Institute of Education libraries in this University and of the Department of Education and Science library who have shown great patience in meeting my frequent requests.

I am particularly grateful to Mrs. Vivienne Greenhalgh of the University Department of Education who has worked on this project as research assistant and who has made many valuable suggestions. Finally I would like to thank Mrs. Edith Brass for her skill and good humour in turning my manuscript into a typed draft.

University of Leeds   PETER GOSDEN
January, 1971

Contents

I INTRODUCTORY

1. The Growth of Teachers' Associations — 1

II SALARIES AND CONDITIONS OF SERVICE

2. Salaries in the Years before Burnham, 1902–1918 — 21
3. Salaries between the Wars — 45
4. Salaries since the Second World War — 60
5. Equal Pay — 102
6. Superannuation — 132
7. Security of Tenure, 1868–1939 — 154
8. Tenure and Conditions of Service since 1939 — 178

III TRAINING, REGISTRATION AND ADMINISTRATION

9. Training Elementary Teachers before 1914 — 194
10. Training Secondary Teachers before 1914 — 214
11. The Teachers' Registration Issue — 235
12. Training between the Wars — 266
13. Training and Supply since 1944 — 283
14. The Administration of the School System — 313

Bibliographical Note — 355

Index — 361

Abbreviations

S.I.C.   Schools Inquiry Commission.
              Chairman: Lord Taunton.

Cross Cssn.   Royal Commission to inquire into the working of the
              Elementary Education Acts in England and Wales.
              Chairman: R. A. Cross.

Bryce Cssn.   Royal Commission on Secondary Education.
              Chairman: J. Bryce.

P.R.O.   Public Record Office.

T.E.S.   *The Times Educational Supplement.*

I
The Growth of Teachers' Associations

Since the beginning of the nineteenth century there has been a steady increase in the number of persons following the occupation of teaching. Along with this increase in the number of teachers there has also been a proliferation of the varieties and forms of teaching which have been undertaken. The dual nature of this growth has been mirrored in the development of associations of teachers; these have expanded their membership, and sufficient separate organisations have emerged and flourished to represent the standpoints of the groups engaged in various forms of teaching. The nature of the occupation of teaching is itself very varied, the interests of those teaching in one sort of school or institution may often appear to be different from and even to conflict with those teaching in other circumstances. It should not therefore cause surprise to find the various teachers' organisations pressing different and even opposing views upon the government, the local authorities and the public generally, from time to time. Most of the main associations seem to have been founded at a time when the state had begun to show greater interest in that particular field of teaching in which their members were involved. This may be seen in the later emergence of organisations for secondary by comparison with those for elementary teachers.

The largest single group of teachers in the later nineteenth century were those working in public elementary schools and it is not surprising that these were the earliest to organise themselves effectively. Appropriately enough, the National Union of Elementary Teachers was founded in the same year as W. E. Forster's famous Education Act was passed, 1870. This was by no means the first association to be established among elementary school teachers but it was the first serious attempt to establish a national union on non-sectarian grounds. The elementary school system had been entirely organised on a denominational

Table 1.1. *Number of persons shown in the Census Returns for England and Wales as teachers*

Date	Male	Female	Total
1891	50,628	144,393	195,021
1901	58,675	171,670	230,345
1911	68,670	183,298	251,968
1921	68,855	187,352	256,407
1931	79,465	181,806	261,271
1951	119,270	182,409	301,679
1961	183,240	261,660	444,900

Table 1.2. *Number of teachers returned as employed in public elementary schools (1951 and 1961 primary and secondary modern schools) in the Annual Reports of the Education Department or the Board or Ministry of Education*

Date	Number of teachers
1891	105,143
1901	149,804
1911	164,271
1921	166,539
1931	171,490
1938	172,674
1951	179,115
1961	216,331

basis before 1870; the schools themselves were established by the different religious bodies with the aim of forwarding—or at least maintaining—the position of the particular denomination. The government inspectorate was recruited and organised on a similar denominational basis. It is not surprising, therefore, that the earlier associations of teachers were also denominational and quite often patronised by the denominational society or its leading members. The British Teachers' Quarterly Association—or British Society of Teachers as it was commonly known—received some assistance from the British and Foreign Schools Society such as free use of accommodation for meetings. Among teachers working in the National Society's Schools, associations tended to grow up based upon units of Church organisation such as the diocese or the deanery, sometimes with clergy as members and possibly with the bishop of the diocese as patron.

The Growth of Teachers' Associations

The pattern of development followed by teachers' organisations during the middle years of the nineteenth century seems to have been largely conditioned by the policies followed by the Committee of Council for Education. The tremendous impetus which the Minutes of 1846 gave to training teachers both under the pupil-teacher apprenticeship system and in training colleges did much to encourage elementary school teachers to think of themselves increasingly as members of a profession with skills and interests of their own which were not necessarily shared by such other groups as the clergy. Some idea of the reaction of the more alert and perceptive churchmen to the spread of these ideas among teachers may be gained from these remarks of Dr. Frederick Temple who, when asked before the Newcastle Commission whether he thought it a good thing to train schoolmasters in a separate college or whether this was open to the same objection as training clergy in isolation, said that 'the profession of schoolmaster is something so very much more definite than that of clergymen, that the evil of training them separately is very much lessened. I think that it is a better system than any other which you would devise.' He felt that the drawback was that it gave them 'too exalted a notion of their own position and of what they have to do and that they gradually acquire a sort of belief that the work of a schoolmaster is the one great work of the day and that they are the men to do it'.[1]

Nationally recognised training and qualifications led to the appearance of non-local associations of teachers—although still denominational. The General Associated Body of Church Schoolmasters in England and Wales held its first Annual Meeting in 1853. The findings of the Newcastle Commission and the Revised Code of 1862 constituted an attack upon the position which elementary teachers thought they had secured and it led to further efforts to bring teachers together in organisations which crossed denominational boundaries. These efforts remained largely unsuccessful to begin with, but by the end of the decade, common problems, common qualifications and common aspirations were at least sufficient to lead to the establishment of some local non-denominational groupings. Early in 1870 two proposals for non-denominational and national organisations were suggested. One of these originated with the London associations connected with the British and Foreign, Wesleyan and Church teachers respectively, the other came from the Associated Body of Church Schoolmasters. In June, 1870, a meeting of teachers was held at King's College, London, and agreed to accept resolutions on the lines of the proposals put forward. The first conference of the National Union of Elementary Teachers took place in the following September and in a document issued subsequently the objects of the new Union were set out: 'to unite together, by means of local associations, public elementary teachers throughout the Kingdom, in order to provide a machinery by means of which teachers may give expression to their opinions when occasion requires, and may also take united action in any matter affecting their interests.' That it was a non-sectarian body pledged to pursue purely professional and educational ends was made clear by the President in 1872. 'It is just in proportion to the breadth of the platform on which we meet that our strength consists, and our influence is felt. We don't meet here as *Church* teachers, *British* teachers, *Wesleyan* teachers, or *Catholic* teachers, but simply as TEACHERS; and so long as we continue to drop these distinctive peculiarities, we shall be able to show an undivided front, and become an undaunted power for the advancement of our professional interests and aims.'[2]

The central organisation set up by the new Union consisted of a Standing Committee whose members were drawn from the local associations of London teachers along with the secretaries of other local associations. The main unit of organisation was the local association; and such associations could be formed in a district by any five elementary teachers. By the time the annual conference met in 1871 there were forty-eight local associations of the Union with more than 2,000 members in all.

The interests of education and the interests of teachers have always been viewed by the Union as very closely related, to forward the one has often led to an improvement in the other. In his work on *The School Teachers*, Asher Tropp listed nine basic aims which the N.U.E.T. sought to achieve from the beginning:[3]

1. Control of entrance to the profession and teachers' registration.
2. The recruitment of teachers to the Inspectorate.
3. The gaining of a right of appeal.
4. Superannuation.
5. The revision of the education code.
6. The gaining of security of tenure.
7. Freedom from compulsory extraneous duties.
8. Adequate salaries.
9. Freedom from 'obnoxious' interference.

Most of these aims have been achieved in course of time, mainly through bringing pressure to bear on the state. Elementary education was a service whose provision was enforced by the state even if the state did not bear the whole of its cost; it is not surprising, therefore, to find that the Union has exerted its influence with most success in the political field. From the earliest days the Union worked through deputations and memorials to the Education Department in Whitehall and to Parliament. Later on the Union secured representation in the Commons. In 1886 it first managed to get a teacher candidate adopted by one of the parties but in the actual election he was defeated. It first met with success in this matter in 1895 when two of its supported candidates were actually elected, Ernest Gray for West Ham (North) and James Yoxall for Nottingham (West); party political neutrality was maintained for the successful candidates bore the colours of opposing parties.[4] Even after securing the return of its own teacher representatives to Westminster, the Union continued the policy which had served it well hitherto of interviewing rival candidates before elections and soliciting their support for the reforms which it was seeking. Similar tactics were employed to influence the larger school boards; candidates were 'interviewed' before elections and teacher-representatives were actually put forward for election—although after 1875 these could not be elementary school teachers still in service and tended to be drawn from teachers in private schools or from among former teachers. The Report from the Select Committee of the Commons on School Board Elections gave some indication of the way in which the N.U.E.T. had come to build up its influence in the large cities by canvassing and generally supporting favoured candidates for the boards and by opposing others. The system of cumulative voting employed in electing school boards tended to give great weight to minority groups in the electorate and the teachers certainly showed that they knew how to make full use of their influence here.

From the early years of its existence, therefore, the National Union of Teachers—as it was called from 1889 when it dropped Elementary from its title—has made full use of the ways open to sectional groupings under democratic forms of central and local government to bring pressure to bear on the authorities. It has continued to maintain a flow of teacher representatives in the House of Commons and has established a relationship with the Department of Education and Science which ensures that it will be consulted on matters of major concern to the schools and teachers. Since the abolition of directly elected school boards in 1902, the Union and its local associations have developed working relationships with the multi-purpose county and county-borough authorities, many of which co-opt teachers who are N.U.T. members to their education committees.

The Union has made considerable efforts to make itself the professional organisation for all teachers, regardless of the type of school in which they serve. In order to attract and accommodate the various groups of teachers with special interests within its ranks, it has from time to time established machinery to meet these needs as when it set up a secondary schools committee in 1909 when local authorities were establishing numerous municipal secondary schools. But in spite of these efforts it has not succeeded in preventing particular groups of teachers even within the elementary field from breaking away and establishing their separate associations, the National Association of Schoolmasters and the National Union of Women Teachers being two examples of these. It has also never succeeded in persuading the secondary teachers to abandon their separate associations. Thus today the National Union of Teachers is by far the largest of the teachers' associations but it does not by any means occupy the whole field. Approximately two-thirds of its members are women.

Table 1.3. *Membership of the National Union of Teachers*[5]

Date	Number of Members
1891	18,072
1901	45,154
1911	72,400
1921	115,577
1931	142,772
1938	155,282
1951	189,717
1961	237,964
1969	294,567

The association of teachers which contrasts most strongly with the N.U.T. in both size and methods of influencing public policy is the Headmasters' Conference. This small association, limited even today to fewer than two hundred heads of leading secondary schools, was founded in 1869, the immediate cause of its foundation being the attempts made by the state in the 1860s to introduce a greater measure of order and efficiency into secondary education. The government had received reports from two commissions of inquiry, one confined to the seven great public schools and the other which looked at about 800 other endowed schools. It brought forward separate legislation to deal with the seven (the Public Schools Act, 1868) and the rest (the Endowed Schools Act, 1869). Many headmasters were considerably annoyed that for purposes of inquiry and legislation a lot of the leading public schools had been classified with the whole range of miscellaneous endowments while a few schools had been favoured by being accorded separate treatment. E. W. Benson, headmaster of Wellington College, wrote to Dr. Temple who was supporting the Endowed Schools Bill: 'You think our connexion will not be weakened by severance from the category of Public Schools and union with decayed grammar schools, consolidated doles of parish bread and hitherto scholarless school houses. Half our boys are brothers of Eton, Harrow, Winchester, Rugby boys—and they will mind it—and their parents will. . . .'[6] Early in 1869 there was correspondence among headmasters of a number of public schools about organising a deputation to meet Forster, then Vice-President of the Council, about the proposed measure and a number of them did in fact meet at the Freemasons Tavern in London where they discussed the Endowed Schools Bill, framed resolutions and organised a deputation to go to see the Vice-President. Much of the initiative for this meeting seems to have been taken by J. Mitchinson, headmaster of the King's School, Canterbury, but one of the leading headmasters present was Edward Thring of Uppingham. The latter proposed that those attending should meet regularly and invited them to meet at Uppingham the following December. In the autumn he sent invitations to the two dozen or so who had been present at the meeting in London and to a number of other headmasters. The question of the relationship with the seven schools officially 'public' was resolved by sending their heads invitations to join. According to Thring in his opening address to the conference, the main object of the gathering would be to put forward with one voice 'pronounced opinion from the most important profession in England'.[7]

In its early years the Conference was much concerned with the connected questions of training teachers for work in secondary schools and the registration of teachers. Mrs. Sydney Webb seems to have been somewhat less than objective when in her review of teachers' organisations in 1915 she passed rapidly over the Conference as of little importance and 'of minor interest' with 'its private discussions of the domestic problems of boys' boarding schools; its public deliberations on such issues as the relation of the public school curriculum to the requirements of the Universities of Oxford and Cambridge, of the War Office, of the Admiralty, and of the Civil Service Commission, the sphere of athletics and of the cadet corps, or the rival claims of Greek and Science and the place of Bible teaching and religious services in the school life of the rich man's child'.[8] Quite apart from the enormous influence Conference schools exerted by way of example followed by the municipal secondary schools as well as by the smaller endowed grammar schools in the present century, the immediate cause of its foundation—proposed action by the state in the field of secondary schooling—has provided a topic to which the Conference and its members have returned time and again. It would be useless for so small a body to attempt to influence the government of the day by seeking to bring mass electoral pressure in the ways that the N.U.T. can use successfully, but it has certainly succeeded in influencing policy in other ways, by submitting memoranda, by argument and by personal contacts with officials of the Board and later Ministry of Education and H.M.I.s.

The organisation of the H.M.C. is naturally not complicated, the main features being a committee and an annual meeting of members. The eligibility of a headmaster to become a member is decided by the committee and the Conference on the basis of such considerations as the academic standing of a school as measured by such factors as the proportion of boys going on to the universities, the amount of independence enjoyed by the governing body of the school and the standing of the individual headmaster among his peers.

Most of the members of the Conference are also members of the rather larger Incorporated Association of Head Masters. This Association now consists pre-eminently of the heads of grammar and public schools along with the headmasters of numerous comprehensive and modern schools. As with other organisations, the immediate cause of foundation seems to have been in some measure due to a feeling of a mutual need among headmasters of local endowed grammar schools to make their voices heard by the government and local authorities in view of the situation created by the passing of the Technical Instruction Act and the creation of Technical Instruction Committees in counties and boroughs. The arrival of the new committees with power to grant aid to existing secondary as well as technical schools naturally had the effect of causing headmasters of the existing endowed schools to seek an effective medium for pressing their views. In its early years this association was concerned with such problems as the interpretation and application of trust deeds, relationships between headmasters and governing bodies, the conditions of service and salaries of assistant masters. From 1902 the I.A.H.M. became increasingly concerned to uphold the supremacy of the headmaster in his own school and to ensure that the new local education authorities did not interfere with the internal administration; in this respect the association was supported by the Board of Education under Morant. The concept of the grammar school held by members, both those who were heads of endowed grammar schools and those who became heads of the new county secondary schools, was really derived from the ethos and practices of the public schools and it is interesting to notice that from 1898 until 1924 the presidents of the I.A.H.M. were members of the H.M.C.[9] Although a good deal larger than the H.M.C., the Association cannot of its nature ever be a mass organisation, by 1910 it had 496 members, in 1960 1,263 and by 1968 1,586 ordinary members.[10]

Up to the middle years of the nineteenth century the headmasters of most endowed grammar schools were usually clerics; the schools were generally small with only one or two assistants. In these circumstances an assistant mastership was often regarded not so much as a career in itself as a preliminary stage to having a school of one's own. The obvious analogy being that of the curate who might expect in due course to obtain a living of his own. The reorganisation and growth of the grammar schools which sprang from the activities of the endowed schools commissioners after 1868 brought with it a considerable increase in the number of assistant masters and a much more consciously professional attitude towards the work. This consciousness of being a segment of the teaching profession with distinctive interests which needed a permanent form of organisation to represent it led to the formation of the Assistant Masters' Association in 1891. The catalyst proved to be an inquiry by a Parliamentary Select Committee which had been appointed by the Commons in 1891 to report on two rival bills for the formation of a register of teachers. This brought home to assistant masters in secondary schools the fact that they were the only section of the educational world which had made no attempt to form an association to represent its views.[11]

The objects of the Association were outlined in its rules as—

'A. To form a body which shall protect and further the interests of assistant masters in secondary schools: (a) by obtaining for teachers in secondary schools the status and authority of a learned profession, (b)

by securing a high standard of qualification for registration, (c) by making the employment of non-registered teachers in secondary schools illegal, (d) by securing the abolition of the present system of "dismissal at pleasure", (e) by making an audited and detailed financial return compulsory on all schools aided by public money, (f) by doing all such other lawful things as may conduce to the welfare of assistant masters and the advantage of education.
B. To establish a Legal Fund.
C. To establish a Provident Fund.
D. To establish an improved Agency System.'[12]

Security of tenure was probably the most perplexing and worrying single issue that confronted assistant masters. Just as an incumbent in a parish living might employ curates to assist him so, the custom was, headmasters might employ assistants on similar conditions, generally dismissable at pleasure. It was even held in some schools that the engagements of assistant masters were *ipso facto* terminated by the resignation of the headmaster. One of the earliest successes of the Association was to challenge successfully, in 1898, the governors of the endowed grammar school at Grantham when they followed this custom.

The establishment of county secondary schools after the Education Act of 1902 led to a large increase in the number of assistant masters eligible for membership and of actual members and to the beginnings of a change in the main preoccupations of the Association. The relationship between the masters and their employers became increasingly a matter of the relationship between masters and a public authority rather than between masters and headmasters or bodies of trustees. Negotiation of salary scales increased in relative importance, the negotiations being with individual counties and county boroughs until the end of the First World War when this process gave way to the negotiation of national scales.

From the beginning the headmistresses of girls' secondary schools and their assistants formed quite separate associations from those of their male counterparts. Soon after the foundation of the Headmasters' Conference, Miss Buss, the headmistress of the North London Collegiate School for Girls, invited headmistresses of other public secondary schools for girls to a meeting at her house in December, 1874. There were at that time very few secondary schools for girls in any modern meaning of that term; private venture boarding schools intent on imparting the veneer of culture or accomplishment remained the

Table 1.4. *Membership of the Incorporated Association of Assistant Masters*[13]

Date	Number of Members
1891	72
1901	1,593
1911	3,259
1921	6,752
1931	9,034
1938	10,921
1951	16,644
1961	26,000
1968	29,400

generally accepted form of education for the daughters of professional and middle-class families. Only three of the Girls' Public Day School Company schools had been opened and very few secondary schools for girls had been reconstituted out of endowments as yet. The Association of Head Mistresses was formed in these circumstances as a pioneering organisation with the aim of encouraging and cultivating a worthwhile education for girls. 'The first object Miss Buss had in drawing her friends thus together was to form in the women teachers of England a true professional spirit, a spirit informed by high ideas of work and character, holding that education involved much more than learning, and that future good should always be held of more importance than any immediate advantage. Miss Buss and Miss Beale (the Head of Cheltenham Ladies' College) stood out conspicuously as the great leaders, Miss Buss in her far-sighted wisdom and forethought, Miss Beale as an idealist and scholar. Both commanded the loving respect of all other heads, both were generously ready to help the weaker, less distinguished mistresses by their sympathy and counsel.'[14]

Unlike the Headmasters' Conference, the Headmistresses' Association did not attempt to become exclusive but expanded steadily as the number of girls' secondary schools grew; thus there was no need to found yet another organisation twenty years later for the 'other' heads as in the case of the men. Another marked difference was the concern shown by headmistresses that those women seeking to teach in their schools should not only be graduates but also that they should have received training in secondary teaching. Institutions to train women graduates for this work were established and training for graduate teachers in girls' schools became the general and accepted practice years before it became widely accepted in boys' schools.

The declared objects of the Association in the early years of the twentieth century were:

'To support and protect the status and interests of women in education generally and secondary education particularly . . .

To provide facilities for intercourse and exchange of ideas between Head Mistresses, Assistant Mistresses and Governors, Managers and other officers of schools and other educational institutions, parents or other persons engaged or interested in educational pursuits or subjects in regard to the same.

To consider all questions affecting the interests of the profession of education and to initiate and watch over, promote or oppose general or particular measures in Parliament or elsewhere affecting such profession, or the interests of persons engaged in the same, and to promote or procure changes of the law, or of the administration of the law relating to such profession, or to schools, colleges and other educational institutions and matters.' Membership of the A.H.M. increased from 13 members in 1874 to some 330 in 1911 and rose steadily to 964 by 1967.[15]

The inspiration for the foundation of the Association of Assistant Mistresses in Secondary Schools came from members of the Head Mistresses' Association, some of whom seem to have spread the idea among their staffs. Some of the staff of the North London Collegiate School, where Miss Buss was known to favour the formation of an Assistant Mistresses' Association, were particularly active in the moves leading to the foundation of the A.A.M. in 1884.[16] An inaugural meeting was held at Westminster on 15th January of that year, 180 assistant mistresses were present from all over the country and Mrs. Hankin of Edgbaston High School was elected president, the first secretary being Miss Ingall from Manchester High School. The objects of the Association were to be to discuss educational questions, to improve the position of teachers in regard to such matters as salaries and hours of work and to afford opportunities to mistresses to meet together socially.[17] A further meeting held in Birmingham in April, 1884, was attended by 372 mistresses from seventy-five schools. It was then resolved to organise the Association through a system of branches and five groups were formed, Yorkshire, Lancashire and Cheshire, Midland, South-Western and London and South Eastern. Foreign and colonial correspondents were appointed to obtain information concerning openings for teachers overseas and steps were taken to form a register of vacant posts to assist members in finding work at home.[18]

The first annual general meeting of the Association was held at the

North London Collegiate School in January, 1885, by invitation of Miss Buss. From its earliest years the Association was characterised by its attention to educational matters. The Presidential Address at this 1885 meeting for instance developed a number of points on the theme of the wise use of school holidays by pupils. The early Annual Reports record branch meetings on such questions as 'The Personality of the Teacher', 'On School Books' and 'The Vocation of Teaching', on which topic Miss Beale gave a paper. At the 1887 meeting the President pointed out that its usefulness and the need for such a society were shown alike in the benefits to members and to Head Mistresses, many of whom would, from time to time, be chosen from among its ranks; mistresses would benefit from the papers read at branch meetings, and 'fortified with this knowledge' they would better meet the difficulties that awaited them in their careers.[19]

The considerable endeavours made by members to improve their professional capacities must not be taken to indicate any lack of interest in such matters as salaries or tenure. In 1892 a joint committee on salaries was set up with the Head Mistresses and at the annual general meeting in the same year the President urged that 'Another way in which some of us can be public spirited would be to follow a suggestion that has been made by a Head Mistress, that, when applying for a Headship, we should, for the sake of future staff, be careful to inquire what sum of money will be set aside for salaries, and that, if the amount be as scandalously small as is frequently the case, we should refuse to entertain further negotiations for appointment. Were governing bodies to find, by constant refusals of this nature, that they could not meet with women willing to undersell themselves and their colleagues, they would be compelled to offer better terms.' The Association was also concerned to ensure that the rights of women were not overlooked in educational matters in the years before the franchise was extended to women. Annual Reports at the turn of the century indicate that the Association was pressing for representation for women on the consultative committee of the Board of Education and on any future education committees which might come to be established at the local level.

As with the Assistant Masters' Association, the Assistant Mistresses' Association was offered more scope with the provision of secondary school education for girls by counties and county boroughs after the Act of 1902. In the early years the bulk of the members taught in endowed high schools and the schools established by the Girls' Public Day School Company.

Table 1.5. *Membership of the Association of Assistant Mistresses*[20]

Date	Number of Members
1891	448
1901	636
1911	1,229
1921	5,157
1931	7,210
1938	8,946
1951	12,114
1961	17,233
1969	20,892

The I.A.H.M., A.H.M., I.A.A.M. and A.A.M. together form the Joint Four which represents them nationally on matters of common concern to all secondary teachers. In recent years local Joint Four organisations have also been established to represent the common views of members of these secondary associations to local authorities; they have, for example, been active in representing the views of secondary teachers on the reorganisation of modern and grammar schools into comprehensive units. On the other hand, in national salary negotiations representation is offered not to the Joint Four organisation but to each of the four associations separately; the I.A.H.M. and A.H.M. each has one representative on the Burnham Main Committee while the I.A.A.M. and the A.A.M. each have two.

The first permanent machinery for co-operative effort between these four associations was set up in 1906 when the Federal Council of Secondary School Associations was established. Historically there has been a contrast between the one principal and highly centralised organisation of elementary teachers and the diversified secondary associations where feeling in favour of merging into one organisation has never been strong enough to set aside hesitations over losing the opportunity to express views on questions particular to the different branches of the profession.

Teachers in technical institutions did not fit readily into either the N.U.T. or the secondary associations. Technical institutions developed rapidly in the last decade or so of the nineteenth century but those who taught in them were slow to organise, possibly because of their very diverse antecedents and their lack of common qualifications. The need for some organisation became more apparent after the Act of 1902 and the establishment of local education authorities which frequently co-opted representatives of the existing teachers' associations to membership of committees but on which the unorganised technical teachers tended to remain unrepresented. In October, 1904, a meeting of about two hundred teachers from technical institutions in the London area set up a committee to draft the rules for what was to become the Association of Teachers in Technical Institutions. The Association grew up as an amalgamation of district organisations, for instance, in 1905 the local West Riding of Yorkshire Association of Teachers of Science, Art and Technology applied for membership of the new London centred organisation and in the same year the Association of Teachers of Domestic Science affiliated with the A.T.T.I.[21]

The aims of the A.T.T.I. included the promotion and safeguarding of professional interests in such matters as tenure, salaries, pensions and registration, but they also included the 'interchange of ideas regarding methods of technical teaching', 'to lay the views of teachers in technical institutions before the educational authorities and the public' and the 'advancement of technical education generally'. According to the President in his address to the general meeting of 1907 in Leeds, 'The authorities view our Association with favour, though they are a little on their guard lest we should develop into a Technical Teachers Trade Union and become the T.T.T.U. instead of the A.T.T.I. They need have no fear, I think, as if such an unfortunate result should come about there would be inevitably a breaking-up of the Association—a catastrophe we should all deplore.'[22]

The growth of this Association has been largely governed by the growth of technical institutions. In 1911 it had about 1,100 members, in 1951 it had 4,625 while in 1961 the total had increased to 12,004.[23] For many years the Association had its offices at 29 Gordon Square with the secondary organisations. In the 1930s there were talks between all of the Gordon Square associations and the N.U.T. with the aim of creating a unified organisation. The only positive outcome of these discussions was that a joint scheme of membership between the A.T.T.I. and the N.U.T. was agreed upon in 1940. In due course the A.T.T.I. moved its secretariat to Hamilton House, the N.U.T. building. In 1959 the N.U.T. disbanded its committee on Further Education and agreed to the A.T.T.I. proposal that it should be accepted as the advisory authority on all aspects of this.[24]

The breakaway from the N.U.T. of two groups, the National Union of Women Teachers and the National Association of Schoolmasters, has had significant consequences during the present century. The N.U.W.T. had its origins in the feelings that produced various sectional organisations of women teachers between 1900 and 1914 with the aim of levelling up the woman's status 'to that of her male fellow-professionals and fellow citizens'.[25] Most of these organisations operated within the N.U.T. and sought to impress upon the Union their aims; among these were the National Federation of Women Teachers and the Women Teachers' Franchise Union. The N.U.W.T. broke away from the larger body in 1909 because at that time the N.U.T. would not accept the policy of equal pay for men and women. In 1919 the N.U.T. gave way on this issue but the separate union was a more effective medium for propaganda purposes and gained more notice in the press than might have been the case had they remained a protesting minority in the larger association. One of the rules adopted by the N.U.W.T. was that none of its members might also be a member of the N.U.T. The organisation was finally disbanded in 1960 after its battle had been won.

An early consequence of the acceptance by the N.U.T. of the aim of equal pay was the formation of the National Association of Schoolmasters whose members were determined to fight this principle. Men teachers formed societies of their own as pressure groups within the N.U.T. in some parts of London and in other localities such as Cardiff and Leeds. In the troubled years immediately after the war at the Cheltenham conference of the N.U.T. in 1919, a group of men teachers met together to form a National Association of Men Teachers. These were all active members of the N.U.T. and their aim was not to secede from it but to act as a pressure group to protect the interests of men within the Union. In 1920 they held their first annual meeting at the N.U.T. conference at Margate and changed their title to the National Association of Schoolmasters. In 1922 they broke away from the N.U.T. because of the preponderance of women members in the Union and the immediate aim of the new Association became to gather all men teachers together in one union and to reduce the N.U.T. to an organisation for women only. It saw the pattern of professional organisation among teachers as essentially federal so that there would be separate unions for the various sections of the teaching profession with a common council on which all organisations would have one vote and which could only act if all the members of organisations were in agreement; where such agreement was lacking each association would act on its own.

Table 1.6. Membership of the National Association of Schoolmasters[26]

Date	Number of Members
1940	8,629
1950	13,163
1960	22,651
1961	31,344
1962	31,887
1963	33,252
1964	35,457
1965	37,538
1966	38,895
1967	39,256
1968	39,967
1969	44,945
1970	50,000 (approx.)

As may be seen from table 1.6 the N.A.S. has made a good deal of headway in recent years and has now achieved representation on the Burnham Main Committee. It may be that many of its members have joined because of the dissatisfaction which they felt at the N.U.T.'s record on salary negotiations. There have been bitter feelings between the N.U.T. and the N.A.S. and members of the latter may not belong to the former. The membership secretary of the N.U.T. has estimated that the two organisations have spent £1¼ million on fighting each other since 1921.[27]

There are a number of other associations of teachers which engage in negotiations regarding salaries or conditions of employment, but none of them are very large. The largest is the National Association of Head Teachers with about 15,000 members drawn mainly from among heads of primary and secondary modern schools; most of the members also belong to the N.U.T. The N.A.H.T. does join with the H.M.C., I.A.H.M. and A.H.M. to form the Joint Council of Heads which meets three times a year at Gordon Square.

Other organisations which are represented on the Burnham Technical Committee include the Association of Principals of Technical Institutions, the National Society for Art Education and the National Federation of Class Teachers. The Association of Teachers in Colleges and Departments of Education in fact represent the principals and other teachers in the Colleges of Education on whose behalf it negotiates salary scales with the employers' organisations in the Pelham Committee. Negotiations concerning conditions of employment for the staffs of Departments of Education are handled by the Association of University Teachers in the same way as those of members of other university departments.

A group of teachers' associations with which this study will not be concerned is the subject associations, the Historical Association, Mathematics Association, Classical Association and the like. These are concerned with the study of a particular subject, with keeping their members abreast of recent developments arising out of current research and with methods of teaching in schools and colleges. They seldom if ever enter the field of 'teachers' politics' or become involved in issues affecting the employment of teachers by the public authorities. It is of some interest to notice in passing, however, that at least two of the contemporary associations were founded partly to assert claims to a higher status for members. Modern Language teachers sought to find through organising themselves additional strength for their claim to be treated on a level of parity with well-entrenched classics teachers. The Association for Science Education was known until recently by its earlier title of Science Masters' Association and as such it had been founded by masters teaching in public schools in the late nineteenth century to claim for the study of science in such schools the place they felt was its due and to claim for themselves salaries and conditions of service equal to those offered to masters teaching traditional and revered subjects.

Neither the College of Preceptors nor the Teachers' Guilds developed in such a way as to become important professional associations for teachers in the twentieth century. The College of Preceptors was set up in 1846 by a group of proprietors of private schools and was incorporated by royal charter three years later. The intention was that individual teachers should constitute themselves a learned profession and—as with law or medicine—have powers of self-regulation. The failure of this ideal to flourish and the growth instead of the N.U.T. and the secondary and technical associations has probably been largely due to the growth of teaching as a predominantly salaried occupation from the late nineteenth century, most teachers being employees and not fee-charging, independent proprietors of small businesses in the way that the solicitor and general practitioner tended to be. Even so, the College of Preceptors has survived and fulfilled a useful role if very different from that envisaged by its founders. The Teachers' Guilds have not survived. The main aim of the founders of the national Teachers' Guild was to draw all of the profession into one organisation which would both encourage the study of education ('to circulate information regarding educational methods and movements in England and elsewhere, and to assist in the establishment of educational libraries and the exhibition of school books and apparatus') and would also act as a philanthropic organisation, encouraging and aiding thrift among teachers and the establishment of 'Teachers' Homes and Homes of Rest for invalid and aged teachers'.[28] Many local guilds were also active in the late nineteenth and early twentieth centuries. The Teachers' Guild movement ran down as more specialised agencies took over the various activities which the movement offered from facilities for studying education to facilities for providing for sickness or old age.

NOTES

1. Royal Commission to Inquire into the State of Popular Education in England, 1861, vol. XXI, pt. 6, p. 363.
2. D. F. Thompson, *Professional Solidarity among the Teachers of England*, 1927, p. 77, quoted from N.U.T. Annual Report, 1872, p. 19.
3. A. Tropp, *The School Teacher*, 1957, p. 113.
4. Thompson, op. cit. p. 174.
5. N.U.T. *Annual Reports.*
6. D. Newsome, *A History of Wellington College, 1859–1959*, 1959, p. 140.
7. *T.E.S.*, 7th October, 1966, p. 775; A. C. Percival, *The Origins of the Headmasters' Conference*, 1969, chapters 2 and 3.
8. Mrs. S. Webb, *New Statesman*, Special Supplement, 'English Teachers and their Professional Organisations', 25 September, 1915, p. 14.
9. G. Baron, 'Origin and Early History of the Headmasters' Conference, 1869–1914', *Educational Review*, June, 1955, p. 228; G. Baron, 'The Secondary Schoolmaster 1895–1915: a study of the qualifications, conditions of employment and professional associations of masters in English secondary schools', unpublished Ph.D. thesis, London, 1952.

10. I.A.H.M., *Lists of Members*; I.A.H.M. Register of Members, 1968, p. 7.
11. I.A.A.M. Annual Report, 1896, p. 22.
12. Ibid., p. 10.
13. I.A.A.M., Annual Report and Annual Lists of Members.
14. E. Day, *Two Leaders*, 1910, quoted by Webb op. cit., p. 15.
15. A.H.M. *A Summary of the Work of the Association of Head Mistresses*, 1911, p. 3; The A.H.M. Report, 1968, p. 7.
16. Report of the 22nd Annual Conference of Educational Associations, 1934, p. 111, paper by G. A. Richardson on the History and Aims of the A.A.M.
17. *Journal of Education*, 1 March, 1884, p. 131.
18. Ibid., 1 May, 1884, pp. 195-6.
19. A.A.M. Annual Report, 1887, p. 10.
20. A.A.M. Annual Reports and as supplied by the A.A.M.
21. A.T.T.I. Proceedings, 1904-5.
22. A.T.T.I. Proceedings, 1907.
23. Figures for 1951 and 1961 supplied by the Finance Officer of the A.T.T.I.
24. *Education*, 23rd March, 1959, p. 648; the present study is primarily concerned with school teachers' associations and no attempt is made to follow the work of the A.T.T.I. in this volume. A detailed study of the association is certainly needed.
25. Webb, op. cit., p. 8.
26. Figures supplied by the N.A.S.
27. *Education*, 3rd April, 1959, p. 709.
28. Webb, op. cit. p. 14.

2

Salaries in the Years before Burnham, 1902—1918

I. LOCAL NEGOTIATIONS

The pattern of salaries actually paid to teachers in this country has always been quite complicated for a number of reasons the most important of which today is probably the varied nature of the posts which qualified teachers hold. On the eve of the passing of the Education Act of 1902 the position was a great deal more complicated because the thousands of bodies then employing teachers all had their own ideas on the correct salaries to offer; there was no central and usually no local negotiating machinery. In the broadest sense it would probably be true to say that salaries in the large towns with active school boards were a good deal more favourable for elementary school teachers than those offered to similar persons in rural areas where voluntary schools predominated. Since elementary school teachers were often quite well organised in the larger cities, they were able to formulate demands and to bring pressure to bear in support of them. They were able to make their presence felt in school board elections and candidates returned with the aid of teachers were not likely to be unsympathetic to their requests. Moreover, the school boards were in a position to raise from the rates the necessary funds to pay reasonable salaries to teachers and were thus much better placed than the voluntary schools which had no such elastic source of revenue and were really dependent upon charity in some form or other to supplement such government grants as they could obtain. The small rural school boards usually offered salaries not very much different from those of rural voluntary schools for while they might have the authority to raise the rates and pay higher salaries, the members of such boards usually felt it was their duty to limit any demand upon the rates so far as possible and the teachers themselves were often not organised. Tables 2.1 and 2.2

although not directly comparable, give some idea of the relative differences between the payments which heads of elementary schools might expect under a large city school board—Leeds—and in rural board or voluntary schools in Devonshire.

Table 2.1. *Leeds School Board Salaries for Elementary School Head Teachers, 1902–3*[1]

Annual Average Attendance	MEN		WOMEN	
	Minimum	Maximum	Minimum	Maximum
	£	£	£	£
over 800	230	260	–	–
601–800	220	250	–	–
401–600	200	230	–	–
301–400	180	210	110	130
201–300	160	190	100	120
100–200	150	175	100	110
Below 100	150	175	90	100

Augmentation of fixed salary of 1s. per unit of annual average attendance allowed to head teachers upon the special vote of education committee after consideration of reports upon school work.

Table 2.2. *Salaries of Head Teachers in Board and Voluntary Schools in Devon, 1903.*[2]

£	BOARD		VOLUNTARY	
	Men	Women	Men	Women
150 and over	1	–	2	–
125–49	9	–	18	–
100–24	42	–	40	–
90–9	14	–	18	–
80–9	14	6	11	19
70–9	5	19	8	44
60–9	–	19	1	54
50–9	–	2	1	10
40–9	–	1	–	1

The contrast is perhaps even more marked if the salaries paid to head teachers of Devon schools are compared with the salaries paid to trained certificated assistants in the board schools of Leeds.

Table 2.3. *Leeds School Board. Salaries for Trained Certificated Assistants, 1902–3*[3]

	MEN		WOMEN	
	Minimum	Maximum	Minimum	Maximum
	£	£	£	£
(a) With B.A. or B.Sc.	90	120	80	90
(b) With First Division in both parts of Cert. Exam.	85	120	75	90
(c) Others	80	120	70	90

That salaries paid in most elementary schools were very low is one of the few general statements that may be made with assurance. This is seen if the salaries shown here are compared with the average annual earnings of male salaried employees which varied between £125 and £140 in the years before the First World War. A similar statement would be true of salaries in secondary schools. The multiplicity of the employing bodies excluded the possibility of any effective general negotiations for salary improvement even if the associations of secondary teachers had themselves been in a sufficiently strong position to pursue them. The poverty of many of the endowed secondary schools was an important factor in ensuring that the salaries offered to the great majority of teachers remained very low. The Bryce Commission, 1895, gathered a certain amount of evidence on the average salaries of assistant masters in secondary schools from the accounts returned to the Charity Commission. These showed that the average salary of 899 masters forming the staffs of 190 first and second grade endowed schools amounted to £105 per annum.[4] The only exception to low salaries in endowed secondary schools was among the headmasters of some of them who were quite comfortably off. The Bryce Commission found that in a sample of ten schools with about 100 scholars each, the stipends of the headmasters totalled £4,175 or an average of £417 10s. each while the 43 assistant masters received a total of £4,597 or an average payment of £106 18s.[5]

Little was done to improve the position of assistants in secondary schools before 1902, and there are numerous references to the paucity of salaries by inspectors and other observers. W. H. D. Rouse wrote an article in the *Contemporary Review* in 1900 in which he examined the later fate of 60 assistants: 'Four of these have got schools of their own, and eight have become curates; amongst the others are a barrister, a solicitor, a gold digger, a professional tenor, a book-maker (not literary), and a grower of tomatoes. Two are out of work and cannot find any; one poor old man shot himself; twenty-four only remain as they were, and fifteen have completely disappeared, leaving no trace.' Rouse commented that the prospects could not possibly compensate for the poor salaries offered. 'Can one wonder that there is . . . a feeling of deep discontent in the teaching profession? It is not everyone who can get a boarding house; and those who do, naturally, try to make the fat years swallow up the lean, and stick to it as long as they can. The majority of members cannot hope for a boarding house; neither can they hope for a post in one of the half-dozen schools which are comparatively rich. . . . Still less can the average assistant hope for a headmastership of his own. In the smaller schools such a post is a very doubtful gain; it brings great risk and small profit. And it should not be forgotten that at present all the chief headmasterships are given to clergymen, in spite of the law which makes laymen equally eligible.'[6]

The most important administrative development which changed the whole structure of educational organisation from 1902 was the establishment of local education authorities in the modern sense. The county and county borough councils became responsible for most educational provision. The consequence of this which most immediately concerned teachers' associations was that there now existed large public bodies of employers all over the country with whom they could negotiate on behalf of their members. This was especially important for the elementary teachers in county areas where teachers were now paid by the county council instead of by thousands of separate bodies of school managers or small rural school boards. In the large cities which had had strong school boards there had already existed for board school teachers a unified pay scheme, but here too the Act of 1902 had the effect of drawing the voluntary school teachers into the same pay structure as the board teachers had enjoyed since the salaries of both groups now became the responsibility of the county borough council.

The change in the administrative structure did in fact bring about an improvement in the majority of cases in the salaries of assistant and head teachers in county areas and in voluntary schools in county boroughs. The position in the two contrasting areas of Devon county and Leeds county borough illustrate this. In Devon the average salaries of adult assistant teachers—usually women—had been £45 for certificated, £40 for uncertificated and £27 for supplementary.[7] The following scales were introduced by the county council related to qualifications:

Table 2.4

	Men £	Women £
Trained certificated	80 × 5 – 110	70 × 5 – 95
Untrained certificated	70 × 5 – 110	60 × 5 – 95
Uncertificated	55 × 2½ – 75	40 × 2½ – 60
Supplementary	40 × 2½ – 45	20 × 2½ – 45

Such scales were only paid where the number of pupils justified the employment of appropriately qualified assistants.

The salary scales for assistant teachers in the elementary schools of Leeds, whether voluntary or council, in 1908 were:[8]

Table 2.5

	Men £	Women £
Trained certificated	90 × 5 – 160	80 × 5 – 110
Untrained certificated	75 × 5 – 140	65 × 5 – 90
Uncertificated	55 × 5 – 65	45 × 5 – 55
Supplementary	35 × 5 – 50	25 × 5 – 40

From 1903, when the city council took over board and voluntary schools, fixed salaries, depending on the size of the school, had been paid to head teachers. In 1908 the maxima for men varied from £175 for the smallest schools to £330 for the largest, headmistresses were paid maxima varying from £115 to £175.

Associations of both elementary and secondary teachers adapted their tactics to attempting to improve salary levels in the new situation. The N.U.T. concerned itself mainly with the position of those grades of elementary school teachers who had some sort of qualification. Until the inter-war years four grades of teacher were to be found in the elementary schools, trained certificated, untrained certificated, uncertificated and supplementary. The first three grades all followed the same course of training, study and examination until their eighteenth year when they took the Board of Education's Preliminary Certificate Examination which qualified them for admission to a training college and for recognition as uncertificated teachers. Some went straight to training colleges at that stage and became trained certificated teachers; others took posts in schools as uncertificated teachers, in their spare time working for the Acting Teachers' Examination, and if successful they became certificated teachers but without college training; the rest remained as uncertificated teachers and formed a permanent class of the teaching service. Supplementary teachers differed from the others in that they did not need to have any academic qualification at all; they were simply approved by an H.M.I. for the particular school in which they were employed and their recognition could be withdrawn at any time. Thus they formed only a local supply of teachers and were mainly employed in rural areas, the majority being women who lived with their parents.[9] The N.U.T. was naturally anxious to eliminate the supplementary grade from the school scene and to ensure that authorities would have to employ qualified persons instead at appropriately higher rates. Pressure centred, therefore, on the rates to be paid to heads and assistants who were certificated.

In the years before the First World War salary negotiations were naturally carried on at the local level by the local association which was itself affiliated to and supported by the N.U.T. nationally. Local associations pressed for the introduction of progressive salary scales where these had not yet been introduced to replace the fixed wage arrangements which had been followed by many voluntary schools and some school boards before 1902. The N.U.T. prepared and circulated information on existing scales of salaries for the guidance of local associations and—it was hoped—of the local authorities. The guidance came to include minimum suggested scales for elementary school teachers and advice on the features which should form part of every scale such as that council and voluntary teachers should be treated alike; that part service under other authorities should count in determining the teacher's place on the scale; and that 'every scale should be drawn with sufficient elasticity to meet the great variety of needs, particularly in small schools, and should recognise the many years spent by the teacher in training for his office, and the responsibilities and obligations he has subsequently to discharge.' The attempts which the Union made to enforce claims for higher salaries in some rural areas tended to be rendered less effective by the existence of considerable numbers of supplementary teachers who were prepared to work for much less than the N.U.T. claimed for its members.

There was an increase of about nine per cent in the level of retail

Salaries in the Years before Burnham, 1902–1918

prices between 1910 and 1913 which followed a long period of stability. It was sufficient to cause a great deal of discontent among members of the N.U.T. and to lead to the setting up of a special salaries committee in 1913, to undertake a national campaign to secure improved salaries. The campaign met with a considerable measure of success for there was some improvement in 149 out of 321 L.E.A. areas.[10] It led directly to the best known clash of the time between the Union and a local authority in the case of Herefordshire. Here the authority declined to establish any sort of county scale of salaries and in 1910 passed a formal resolution incorporating this policy. Representations from the local teachers' association were of little avail although in 1913 the county did set up a special committee to look at the salary position and in particular to determine whether the county paid much lower salaries than other authorities as the teachers claimed. This committee decided not to establish any scale although it did recommend that certain salaries should be increased. The Union was not prepared to accept this position and organised a strike of indefinite duration which led to the closure of about fifty schools. The eventual outcome of this season of hostilities was that the authority conceded a scale but at much lower rates than the teachers had demanded.

The overall picture of salaries paid to certificated and uncertificated teachers is shown in Table 2.6. The contrast between salaries paid in London and the county boroughs on the one hand and in county areas on the other may have been due in part to variations in the cost of living but a major influence was the fact that the teachers' associations had had considerable influence with the large school boards before 1902 while they had found it almost impossible to influence salaries in rural areas and small towns. In other words the higher salaries were to be found where the influence of the teachers' associations had been felt longest and where it had been stronger.

The new administrative structure of 1902 came to have a beneficial effect upon the salaries of many secondary school teachers also. The influence of the new local education authorities made itself felt in three ways. In the first place, counties and county boroughs were empowered to establish their own secondary schools. This they did in considerable numbers. Salary scales for heads and assistants had to be provided and those for assistants were often a good deal more generous than the salaries payable in the endowed schools. Secondly, some authorities required the governors of endowed schools which they aided to pay approved salary scales as a condition of grant aid. Thirdly,

Table 2.6. *Salaries paid to Certificated and Uncertificated Teachers 1910–14*[11]

Type of Local Education Authority and Year	Expenditure on Teachers' Salaries per unit of Average Attendance	AVERAGE SALARIES					
		Certificated Teachers				Uncertificated Teachers	
		Head		Assistant			
		Men	Women	Men	Women	Men	Women
London:	s. d.	£	£	£	£	£	£
1910–11	77 6	282·4	202·9	156·5	115·0	82·3	61·6
1911–12	80 10	285·3	204·8	158·6	116·2	83·4	61·7
1912–13	84 7	287·6	207·3	160·1	117·6	87·0	62·0
1913–14	(a)	290·0	209·3	160·6	118·7	89·9	62·9
County Boroughs:							
1910–11	55 9	227·2	137·3	124·6	88·4	64·8	53·7
1911–12	56 11	227·2	138·0	125·5	89·6	66·4	54·4
1912–13	57 2	227·4	138·7	126·4	90·4	68·0	55·4
1913–14	(a)	227·6	139·7	127·8	91·7	70·3	56·3
Urban Districts:							
1910–11	59 0	231·2	150·8	135·4	101·2	72·2	58·7
1911–12	60 10	234·2	154·6	139·6	103·4	73·3	59·5
1912–13	62 3	236·7	155·8	141·4	104·7	75·8	59·9
1913–14	(a)	238·1	157·5	142·1	105·8	77·6	60·7
Boroughs:							
1910–11	54 10	202·0	126·4	115·0	87·3	66·4	56·6
1911–12	55 5	201·8	127·0	115·8	88·3	67·5	57·2
1912–13	59 4	202·3	128·0	116·8	89·8	69·4	57·9
1913–14	(a)	202·2	128·9	118·3	91·0	71·0	58·6
Counties:							
1910–11	51 10	145·7	99·7	101·9	78·9	64·2	54·5
1911–12	53 1	146·3	100·4	102·1	79·7	65·3	55·3
1912–13	54 6	147·2	101·5	103·0	81·1	66·3	56·1
1913–14	(a)	148·7	103·2	104·3	82·9	68·0	57·1
Total:							
1910–11	57 2	176·2	123·0	127·5	92·4	65·2	54·8
1911–12	58 8	177·0	123·9	128·5	93·6	66·4	55·5
1912–13	60 3	178·0	125·2	129·3	94·6	67·7	56·3
1913–14	(a)	179·5	126·9	130·2	96·0	69·6	57·0

(a) Figures not available

the salaries offered by the authorities came after some years to have an indirect effect on other endowed schools through the operation of the mechanism of the labour market.

From 1902 until the First World War the secondary associations were campaigning to improve the salaries of their members. The most active association was probably that of the Assistant Masters. In 1904 the Council of this Association adopted a salary scheme which it urged upon local authorities and, where possible, upon governing bodies of endowed schools. The scheme stated:

'1. That in every secondary school there should be a definite scheme of salaries including provision for increments.

2. (a) The lowest salary paid in any secondary school to any master registered in Column B should be at least £150, rising by automatic yearly increments of £10 to at least £300.

(b) Salaries on a higher scale than the one suggested above should be paid to members who are specially qualified by attainment or experience and to holders of the following posts (1) second master, (2) heads of departments, (3) head of lower school.

(c) So far as can be done without injury to the interests of the school, these better paid posts should be given to members of the staff of long standing and of meritorious service.

(d) In fixing the salary of an assistant master regard should be had to experience gained in any efficient school.

3. A pension scheme is an essential part of any sound scheme for the remuneration of masters.

4. The school authority should recognise that the assistant master is not liable at common law for the payment of a substitute in cases of ordinary illness.

5. When residence is designed to be partly payment for teaching services some deduction may be made on account thereof from salary, but where residence involves further important duties and responsibilities no such deduction should be made.'[12]

The situation that confronted the secondary associations may be illustrated by reference to the I.A.A.M.'s survey of salaries paid in 123 schools in 1904[13] (see Table 2.7, p. 30). The impression of low salaries given by the I.A.A.M. surveys is confirmed by other contemporary evidence. Professor Sadler was commissioned by a number of local authorities to survey the secondary schools in their areas when they became responsible for this form of school provision and in his reports he usually gave the current salary position. Salaries at the secondary school at Southend were said to be fairly typical; this was a large school for the time with seventeen assistants of whom seven were graduates. Their average salary amounted to £124 11s. 2d., the highest salary being £177 10s. 0d. and the lowest £85.[14] Four years later Norwood and Hope in their book on the *Higher Education*

Table 2.7

Amount of Salary	Number of Masters paid at this rate
Under £100	6
£100–120	31
£121–140	38
£141–160	38
£161–200	45
£201–250	20
£250+	14

of Boys in England found the average salary paid to non-resident masters was just over £120.[15]

One of the main methods employed by the I.A.A.M. in its salary campaign was to seek sympathy by arranging suitable publicity for the position in which assistant masters found themselves. In 1904 an article appeared in the *Yorkshire Post* based on information supplied by the Association and entitled 'Secondary Education: the Supply of Assistant Masters'.[16] The article gave an analysis of salaries paid in thirty-two secondary schools in the West Riding. The average salary paid to assistant masters was £150 8s. 11d. but if the Grammar Schools of Leeds and Bradford along with Giggleswick and Sedbergh were excluded this average dropped to £116 0s. 6d. for the remaining twenty-eight schools. The salaries of headmasters were shown to be much higher, but this was of small comfort since not more than one in six or seven could now expect to become a head; 'the profession is a lottery, which clever young men enter in the hope of picking up one of the prizes, and which the man of good average ability eschews, unless he is careless of his future'. By way of comparison the writer pointed out that the school attendance officer under the Leeds authority was to be paid £121 6s. 8d. per annum and a cashier in the City Accountant's Office was sure of £140 annually. The *Journal of Education*, commenting upon the situation revealed by this article, stated that 'The cruelty of the position is apparent when it is remembered that a schoolmaster is an educated man, for whom the bare necessities of life are more numerous than those of an artisan; that he has little or no prospect of an increase in salary; that he has no pension in the future; that he ought to marry'.[17] Perhaps the worst feature of the situation was the absence of any sort of progressive scale of salaries and the payment of a fixed wage without any promise of betterment.

Salaries in the Years before Burnham, 1902–1918

The first major success that the secondary teachers met with in their campaign for proper salary scales was in 1906 with the adoption by the London County Council of a scale of salaries for assistants on the lines of that put forward by the I.A.A.M. The new salary scale was to be paid in the Council's own schools and governing bodies of endowed schools in the area were urged to do likewise. The scheme provided for assistant masters to be paid on a scale from £150 to £300 by £10 increments with the maximum at £350 for those holding posts of special responsibility. The scale for assistant mistresses was from £120 to £220 with the possibility of a maximum of £250 in special cases. To be placed on these scales teachers had to be graduates and normally to hold a university certificate or diploma in education or to give evidence of one year's satisfactory teaching experience.[18]

A number of other authorities followed London in establishing scales but not usually on such generous lines. As part of their continuing campaign, in 1910 the I.A.A.M. sent a letter to all local authorities asking for particulars of salaries in all the secondary schools they maintained. The replies to these letters showed that sixty-two authorities out of one hundred and twenty-one possessing powers to run secondary schools had introduced scales for secondary assistants. The scales offered:

(a) initial salaries of £100 or less in 6 areas
　　　　　　　　　　£101 to £130 in 37 areas
　　　　　　　　　　£131 to £150 in 15 areas
　　　　　　　　　　Over £150 in 5 areas
(b) annual increments of £5 or less in 6 areas
　　　　　　　　　　£5 to £10 in 25 areas
　　　　　　　　　　Over £10 in 31 areas
(c) maximum salaries of £200 or less in 41 areas
　　　　　　　　　　£201 to £250 in 18 areas
　　　　　　　　　　£251 to £300 in 2 areas
　　　　　　　　　　Over £300 in 1 area.[19]

A complete analysis of all salaries paid to head and assistant masters and mistresses in grant-aided secondary schools was published by the Board of Education in 1911 and is reproduced in Table 2.8. Perhaps one of the most striking features it reveals is the very large differential between heads and assistants, headmasters being paid on average 2·6 times more than their assistants while headmistresses receive an average

Table 2.8. *Salaries of Head and Assistant Masters and Mistresses in Grant-aided Secondary Schools on 31st January, 1911*

Salary per Annum	Head Masters		Assistant Masters		Head Mistresses		Assistant Mistresses	
	No.	%	No.	%	No.	%	No.	%
Under £60	—	—	10	0·2	—	—	34	0·9
£60 and under £80	—	—	33	0·8	—	—	88	2·3
80 ,, 100	—	—	77	1·9	—	—	277	7·3
100 ,, 120	—	—	234	5·9	—	—	1,169	30·8
120 ,, 140	—	—	513	12·8	—	—	1,308	34·4
140 ,, 160	—	—	847	21·2	1	0·4	535	14·1
160 ,, 180	2	0·4	795	19·9	2	0·8	244	6·4
180 ,, 200	3	0·6	562	14·0	8	3·1	79	2·1
200 ,, 220	3	0·6	456	11·4	26	10·0	41	1·1
220 ,, 240	8	1·5	186	4·6	12	4·6	20	0·5
240 ,, 260	30	5·5	143	3·6	33	12·7	3	0·1
260 ,, 280	31	5·7	48	1·2	19	7·3	—	—
280 ,, 300	23	4·2	28	0·7	17	6·5	1	0·0
300 ,, 350	91	16·8	51	1·3	50	19·2	—	—
350 ,, 400	81	14·9	15	0·4	35	13·5	—	—
400 ,, 450	77	14·1	3	0·1	23	8·8	—	—
450 ,, 500	52	9·6	—	—	4	1·5	—	—
500 ,, 600	57	10·5	1	0·0	20	7·7	—	—
600 ,, 700	35	6·5	—	—	6	2·3	—	—
700 ,, 800	22	4·1	—	—	2	0·8	—	—
800 ,, 900	14	2·6	—	—	1	0·4	—	—
900 ,, 1,000	2	0·4	—	—	—	—	—	—
1,000 and over	11	2·0	—	—	1	0·4	—	—
Total	542	100·0	4,002	100·0	260	100·0	3,799	100·0
Average Salary	£438		£168		£332		£123	

2·7 times more than assistant mistresses. Even after ten years of campaigning by the secondary associations, the salaries paid to assistants still looked miserably low. An important reason for the great disparity between the salaries of heads and assistants in the secondary schools lay in the clerical tradition which had surrounded secondary education in the nineteenth century. A clerical headmaster with two or three assistants would have been a fairly typical staff for many endowed grammar schools. The schools were small and the assistant masters were in much the same position as curates in parishes, poorly paid but standing a very fair chance of getting a 'living' or headship of their own before too many years had passed. The growth of the schools meant that the prospects of achieving a headship became much less good and that for many an assistant mastership would represent a total career. During the first part of this century the secondary associations were fighting to get this new state of affairs reflected in the salaries offered. The associations of headmasters and headmistresses both came to show increasing concern over the inadequacy of assistants' salaries and to urge improvements.

The rise in the cost of living which became noticeable after 1910 and the increased efforts of the elementary school teachers at that time led to an intensification of the salary campaign conducted by the secondary school associations. In 1911 the I.A.A.M. raised its target when the council resolved 'That the lowest salary paid in any secondary school to an assistant master should be £150 rising by automatic yearly increments of at least £10 to £300; and then by similar increments of £15 to at least £450'.[21] A memorandum setting out the case for an improvement in salaries was sent to every member of the Commons immediately before the debate on the education vote in the same year; this drew attention to the power of the Board of Education to help 'by increasing the grants now made to secondary schools, and insisting that the increase be used solely for the purpose of augmenting Assistant Masters' salaries'. By 1914 a subcommittee of the executive had been formed to deal with the salaries issue and an inquiry was undertaken in all aided and maintained schools. The subcommittee collected suitable material for the campaign, issued specimen literature to branches, compiled suitable articles for use by newspapers and prepared applications to local authorities for salary increases. About fifty local campaigns were started of which fifteen were fruitful in that they resulted in the establishment of satisfactory scales or the improvement of old ones. In the words of *The A.M.A.* 'In every case the Sub-Committee has kept in close touch with the campaigners, and there seems to be general satisfaction at the fact there there is a central body to combine isolated units, to give individual schools the experience and cohesion of the whole body, and to break down that feeling of insecurity that has prevented men from asking for their deserts.'[22]

The campaign was halted with the outbreak of the World War. The chairman and secretary of the subcommittee on salaries reported in 1915 that according to a survey they had conducted the average salary paid in England and Wales was £175·52 and the average number of years in service was twelve. Among the local authorities there was only one, London, with a scale in which the ordinary maximum payable after fifteen years of service was £300. The authors of the report commented that two points stood out clearly, namely, '(1) the enormous disparity in the scales of different men with the same qualifications, engaged in precisely the same work and in similar areas, and (2) the parochial principle of disregarding, wholly or in part, service in other areas, so that a man cannot move to another district without throwing away the value of the whole or part of his previous service.'[23]

Undoubtedly the elementary and secondary teachers' associations were able to bring about considerable increases in the salaries of their members between 1902 and 1914. A much larger number of teachers in both elementary and secondary schools now had progressive salary scales in place of fixed wages. The enormous reduction in the total number of employing bodies under the Act of 1902 had enabled the associations to identify an employer with whom they could negotiate and endeavour to put pressure on in a way that only the elementary teachers' associations in the larger cities could do before. In this way the associations were fortunate in being aided by circumstances. But it is worth looking a little more closely at the new pattern of local administration, for in one way it did not favour the teachers' cause. The new local education authorities were multi-purpose bodies, education was only one of their functions and they had to meet the calls of many other public services on the town purse. In the words of the creator of the new system, Robert Morant, it was, indeed, a virtue of the multi-purpose authority that it would have to weigh the demands of education against other public needs. He had sought to avoid having authorities responsible for education only since 'there is the mistake of getting together a lot of people whose sole (or main) hobby is education and letting a body of such folk have the run of the public purse. It becomes a matter of "There's nothing like leather". Education lends itself particularly to the development of extravagances.

'Ordinary common sense restrictions, such as would be obvious to an ordinary person, are wholly overlooked; and so-called education fads and extravagances of all kinds and out of all proportion to the rateable capacity of the town and its useful needs in other directions, became the normal course of policy with school Board members.

'All this is avoided, without any real educational needs suffering at all, if all education is part of the ordinary municipal purse.'[24]

The members of county and county borough councils included many whose main interests lay outside the educational field and in the years following 1902 they found themselves faced with the need to raise an increasing proportion of the finance education needed from the rates since the government grants failed to expand in proportion to the growth of total educational expenditure. In the financial year 1905-6 Exchequer grants met 53·9 per cent of the total cost but by 1911-12 the grants met only 48·2 per cent of total educational expenditure.[25] The pressure on local rates became increasingly severe and the cost-consciousness and complaints of the local authorities grew markedly. In 1911 the Treasury appointed a committee under Sir John Kempe to inquire into the changes in the relation of local to central taxation since 1901. The committee reported in 1914 and found the complaints of the local authorities justified. It recommended that any reform of the system should 'provide for an automatic expansion of the government grant concurrently with an increase in the local expenditure which it is intended to aid.' The genuine financial stringency with which education authorities were faced before 1914 served to harden their attitude towards the claims of the teachers.

The general development of such ancillary services as medical inspection and school meals in this period increased the size and unpopularity of the education rate. Comments on education and the rates which appeared in the *Journal of Education* in 1909 also pointed to other expensive developments such as the gradual abolition of supplementary teachers and their replacement by trained teachers, requirements of the Board for smaller classes and the provision of accommodation on a more generous basis than hitherto necessitating the building of new schools. The *Journal* concluded that 'education is not really popular, and that a new generation must arise which has known the practical value of the school and institute before the education rate will be cheerfully paid'.[26] The weight of the local burden and the reluctance of local authorities to increase it further led the teachers' associations to urge that more generous grants should be paid by the Treasury. At each of the N.U.T.'s annual conferences from 1908 to 1912 resolutions were passed calling the attention of the Board to the heavy burden on the local rates and expressing the view that the cost of education should be met by larger and more equitable government grants, particularly to localities heavily rated for education purposes, and that such grants should rise automatically as new and increased responsibilities were placed on the local authorities.[27] In October, 1913, a conference of ten national associations of teachers (including the N.U.T., the four secondary associations and the A.T.T.I.) met with the object of securing further financial aid from the government, and it was resolved that a deputation should call on the President of the Board to urge that a substantial proportion of any further grants of public money to local authorities 'should be definitely assigned to the specific purposes of improving the staffing of schools and increasing the stipends of teachers'.[28] The outbreak of war led to the deferment of measures to adjust the grant position.

II. ESTABLISHING NATIONAL SALARY SCALES

The salary campaigns of the teachers' associations were suspended when war began. Widespread unemployment and falling incomes seem to have been expected in this country, but in fact wartime boom conditions rapidly developed, with consequent increases in prices and in the wages of most groups of workers. By 1916 the level of prices had risen 40 per cent or so above that of 1914. Extreme discontent among members led the N.U.T. to re-open its salary campaign in July, 1916. In October the Executive of the Union resolved that, 'In view of the present heavy strain upon the salaries of teachers and of the difficulty experienced in obtaining from local authorities adequate financial relief, this Executive resolves to initiate and develop a national movement to secure an immediate and substantial increase in teachers' salaries'.[29] The secondary associations began by this time to pursue vigorously a policy of seeking 'war bonuses' to meet the increase in the cost of living. Many authorities were, in fact, paying such bonuses and more came to do so, but these differed widely in amount and were awarded on apparently conflicting principles. Most of the associations were active in revealing the 'meagre and capricious nature of local payment';[30] a list of areas where the bonuses were being paid which was published in the *A.M.A.* in December, 1916, showed that they usually amounted to payments of no more than £5 to £10 yearly. The vigorous publicity activity undertaken by the associations and their representations to the Board of Education were influential in causing the government to introduce higher grants to the local authorities in 1917.

The President of the Board of Education by this time was H. A. L. Fisher. In introducing the education estimates in 1917 which provided for higher grants, he told the Commons, 'I do not expect the teaching profession to offer great material rewards—that is impossible; but I do regard it as essential to a good scheme of education that teachers should be relieved from perpetual financial anxieties, and that those teachers who marry should be able to look forward to rearing a family in respectable conditions. An anxious and depressed teacher is a bad teacher, an embittered teacher is a social danger.... The first condition of educational advance is that we should learn to pay our teachers better. If we do not take this step, we shall not be able to keep the profession at its present level in numbers and quality; still less shall we be able to extend its sphere or to deepen its influence, and steps should be taken now if the fruit of the investment is to be reaped after the war.'[31] The machinery Fisher used in his early efforts to improve the rewards of teachers was adapted from the Report of the Kempe Committee. This had proposed a grant formula which included 40 per cent of all approved expenditure; Fisher now offered local authorities 60 per cent of their expenditure on teachers' salaries in elementary schools. A few months later, in June, 1917, he appointed a departmental committee to enquire 'into the principles which should determine the construction of scales of salary for teachers in elementary schools' and another committee to undertake a similar task for teachers in secondary and technical schools, schools of art and training colleges.

Both of these committees collected a great deal of evidence from officers of the Board of Education and of the local education authorities, from representatives of the different teachers' associations and from individual teachers. The Reports from these committees were both published in 1918 and contained a mass of details showing the salaries paid in different parts of the country and in different types of school. The Elementary school salaries report suggested that payment by salary scales in place of a flat wage should be universal and that the scales of all areas should be based on common principles, such as the need to obtain a supply of suitable recruits and the reasonable assurance for teachers of a remuneration which would enable them 'to live appropriately without financial embarrassment'. The application of the same principles in the circumstances of different areas 'will produce a diversity of results' and national scales were not, therefore, recommended.[32] The Report on principles governing the salaries of secondary teachers came nearer to advocating something like a national scale, but stopped short of such an arrangement on the grounds that compulsion to pay the higher salaries of a national scale would cause the collapse of some secondary schools unless additional finance could be made available. 'A national scale in fact implies a national guarantee, and it is difficult to see how the teacher can have real security in all cases till that is forthcoming. How far this is likely to occur we cannot say, as it is no part of our duty to discuss the sources from which the amounts required should be provided.'[33] The committee did suggest that there should be scales in which a minimum initial salary for teachers of the graduate class in all secondary schools in receipt of public money should be fixed by the Central Authority, and that a further minimum sum should be centrally prescribed for a point part of the way up the scales. The nearer approach to a national scale in the secondary report may have been due to the pressure from the secondary teachers. At its meeting in January, 1918, the I.A.A.M. Council resolved 'that this Council advocates a National Salary Scale with an initial salary of £160 per annum, rising by increments of at least £15 to £600, and considers essential the immediate introduction of a compulsory minimum scale of £160, rising by at least £15 to £450; these scales to be supplemented by an additional allowance in the districts where the cost of living is high'.[34] The Annual Report of the Association for 1918 expressed the view that the Departmental Committee's Report had been very weak in dealing with the question of a national minimum scale.

Through improving the grant arrangements and through the advice given by the Departmental Committees' Reports, Fisher hoped to bring about the necessary improvement in salaries. He was opposed to the suggestion that teachers should be paid entirely by the state—a suggestion of which a good deal was heard at the time—and told the Commons, 'I do not so much fear the enslavement of the public intellect through a corps of state teachers . . . But I do fear a very great and abrupt decline in the local interest in education if the control of the teaching body, and payment means control, is withdrawn from the local authorities and vested in Whitehall'.[35] The only demand from the teachers' associations that the central government could meet without weakening the position of the local authorities was their frequently expressed desire for a comprehensive superannuation scheme. The Teachers' Superannuation Act of 1918 did introduce a generous non-contributory scheme which had the effect of making teachers in grant-aided elementary and secondary schools eligible for pensions on much the same conditions as civil servants.

But none of these palliatives succeeded in meeting the discontent among teachers over the salary issue. During 1918 and 1919 there was an increasing measure of militancy, with strikes in more than thirty areas. The strikes were usually called by local associations of elementary teachers who then looked to the N.U.T. for support. There was already a shortage of trained teachers, and the implementation of the Education Act of 1918 would add to the demand for them. Teachers believed that the increased grants to local authorities were not being fully applied to the augmentation of their salaries. An article in *The A.M.A.* in 1918 claimed that the salaries of officials had been increased and some of the money had been used 'improperly' to reduce school fees, and allocated to the general reserve and to the reduction of the rates.

Early in 1919 a joint committee of the A.M.C., the C.C.A. and the A.E.C. was established, to consider establishing common scales throughout the country. The committee met a number of times but it did not attempt to consult with teachers' organisations as its members were unable even to agree among themselves. The growing scarcity of teachers was the most important single factor behind the resolution carried by the Association of Education Committees at its Annual General Meeting in June, 1919, 'That this Association is of opinion that a National Scale of Salaries for Teachers (Elementary and Secondary) is a matter of urgent necessity, and asks the Board of Education to summon a conference at the earliest possible date, of representatives of Associations concerned in the administration of education and of the recognised teachers' organisations, with a view to the preparation of such a scale without undue delay'.[36] This initiative on the part of the A.E.C. did in fact lead to the establishment of the Burnham machinery. Fisher responded to the A.E.C.'s invitation by setting up the Standing Joint Committee on Salaries. He told the Commons that, 'In spite of all the efforts which have been made by the Board to improve the position of the teacher . . . in spite of the fact that the system of elementary school finance is now based on a principle definitely framed to encourage educational authorities to be liberal in their salaries; and in spite of the very liberal superannuation which has now been granted to teachers in elementary and secondary schools, there is still considerable unrest, and this unrest has been giving me very serious concern. There have been strikes here and strikes there and the work of the local education authorities, whose attention ought now to be engaged in tackling the very difficult problems created by the Education Act, is greatly embarrassed by these salary disputes. I have accordingly endeavoured to find some means by which these disputes may be minimised, and the atmosphere generally sweetened.'[37]

The Standing Joint Committee consisted of twenty-two representatives of the local authorities and twenty-two representatives of the

N.U.T. and its object was to secure a solution of the salary problem in public elementary schools. Committees were also set up soon after to deal with the salaries of secondary and technical school teachers. Fisher suggested that the elementary committee should begin by drawing up a provisional minimum scale and this it issued in November, 1919. The scale was accepted by the N.U.T. and by the great majority of the local authorities. By the beginning of 1921 Standard Scales I, II, III and IV for elementary schools had been formulated and had replaced the provisional minimum; by this time also a national scale had been formulated for secondary and technical teachers and was accepted both by the associations of teachers and of the local authorities.

To what extent did the establishment of national scales for salaries represent a measure of success for the teachers' associations? The view has been expressed that it was 'the final result of the agitation for better salaries' and that the first national scales 'culminated the salary campaign of the National Union of Teachers'.[38] Yet the setting-up of national negotiating machinery took place on the initiative of the local authorities, and the willingness of the N.U.T. to accept national in place of local scales was by no means obvious even as late as 1919. The salaries campaign of 1913 and the following year, which was resumed in 1916, was aimed at improving local authority scales for qualified elementary teachers. By 1919 some members and local associations were pressing the N.U.T. to seek a national scale; some nineteen motions on these lines were received for discussion at the Easter Conference of that year.[39] A letter in *The Schoolmaster* of 5th April, 1919, stated that 'it is high time that the Union demanded from the Government a national scale, instead of encouraging little strikes against Local Education Committees, whose scales, when very reluctantly granted, are not worth accepting'.

The case against a national scale was argued strongly in an editorial article in the N.U.T.'s journal in May, 1919.[40] The West Riding Education Committee had just resolved that there ought to be a national scale and this was by way of reply. The journal argued that there had not been enough clear thinking by those teachers who urged the promotion of a national scale. It was not at all certain that the worst-paid would be raised to the level of the best-paid. It concluded that the West Riding had in mind an average scale, 'one which would mean levelling down as much as levelling up', and that although a national scale might come eventually, 'the question of whether its coming should be hastened by teachers is one which needs to be well-weighed'.

Certainly the oldest, most well-established and influential local associations of the N.U.T. tended to be those of London and the big provincial cities, where local negotiations had brought a fair measure of success to teachers since the days of the large school boards. These appeared to have less to gain from a national scale—or scales—than teachers who lacked a tradition of successful local organisation and negotiation in such areas as rural Dorset or Wiltshire. The strength of the better established local associations may also be seen, perhaps, in the desire of the N.U.T. to regard national scales as minima when they were eventually settled, so as to leave room for local pressure to be brought to bear to improve them where possible.

The secondary associations, on the other hand, actively sought national scales at least for assistant teachers. One factor behind this attitude may have been the greater mobility which an ambitious secondary teacher had to show if he wanted to progress in his career, for while an elementary assistant might expect to get a headship under the same authority, there would be far fewer local opportunities for promotion for secondary assistants. An authority might have a hundred elementary schools, most of them with only a few assistants, while it might have only two or three secondary schools with possibly as many as twenty assistants each. A man who expected to have to move from one authority to another naturally wanted his earlier service to be recognised for incremental purposes, and would probably also favour a nationally accepted salary scale. Another important factor which influenced the secondary teachers to press for a national scale was that their limited numbers reduced their bargaining strength in any particular locality. Strikes were much less likely to be effective for them than for the elementary teachers. Before the war their tactics had been largely confined to collecting, tabulating and circulating information on salaries, setting such information alongside salary scales offered abroad or in other occupations in this country such as Civil Service appointments, and sending copies of these comparisons to members of local authorities responsible for salary scales with arguments for improvement. These tactics met with some success—as in Essex in 1912 —but argument was likely to be more effective at the national level than in dealing with those more reluctant local employers who refused to listen. Certainly by 1918 the secondary associations were seeking a national scale, the most active association in this respect being the I.A.A.M. The chairman of that organisation outlined its policy as seeking a national scale with pensions and salaries provided directly by the state to encourage mobility.[41] In 1919 the Board of Education received a deputation from the I.A.A.M. which proposed a national minimum secondary scale for assistants starting at £200 and rising to £600 by £20 steps; it also put its suggestion that the Board should take over responsibility for teachers' salaries, leaving local authorities to provide buildings and equipment.[42] The representatives of the Assistant Mistresses also urged the establishment of national scales for secondary teachers in their evidence before the Departmental Committee of 1918.[43] Thus it might be fair to conclude that in 1919 some of the elementary teachers were less anxious to change to national scales and negotiations than the secondary teachers. Local negotiations had served some of the N.U.T. associations reasonably well and they were not keen to leave the proven method for the unproven. At the same time the secondary associations had done less well in local negotiations and were much more anxious to see a national scale and national negotiating machinery established.

NOTES

1. Leeds School Board Year Book, 1902, pp. 37–8.
2. R. R. Sellman, *Devon Village Schools in the Nineteenth Century*, 1967, p. 103.
3. Leeds School Board, op. cit., p. 38.
4. Bryce Cssn., vol. IV, 1895, p. 539.
5. Ibid., p. 538.
6. W. H. D. Rouse, 'Salaries in Secondary Schools', *Contemporary Review*, August, 1900, pp. 275–80.
7. These figures relating to salaries in Devon are from Sellman, op. cit., pp. 148–9.
8. City of Leeds Education Committee Handbook, 1908, p. 162.
9. Report of the Departmental Committee for Enquiry into the Principles which should determine the construction of scales of salary for Teachers in Elementary Schools, Cd. 8939, 1918, vol. I, paras. 26 and 27.
10. A. Tropp, *The School Teachers*, 1957, p. 269.
11. Board of Education, Report for 1913–14, Cd. 7934, 1915, p. 74.
12. I.A.A.M., Annual Report, 1903, p. 29.
13. I.A.A.M., Annual Report, 1904, p. 30.

14. M. E. Sadler, *Report on Secondary and Higher Education in Essex*, 1906, p. 374.
15. C. Norwood, and A. Hope, *The Higher Education of Boys in England*, 1909, p. 239.
16. *Yorkshire Post*, 10 March, 1904, p. 8.
17. *Journal of Education*, June, 1904, p. 396.
18. I.A.A.M. Annual Report, 1906, p. 9.
19. I.A.A.M. Annual Report, 1910, Supplement II, p. 13.
20. Board of Education, Statistics relating to annual income and expenditure in certain secondary schools in England (excluding Wales and Monmouthshire), Cd. 5951, 1911, part II, p. 17.
21. I.A.A.M. Annual Report, 1911, p. 74.
22. *The A.M.A.*, October, 1914, p. 152.
23. A. Blades and G. D. Dunkerley, 'Salaries and Conditions of Service in Secondary Schools', *The A.M.A.*, September, 1915, pp. 144–7.
24. P.R.O. Ed. 24/14, Points against Ad Hoc by R.L.M.
25. Ministry of Education, *Education 1900–1950*, Cd. 8244, 1951, p. 25.
26. *Journal of Education*, January, 1909, pp. 18–19.
27. N.U.T. Annual Report, 1912, p. LXXXVIII.
28. N.U.T. Annual Report, 1914, p. LXXI.
29. 'The Fight for Salary Scales', *The Schoolmaster*, 20th March, 1953, p. 417.
30. I.A.A.M. Annual Report, 1917, p. 6.
31. Hansard, H. of C., 19th April, 1917, cols. 1896–97.
32. Report of the Departmental Committee, Cd. 8939, 1918, vol. I, p. 7.
33. Report of the Departmental Committee for Enquiry into the Principles which should determine the fixing of Salaries for Teachers in Secondary and Technical Schools, Schools of Art, Training Colleges and other Institutions for Higher Education (other than University Institutions), Cd. 9140, 1918, vol. I, p. 11.
34. *The A.M.A.*, January, 1918, p. 15.
35. Hansard, H. of C., 19th April, 1917, col. 1897.
36. P. Sharpe, 'The Burnham Committee', *Education*, 16th June, 1944, pp. 725–26.
37. Hansard, H. of C., 12th August, 1919, cols. 1231–2.
38. D. F. Thompson, *Professional Solidarity among the Teachers of England*, New York, 1927, pp. 261, 265.
39. *The Schoolmaster*, 4th January, 1919, pp. 10–12.

40. *The Schoolmaster*, 24th May, 1919, p. 807.
41. *Journal of Education*, November, 1918, pp. 677–8.
42. *The A.M.A.*, October, 1919, p. 88.
43. Report of the Departmental Committee, Summaries of Evidence, Cd. 9168, 1918, vol. II, p. 73.

3
Salaries between the Wars

The Standing Joint Committee between the local authorities and the N.U.T. completed its first task rapidly and issued a report on 21st November, 1919, recommending a provisional minimum scale for a college-trained certificated male teacher of £160 rising to at least £300; the provisional minimum scale for women extended from £150 to £240. Head teachers received somewhat higher salaries, the actual amount depending on the grading of the school. The committee, under the chairmanship of Lord Burnham, then proceeded to formulate complete scales for heads and assistants, the scales being based on the teachers' qualifications. Four sets of scales were evolved to cover the supposed difference in the cost of living in different parts of the country, the highest Standard Scale (IV) being payable in the metropolitan area and the lowest (I) by rural authorities. The introduction of four scales, rather than the more recent system of one scale with a cost-of-living allowance for the metropolitan area, was certainly a way of making the new national machinery more acceptable to the elementary teachers and the authorities, even if it was not entirely justified on the alleged grounds of variations in the cost of living. It enabled the committee to recommend Standard III scale payments in line with what teachers could in fact negotiate on a local basis in the large provincial cities without encountering the implacable hostility of the more remote rural authorities, who would certainly have not been prepared to accept such high figures for their teachers' salaries along with the sudden increase in costs that would have been involved. In a sense the four Standards arrangement for salaries provided an easier transition from the multiplicity of locally fixed scales to the post-Second World War period when a uniform system was accepted by both sides. The difficulty with which the teachers' associations representatives were faced becomes clear when the scales actually being paid in a few of the large cities in 1920 are set alongside the Standing Joint Committee's proposals; in Birmingham, for instance, trained certificated male assistants currently enjoyed a maximum salary £5 above

Table 3.1. *Scales for college-trained certificated assistant elementary school teachers*[1]

Standard Scale	Men				Women			
	£	s.	£ s.	£	£	£ s.	£
I	172	10 × 12	10	325	160 × 12	10	260
II	172	10 × 12	10	340	160 × 12	10	272
III	182	10 × 12	10	380	170 × 12	10	304
IV	200	× 12	10	425	187 × 12	10	340

Table 3.2. *Scales for uncertificated assistant elementary schoolteachers*[2]

Standard Scale	Men			
	£ s.	£ s.	£*	£†
I	103 10 × 7	10	160	204
II	103 10 × 7	10	160	204
III	109 10 × 7	10	180	228
IV	120 × 7	10	200	255

Standard Scale	Women		
	£ £ s.	£*	£†
I	96 × 7 10	150	164
II	96 × 7 10	150	164
III	102 × 7 10	160	182
IV	112 × 7 10	170	204

* Appointed on or after 1st April, 1914.
† Appointed before 1st April, 1914.

The scales for college trained certificated head teachers varied from maxima of £357 10s. (men) and £286 (women) in the smallest schools in Standard I areas to £637 10s. (men) and £510 (women) for the largest schools in Standard IV areas.

that now suggested for Standard Scale IV.[3] In these circumstances not only were the four sets of national scales understandable but so too was the desire of the N.U.T. negotiators, and particularly Yoxall, the General Secretary, to regard the recommended scales as standards which might be improved upon by local negotiation instead of as absolute figures which were not to be changed at the local level. The local authority associations were not prepared to accept this view since they felt that one of the main purposes of the national negotiations was to eliminate the competitive bidding-up of salaries by a few over-anxious authorities.

The 'fairness' or adequacy of any salary scales is generally a moot point with contemporaries and so it has been with the first Burnham Scales. The generally held view seems to be that the Scales marked a considerable advance for elementary school teachers' salaries. Tropp pointed out that the Report of the Committee on National Expenditure in 1931 showed that when the standard scales were recommended the cost of living was 164 per cent above pre-war, while the standard scales meant extra remuneration for elementary teachers of 159 per cent above the pre-war average.[4] The cost of living was at a peak in 1920 and began to fall rapidly soon after; teachers gained considerably from this trend in the next two decades, for the salary reductions that followed were proportionately a good deal smaller than the rise in the value of money (see Table 4.2). An editorial in the *Times Educational Supplement* two days before the acceptance of the Standard Scales at the N.U.T. special conference by a two-to-one majority suggested that there were two points which should be made when considering whether teachers were better or worse off than they were before the war: firstly that teachers would be protected against any fall in salary in the near future regardless of any possible fall in the cost of living, and secondly, 'that pensions are not only certain—and it must be remembered that the average tax payer and rate payer has no pension and is well aware of the fact that a teacher has a pension—but are fixed with reference to salaries which have been settled at a moment when prices are beginning to decline from their highest point'. The paper went on to express the view that teachers had been 'remarkably successful'.[5] There was a good deal of truth in this comment, but it needs to be qualified in that the settlement represented a much greater improvement for some groups of teachers in some areas than it did for other elementary school teachers in other areas.

The Joint Standing Committee for salaries in secondary schools consisted of 26 representatives of local authorities and 26 representatives of teachers associations with Lord Burnham as chairman; it was set up in May, 1920 and reported on the following 1st October. There had been some delay in setting up this committee and the teachers' position was said to be becoming 'almost desperate'.[6] The I.A.A.M. had claimed a national salary scale for assistant masters of £300 to £800 by steps of £30 and at the beginning of 1920 suggested that the first step should be to institute immediately a minimum scale of £300 to £600. The Association of Assistant Mistresses claimed a scale for graduate mistresses of £300 to £600 by steps of £20. The Association of Head Mistresses recommended a similar scale for assistants and for heads of schools with fewer than 300 pupils £600 to £800 by steps of £50, with a scale reaching to £900 at the maximum for headmistresses of schools with more than 300 pupils. In the previous year the I.A.H.M. adopted a resolution advocating a minimum salary of £800 for head masters and the abandonment of capitation payments. National scales were recommended for assistant masters and mistresses.

Table 3.3. *Scales for Assistant Masters and Mistresses in Secondary Schools*[7]

I GRADUATES					
Men			Women		
Minimum	Increment	Maximum	Minimum	Increment	Maximum
£	£	£	£	£	£
250	15	500	225	15	400

II NON-GRADUATES					
Men			Women		
Minimum	Increment	Maximum	Minimum	Increment	Maximum
£	£	£	£	£	£
190	12 10s.	400	177 10s.	12 10s.	320

There were additional payments of £50 for a good honours degree and up to £50 for a post of special responsibility in a school. Slightly higher scales were payable in London.

Although these scales were unanimously recommended by the Joint Standing Committee there was a good deal of criticism of particular points from members of both the A.A.M. and the I.A.A.M. Members of the Association of Assistant Mistresses believed the commencing points of the scales were much too low, particularly for non-graduates, and they were also disappointed to find that the principle of equal pay for men and women had not been granted. Both of the assistant teachers' organisations considered that the maxima were too low.[8] Even so the executives of all four secondary associations recommended acceptance of the Report as did the local authority associations. Most of the authorities adopted the new scales but quite a number did so from

1st April, 1921 instead of from 1st September, 1920, which had been the recommended date. The governing bodies of many endowed schools were not directly parties to the agreement even though some of them received a block grant from a local authority. Only where the local authority assumed direct responsibility for any deficit in the running expenses of a school did the Report have immediate application. Nevertheless, the pressure of the market soon led most schools not controlled by the agreement to adopt the scales or scales slightly more favourable in some cases. It is interesting to note that G. D. Dunkerley who was Organising Secretary of the I.A.A.M. and Secretary to the Secondary Teachers' Panel in the Standing Joint Committee, wrote with a co-author two years later that, 'The general opinion expressed by the Associations of Teachers responsible for the negotiations was that, while these scales in themselves would not make the remuneration sufficiently attractive at the cost of living then prevailing, yet, as the latter diminished, the teachers would be placed relatively in a more favourable position.'[9] Certainly there is no question but that the adoption of national scales was of great value to most secondary school teachers. The contrast between the pre-war and post-war position was very marked, as Dunkerley and Kingham themselves stated when they pointed out in the early twenties that 'until the last two or three years the prospects of Secondary School teachers, where any such existed, were unsatisfactory in the extreme; in far too many cases there was nothing that could be described as prospects—a state of affairs which acted as a thorough blight on the profession'.[10]

The Burnham Secondary Committee found the position of head teachers too complex for it to be able to prescribe scales; accordingly it recommended that head masters should be paid on scales devised by local authorities to suit the circumstances of their own schools but that no scale should have a minimum point below £600 per annum. A considerable number of authorities did not hasten to lay down scales for heads and a number continued for some while to pay salaries below the minimum figure of £600. In their efforts to get this minimum salary accepted, the I.A.H.M. decided that after March, 1923, no person who accepted appointment to a headship at a salary below £600 per annum would be admitted to membership of the Association.[11] The Association sought to persuade the Board of Education to bring pressure to bear on authorities that were failing to pay the minimum, but the Board's response was far from satisfactory.[12]

The Board itself, as well as local authorities and teachers, began to come under pressure to reduce expenditure on education in the early 1920s and the teachers' associations were to be concerned with defending the salary position gained in 1920 for much of the period between the two wars. The fall in cost of living from the high level reached at the time the first Burnham scales were negotiated, along with periodic economic crises of depression, formed the background against which the associations had to fight their defensive battles. Any success they met with in preserving the post-war position meant some gain in the real income of their members all the while the value of money continued to increase—as it did until about 1935.

As early as 1921 the Board of Education suggested to the teachers' associations that their members should surrender part of their salaries and contribute towards the cost of their pensions. The proposal met with a negative response. Early in 1922 the Committee on National Expenditure (Geddes Committee) issued its First Interim Report, on which it had been working for much of 1921.[13] The Report pointed out that the bill for teachers' salaries was two-and-a-half times the pre-war figure, that the cost of living index stood at 161 in September, 1920, when the Burnham scales were fixed but had since fallen to 103, and that wage reductions on the ground of the falling cost of living had been accepted by most other classes of the community. It went on, 'We see no way of making the reductions necessary in the national expenditure without, among economies in many other directions, reducing the expenditure on elementary education. This can only be done by raising the lower age limit, by putting more pupils under one teacher, and paying the teachers less, and we think the teachers and Education Authorities should be asked to face this fact.'[14] Associated with the cost of salaries was that of pensions, under the Superannuation Act of 1918; since this Act offered pensions on a scale broadly similar to those of the civil service to teachers on a non-contributory basis, there was a rapidly increasing Treasury commitment.[15]

The government of the day decided not to raise the age of entry to schools and not to cut teachers' salaries, but it did propose to go ahead with a School Teachers (Superannuation) Bill. The vigorous opposition of the teachers' associations to this, particularly the N.U.T., is discussed elsewhere (*infra* chapter 6).

But however annoyed the teachers might have been by the superannuation measure, more troubles were to come, for the Geddes Committee's suggestion that teachers should be paid less was translated into a positive suggestion through the Burnham Committees that they should accept a voluntary abatement of 5 per cent of their salaries for the fiscal year 1923-4. The matter was first put to the Burnham Committee for elementary schools and was accepted by the N.U.T. at a Special Conference late in 1922. The acceptance of this 'voluntary' cut in pay by the N.U.T. seems to have been in the hope that it would prevent the disintegration of the Burnham scales, the possible dissolution of the Burnham Committee and further demands for even more severe reductions. The Authorities' Panel in the Committee, when asking for the reduction, pointed out that many authorities had already banded together to try to obtain reductions on a local basis, and that some of them were suggesting figures as high as 20 per cent.[18] At a meeting in January, 1923, the teachers' representatives on the Burnham Secondary Committee were asked whether they were prepared to make an offer along the same lines as the elementary teachers; they agreed to recommend the 5 per cent reduction to their associations.

A small number of local authorities nevertheless took matters into their own hands and tried to abandon the Burnham agreements. In an effort to check this trend, the N.U.T. found it necessary to undertake strike action in Lowestoft, Gateshead and Southampton. These authorities attempted to impose cuts which would have the effect of reducing the salaries of their teaching staffs below the payments agreed under the reduced national scales. In Lowestoft the strike lasted for eleven months, while in Gateshead and Southampton the strikes lasted for two-and-a-half and three-and-a-half months respectively.

The secondary associations were also engaged in defensive action at this time. South Shields education authority dismissed teachers in its secondary schools and refused to reappoint them except at a reduction of 15 per cent of their salaries. The I.A.A.M. advised its members concerned to refuse re-engagement and promised them full financial support, but in less than three weeks the majority of the staff had returned to work, apparently influenced by the belief that the authority would find it easy to fill the vacated posts since no qualifications were laid down as necessary for a secondary school teacher, and staff needed to be very weak before the Board of Education would refuse a grant. In Cardiganshire the N.U.T. and the secondary associations supported their members who resigned when the authority adopted a scale for secondary schools which was much inferior to the Burnham agreement. The I.A.A.M. wrote to intending applicants informing them of the position, and three schools which were unable to appoint suitable staff were closed for a term in 1923. The dispute dragged on for a number of years before Cardiganshire came to adopt fully the Burnham scales.[19]

The original Burnham Report on the salary scales which were in 1923 reduced by 5 per cent was itself due to expire in March, 1925. Negotiations for a Report to come into force on 1st April were undertaken in May, 1924. The authorities sought considerable further reductions, initially of 15 and later of 10 per cent in salary levels. The teachers' panel refused to agree to any further reductions and in the autumn both sides agreed to accept the arbitration of Lord Burnham. The position in which the teachers' associations found themselves was certainly very difficult and their members were regarded with envy and hostility by many newspapers and by large sections of the public.[20] Their position was described in the *Contemporary Review* in these terms: 'In place of the strong support in the major part of the better class press, they found themselves confronted with a growing attack on their whole salary position. The less scrupulous journals represented them as war-profiteers in salary, who were luxuriating in incomes double or treble those received before the War. The whole case on which the amelioration of the teachers' position rested, the fact that the improvement in their salaries was a very much overdue pre-war adjustment, became forgotten or deliberately ignored, and the teachers were ranked indiscriminately with all the many industrial groups that had, since the War, been fighting the wage question.'[21] The immediate outcome of the arbitration was favourable to the teachers, for Lord Burnham recommended new scales which involved a reduction of existing salaries by rather less than 1 per cent.

Most local education authorities accepted the award within two months of its being announced, but by the following December the elementary scales had still not been adopted by Carmarthenshire, Croydon, Essex, Harwich, Newcastle-under-Lyme, Pembroke (borough) and Wimbledon. Under the conditions agreed for seeking arbitration, the Burnham Committee suggested to the President of the Board of Education that he should take action against the authorities which did not conform. In February, 1926, the Board issued a regulation requiring payment on the agreed scales by all authorities and by March only Essex and Carmarthenshire maintained their refusal to pay. Essex County Council sought the opinion of counsel as to the legality of the Board's regulation of February. W. M. Upjohn, K.C., expressed the opinion that the Board of Education's regulation was illegal. The Board's reply came in July, 1926, when Lord Percy, the President announced that new draft regulations had been framed which would have the effect of safeguarding the payment of the Burnham scales since the government grant would be adjusted to ensure that no authority benefited financially from paying less than the scale suggested. This ensured that the Burnham scales were now in effect compulsory.

The economic crisis of 1931 again led to a situation in which the teachers' associations found themselves defending the existing salary scales against urgent and powerful demands for reductions. The settlement of 1925 had been for a period of six years and could be terminated by one year's notice from either the teachers' or the authorities' panel of the Burnham Committee; the latter gave notice in 1931 that the present award should end on 31st March, 1932. Accordingly the committee on elementary teachers' salaries met and the authorities pressed the teachers' representatives to accept that there should be a reduction in the total amount spent on salaries. The teachers refused to accept this as a principle around which more detailed negotiations should take place, and the committee therefore adjourned indefinitely. In the summer of 1931 the May Committee on National Expenditure published its report.[22] The Committee recited the main events in the story of teachers' salary negotiations since the War and commented astringently on the failure of the government to impose in full the cuts suggested by the Geddes Committee, adding that 'In the present financial situation, it appears to us essential that the Government must itself assure to the negotiating body that grants will only be paid on the assumption that there is an overall cut in the total cost [of salaries] of the prescribed percentage. In this connection we might point to the position of the police. Like teachers they are engaged, paid, promoted and retired by local authorities, aided by a percentage grant from the state. Yet in their case the state fixes the salaries. We do not see any fundamental reason why if the fixing of salaries by the state is appropriate in the case of the police it should be inappropriate in the case of teachers.' The prescribed percentage cut suggested was twenty, after the committee had explained that the continuing fall in the cost of living pointed to a reduction 'in the neighbourhood of 30 per cent'.

All the teachers' associations did what they could to oppose the threatened reductions. They protested particularly against what they considered to be the misrepresentation of their position by the May Report. The leader of the Secondary Teachers' Burnham Panel, W. Jenkyn Thomas, in a letter challenging the May Committee's arguments, quoted from the 1923 Memorandum of the Association of Education Committees which had criticised the Geddes proposals. 'The teachers who urged insistently in August, 1920, the excessive cost of living were given their option of a sliding scale of salaries, high at the moment but falling as prices fell, or a scale based upon normal prices, to continue unaltered for a period of years. They chose the latter, and thereupon the then cost of living ceased to be a factor in settling the

Table 3.4. *The average salaries of teachers, 1914–30*[23]

	GRADUATES			NON-GRADUATES		
	Men £	Women £	Men and Women £	Men £	Women £	Men and Women £
Average salary at:						
31st January, 1914	225	151	194	165	123	139
31st March, 1922 (first year of Burnham scales)	451	343	400	357	272	301
31st March, 1923 (second year of Burnham scales)	461	359	413	376	289	319
31st March, 1924 (5% reduction)	442	348	399	365	382	310
31st March, 1930	436	366	420	384	297	326

scales. They were calculated upon normal conditions.'[24] In spite of the opposition, the government made it clear that it was going to exact a reduction of 15 per cent in salaries and that the entire benefit of this saving was to go to the Treasury, the local authorities to feel no benefit. In August, 1931, Sir George Lunn, the leader of the authorities' panel urged on the teachers' associations the need to resume meetings of the Burnham Committees so as to ascertain what the national situation required by way of a reasonable reduction. At the same time the authorities made it clear that they had not been seeking a reduction in the expenditure on salaries so that the entire benefit should go to the central government. Thus on 15th September, the day after the National Economy Bill was given its second reading in the Commons, the A.E.C. sent a letter to the Prime Minister, the president of the Board of Education and to all M.P.s, protesting against the undue severity of the proposed cut. The teachers' associations maintained vigorous pressure—as did other sections of the community who were threatened—and they achieved a measure of success. On 21st September the Prime Minister announced in the Commons that the government had decided that 'the simplest way of removing just grievances is to limit the reductions as regards teachers, police and the three Defence Services, to not more than 10 per cent.'[25]

The Burnham Committee met again in November in an attempt to draw up scales which would apply from April, 1932, and to inquire into the possibility of varying the relative shares of the loss to be borne by particular groups of teachers, within the context of the 10 per cent reduction in the total of salaries paid which had been ordered. Any attempt to vary the scales then would, of course, have involved reducing the salaries of some teachers by more than 10 per cent; this was felt to be too difficult and too invidious an exercise and it was not undertaken. The Burnham Committees formally extended the scales of 1925 to 31st March, 1933, and the cuts required were, therefore, deducted proportionately from these scales.

Once the cuts had been imposed, the teachers' associations pressed for the restoration of full salaries. One consequence of the cuts which was particularly painful was the injustice which arose from the permanent reduction in the superannuation benefits of those due to retire, whose pensions would be calculated on the basis of salaries reduced temporarily to meet a short-term financial crisis. The permanent sacrifice inflicted in this way on a minority was stressed at the I.A.A.M. Council Meeting at the beginning of 1932.[26] The Burnham Committee extended the 1925 scales for a further year in March, 1933, and during the year the teachers' associations developed their campaign for the restoration of full salaries. On 23rd November a deputation from the N.U.T. was received by the Prime Minister, which presented a petition with 200,000 signatures, asking for the resumption of full salaries. In the course of the interview the Prime Minister gave the assurance that the reduced salaries would not be taken as a basis for normal negotiations. In their campaign the teachers were supported by some local authorities.

In the spring of 1934 the government announced that half of the cut would be restored on 1st July. This partial restoration aroused more alarm among teachers at the prospect of a 5 per cent cut now becoming a semi-permanent feature. The Joint Four Secondary Associations wrote to the President of the Board of Education expressing this concern in April, 1934. In their letter they pointed out that this action was difficult to reconcile with the assurances repeatedly given that the cuts were purely a temporary expedient.[27] The other half of the 1931 cut was finally restored from July, 1935.

The passing of the emergency led to attention being focussed on the shape and form of the salary structure, which had remained unchanged since 1920. The arrangement of having four standard scales for elementary school teachers based on the area in which they worked had served a useful purpose in enabling the machinery of national negotiations to take over from an extremely varied pattern of local payments with less friction than might otherwise have arisen. The disadvantages of the system became increasingly apparent with the passage of time, while the general acceptance and working of the Burnham system itself made the existence of as wide a variety as four separate standards less necessary. In 1931 Dr. J. Graham had submitted a memorandum on the structure of teachers' salary payments to the executive committee of the A.E.C., in which he criticised some of the consequences of the way in which the standard scales worked. He wrote, 'The Scale IV authorities get the cream, the Scale III authorities get the Grade A milk, and the Scale II and Scale I authorities share what is left'.[28] The N.U.T. was pressed by many of its members to seek the abolition of the lower standard scales, and in the Burnham negotiations which opened in the autumn of 1935 the Union also pressed for this. In its Report of January, 1936, the Burnham Elementary Committee abolished Standard Scale I, the lowest, but recommended the continuation of the other three for the period to be covered by the Report, 1936-9.

Although no other significant changes were made in the late 1930s, the teachers' associations were formulating salary policies in these years which were to have significant consequences in the period of reconstruction after the Second World War. The policy evolved by the N.U.T. was to be particularly important, for many of the ideas set out in the Union's memorandum on Salary Policy in 1939 came to be accepted by the remodelled Burnham Committees five years later. The principle underlying this memorandum was that 'salaries of teachers should depend upon qualifications, length of service and special responsibility, and not upon the sex of the teacher or type of school or area in which service is rendered'.[29] The ultimate aim, therefore, was not only the abolition of the separate standard scales for elementary teachers in different areas but also the abolition of the separate scales paid in the secondary and technical schools. The influence of the large female membership of the Union might perhaps be seen in the removal of 'the sex of the teacher' from among the criteria determining salary. The immediate aims of the Union were listed as:

> The restoration of equality of increments between men and women;
> The securing for women teachers of the highest possible proportion of the men teachers' salaries up to 100 per cent;
> The elimination of Scale 2;
> The highest obtainable degree of co-ordination between elementary scales and those in elementary and technical schools in respect of both graduates and non-graduates;
> The elimination of the 'probationary' halt;
> Improved scales for uncertificated teachers;
> The elimination of miscellaneous anomalies.[30]

While the main preoccupation of the associations representing the various groups of teachers had been with defending the existing position against attacks on their salaries it had not been difficult for them to stand united; it was only to be expected that differences would appear in the more positive task of planning possible future developments. The associations representing secondary teachers were scarcely likely to urge the abolition of their own distinct salary scales. The Salaries Sub-Committee of the I.A.A.M., for instance, reconsidered the principles on which the secondary schoolmasters' salary should be based and rejected the suggestion of the common scale for all qualified teachers.[31] The possible consequences of such a scale had been examined by A. Gray Jones in an article in *The A.M.A.* in February, 1937; he concluded that the secondary teacher 'would inevitably be cast for the part of Peter—the Peter who was robbed to pay Paul'.[32] The precursors of the later difficulties between teachers' associations had arrived.

NOTES

1. Board of Education, Report of the Standing Joint Committee on Standard Scales for Teachers in Public Elementary Schools, 1920, p. 2.
2. Ibid., p. 4.

3. *T.E.S.*, 4th November, 1920, p. 584.
4. A. Tropp, *The School Teachers*, 1957, p. 212.
5. *T.E.S.*, 4th November, 1920, p. 587.
6. *Journal of Education*, July, 1920, p. 437.
7. Board of Education, Report for the Year 1919–20, 1921, p. 3.
8. *Journal of Education* t December, 1920, p. 779.
9. G. D. Dunkerley and W. R. Kingham, *The Assistant Master*, 1923, p. 59.
10. Ibid., p. 55.
11. *Journal of Education*, February, 1922, p. 141.
12. *T.E.S.*, 25th March, 1922, p. 141.
13. First Interim Report of the Committee on National Expenditure, Cmd. 1581, 1922.
14. Ibid., p. 111.
15. Ibid., p. 120.
16. Report of the Select Committee on Teachers in Grant-Aided Schools (Superannuation), 1922.
17. Tropp, op. cit., p. 220.
18. *The Schoolmaster*, 8th December, 1922, p. 855 and confirmed by verbatim records of the Burnham Committee.
19. *The A.M.A.*, June, 1922, p. 93; *The A.M.A.*, September, 1923, pp. 164–9 and September, 1924, pp. 196–204.
20. In the leading article in the *Daily Mail*, 25th September, 1924, teaching was described as a 'parasitic' pursuit. It continued, 'The teachers like to identify themselves with the cause of education, but their rate of pay has nothing to do with educational efficiency, nor does it bear any real relation to their qualifications, or to their outlay in preparing themselves for their career. The elementary schoolmaster is not required to be a person of high accomplishment and he gets his training cheap.' *The Schoolmaster*, 10th October, 1924, p. 538.
21. S. Rowland, 'The Schoolmaster's Position', *Contemporary Review*, November, 1924.
22. Report of the Committee on National Expenditure, Cmd. 3920, 1931.
23. Ibid., p. 50.
24. *T.E.S.*, 22nd August, 1931, p. 329.
25. *Hansard*, H. of C., 21st September, 1931, col. 1271.
26. *Journal of Education*, February, 1932, p. 125.
27. *The A.M.A.*, January, 1935, p. 24.

28. *T.E.S.*, 31st January, 1931, p. 41.
29. N.U.T. Annual Report, 1939, p. CVII.
30. Ibid., p. CXII.
31. *The A.M.A.*, January, 1938, p. 33.
32. *The A.M.A.*, February, 1937, pp. 658–60.

4
Salaries since the Second World War

The two most striking developments in the salary structure during the last quarter-century were the establishment of a common scale for all qualified teachers employed in local authority schools in 1945, and the later introduction of differential payments for the more highly qualified teachers dealing with more advanced work and with older pupils. The table of salary indices on page 94 and the subsequent note show the extent to which the introduction of the common or basic scale for all qualified teachers favoured the sectional interests of the great majority serving in the former elementary schools, while the reintroduction in different ways of differentials has favoured the graduate and the secondary school assistant. It would be straightforward if one could explain the developments of 1945 by saying that the union representing the certificated elementary teachers was then in the ascendant and that the adoption of the basic scale was due simply to the influence of the N.U.T. on public policy in this field. It would also be a simple and uncomplicated explanation to say that the changes since that date which have sought to attract more good graduates back to the schools marked the increasing influence of the Joint Four. Although there might be some truth in either of these statements, neither can be said to offer anything approaching an adequate explanation of the actual course of events, in spite of the opinions expressed by some teachers. As in earlier years, the influences exerted by the teachers' associations were mingled with other influences to produce the pattern of salary settlements which have followed the Second World War.

I THE ESTABLISHMENT OF A COMMON SCALE

During the years following 1939, as in previous wars, much attention was given to replanning the whole system of education. The educational doctrines which found widespread and official favour at that time stressed the equal importance to be attached to the education of all children. 'The keynote of the new system will be that the child is the centre of education and that, so far as is humanly possible, all children should receive the type of education for which they are best adapted.... If this choice is to be a real one, it is manifest that conditions in the different types of secondary schools must be broadly equivalent.'[1] From this it could be said to follow that all teachers should be paid on a common salary scale, however dull or gifted, old or young their pupils might be.

The first official report to spell out in terms of the salary structure the consequences of secondary education for children of all abilities was that of the Spens Committee in 1938. This report did not go so far as to suggest a common scale for all teachers, but it did suggest that the type of school in which a teacher was serving should no longer determine automatically the salary scale applicable. If grammar and modern schools were to be recognised as of equal worth, as varying forms of the same secondary stage of education, then the principles on which teachers' salary scales were based would have to be changed. 'At present these two forms of secondary education are sharply divided by the fact that the basis of the teachers' remuneration is the type of school in which he serves. So complete a differentiation cannot be maintained indefinitely, if the salaries of teachers are to be in any way consistent with parity of schools in the secondary stage.' The Spens Committee recommended that 'There would still be two scales of salary for teachers in grammar and modern schools, but these would no longer be "elementary" and "secondary"; a proportion of posts on the higher scale would be allocated to each type of school.' The Committee added that 'in the grammar schools the proportion of posts on the higher scale would be larger owing to the preponderance of more advanced work'.[2]

One effect of war-time conditions was to encourage an egalitarian outlook in the world of education, and this explains why the McNair Committee, reporting in 1944, went the whole way in recommending one basic scale for all who were 'qualified' and 'that the Board of Education should recognise only one grade of teacher, namely the grade of "qualified teacher", and that, subject to the Board having discretion to accord such recognition to persons with good academic or other attainments, a qualified teacher should be a teacher who has satisfactorily completed an approved course of education and training.'[3]

Such a movement as was now apparent in 'official' thought had long been sought by the National Federation of Class Teachers. The Federation expressed its policy on this issue in five points first accepted in 1929; these were:

(1) The teaching profession is an essential unity;
(2) The adequate remuneration of the class teacher is the basic principle of salary policy;
(3) There is no justification for differentiations in different types of schools;
(4) There should be only one Burnham Committee;
(5) Additions should be made to the basic scale for posts of special responsibility.[4]

The Federation pressed these aims at N.U.T. conferences from 1929. In the early years the executive of the Union was not willing to accept it; in 1931 the general secretary, Mander, urged the conference to leave the executive 'with a free hand and a strong hand to face the future' and he opposed the idea of fusing the elementary and secondary Burnham committees on the grounds that 'the strength of the Union resides in the Elementary Panel where the Union has a strong and coherent body'. Resistance to economy cuts and attempts to have the cuts restored occupied the main effort of the N.U.T. in the years following 1931. Up to 1938 the demand for one scale and one committee was still being rejected by the conference on the advice of the executive, but in the next year the position changed. By the spring of 1939 the N.U.T. executive had changed its mind on this issue and put forward to the annual conference at Llandudno a Memorandum on salary policy incorporating the principles advocated by the N.F.C.T. On 20th May, 1939, copies of the Memorandum were sent to Sir Percival Sharp, Secretary of the authorities' panel, with a letter asking the panel to join in a 'friendly discussion of the issues raised'. In his reply Sharp indicated that the authorities' panel was prepared to accept the invitation, but the international crisis and the outbreak of war prevented matters from being taken further at that time.

During the first four years of the war, salary activity of the teachers' associations and the Burnham machinery was largely confined to seeking and recommending war allowances to meet increases in the cost of living which arose out of war-time conditions. These allowances, the first of which was agreed in 1940, applied either only to teachers who were on lower salary scales or applied more generously to the less well-paid. The allowance payable from April, 1941, for instance, amounted in the case of men to £26 p.a. on salaries up to £262 10s. to £13 on salaries exceeding £262 10s., but not above £370, and no addition was to be made to salaries of more than £370. Since these additional payments were designed to meet increases in the cost of living and, by implication, to alleviate any hardship, there was some justification for concentrating the relief they gave on the lowest paid; but an incidental effect was to narrow the range of salaries and to move nearer to a greater equality. Although unintentionally so, it was certainly in line with the sentiments officially expressed by the Board of Education in 1941 in *Education after the War*. 'It is clear that, if a policy is to be adopted to secure a greater unification of the educational system and to break down the old distinctions too often redolent of social prejudice, it will be desirable to unify, as far as may be, the teaching profession and to find some alternative to a series of differentiated scales which are based on distinctions it is desired to remove.'[5]

The Education Act of 1944 provided for a different statutory system of education in three stages, primary, secondary and further; the division between primary and secondary was to be at the age of eleven. Thus both the elementary and secondary codes as they had existed hitherto were superseded, and all schools providing for children over the age of eleven were to fall within the orbit of the new secondary code. It followed from this that the position of the separate Burnham elementary and secondary committees would need to be reconsidered. Section 89 stated: '(1) The Minister shall secure that for the purpose of considering the remuneration of teachers there shall be one or more committees approved by him consisting of persons appointed by bodies representing local education authorities and teachers respectively, and it shall be the duty of any such committee to submit to the Minister, whenever they think fit or whenever they may be required by him to do so, such scales of remuneration for teachers as they consider suitable; and whenever a scale of remuneration so submitted is approved by the Minister, he may by order make such provision as appears to him to be desirable for the purpose of securing that the remuneration paid by local education authorities to teachers is in accordance therewith.' Thus the Act left the future committee arrangements to be decided by the Minister, but it did meet the demands of virtually all the teachers' associations in that it provided for the enforcement of future recommendations from the Burnham machinery by statutory order. Thus no longer would it be possible for individual authorities to pay less than

Burnham and for the teachers' associations to have to undertake campaigns against such wayward L.E.A.s to bring them into line.

Although all the teachers' associations found themselves united in welcoming statutory enforcement, their reactions to the Minister's reconstruction of the committee system were mixed. Mr. Butler as Minister, announced the new arrangement in the House of Commons on 4th May, 1944, but his 'provisional conclusions' had already become known the previous month.[6] The Burnham elementary and secondary committees were to be abolished and their work was to pass to a new committee, the Burnham main committee, consisting of both a teachers' and an employers' panel. The teachers' panel had 26 members, 16 from the N.U.T., 4 from the A.T.T.I., 2 from the I.A.A.M., 2 from the A.A.M., 1 from the I.A.H.M. and 1 from the A.H.M. The new panel was thus dominated by the N.U.T.'s representatives who, with their associates from the A.T.T.I., held more than three quarters of the places and the spokesman for the teachers' panel was the general secretary of the N.U.T. The reaction of the secondary teachers' associations to losing the Burnham secondary committee, where their voices had been heard hitherto, and forming less than a quarter of the new teachers' panel of the main committee could scarcely be cheerful. Their fears had already been expressed in an editorial article in *The A.M.A.* in March which discussed the future structure of Burnham, pointing out that before the war there were about 200,000 teachers in England and Wales and the number of heads and assistants in secondary schools was no more than 25,000. 'In a single committee the representatives of teachers in the existing secondary schools would be a minority'; it would be unwise to place on one committee the responsibility for all schools. 'When all post-primary schools are in fact secondary schools, when real changes and not changes in nomenclature only have been effected, the position will be different.'[7]

The representatives of the four secondary associations had expressed the view to Mr. Butler that it would be impossible for one committee, comprising an authorities' and a teachers' panel, each panel having its own leader and only the two leaders being permitted to speak at meetings of the full committee, to function successfully. They suggested to the Minister that it would improve both confidence and efficiency to establish a number of committees whose members would have specialised knowledge of the problems of the different types of school, i.e. primary, grammar, modern and technical. The work of these committees could be co-ordinated through a Burnham co-ordinating committee upon which each of the sectional committees would be equally represented and in the proceedings of which their representatives would have a direct voice. In fact these suggestions were put on one side by the Minister and he offered the Joint Four minority representation on the new main committee. The secondary associations believed that refusal would be interpreted as unwillingness to take part in a reorganisation generally held to be an essential part of the reform outlined in the new Education Act, and feared that the Minister would proceed with his plans without their assistance. Reluctantly they agreed to participate, but stated that 'since the proposed reconstruction and suggested procedure apparently offered no opportunity for the expression of minority views through the machinery of the Burnham Committee, our constituent association will undoubtedly feel that they must reserve the right to use other means of making their opinions known'.[8]

The influence of the Joint Four appears to have been negligible in the negotiations which led to the first report from the new Burnham main committee, and it is in the years of its operation, 1945–8, that the accompanying tables show the greatest departure from normal in the differentials between the salary grades there illustrated, the biggest loser being the graduate assistant in the grammar school. These were also years when feeling between the secondary teachers and their associations and the N.U.T. was very bitter.

At the outset of the negotiations the teachers' panel incorporated their claim in an agreed document which set out the following principles in the preamble: 'That salaries of teachers should not be differentiated solely on account of sex or type of school, or in respect of area, except as between areas of the London type and the rest of the country.

'That all salaries should be related to a basic scale to be fixed for all qualified teachers.

'That departures from the basic scale should only be made on account of the possession of qualifications additional to, or less than the basic qualification referred to above, or upon appointment or posting to a position of special responsibility.'[9]

The initial unity thus exhibited by the members of the teachers' panel disappeared in the face of the pressures set up by the negotiations. The first task which the Burnham main committee had to undertake was to negotiate a basic scale for qualified assistant teachers, who were to be regarded as similar to the existing certificated teachers. At this stage no difficulties arose within the teachers' panel. One of the

I.A.A.M. representatives said later, 'We were all anxious to improve the salary position of teachers in this category and certainly on the secondary side we have always recognised the importance of the work that is done in the primary schools. A sound system of secondary education requires for its foundation a sound system of primary education.'[10] The new basic scale for men was agreed at £300 increasing by £15 to £525. This was a considerable improvement on existing salaries for non-graduate assistants, but it did not bring any improvement in real income by comparison with the certificated teacher in 1938 if allowance be made for the rise in the level of retail prices.

The differences between the teachers' associations arose over the additions to the basic scale to be made for the possession of additional qualifications or for holding posts of special responsibility. In their initial bid the teachers' panel had claimed a graduate addition of £75 at the minimum and £100 at the maximum. The authorities had initially argued against paying any addition, claiming that while graduation was an important additional qualification there was no need for a special payment for it as such, since graduates would stand a good chance of receiving this in the form of remuneration for posts of special responsibility. Eventually the majority of the teachers' panel lowered their bid for a graduate addition to £15 at the minimum and £45 at the maximum, the cost being met partly by a reduction in the number of posts of special responsibility the authorities were prepared to offer. The authorities' panel then offered a graduate addition of £15 to £30 for men (women to receive the then usual proportionate rate of four-fifths of the men's payment) and this was accepted by the majority of the teachers' panel, the representatives of the Joint Four dissenting. The scheme for special allowances permitted additions for special responsibility of not less than £50 or more than £100; in the case of graduates the graduate allowance was to be deducted, so the allowances to such teachers with maximum scale salaries ranged from £20 to £70.[11]

The ratification of this provisional agreement by the teachers' panel marked the opening of public hostility between the teachers' associations. One cannot help noting that the inauguration of the official 'unification' of the teaching profession led to more bitterness between elementary and secondary teachers and their associations than had probably ever been seen before. The representatives of the secondary teachers, outvoted in the Burnham teachers' panel, decided to put their case before a wider public, and the following letter appeared in the *Times Educational Supplement* in November, 1944:[12]

Sir, The provisional proposals agreed by the Burnham committee are being submitted to the constituent associations and therefore must be regarded as *sub judice*; detailed comment must be postponed until these bodies have made known their views. The six representatives of the four secondary associations are, however, so convinced that the implementing of these proposals would militate against the present and future efficiency of the existing secondary schools that they are unable to commend these proposals to their constituents.

The maintenance and improvement of the standard of the existing maintained and aided secondary schools depend on their power to attract to their service suitable men and women of the highest qualifications. The proposals of the Burnham committee have increased our misgivings for the future development of these schools, and it is for this reason that the six representatives of the four secondary associations are unable to give them support.

The annoyance felt by the N.U.T. at the publication by the Joint Four of their grievances soon found expression in *The Schoolmaster*, where particular concern was shown over the impressions feared to have been created:[13]

> and among the impressions created by the letter ... in the minds of members of the National Union of Teachers as well as in the minds of teachers generally was that in some vague way the Union representatives on the Burnham committee had sold the pass and given representatives of the Four Secondary Associations grounds for protest against their action.

The I.A.A.M. sent a circular to branches on 23rd November outlining the advantages if L.E.A.s could be persuaded to advise their associations, and through them the Authorities' Panel, that the suggested scales should be improved in certain directions. Local action might include deputations to councillors, directors, etc.; letters might also be sent to M.P.s, particularly university members, on the graduate issue. The N.U.T. regarded this as another attack on the leading position it had secured in the new Burnham machinery and *The Schoolmaster* complained that the I.A.A.M. was trying to edge forward on its own narrow front while sheltering behind the main proposals. On the campaign to influence local authorities it commented that 'the teaching profession simply cannot afford to educate local authorities in the art of rebellion against their appointed leaders'.[14]

The provisional agreement was accepted by a special salaries conference of the N.U.T. on 5th December, 1944, when 2,000 voted in favour of acceptance and 3 against. This ensured that the suggested scales would come into force. At the conference itself those delegates expressing the views of the National Federation of Class Teachers thought that the difference between the salaries of heads and assistants was too wide, while those expressing the views of the National Association of Head Teachers thought they were not wide enough, particularly in the smaller schools. The attitude of the N.U.T. in the salary negotiations appears to have been that the highest priority must be accorded to securing adequate remuneration for the majority of its members, that is, to securing the best possible basic scale for the qualified teacher grade. In spite of the suspicions the secondary teachers came to form later, the Union's attitude in the negotiations to the graduate and special responsibility additions was certainly not one of opposition; it was in fact benign towards them but did not regard them as being so important, and so well worth fighting for, as the basic scale. One consequence of the N.U.T.'s acceptance of the authorities' proposals for very small differentials in the 1944 negotiations was to set back for many years any hope the Union might have had of being accepted by all school teachers as the natural representative of their interests; it suffered from having become thought of as unsympathetic to the claims of the more highly qualified. But it might equally well be argued that the pressures in the opposite direction from a group such as the National Federation of Class Teachers could not have been ignored without danger to the internal unity of the N.U.T. The local authority negotiators seem to have viewed the attempt to achieve an overall agreement for primary and secondary teachers as a continuation of the elementary salary scales, increased to allow for inflation but offering as little additional reward to the more highly qualified teachers as the pre-war elementary scales had offered.

From the beginning of 1945 the secondary associations mounted continuous pressure to improve the lot of their members, and over the next fifteen years or so many of their aims were achieved, as the inadequacy of the attractions of teaching for the more able men and women who obtained good degrees became increasingly evident to many in the local authorities and the ministry. In other words market forces worked in favour of the more highly qualified graduate teachers, and the need for differentials which favoured them came to be increasingly widely recognised by those concerned with the supply of teachers for the schools. A statement issued by the Joint Four early in 1945 pointed out that the new scales would not attract highly qualified men and women into the profession. It claimed that for headmasters and headmistresses of existing secondary schools the new scales gave a lower maximum for 59·3 per cent of headmasters and for 53·09 per cent of headmistresses.[15] 'The assessment of salaries solely on a capitation basis, irrespective of the scope and nature of the work carried out in the school, is a retrogressive step which involves special hardship on the smaller schools, hinders mobility in the profession, and introduces the new and unwelcome feature of a salary fluctuating annually in accordance with the number of pupils beyond the statutory school-leaving age.' The statement went on to criticise the smallness of the graduate addition and the small number of special responsibility posts provided for. Four main proposals were put forward:[16]

(1) A revision of the proposed formula for assessing the salaries of head masters and headmistresses;
(2) A substantial increase of the 'graduate' addition payable to all graduate teachers irrespective of the type of school in which service is given;
(3) A mandatory scheme of additional payments in respect of high academic attainments, service of exceptional value, and special responsibility, directly related to the nature of the work and the age of the pupils; and
(4) The abolition of the 'merger' clause (under which graduates holding posts of special responsibility lost their graduate allowance).

It is interesting to notice that each of these aims was subsequently achieved in one way or another.

Some of the secondary teachers certainly seem to have hoped to bring about an amendment of the new scales before they came into effect, possibly through parliamentary pressure, and the grievances of the secondary school teachers were given an airing in the House of Commons.[17] On 20th February, 1945, in a debate on teachers' salaries, Kenneth Lindsay, who represented the English Universities, put the secondary associations' case against the new agreement. He argued that the common scale of salaries for all teachers, primary and secondary, 'degrades the graduate degree and thereby will discourage recruitment', that the scale slowed down the accretion of salaries, that it diminished the income of the majority of secondary heads and that it created a new series of anomalies. He put forward the proposals of the Joint Four and claimed that they would require only another 2 per cent increase on the salary bill, which had already been increased by 48 per cent. One of the members for Cambridge University, K. W. M. Pickthorn, expressed the feelings of grammar school masters. 'First of all they think that these scales will reduce the maximum salaries of grammar school headmasters, not the existing ones, who have a kind of vested interest, but those who have a prospective interest in the top grammar school salaries; they think they are going to suffer. The second thing they fear is that the secondary schoolmasters in general will have, I will not say lower salaries than before . . . but certainly that compared with other kinds of schoolmasters they will have lower salaries than before these scales.'

The official reaction of the N.U.T. to these complaints against the new scales was given in editorial comment printed in *The Schoolmaster* on 1st March:

> For many weeks the effect of an unprecedented sectional campaign, carried out by the Associations representing the most highly paid section of the teaching profession, had gathered momentum in the House. Consequently, it was in every way desirable that the critics should be brought into the open and given an authoritative answer. The spearhead of the attack was constituted by the University members, who reflected very faithfully the attitude of the Secondary Associations who had briefed, or may we say, over-briefed them. The main ingredients of their speeches were inaccurate or exaggerated descriptions of the scales, prejudice against the new Burnham Committee, hostility towards the N.U.T., and a wishful, cynical and ignorant disbelief in Mr. Butler's new Education Act.

In fact, in 1944 and 1945 the education policy which was being followed by the government seemed to those operating it to require an egalitarian salary policy and the removal of differential scales or payments. Mr. Butler as the responsible minister did not say this in defence of the agreement—he seemed to find the task of defending the new scales unpleasant and difficult; but in 1947 the chairman of the Burnham committee, Lord Soulbury, did reveal something of the thinking behind the government's attitude. Speaking as 'the man in the street', he commented, 'I think I should be right in saying that the teachers in the secondary schools were not entirely satisfied with the settlement of 1945; they felt that it was less favourable to them than to the teachers in the primary schools. So it was, but my recollection is that the differentiation was deliberate and designed to conform to what was understood to be the policy of the Minister of Education. By the 1944 Education Act a large number of elementary schools were to become secondary schools and it was thought desirable to treat the teaching profession as a unified whole and facilitate mobility of transfer between the old and new secondary schools and between primary and secondary schools.

'My own view, though of course I did not and could not express it at that time, was that on the whole and in the changing circumstances of our educational system the settlement was not unreasonable. We had before 1945 a very small though a very good system of secondary education; perhaps the best in the world. The same could not, I think, be said of our elementary system and—public resources not being unlimited—it seemed good policy to use the money now available to stimulate the attractiveness of the primary and new secondary schools. The inevitable result was to make a comparison of the benefits gained by the primary and secondary or grammar school teachers unfavourable to the latter.'[18] The weakness in this theory, which became apparent in due course was that, far from able persons being drawn to other types of school, many of them were not drawn to the schools at all. Education can never be viewed in isolation from its surroundings, and the years of full employment certainly ensured plenty of openings outside the schools for the more able men and women.

II THE WIDENING OF DIFFERENTIALS

The Burnham Reports of 1948, 1951 and 1954 the main features of which are summarised in Table 4.1, all introduced additional differential payments and showed a movement away from the position established by the 1945 settlement. Sir William Alexander pointed to this change of sentiment when he wrote that 'The immediate post-war situation created a levelling process in the salaries of teachers which may well have accorded with the mood of 1945 but as the years have passed there has been increasing recognition of the wide range of responsibilities within the teaching profession which necessarily require schemes of differentials which would enable Local Education authorities to meet the needs of the different posts in schools.'[19] But while the

Reports of these years had this feature in common, they appear to be groping and uncertain by comparison with the developments of 1956 and later, when the differentials became both larger and more systematic in their application. In 1948 the first payment for good honours was introduced but was confined to holders of a Class I degree. In 1954 this definition was widened and a payment of £30 yearly was offered to those with either first or good second class degrees. The graduate addition itself had been increased to £60 by 1951 and remained at that level until 1956. Both of these differential payments have remained as part of the salaries structure; by 1963 the good honours payment had reached £120 while the graduate addition stood at £100. Neither of these payments was further increased in the awards of 1965 or 1967.

Special responsibility allowances had been recommended by the Spens and McNair committees, but comparatively few were actually paid in the years between 1945 and 1948. They were paid by local authorities in accordance with a variety of local schemes and some systematisation seemed to be necessary. In 1948 the agreement laid down that these responsibility allowances should be attached to $12\frac{1}{2}$ to $17\frac{1}{2}$ per cent of full-time posts under each authority and that the individual payments might range from £50 to £150. In 1951 the teachers' associations pressed for the scheme to be made more specific, and the number and range of payments came to depend largely on the pupil unit total of a school,[20] the minimum payment for any teacher who was granted an allowance being fixed at £40. The form of these provisions gave local authorities a great deal of room for manœuvre but failed to satisfy the more highly qualified teachers simply because the prospects the individual had of gaining an allowance for himself remained vague and uncertain; thus allowances as offered under this scheme could hardly serve as bait to attract good graduates to the schools when they were considering which career they should pursue. It was the basic scale plus the personal additions which they looked at, for these alone were certain. The 1956 agreement changed all this and introduced the much more rigid type of allowance scheme which still exists. Each school was to have a certain number of head of department posts ranging from A (£125) to D (£350) and a number of graded posts each worth £75, £125 or £175; the number of such posts depending upon the unit total of each school. The unit values attaching to pupils aged from 13 to 15 were increased from one to two in order to improve the financial prospects of heads of secondary modern schools. Sir William Alexander, secretary of the authorities' panel told a press conference that 'The key reform of the 1944 Act was that it envisaged secondary education for all children. If that is to be a reality, all secondary schools must be treated as secondary schools. We believe ... that, in the educational field, nothing is more important during the next ten years than that the secondary modern school should improve its standing.'[21] The impact of the great increase in the differentials offered in the 1956 settlement may be judged from the Table of Salary and Price Indices. The principal beneficiary of the four specimen salary positions there examined was the graduate assistant in the grammar school, whose salary index moved from 178 to 255, by comparison the salary index of his non-graduate colleague in the primary school—the main beneficiary of the 1945 agreement—moved rather less, from 191 to 237 (1920=100). The widening of differentials did not pass unobserved; the *Times Educational Supplement* commented, 'If a professor gets rather over £2,000 then it does not seem unjust for a head of department in a large grammar school to earn £1,400. A reasonable hierarchy of educational salaries has at last been established.'[22]

Since 1956 the actual figures have grown larger, partly reflecting the effect of inflation and partly reflecting a real improvement in the standard of living of teachers. The structure of teachers' remuneration had changed but little by 1971, the principal exception to this being the replacement of the head teachers' allowances by separate salary scales for heads in 1965. The head teachers' scales were still related to the unit totals of their schools in much the same way as the allowances had been except that there were only 13 scales whereas the number of groups for allowances had grown to 27.

A form of differential payment which did not find its way into the salary arrangements during this period in spite of its being advocated by many was a special bonus or higher scale for persons possessing qualifications in subjects where there were especially difficult and persistent shortages, as in some branches of science and mathematics. In fact the authorities have often used the special responsibility allowances to favour persons 'so qualified'. It has been noticeably easier for a young man with an honours degree in physics to find a post with a substantial allowance than it has been for a man equally well qualified in history. But this covert use of the salary arrangement has never been written into a Burnham Report. This has meant that while above-average allowances could be used to tempt a mathematics teacher to one school rather than to another, the covert nature of this differential has made it of little value in attracting young mathematics graduates to teaching as a career, for good fortune in the distribution of allowances could hardly be given a cash value to an outsider and potential entrant. The absence of any overt subject differential was certainly partly, possibly entirely, due to the united opposition of all the teachers' associations to such payments. The secondary associations strongly favoured the introduction of greater differentials for the well-qualified, but were opposed on grounds of principle to any subject differentials. The authorities' panel doubtless realised the united opposition of the teachers to any formal subject payments and tried to meet the subject shortages apparent in the late '40s and early '50s through the system of leaving the payment of discretionary special allowances to each authority. Certainly in the negotiations before the 1951 Report the authorities' panel maintained their preference for flexible allowances rather than a substantial increase in the graduate allowance.

Some critics believe that both the Ministry and the local authorities thought that there were already enough arts graduates and that there would be enough mathematics and physics graduates by 1960. Thus the employers sought to follow a policy of paying a small graduate allowance and eking it out with special responsibility payments until the shortage passed.[23] By 1954 the Minister of Education, Florence Horsburgh, was encouraging the local authorities to make full use of the provisions of the Burnham Report which enabled them to grant special allowances. She was particularly concerned about the need to attract and retain in the schools well-qualified graduates, above all in science and mathematics, having received in November, 1953, a report from the N.A.C.S.S.T. on 'Graduate Teachers of Mathematics and Science' which viewed the shortage as constituting 'a national problem'. Her successor, Sir David Eccles, described the steps he had taken to deal with the supply problem when he addressed the I.A.A.M. Council meeting in December, 1954. 'A month ago I made the first move. It was, I am told, unique. Hitherto, Burnham has always come to Curzon Street, but this time Curzon Street has gone to Burnham. I have asked the Committee to assess the results of the pool of special allowances and to recommend what more should be done. In my letter to the Burnham Committee I have asked them to look at the position of all teachers engaged in more responsible or advanced work, and I have mentioned particularly the importance of offering career prospects adequate to attract enough teachers of distinguished quality. So now the ball is in the Burnham Court, and I am going to be interested to see what return they make.'[24] He did not have to wait long, for in February,

1955, the Burnham Committee agreed a set of amendments to the 1954 Primary and Secondary Report which included recommendations specifying the ranges of allowances to be paid according to the extent and nature of the advanced work undertaken; advanced work being defined as work above G.C.E. 'O' Level. Thus by the middle of the 1950s the unsoundness of the premises on which salary policy had been based was becoming clear to the Ministry and employers, and their changed view of the situation was the most important factor which led to the more clearly defined career structure incorporated in the 1956 agreement.

The failure of the policies followed in 1945 and the succeeding decade to attract able graduates to the schools was fully documented by the Crowther Report which was published in 1959. The figures gathered by the Central Advisory Council showed the decline in the recruitment of good graduates to teaching during the years when differentials were small or uncertain.[25] The grammar schools generally and their sixth forms in particular were found to be living on the abilities of staff recruited in the thirties for 'that period of so much distress in English life was a golden age for recruitment to grammar schools'. The Crowther Report pointed out that 'the great difference between the university graduate and the student leaving a training college is that there is severe competition from many quarters to secure the services of the former, and that it is therefore necessary to offer much more pay to get him into teaching'.[26]

The management, and more particularly the Ministry of Education, continued to emphasise the importance of adequate differentials in the early 1960s. In 1961 in the first of the 'pay freeze' crises when the Minister had to ask the Burnham Committee to reduce the cost of its proposals, he was particularly anxious that the reduction should be achieved by cutting the proposed new basic scale. He told the Committee that 'to attract the highly qualified entrant, the rewards for higher qualifications and for higher posts of responsibility in primary and secondary schools require special attention. I therefore want to see the Committee's current proposals on differentials retained in full, or better still increased, in any revised scheme.'[27] A few days later the Minister elaborated on this theme in the Commons debate on teachers' salaries. 'It is perfectly clear,' he said, 'that we have reached a situation where our real shortages inside the teaching profession are in graduates. It is teachers of science, mathematics and other subjects of which we are really short.'[28] By the 1960s this view found a good deal of support outside educational circles. According to *The Economist*, 'There is no shortage of entrants to the profession on the basic scale, but severe shortages exist higher up (particularly among graduate teachers of science and mathematics); and the normal professional expectation of good salaries in the top jobs has been steadily eroded by the N.U.T.'s own policy. The country now gets increasingly little return for training and re-imbursing young women teachers, 15,000 of whom left to get married last year, most of them with less than three years' service. It is patently more desirable to give substantial inducements both to graduates (thus raising the status of the profession) and to those following a career who stay in the schools for five years or more.'[29]

III TEACHERS AND THE SALARY STRUCTURE

The sense of betrayal and frustration felt by many of the more highly qualified secondary teachers after the 1945 settlement showed itself not only in the campaigns mounted by the traditional secondary associations but also in the foundation of the Graduate Teachers' Association. Before the 1944 Act the secondary associations had represented the majority of teachers in the existing secondary schools. The reclassification of senior elementary schools as secondary by the Act meant that the separate identity of the better qualified and mainly graduate staffs of the pre-war secondary schools was felt by many of them to have become submerged, and the possession of a degree was seen by these teachers as a distinguishing qualification which might again give them an identifying badge within the larger group of qualified teachers. Hence the attempt was made to build up an association to represent the interests of graduate teachers; it emerged in 1947. The Association failed to obtain representation on the Burnham Committee but it had some influence as a pressure group for a few years around 1950. Its existence may have had a stimulating effect on the secondary associations, especially on the I.A.A.M., which felt its rivalry most keenly. In the November–December issue of 1947 the editor of *The A.M.A.* claimed that it was untrue to suggest that the Graduate Teachers' Association would be more effective than the existing bodies. Its decline set in with the increase of differential payments and the greater measure of satisfaction with existing arrangements which these produced among graduates.

During the decade after 1945 the I.A.A.M., the most vocal and active of the four secondary associations, became increasingly critical of Burnham agreements and the negotiating machinery. It had protestingly accepted the awards of 1948 and 1951, but in October 1953 the measure of its discontent was shown when the 300 members of Council voted unanimously to reject the Burnham proposals, which made no provision for improvements in the graduate addition or the special allowances' scheme, and proposed £30 for a first class honours degree, which was described by the Association as 'less than a palliative'.[30] The following January the Council was asked for the first time in its history to approve in principle the taking of strike action in support of salary claims. In support of the motion it was argued that grammar school teachers needed to show that they were not a 'spiritless body of men' but that they were prepared to be fighting advocates of a course which they regarded as not only just but vital. Against the motion it was urged that strike action was the weapon of industrial disputes and that the demand for such action might divide the Association. The motion was narrowly defeated by 149 to 143 votes. By January, 1955, the I.A.A.M. Council had suppressed its fears of being thought 'trade unionist' or 'unprofessional' to the extent that it was prepared to approve that strike action might be taken as a last resort, and to instruct the executive to consider the most effective ways of raising a long-term fund in support of the Association's policy on salary and other issues.[31] About this time also the Association was seriously considering whether it should withdraw from the Burnham Committee, since the procedure adopted in each set of negotiations entailed the settlement of the basic scale first, and the total cost of this resulted in there being very little hope of any adequate consideration of the market conditions applicable to the graduate case. In deciding against withdrawal the I.A.A.M. executive was influenced by the consideration that not only would its influence on salary negotiations be weakened, but it would risk being relegated to a fringe position in educational politics, where it would be less frequently consulted by the Ministry and local authorities. Furthermore it was possible that the unity of the Joint Four might be jeopardised, as the I.A.H.M., A.H.M. and A.A.M. were thought to be against secession from Burnham.

The four secondary associations on their own were unable to take any decisive action to help their members' salaries. The best they could do was to make their case known as widely as possible and seek public and political sympathy, hoping thereby to change the climate of opinion in their favour. Taking advantage of the shortage of teachers in some subjects, they stressed the economic value of the work their members were doing and the impossibility of recruiting enough highly-qualified graduates for the more advanced teaching in the different subjects at existing rates of pay.[32] The change in official policy and the consequent marked growth in differential payments in the later 1950s has already been discussed, and it would probably be an exaggeration to describe the influence of the secondary teachers' associations on this development as more than marginal. Nevertheless, after the lean years the welcome which the secondary associations gave to the scheme for differential payments in the 1956 Burnham agreement was a hardly surprising. For the N.U.T. the 1956 agreement came at a time when dissatisfaction among its members with both salary scales and general conditions of service was acute. The widespread feeling among teachers that their purchasing power had declined, and that the gap between them and manual workers had narrowed, was intensified by the government's proposal that teachers should contribute an extra one per cent to the cost of their pensions; it was seen as an attempt to impose a cut in salaries on a section of the community already badly paid.[33] At the 1955 Annual Conference discontent with salaries found expression in a resolution instructing the Executive 'to develop immediately a more militant Salaries Campaign, clearly incorporating minimum figures of £500–£1,050'. The following year Conference attempted further to bind the leadership by deciding that these figures were not to be assumed as merely bargaining figures, which was to be interpreted to mean that the representatives on the Burnham Committee could not accept figures less than these. In his address to the Conference the President spoke of the disillusion among teachers stemming from the under-valuation of the profession. 'Anyone looking at the educational scene today cannot fail to be impressed by the fact that the teaching profession is labouring under an acute feeling of frustration and bitter dissatisfaction. It is certainly more acute than it has been for thirty-five years at least—possibly more acute than ever before in our history. We emerged from the war with high hopes and with universal promises of better things ringing in our ears. A new Act was on the Statute Book and a new day was dawning. But steadily and apparently inescapably conditions have deteriorated ever since. Wages have declined in value until each one of us can look and see unskilled and socially unimportant jobs being better paid; the actual classroom work of teaching has steadily become more exacting and more exhausting; and duties outside the classroom have become more oppressive.'[34]

The 1956 agreement itself seems to have marked the beginning of a new set of difficulties for the N.U.T. These difficulties have not arisen directly out of the increases paid mainly in grammar schools, but out of the way in which the agreement upgraded salary prospects in the secondary modern schools. The N.U.T. was probably as strongly represented in the modern as in the primary schools, thus in an immediate sense the successful attempt which the authorities' panel made to upgrade the salary opportunities in the modern school favoured one section of the Union's membership without offering any compensation to their often identically qualified colleagues in the primary schools. The probable difficulties had been apparent to N.U.T. members of the Burnham Committee during the negotiations, and they resisted the proposal of the authorities' panel to upgrade the modern schools by increasing from one to two the number of units scored by a school for each pupil between the ages of 13 and 15. The Union argued that all children of compulsory school age should be similarly rated in terms of units. In addressing the special conference of the N.U.T. called to approve the new salary agreement, Sir Ronald Gould explained, 'The Teachers' Panel welcomed the increased allowances, though they were still inadequate, but they did not wish to see any change in the relativities between secondary modern schools on the one hand and primary and grammar schools on the other. Indeed, the disturbance of relativities was anathema to some of my colleagues. So we decided to submit new proposals, increasing the allowances but keeping the existing unit values, or, if you like, refusing to agree to a device which would discriminate between primary and secondary modern schools'.[35] Nevertheless, the Authorities' Panel insisted upon the up-grading of the secondary modern school. The National Association of Head Teachers, whose members were mostly in primary and modern schools, reacted in a manner similar to that of the N.U.T. At its conference to consider the new Burnham Award it expressed serious concern that further discrimination had been shown in the differentials paid to heads in different types of schools to the disadvantage of primary school heads. 'Delegates unanimously deplored that the memorandum of the N.A.H.T. which showed no discrimination had not been adopted by the Burnham Committee, and instructed the Council to press for its adoption.'[36]

The increase in differential payments and their widespread application in the modern schools had the effect of introducing into N.U.T. salary policy documents and conference debates from this time on an increasing emphasis once more on the importance of the basic scale. A memorandum produced by the executive on the instructions of the Union's conference in 1957 spoke of the basic scale as 'symbolic of the fundamental unity of the teaching profession', claimed that the scales had become 'top-heavy' and suggested that the basic element needed to be substantially increased. The pressure for this renewed emphasis within the N.U.T. came especially from the National Federation of Class Teachers, whose president complained after the 1956 Award that the basic scale had failed to unite the profession. 'Indeed, there appears to be a greater disunity than ever before in our profession, and it is all due to the fact that a tremendous superstructure has been imposed on the basic scale.'[37] The notion that the basic scale was a symbol of unity has found its way into numerous Union statements since 1956. In the memorandum on salary policy put to and accepted by the annual conference at Easter, 1961, for instance, it was said that the basic scale 'symbolises the unity of the teaching profession because every teacher is affected by the level of payment; the basic scale also recognises that teachers perform a service of inestimable value to the community, whatever the type of school'. The same document reviewed the Union's objections to the extra unit weighting given to pupils between the ages of 13 and 15 and suggested that all children up to the age of 15 should be rated at $1\frac{1}{2}$ units each.

During the 1960s the leadership of the Union has come under increasing pressure from a large section of its membership to give more emphasis to improving the basic scale and securing the removal of the so-called primary-secondary differential. At the 1963 Annual Conference, for example, a motion instructing Union representatives that unless a satisfactory agreement was reached in these two respects they should not include a provisional settlement which allocated money to increasing any of the differential payments received considerable support, and has also been pressed at subsequent conferences. By the autumn of 1967 the Union was obliged to take some action, and it instituted a series of sanctions in eighteen selected areas in line with the programme of action laid down at a special salaries conference held in May, when negotiations in the Burnham Committee had virtually broken down. The sanctions, which took the form of refusing to supervise school meals and refusing to work with unqualified teachers, were the most far-reaching the Union had applied for some forty years. An N.U.T. statement listed the objectives of the sanctions as the achievement of a much improved basic scale, the removal of the primary-secondary differential, and immediate action by the government and L.E.A.s to meet Union policy on school meals and unqualified persons.[38] At the end of November the dispute between the N.U.T. and the local authorities lost some of its force when both sides agreed to recommend to the Burnham Committee the establishment of a working party 'to examine the principles underlying the structure of the basic scale and to review the arrangements relating to the unit total system'. Both sides also set up working parties to consider ways of ending compulsory school meal duties and the issue of unqualified teachers. The salaries working party included representatives of the N.A.S. whose views were very different from those of the N.U.T. The General Secretary of the former was quoted as saying that the working party was predoomed to failure. 'The N.U.T. is for the basic scale and supports the primary teachers. We don't regard the primary thing as the most important problem. And we want to strengthen the career structure.' The working party did indeed fail in its task of considering the primary/secondary differential. There was a failure to agree on the amount of representation to be offered to the N.A.S., and when an additional representative from the Association declined to withdraw from the meeting of the working party on 1st April, 1968, the chairman was obliged to adjourn the meeting *sine die*.[39] Matters were, therefore, referred back to the full teachers' panel of Burnham. The N.U.T. accepted a settlement the following autumn which had the effect of increasing the unit value of pupils under the age of 13 from 1 to $1\frac{1}{2}$ units each, at a total cost of about £4,000,000. Introducing an article giving details of the settlement, *The Teacher* wrote, 'After many years of argument the primary-secondary differential, which long bedevilled the educational system, is ended.' The N.U.T. must certainly hope that this is so, but the letters from primary teachers which appeared the following week gave little hope that it would be taken in this way.

Relations between the N.U.T. and the N.A.S. are probably the worst among the teachers' associations at the present time. The N.A.S. was opposed to that equal pay for women teachers which was so eagerly sought by the N.U.W.T. and formed part of the official policy of the N.U.T., with its predominantly female membership.[40] Equal pay was agreed to by the local authorities and by the Minister of Education, and in 1955 a scheme came into effect which brought the salaries of women into line with those of men by stages, full equality being achieved by 1st April, 1961. The N.U.W.T. dissolved itself on having attained its object. With the settlement of the equal pay issue and the continued growth of the N.A.S. as an organisation with a distinctive viewpoint and interest in the salary field, the Minister agreed to its representation on the teachers' panel in 1962, when the Association was granted two places. At the same time the National Association of Head Teachers was granted representation for the first time on the panel, being invited to appoint one member.

The N.A.S., having failed to prevent the coming of equal pay, turned its attention increasingly to the improvement of the career prospects of those who were likely to spend a lifetime working in the schools, as distinct from the very large number of young women teachers whose average period of service before marriage and child-bearing was very short. In 1965 continuous service increments were given precedence over all other N.A.S. salary demands save that for an adequate scale. In 1967 the N.A.S. conference deplored D.E.S. advertisements for married women to return to the classroom, on the grounds that they portrayed teaching as 'a spare-time occupation for married women'. In a statement at its 1968 conference, the Association claimed that 'the costly business of training teachers can be made more effective only by increasing the proportion of men in training and by encouraging long-serving career teachers'. At the same conference the Association decided to affiliate to the Trades Union Congress, two years before the hitherto less militant N.U.T. decided to do so. Much of the influence of the N.A.S. in the last few years has been due to the attraction of its methods to teachers who have grown increasingly restive at the apparent failure of the established machinery and the N.U.T. to secure for them what they consider their fair share of the general prosperity. The apparent conversion of the N.U.T. to more militant methods in 1969, and the results these produced, owe much to the development of the N.A.S. since the settlement of the equal pay issue.

It would not be unfair to say that the other associations have not always found it easy to work with the N.A.S. Already in 1962 there were signs of the difficulties that lay ahead, for in the course of the salary negotiations of that summer the N.A.S. circulated to its members accounts of the proceedings of the Burnham Committee and of the teachers' panel before a report had been agreed, and while the other member associations regarded the proceedings as confidential. On 28th September, members of the teachers' panel representing the other associations, N.U.T., A.T.T.I., I.A.A.M., A.A.M., I.A.H.M., A.H.M.,

N.A.H.T., agreed to publish a joint statement on procedure, reaffirming their belief in the established practice. 'The representatives of the seven associations are unanimously of the opinion that the publication of *ex parte* accounts of the proceedings of the Teachers' Panel and the Burnham Committee would undoubtedly damage present salary prospects and place such a strain on negotiation that there would be great risk of complete breakdown.' The leader of the Authorities' Panel communicated the view of his Panel that they were not prepared to continue the negotiations unless the proceedings were treated as confidential by all those participating. The immediate solution to this particular difficulty was that the Burnham Committee agreed to set up a working party to consider its procedures and conventions after the completion of the current set of negotiations which, all then agreed, should be confidential.

Membership of the teachers' panel was revised further in 1966 when both the N.A.H.T. and the N.A.S. asked for further representation. The N.A.S. representation was increased by 1 and the A.T.T.I. membership of the panel decreased from 4 to 2. Working difficulties similar to those of 1962 still occurred from time to time. At a full meeting of the Burnham Committee on 4th November, Mr. T. A. Casey made a statement on behalf of the N.A.S. which was not authorised by the teachers' panel and the *Times Educational Supplement* printed a report by Mr. Casey giving his version of what took place at the meeting. At its subsequent meeting on 21st November the teachers' panel carried a resolution deploring the N.A.S. action in 'contravening the rule, agreed by all Associations including the National Association of Schoolmasters, which states that "each panel shall normally express one point of view at meetings, and shall appoint a spokesman or spokesmen for the purpose".'

During the second half of the period since the Second World War the teachers' associations have had to adapt their efforts in salary negotiating increasingly to a situation in which the rôle of the central government has become much more explicit and much more active in deciding salary awards. The economic and financial policy currently being followed has long had some impact on teachers' salaries, but recent governments of both parties have felt obliged by the economic situation to take a much more direct and active part in negotiations than formerly. At the same time there was a greater keenness on the part of the central Ministry or Department of Education to have a direct hand in the allocation of rewards to teachers, in order to make the profession more attractive to well-qualified graduates or to some other specialist group. The changes in the Burnham negotiating machinery which were introduced in 1965 by the Remuneration of Teachers Act were rather more a matter of direct contention between the central government and the local authorities than between the employers and their teachers. The Act followed increasing difficulty with the existing arrangements, which culminated in 1963 when the Minister had refused to accept the Burnham Committee's recommendations and the Committee refused to make the changes sought by the Minister. A special Act was accordingly passed imposing ministerial salary scales for a two year period while negotiations concerning changes in machinery took place. The two main changes subsequently introduced in 1965 were that the Secretary of State should be directly represented on the management panels of the committees, and that in cases of disagreement between the panels there was provision for arbitration; when this proved to be necessary the arbitrators were to be appointed by the Minister of Labour. Under these arrangements, the Secretary of State was no longer able to reject the findings produced by the new machinery, the only way of preventing the findings from taking effect being for each House of Parliament to resolve 'that national economic circumstances require that effect should not be given to the recommendations'. Under Section 7 of the 1965 Act any order might be made with retrospective effect. The new arrangements thus met two of the aims which teachers' associations had sought for some years and which were not capable of achievement under the 1944 Act; they provided for arbitration and they made back-dating of awards possible. The 1965 arrangements have limited the position of the local authorities to the extent that governmental representatives have joined the employers' panel. The general negotiating position of the teachers' associations has not been directly affected by this measure, but they now have to contend in a more immediate sense with whatever the central ministry feels to be the correct policy to apply to salary issues.

Since the reconstruction of the salary machinery there have been three sets of full-scale negotiations and an interim settlement. In 1965 and 1967 the teachers' pay claim was submitted to arbitration following complete failure to reach agreement by negotiation. The Teachers' Panel argued its case for more than the 'normal' economic increase in terms of the need to bring teachers' salaries into proper relationship with those of other groups. As Gould told the arbitrators in 1965, 'We seek a revaluation of the teachers' position because we believe this to be essential to the development of the education service and the well-being of the country. Any salary increase awarded, we suggest, must do more than compensate for changes in the purchasing power of money, and do more than maintain the teachers' position vis-à-vis others; to mark the importance of the education service in the modern world it should raise the teachers' position in relation to others. We ask arbitrators to regard their task as an exercise in determining social priorities.'[41] On both occasions the global sum awarded by the arbitrators was marginally higher than the management's offer but fell far short of the teachers' demands. The bitterness and frustration of teachers resulting from their belief that they have been 'under-valued' over many years was one factor underlying the militancy shown by teachers in 1969/70, although the claim for an interim increase was not itself presented or argued in these terms.

The round of negotiations leading to the 1969 Burnham agreement began with a claim submitted by the Teachers' Panel in October, 1968, for a basic scale of £900 rising by ten annual increments of £80 to £1,700, a graduate allowance and a good honours degree allowance of £150 each, and other increases in the above scale payments. At the end of January, 1969, the Burnham Committee agreed provisionally to a basic scale of £860 to £1,600 over fourteen years, which with other increases, including those arising from the revision of the unit total system, would add £33 million per annum to the total salary bill, representing an increase of approximately $7\frac{1}{8}$ per cent over two years. The N.A.S. had earlier dissociated itself from the revised pruned proposals suggested by the teachers' panel, on the grounds that they constituted an 'abject surrender' and departed from the 'common sense approach' of the report of the Economist Intelligence Unit, 'The Economic Status of the Schoolmaster', which the Association had commissioned in 1967. The General Secretary of the N.A.S. accused the management panel of being 'more concerned to appease the N.U.T. to prevent further militancy from them, than to face up to the need for a career structure'. The N.A.S. salary proposals envisaged a basic scale of £850 rising to £1,650 after ten years, and jumping to £1,750 after fifteen years of continuous service. In February the Association began its work-to-rule in sixteen schools to gain publicity for these proposals and to draw attention to the shortcomings of the Burnham machinery. After the suspension of some of its members involved in the work-to-rule the Association staged a series of token strikes and became involved in a protracted dispute with Durham Education Authority. By contrast, the N.U.T. Executive, largely influenced by the belief that in the circumstances of the Government's incomes policy a more favourable settlement would not be achieved if the claim were referred to arbitration or to the Prices and Incomes Board, recommended acceptance of the provisional agreement to a Special Salaries Conference of the Union on 15th February, 1969. The vote in favour of acceptance was 134,833, the vote against 90,791; the latter being much larger than many had expected. By the time of the annual conference two months later it had become increasingly apparent that prices and incomes policy was being openly breached. This factor, combined with the initiative of left-wing teachers within the Union, was largely responsible for securing the defeat of the Executive in two key salary debates, one of which committed it to negotiating 'a substantial salary increase on the basic scale to come into effect by 1 April, 1970'. Among the Executive and rank-and-file members of the N.U.T. there were many who faced the dilemma that they believed that in the national interest the government was right to apply an incomes policy, but also felt that the policy had come to 'mean what you make of it', and in such circumstances, as *The Teacher* commented, 'issues of political principle subside to a whisper'.[42]

During the first week of June the Union launched a nationwide campaign to secure an interim salary award. Marches, demonstrations and public meetings were planned to draw public attention to the inadequate salaries of teachers, against a background of rising prices and the collapse of the incomes policy. Preliminary discussions were also held with other teachers' associations. On 7 June the Executive agreed to recommend that in the event of a breakdown in the negotiations members in selected schools or areas should be called out on extended strike subject to the decision of a special conference. On 9th July a march and mass meeting was organised by the London Teachers' Association, the teachers taking a half-day to attend. In September the Young Teacher Conference (N.U.T.) called for a one-day national strike in support of the Union's claim. The same month all the teachers' associations represented on the teachers' panel agreed to present a claim for a flat-rate increase of £135 to the management panel on 8th October.

Two days before the meeting, full-page advertisements putting the teachers' case appeared in *The Times* and *The Guardian*. The response of the management was to offer an increase of £50, which was unanimously rejected by the teachers' associations and labelled 'derisory'. The N.U.T. Executive decided not to wait for a formal breakdown in the negotiations but to go ahead with its plans for strike action. In November half-day and one-day strikes were organised by local associations, the first taking place at a Corby secondary school where 20 out of 28 N.A.S. and N.U.T. members walked out for the day. During the first two weeks of December some 4,000 teachers were on strike in 250 schools selected by the N.U.T. Executive. The enthusiasm of members was, according to *The Teacher*, 'quite unprecedented in the history of the N.U.T.'. On 15th December the management returned with an offer of an increase of £100 on salaries up to £1,000, tapering to an increase of £60 on salaries in excess of £1,525 a year; an increase which was consistent with the 4½ per cent maximum of the government's revised incomes policy. Again the teachers' panel rejected the offer, the N.U.T. suspecting a plot by the management to split the profession by offering more to the lower paid and by suggesting the reference of the future structure of teachers' salaries to an independent body, a step which the N.A.S. was known to favour. On the same day as the Burnham Committee meeting the N.U.T. Executive decided to impose a compulsory levy on all members from 1st January, and to proceed with a second wave of strikes. There were signs too that the I.A.A.M. was preparing to join in militant action. At its Christmas meeting the I.A.A.M. Council instructed the Executive Committee to cooperate in any form of strike action agreed upon by the teachers' panel, and to organise machinery for collecting contributions to the Schoolmasters' Defence and Legal Assistance Society.

No progress towards reaching an agreement was made at the meeting of the Burnham Committee early in January, and the chairman ruled that the teachers' claim must be submitted to arbitration. The teachers' panel refused to cooperate in the arbitration procedures, believing that to do so would be to place their heads in the 4½ per cent noose. After a senior conciliation officer of the Department of Employment and Productivity had failed to persuade them to accept arbitration, the Secretary of State of that Department and the Secretary of State for Education and Science met the Teachers' Panel. Both ministers gave assurances that the chairman of the arbitration tribunal would be a person of undoubted independence and that the government would accept any award of the arbitrators. They could not give any assurance that the arbitrators would not be tied by the incomes policy, although they somewhat ambiguously pointed to flexibilities in the policy in certain circumstances. The teachers preferred to test this flexibility in negotiation rather than in arbitration and two further meetings of the Burnham Committee were held in February. The management favoured an immediate review of the structure of teachers' salaries, with a new Burnham Report to operate from 1st October 1970 to 31st March, 1972, while the teachers stood by their claim for a flat-rate increase.

Provisional agreement was eventually reached at a meeting of the Committee on 3rd March, 1970. This was against a background of extended area strikes in Waltham Forest, Birmingham and Southwark, involving members of the N.A.S., N.U.T., and I.A.A.M., and a decision of the N.U.T. Executive to impose a ban on the invigilation of public examinations during the summer if the claim had not been met. The agreement, which came after the Secretary of State had personally conveyed proposals from the teachers' panel to the management, offered teachers an interim increase of £120 a year from 1st April, 1970, with a full-scale review of the structure of teachers' salaries, based on 1969 salary levels, to be partially implemented from 1st January, 1971, the overall cost of the two proposals in the financial year 1970–1 to be not less than £42 millions. The teachers gave an assurance that they would take steps to terminate as quickly as possible all forms of industrial action and sanctions. Summing up the outcome of the dispute, *The Teacher* was modestly restrained: 'When the campaign started the teachers were told that they had concluded an agreement for two years and an interim increase was impossible. By hard action this nil offer has been raised to an interim increase of £120 per annum together with the bringing forward by three months of a full scale review which will guarantee in 1970–71 as much money overall as was represented by the teachers' claim, and a guarantee of at least as much again overall in the following year. On any assessment this is a considerable victory.'[43]

One noteworthy feature of the campaign for an interim increase was the degree of unity shown by the teachers' associations. Once negotiations began for the full-scale review of teachers' salaries it was inevitable that the traditional differences in salary policy would again emerge and the year-long truce between the N.A.S. and the N.U.T. would come to an end. Disagreement first arose about the procedure which should be followed in the 1970–1 salary negotiations. At a meeting of the Burnham Committee in April which ratified the provisional agreement of 3rd March it was agreed that a working party should be set up to undertake a review of the structure of teachers' salaries. Subsequently the N.U.T. Executive decided that it wished a salary case to be put to the management side before the working party met, while the other teachers' organisations represented on the teachers' panel favoured forming a working party to hear what the management had to offer on the restructuring of salaries. On 8th June the teachers' panel agreed to go ahead with a salary claim stressing a basic scale of £1,250 rising to £2,200 over ten years. After an eleventh year qualified teachers would reach the graduate's maximum of £2,375. The claim followed closely the salary policy laid down at the N.U.T. Annual Conference, 1970. In reply to this the management panel put forward a scheme for restructuring the salary structure designed to give greater rewards to the more senior teachers.

By the end of 1970 the N.U.T., and therefore the teachers' panel, was still putting the basic scale for all teachers first, while the authorities' panel along with the associations whose representatives formed a minority of the teachers' panel were seeking to move away from this emphasis in the salary structure to one that would favour the long-serving and more senior members of the profession.[44]

NOTES

1. Board of Education, Educational Reconstruction, Cmd. 6458, 1943, p. 9.
2. Board of Education, Report of the Consultative Committee on Secondary Education (Spens Report), 1938, pp. 298–9.
3. Board of Education, Report of the Committee appointed to consider the supply, recruitment and training of teachers and youth leaders (McNair Report), 1944, p. 45.
4. *The National Federation of Class Teachers and its fight for the Basic Scale*, Nottingham, 1945.
5. Board of Education, Education after the War, 1941, p. 63.
6. *T.E.S.*, 22nd April, 1944, p. 193.
7. *The A.M.A.*, March, 1944, p. 61.
8. Ibid., January–February, 1945, p. 40.
9. *The Schoolmaster*, 16th November, 1944, p. 314.
10. *The A.M.A.*, January–February, 1945, p. 40.
11. The main facts concerning the course of negotiations in Burnham

are given in *The Schoolmaster*, 11th January, 1945, p. 21, and in *The A.M.A.*, January–February, 1945, pp. 40–1.
12. *T.E.S.*, 11th November, 1968, p. 547.
13. *The Schoolmaster*, 23rd November, 1944, p. 329.
14. Ibid., 21st December, 1944, p. 393.
15. Particulars obtained from a sample of its members by the I.A.H.M. showed that under the new scales out of 241 aided and maintained schools 56 per cent would lose with an average loss of £82 5s. 44 per cent would gain with an average gain of £76 2s.; out of 23 direct grant schools 91·3 per cent would lose with an average loss of £227 while 8·7 per cent would gain with an average of £82.
16. *T.E.S.*, 17th February, 1945, p. 79.
17. *Hansard*, H. of C., 20th February, 1945, cols. 665–751.
18. Reported in *T.E.S.*, 1st November, 1947, p. 586.
19. *Education*, 30th December, 1955, p. 1075.
20. The concept of unit totals was introduced in 1948 in relation to head teachers' allowances in order to weight the salaries of heads of grammar schools. Each pupil under the age of 15 was to count 1 unit, pupils of 15 to 16 4 units, 16 to 17 7 units, over 17 10 units The allowances added to a teacher's salary if he held a headship ranged from £55 for a school with the smallest unit totals to £900 for the largest.
21. *The Schoolmaster*, 4th May, 1956, p. 456.
22. *T.E.S.*, 4th May, 1956, p. 583.
23. *The Schoolmaster*, 11th December, 1953.
24. *The A.M.A.*, January, 1955, p. 21.
25. *15 to 18*, 1959, pp. 234–5.
26. Ibid., p. 440.
27. Reported in *The Schoolmaster*, 28th July, 1961, p. 162.
28. *Hansard*, H. of C., 1st August, 1961, col. 1409.
29. *The Economist*, 29th July, 1961, p. 439.
30. The I.A.H.M., the A.H.M. and the A.A.M. also rejected the proposals.
31. In view of the financial weakness of the Association strike action was hardly feasible. In submitting his annual statement of accounts for 1953 the Honorary Treasurer explained that since the war it had not been possible to do much more than to preserve the paper value of the Association's Defence and Legal Funds which were to some extent mortgaged to meet the remaining claims arising out of the Cardiganshire and Haverfordwest tenure disputes.

32. Some of the earlier publicity concentrated rather ineffectively on the vague concept of 'fairness'; the later and more effective appeal to the argument of economic efficiency may be seen in *The Grammar School Master's Salary; A National Problem* (1953) and similar publicity material.
33. Cf. *The Economist*, 23rd and 30th May, 1964, for articles comparing the movement of salary levels with the rate of increase in the wages of manual workers, 1938–1955/6; *infra.*, chapter 6.
34. N.U.T. Annual Report, 1956, p. xxxv.
35. *The Schoolmaster*, 18th May, 1956, p. 564.
36. Ibid., 25th May, 1956, p. 609.
37. Ibid., 20th April, 1956, p. 376.
38. *The Teacher*, 8th September, 1967, p. 1.
39. A statement was issued by the leader of the teachers' panel on behalf of all the Burnham parties except the N.A.S., giving an account of the difficulties between the teachers' associations which led to the breakdown of 1st April. This was printed *in extenso* in *The A.M.A.*, June, 1968, pp. 117–18.
40. *Infra.*, chapter 5.
41. *The Teacher*, 23rd July, 1965, Supplement, p. 1.
42. Ibid., 18th April, 1969, p. 2.
43. Ibid., 6th March, 1970, p. 2.
44. The Burnham settlement of 1971, which moved away from the basic scale, was too late to be examined in this study.

Table 4.1. Burnham Reports, 1948–70, a Brief Summary of the Main Features

Date of Report	Basic salary scale for a qualified teacher	Graduate addition	'Good Honours' payment	Training additions	Allowances for posts of special responsibility	Payments for head teachers
1948	£300 to £555	£30	£15 for Class I degree increasing to £30 at the scale maximum	£15 for each year of training beyond 2 up to a maximum of 5 years	To be paid on 12½ to 17½% of full-time posts under each authority and to range from £50 to £150	Additional to total payments under columns 1 to 4 until 1965: school groups based on pupil unit totals (for each pupil under 15 count 1 unit, 15 to 16 4 units, 16 to 17 7 units, 17+ 10 units) 22 groups with allowances from £55 for the smallest unit totals to £900 for the largest
1951	£375 to £630	£60	—	£18 "	Number and range to depend on the pupil unit total of a school; minimum payment for an individual teacher fixed at £40	As in 1948 Report
1952	Special cost of living addition of £40 p.a. to all salaries					
1954	£450 to £725	£60	£30 for all 'good honours'	£18 "	As in 1951 Report	Allowances for the 22 groups increased to range from £100 for smallest to £920 for the largest
1956	£475 to £900	£75	£50	£25	New scheme of (1) Head of Department posts, ranging from A (£125) to D (£350); (2) Graded posts, scaled as I (£75), II (£125) and III (£175)	Unit scores changed to each pupil under 13 1 unit, 13 to 15 2 units 15 to 16 4 units, 16 to 17 6 units, 17 and over 10 units. Allowances to range from £125 to £1,115 for the 22 groups
1959	£520 to £1,000	£90	£75	£30 for each year of training beyond 2 up to a maximum of 6 years	(1) Head of Department posts to range from A (£150) to D (£420); (2) Graded posts from I (£90) to III (£210)	27 groups (5 added to cover heads of largest schools) Allowances to range from £150 to £1,485

Year	Scale			Allowances	Promoted posts	Summary
1961	£570 to £1,170	£100	£100	Up to a maximum of 4 increments	(1) Head of Department posts to raise from A (£545) to E (£165); (2) Graded posts from I (£100) to III (£230)	27 groups ranging from £165 to £1,670
1963	£630 to £1,250	£100	£120	Up to a maximum of 3 increments for each year of training beyond 3 years	(1) Head of Department posts to range from A (£590) to E (£180); (2) Graded posts from I (£110) to III (£250)	27 groups ranging from £180 to £1,770
1965	£730 to £1,400	£100	£120	Up to a maximum of 3 increments; £50 allowance for post-graduate certificate, etc.	(1) Head of Department posts to range from A (£660) to E (£200); (2) Graded posts from I (£120) to III (£300)	11 separate salary scales for heads introduced; 13 scales depending on school unit totals with maxima ranging from £1,600 to £3,850
1967	£800 to £1,500	£100	£120	Up to a maximum of 3 increments; £50 allowance for post-graduate certificate, etc.	(1) Head of Department posts to range from A (£700) to E (£210); (2) Graded posts from I (£125) to III (£315)	13 scales with revised maxima ranging from £1,710 to £4,110
1969	£860 to £1,600	£105	£125	A maximum of up to £3 increments; £50 allowance for post-graduate certificate, etc.	(1) Head of Department posts to range from A (£742) to E (£222); (2) Graded posts from I (£132) to III (£334)	14 scales with revised maxima ranging from £1,817 to £4,583
1970	£980 to £1,720 (special cost of living addition of £120 p.a. to all salaries)					

Table 4.2. Salary and Price Indices

Date	Retail Price Index	Male assistant in primary school (non-graduate)	Headmaster of a primary school (non-graduate)	Male assistant in grammar school (hons. graduate)	Headmaster of a grammar school (hons. graduate)
1920	100	100	100	100	100
1921	91	100	100	100	100
1922	74	100	100	100	100
1923	71	95	95	95	95
1924	71	95	95	95	95
1925	71	96	96	96	96
1926	69	96	96	96	96
1927	67	96	96	96	96
1928	67	96	96	96	96
1929	67	96	96	96	96
1930	64	96	96	96	96
1931	60	86	86	86	86
1932	59	86	86	86	86
1933	57	86	86	86	86
1934	57	91	91	91	91
1935	59	96	96	96	96
1936	60	96	96	96	96
1937	62	96	96	96	96
1938	64	96	96	96	96
1939	66	96	96	96	96
1940	74				
1941	81	Salaries were augmented from time to time			
1942	86	by the payment of cost-of-living additions			
1943	90	during the war			
1944	91				
1945	95	138	124	111	123
1946	98	138	124	111	123
1947	103	138	124	111	123
1948	110	146	133	123	154
1949	114	146	133	123	154
1950	117	146	133	123	154
1951	129	166	149	153	168
1952	139	176	158	161	173
1953	145	176	158	161	173
1954	147	191	177	178	186
1955	153	191	177	178	186
1956	161	237	222	255	230
1957	167	237	222	255	230
1958	172	237	222	255	230
1959	173	263	253	293	270
1960	173	263	253	293	270
1961	181	308	298	338	310
1962	189	308	298	338	310
1963	193	329	321	356	329
1964	199	329	321	356	329
1965	208	368	364	394	381
1966	216	368	364	394	381
1967	223	395	389	417	406
1968	230	395	389	417	406
1969	244	421	412	443	431
1970	256	453	436	467	446

A NOTE ON SALARY AND PRICE INDICES SHOWN IN TABLE 4.2.

A fuller version of this Note appears as 'The Movement of Teachers' Salaries, 1920–68' by Vivienne C. Greenhalgh in the *Journal of Educational Administration and History*, December, 1968, pp. 23–36. The opportunity has been taken to extend to 1970 the statistics given in that article.

I. *Retail Price Index*

This index has been based on the London and Cambridge Economic Service price index which is largely constructed from statistics published annually by the Department of Employment and its predecessor, the Ministry of Labour.

II. *The four career grades for teachers taken here*

The salaries which these index numbers reflect are based on four examples of career structure and would have been paid to male teachers, aged 40 or so, holding the following qualifications and posts:

Teachers with a Teachers' Certificate awarded after two (now three) years of training serving as:

(a) assistant teacher in an elementary (later primary) school,
(b) headmaster of an elementary (later primary) school.

Graduate with good honours degree and a one-year post graduate certificate serving as:

(c) assistant master in a secondary (grammar) school,
(d) headmaster of a secondary (grammar) school.

III. *The typical nature of these four examples*

(a) Assistant teacher in an elementary (later primary) school.

By 1920 it was common for intending elementary teachers to study in a training college for the Teachers' Certificate after a period of preliminary education in a secondary school. This pattern of training was replacing an earlier one whereby a prospective teacher served an apprenticeship in an elementary school as a pupil teacher before taking a qualifying examination for entrance to a training college. Teachers without certificates were also employed in elementary schools and were able, until 1926, to enter for the Acting Teacher's Certificate. In 1920–21 there were 34,243 certificated male teachers serving in public elementary schools; of these 77·6 per cent were college-trained. In addition there were 2,177 teachers who were uncertificated. Today the great majority of primary school teachers are college-trained.

(b) Headmaster of an elementary (later primary) school.

The certificated teacher since 1920 might not unreasonably have hoped to obtain a headship of an elementary or primary school at some stage in his career. The average size of this type of school has always been small; consequently the ratio of head teachers to assistants has been a high one. In 1966 approximately one primary teacher in six was a head teacher while before the Second World War one in four or five had headships. These figures apply to men and women but the chances of promotion for men are much greater than for women. In 1966 about one in three male primary teachers were heads whereas fewer than one in nine women were.

(c) Assistant master in a secondary (grammar) school.

There have been changes since 1920 in the staff composition of a typical selective secondary school. Between 1924 and 1938 the number of male teachers in secondary schools who were graduates rose steadily from 76·3 per cent to 86·9 per cent; in 1966 slightly fewer than four-fifths of grammar school teachers were graduates. Until the late twenties the majority of male graduate teachers were untrained. Since then the position has been reversed and in 1966 approximately 72 per cent of male graduate teachers were trained. The majority of male graduate teachers today have a 'good honours degree', defined in the Burnham Reports as a first or second class honours degree or a higher degree. In 1938 there were 6,992 male graduates teaching in elementary schools while the number employed in secondary schools was 11,286.

(d) Headmaster of a secondary (grammar) school.

The post of headmaster of a selective secondary school has rarely been filled by a non-graduate. In 1966 one graduate in twenty-two serving in a grammar school was a headmaster, which contrasts unfavourably with the proportion of teachers holding headships in primary schools. Against this should be balanced the greater opportunities for graduates to obtain some other post of recognised responsibility such as head of a subject department in a grammar school.

IV. *Calculating the specimen salaries*

In all cases it is assumed that the teacher was aged about 40, as most teachers may expect to reach at least the top of the basic scale by that age.

(a) Assistant teacher in an elementary (later primary) school.

Of the 4 standard scales for certificated teachers in elementary schools which existed from 1920, Scale III salaries were paid by over half the local education authorities and the maxima of this scale is used in this example. The figures in Table 4.3 for 1945 and subsequent years are the various maxima of the basic scale; no element of above-scale allowances is included. There were few special allowances for posts of responsibility in primary schools in the years immediately following 1945. By 1966, however, of 23,619 assistant male teachers serving in primary schools 10,796 received allowances. The proportion of women receiving these allowances was smaller; of 87,767 assistant female teachers 16,456 received allowances.

Table 4.3. *Assistant male teacher with a teacher's certificate awarded after two (now three) years of training and serving in an elementary (later primary) school*

	Date	Salary (£s)
Scale III (Larger cities' scale) maximum		
	1920	380
	1923–5	380 less 5%
	1925–31	366
	1931–4	366 less 10%
	1934–5	366 less 5%
	1935–9	366
	1939	war bonuses were added during the Second World War
Burnham Main Committee basic scale (maximum)		
	1945	525
	1948	555
	1951	630
	1952	670
	1954	725
	1956	900
	1959	1000
	1961	1170
	1963	1250
	1965	1400
	1967	1500
	1969	1600
	1970	1720

(b) Headmaster of an elementary (later primary) school.

Before the war the salary scales for this teacher varied with the number of pupils in average attendance. In the years following 1921 average attendance remained fairly constant at about 250 pupils per school, i.e. Grade III of elementary schools. The scale maxima for a Grade III school in a Scale III area are given in Table 4.4. Between 1945 and 1948 salary scales for primary and secondary heads were grouped according to the number of pupils on the roll of a school. In 1948 a new system of unit totals and head teacher allowances was introduced under which all heads were paid as qualified assistants and also received an allowance which varied with the number and ages of pupils on the roll. According to the Annual Reports of the Ministry of Education the average size of primary school in the years following the Second World

Table 4.4. *Headmaster of an elementary (later primary) school with a teacher's certificate awarded after 2 (now 3) years of training*

Date	Salary (£s)
1920	494
1923–5	494 less 5%
1925–31	474
1931–4	474 less 10%
1934–5	474 less 5%
1935–9	474
1939	War bonuses were added during the Second World War
1945	615
1948	655
1951	740
1952	780
1954	875
1956	1095
1959	1250
1961	1475
1963	1585
1965	1800
1967	1920
1969	2035
1970	2155

War was Group II for head teacher allowance purposes and this allowance has been added to the basic scale maxima to produce the specimen salaries.

(c) Assistant master in a secondary (grammar) school.

The figures in Table 4.5 for the inter-war years are the various maxima of the provincial scale for graduates in secondary schools. Very few responsibility allowances were paid to teachers in these years.

The specimen salaries for the post-war period comprise the maxima of the basic scale plus certain above scale allowances. The figures include the graduate allowance (from 1945), the good honours allowance (from 1954) and the appropriate allowances for variously recognised periods of training and study. Incorporated in the post-war figures are allowances which would typically have been paid to a male graduate responsible for the teaching of a subject moderately widely studied, e.g. geography, history, chemistry or physics. From 1951 these special responsibility allowances gradually grew in importance and came to form a larger element in this teacher's total salary. It is not possible to support with statistical evidence the assumptions made in estimating what addition for special responsibility should be included, but the statistics do make clear that the great majority of graduate teachers can expect to receive some above-scale allowance by the age of 40. In 1966, of a total of 17,854 male graduate assistants serving in grammar schools, 15,241 received allowances, and over half of these were for the post of head of department. There is some evidence to suggest that the specimen salaries in table 4.5 are not unreasonable. An analysis made by the Ministry of Education in 1957 showed the average salaries of male good honours graduates who were deputy heads or heads of departments for subjects other than mathematics and science. In the 40–49 age group the average salary was £1,349. In 1966 the average salary of all graduates aged 40–44 was £2,025.

(d) Headmaster of a secondary (grammar) school.

Before the Second World War the Burnham Secondary Committee only suggested a minimum salary for this grade. Consequently there were considerable variations but a salary of £800 was probably typical for the head of a three-form entry school.

Although there was a wide disparity in the salaries of grammar school heads prior to 1945, they were paid at a higher level than the heads of elementary schools of similar size. The reconstituted Burnham Committee faced the problem of devising a scheme of salaries applicable to primary and secondary heads without at the same time

Table 4.5. *Assistant master in a secondary school who has gained a good honours degree and a post-graduate certificate after 4 years of study*

Date	Salary (£s)
1920	500
1923–5	500 less 5%
1925–31	480
1931–4	480 less 10%
1934–5	480 less 5%
1935–9	480
1939	War bonuses were added during the Second World War
1945	555
1948	615
1951	766
1952	806
1954	891
1956	1275
1959	1465
1961	1690
1963	1780
1965	1970
1967	2085
1969	2214
1970	2334

adversely affecting the salaries of grammar school heads. To achieve this a common grading schedule was adopted for all schools but in addition a head would also receive a sum of £50 for each group of 30 children over the age of 15.

In 1948 separate scales for heads were abolished and the age weighting of older children was further increased under the unit total system of determining the allowances which heads received in addition to the salary paid to them as qualified teachers. The effect of this change was to give a considerable proportionate increase to the heads of schools with sixth forms.

From 1965–9 there were 13 groups of salary scales for head teachers linked to unit totals; a 14th group was added in 1969.

The figures in Table 4.6 apply to the headmaster of a three form entry grammar school with about 60 pupils in the sixth form in 1945.

As the proportion of pupils staying on to the sixth form has steadily increased, some allowance has been made for this factor by adjusting the group number of the school.

Table 4.6. *Headmaster of a secondary (grammar) school with a three-form entry who has gained a good honours degree and a post-graduate certificate after four years of study*

Date	Group No.	Salary (£s)
1920–45		About 800 (see text)
1945		985
1948	XV	1235
1951	XV	1346
1952	XV	1386
1954	XV	1491
1956	XVI	1840
1959	XVI	2160
1961	XVI	2480
1963	XVI	2635
1965	9	3050
1967	9	3255
1969	9	3450
1970	9	3570

5
Equal Pay

The prolonged issue of equal pay between men and women teachers was one expression of the general conflict over the abolition of pay differentials on grounds of sex alone in public employment. In a sense the campaign for equal pay formed part of the wider campaign which included the demand for full political and legal equality, the best remembered phase of which is probably the drive by the suffragette movement to win votes for women in the years immediately prior to the First World War. The close association in the demands for political and economic equality is particularly apparent in the series of developments which led a section of the more active women members of the N.U.T. firstly to form their own pressure group within the Union and later to break completely with it.

The origin of the movement for equality among women members of the N.U.T. seems to have been a demand for equal benefits from the Union's own charitable funds. The subscription to the Benevolent and Orphan Fund was the same for men and women, yet the maximum benefit for men was £30 while that for women was £25. A group of women struggled to reform this and was successful in 1903.

The issue broadened in 1904 to whether the Union should seek equal pay for its women members, and correspondence on this in *The Schoolmaster* led to the formation of the Equal Pay League, an organisation within the N.U.T. of men and women sympathetic to the cause.[1] From 1904 equal pay motions were on the agenda at N.U.T. Conferences, but were rejected by considerable majorities, for while most members of the N.U.T. were women, they were far from constituting a majority either at the annual conferences or on the Executive. The aims of the Equal Pay League were to secure the election of women to the conference and to the executive. In 1906 the name was changed to the National Federation of Women Teachers.

By 1908 the question of the suffrage had become predominant. It was thought that if the N.U.T. could be persuaded to declare itself in favour of votes for women this would carry weight with the government. Thus the question of equal pay took second place while the N.F.W.T. tried to get support for an N.U.T. conference motion supporting the enfranchisement of women teachers. When such a motion eventually came to be debated at the annual conference of 1911 in Aberystwyth, it led to a thirty-minute anti-female suffrage demonstration by men delegates in the conference hall, and the motion was eventually rejected by 40,653 votes to 12,276. The N.F.W.T. maintained the pressure in local N.U.T. associations for the next 3 years.[2] At N.U.T. Conferences at Hull (1912), Weston-super-Mare (1913) and Lowestoft (1914) women's suffrage motions were heavily defeated. In this politically charged atmosphere the cause of equal pay was hardly likely to flourish, and in fact at the Lowestoft conference an equal pay motion was rejected by 58,483 to 11,017.[3]

It was against this background that during the war the N.F.W.T. began to show signs of becoming more than a pressure group trying to operate through the N.U.T. In 1916 the N.F.W.T. held its conference for the last time in the same town as the N.U.T.; after that it took place at a different date and in a different town. In 1914 8 of the 9 women on the N.U.T. executive were also members of the N.F.W.T., but the strong opposition of male members to the achievement of women's aims, along with the increasing determination of the keener women, led towards complete separation. Even after equal pay became part of the official policy of the N.U.T. in 1919, following a referendum of the membership and a majority in favour of 19,965, the leadership remained lukewarm. Indeed, in its issue of 6th December, 1919, *The Schoolmaster* was describing N.F.W.T. members as 'the fierce Hippolytas of the Women's Federation' and as 'wildest Amazons', because of their advocacy of equal pay. Perhaps the most important formal step in the break between the N.F.W.T. and the N.U.T. came at the former's conference at Portsmouth in 1921, when it was resolved that candidates for the central council should not be members of the N.U.T.[4]

At the local level in the years before 1919, where the N.F.W.T. had a considerable measure of strength in an area, it had been able to secure from employing authorities concessions in the direction of equal pay with men. In Swansea the minimum salary for both men and women college-trained certificated teachers was £225 and for non-collegiate teachers £215; uncertificated men and women began at £105, while assistants of both sexes began in the secondary schools at £275. Elsewhere equal minimum rates or equal increments were also obtained, although men proceeded to a higher maximum than women. Arrangements on these lines prevailed in Tottenham, East Ham and Mountain Ash.[5] But these were far from typical, as the Departmental Committee of inquiry into salaries in elementary schools reported in 1918. The Committee found that the maximum difference in the salaries of men and women certificated class teachers in the same year of service might be anything up to £60; sometimes the difference grew at a constant rate from the first year of service, and sometimes it grew rapidly only when teachers were approaching a comparatively advanced stage in their career. The committee also noted that a relatively small ultimate difference was always associated with a low scale for men rather than with a high scale for women.[6]

I SECTIONAL INTERESTS AND THE 4.5 RATIO

As with the salary structure generally, the relationship established between men's and women's salaries in the years 1918 to 1920 remained virtually unchanged for many years. The introduction of a national salary structure for the first time naturally implied the establishment of a national attitude to the question of equal pay. In addition to all the factors which produced the conflicts and struggles over teachers' salaries in these years, the equal pay issue continued to generate further political heat in that it was so closely associated with the extension of the franchise to women at the end of the war and with the general position of women in post-war society.

Women teachers in London were perhaps better organised and keener in their support of equal pay than they were elsewhere. In March, 1919, the L.C.C. considered proposals from its education committee for a revision of the existing scales of salaries for teachers in elementary schools which would have had the effect of further increasing the differential between the salaries of men and women. A petition of protest against this, signed by over 10,000 women teachers, was presented to the meeting and the proposals of the education committee were rejected by the full Council. At this time there were about 18,000 elementary school teachers in London, of whom 12,000 were women. *The Times* commented that the rejection of the scale was 'an unexpected decision. Nor will it escape notice that the success, so far as it goes, synchronises very closely with the extension of the parliamentary vote to women'.[7] The principle of equal pay was not accepted by the L.C.C. at this time, but the new scales adopted in May, 1918, did not increase the differential between men and women.

The Board of Education's Departmental Committee on salaries found itself the first official national body before which the case for equal pay for women teachers was argued. The National Federation of Women Teachers presented a strong memorandum to the committee which made the following points:[8]

(1) It had been possible to obtain a large number of women at a low rate of payment because there had been a dearth of suitable work for them and they had been unorganised. Both of these conditions had now changed. Many careers were now open to women, and competition for the services of educated women would become even keener.

(2) The payment of a higher salary to men would have the effect of preventing rather than securing their services, because if a better quality woman could be obtained at a lower price she would be preferred to the more expensive but inferior man. Higher salaries to attract more able men would tend to reduce their chances of employment.

(3) The expense of raising the salaries of women was no argument, since the Board of Education's duty was to control L.E.A.s and to make state assistance depend on certain conditions, one of which should be the payment of just salaries.

(4) The argument that many women were ready to come for lower salaries was 'immoral' and at the root of all sweated labour. When women were better organised they would not be willing to come for salaries which implied inferior status and quality.

The N.F.W.T. also set out a series of arguments to show the 'unfairness' of the sex differential, namely:[9]

(1) The work of men and women teachers involved equally long training and probation and equal qualifications were required.

(2) The cost of training was the same; where the college fee was less for a woman student she had to supplement this by undertaking housework in the college.

(3) Conditions of service were fixed irrespective of sex and the size of the class did not depend upon the sex of the teachers.

(4) As government grants were paid irrespective of sex, the teachers'

remuneration ought to be on the same basis. The present system led to the strange anomaly that the man teacher was receiving money for work done by his woman colleague.

(5) Payment of salary was not based upon private responsibility or upon the number of dependents.

(6) The education of girls and young children was of equal importance with that of boys and of equal value to the community.

(7) The cost of the necessities of life was the same for men and women. Taxes and local rates were fixed irrespective of sex. The provision of a home with necessary attendance for those who made teaching their life-work was as needful for women as for men.

The Departmental Committee was not persuaded by the N.F.W.T. memorandum. It argued in its report that since the schools could not be staffed entirely by the one sex or the other, the cases of men and women called for separate consideration. The ratepayers and taxpayers could not with justice be asked to shoulder the burden of paying to men or women higher salaries than were adequate, and in the existing circumstances a scale of salaries that was adequate for women was inadequate for men. The Committee could not, therefore, recommend equal payment as a principle on which scales for men and women teachers should be constructed. The Committee recommended that the starting salaries of certificated men and women teachers should be little different, but that at the maximum women should be paid three-fourths of the amount paid to men.[10] It accepted the view put by a number of witnesses that the number and quality of male recruits to teaching before the war had been declining, and that if equal pay were adopted the salaries for men would be lowered and they would be driven further away from the profession. This argument was put strongly by such witnesses as Sir Robert Blair, Education Officer to the L.C.C., who insisted that the services of men could not, in fact, be purchased at the same price as those of women. It was a question of market values. The committee which surveyed the salary position in secondary schools also came to the conclusion that the salary that would attract a woman would not attract a similarly qualified man; given existing economic and social conditions, differences between men's and women's salaries after the first few years of service appeared inevitable.

The attitude of the N.U.T. to equal pay as expressed to the Committee was somewhat equivocal. The Union nominated 5 teachers (3 men and 2 women) to give evidence. One of the men argued in favour of equal pay, another put forward arguments against it, while the third thought that there might be a basis for equality at the beginning of the scale, but after one or two years' service the salaries of men should proceed by considerably increased increments to a higher maximum than those for women. One of the women teachers thought that equal work was worth equal pay but if men and women teachers of the same grade were paid at the same rate the status of men teachers with families to support would be lower than that of women teachers, yet that the maximum paid to men should not be more than £20 greater than that paid to women. The second woman witness, Miss E. R. Conway, who was president of the N.U.T. in 1918, put forward the case for equal pay more strongly.

After the Departmental Committee had reported and before the first report from the Burnham Committee, the War Cabinet's committee on women in industry gave its advice on the equal pay issue in the teaching profession. It accepted the principle of equal pay for equal work and suggested that in view of the arguments advanced by the Departmental Committee in coming to the opposite conclusion, a system of family allowances should be introduced to meet the situation. The principle of equal pay for equal work should be applied, but where it was essential to employ men and women 'it may be necessary for the state to counteract the difference of attractiveness by a payment for the services rendered to the State in connection with the continuance of the race, or, in other words, by the payment of allowances to married men'.[11]

This recommendation was, of course, not in line with the attitude of the employing authorities or the Board of Education, both of which were concerned at the difficulty of attracting sufficient male applicants. The Board told the Cabinet Committee that the supply of men teachers had been less than the demand from the time when intending teachers began to be given a secondary school education, since this gave potential entrants a wider choice of occupation than had previously been the case. At the same time there was little to complain of in the educational level of the women who were being drawn into the profession. The representative of the largest single employing body, the L.C.C., believed that given the actual position in the outside World, 'women must be sought in the women's market and paid generously; men must be sought in the men's market and also paid generously. It is not known that any statistician has estimated the ratio between the two markets and therefore the proportion of three-quarters or some such figure embodied in present scales must be regarded as the result of experience and roughly meeting the needs of the schools'.[12]

The Association of Head Mistresses submitted written evidence to the Committee urging that all professions and callings should be open to women on equal conditions with men. By 'equal conditions' they understood (a) equal pay for equal work; (b) equal opportunities for promotion; (c) equal opportunities in training. The fact that some professions remained virtually closed to women meant that the achievement of equal pay for equal work in those professions that were open to them was difficult, if not impossible, to attain. It had certainly operated to increase the supply of women teachers artificially. Many women who had no natural gift for teaching had entered the occupation because others were closed to them, and they lowered the standard of efficiency and the rates of pay.[13]

The Schoolmaster, commenting on the Cabinet Committee's report, warned that equal pay must mean levelling up women's pay to the level of the men's. If this were not done, the shortage of men teachers would become even more acute. There should be 'a clear warning to the local education authorities that they should not propose, and to the Board of Education not to permit, an equalization by levelling down the pay of men.'[14]

The scales actually recommended by the Burnham Committees fell between the positions advocated by the Board of Education's Departmental Committees and the Cabinet Committee. The provisional minimum scale for certificated assistant teachers in elementary schools, for instance, started at £160 for men and £150 for women, while the respective maxima were £300 and £240, giving a ratio of four-fifths at the maximum in place of the three-quarters ratio recommended by the Departmental Committee. Over a career of 44 years these scales gave women a total of £10,110 and men £12,150; a relative percentage of 83·2 or almost five-sixths. Although there was great variety in the existing scales, the percentage had usually been in the region of 75 in most areas. Therefore the provisional minimum scale did represent an improvement in women's salaries relative to those of men. Sir George Lunn, Chairman of the Authorities' Panel of Burnham, explained this in terms of political pressures. He spoke of the 'huge demands all over the country for equal pay for men and women', adding that 'every Parliamentary candidate was bowing calmly before that demand. There was hardly a man who dared to stand out against that principle.' The N.U.T. agreed to these scales at a special conference on 30th December, 1919.

Miss Conway told the conference that all the women on the Joint Standing Committee were in favour of equal pay and that it was put forward as the policy of the Union, but opposed to them was 'a solid mass of masculine imperturbability'. She felt that they were justified in not breaking off negotiations on this issue as the new scale raised women's salaries even more than those of men.[15] At this time about three-fifths of the N.U.T.'s members were women.

The reactions of the N.F.W.T. and of the N.A.S. to the provisional scale were much less equivocal. At a special conference in January, 1920, the N.F.W.T. agreed to oppose in every possible way 'the imposition of unjust scales of salaries on women teachers'. The Federation protested against a committee containing an overwhelming majority of men deciding a question in which women equally with men were concerned. Only 5 out of 46 members of the Joint Standing Committee were women. To the N.F.W.T. 'the outstanding evil' of the Burnham scales was that the degree of equal pay which had been secured in some areas was swept away.[16] A deputation from the Federation met Fisher to urge the claim for equal pay. He explained that while the government paid grants to local authorities, it was the latter who paid the salaries. If the authorities cared to pay equally for men's work and women's work the government would still pay the grants.

The executive of the N.A.S. protested against the new provisional scale from the opposite point of view. It objected particularly to the low maximum offered to men, to the length of the scale and to the attempt to bind teachers for a 3-year period in times when economic conditions were changing rapidly. It asserted that no salary scale below that claimed by the N.A.S. at its conference, viz. £300 × 25 to £500, would be satisfactory for schoolmasters.[17]

Some of the local groups of schoolmasters were very active in pressing their case, especially the London Schoolmasters' Association, which in 1921 published a volume entitled *Equal Pay and the Teaching Profession* arguing against equal pay from every conceivable angle.

From the establishment of the Burnham machinery until the principle of equal pay in the public services came to be accepted in the 1950s, women's salaries continued to approximate to men's in roughly the proportion of 4 : 5. But there was a marginal deterioration in the position of women's salaries in the Burnham award effective from April, 1925. Demands for reductions in public expenditure by central and local authorities led to the general pressure for reductions of salary levels described above.[18] Now that the political pressures for equal pay seemed to be less strongly felt, the local authorities concentrated their efforts to some extent on trying to lower women's salaries, especially the salaries of young women, for here the employers felt that market forces most favoured them. In the 1924-5 negotiations direct talks between the two panels broke down and Lord Burnham arbitrated. The annual increments in the elementary scales were reduced from a common £12 10s. for both sexes to £12 for men and £9 for women, thus lengthening the period of time taken to reach the maxima, which were themselves only slightly modified. There was provision for the salaries of teachers in post to 'mark time' until their new scale salaries caught up with those payable in March, 1925. The overall result was that in the case of men certificated assistants the amount eventually lost by comparison with existing scales did not exceed £10 in any one year, and generally much less; for women the amount varied from £1 to £41.[19]

The reactions of the teachers' associations were predictable. As a party to the Burnham negotiations which it felt it had to honour, the attitude of the N.U.T., as expressed by its General Secretary, was that teachers had done well to avoid any worse cuts in the circumstances and that they should use the years immediately ahead to influence the authorities towards a reversion to the previous position, where the salaries of men and women would be more nearly equal. The N.A.S. complained of the cuts in men's salaries and of the N.U.T. showing too much solicitude for women's salaries because it had passed a resolution which 'deplored the lowering of the status of women teachers by the change of increment to £9'. The N.U.W.T. felt that if a lowering of salaries was unavoidable, the burden should have been shared evenly between men and women, and criticised the N.U.T. for consenting to the new scales.[20]

II THE EQUAL PAY ISSUE AFTER 1920

While the three decades following the first Burnham agreement saw little change in the actual salary differential between men and women teachers, this was the period when both the N.U.W.T. and the N.A.S. grew into national teachers' associations quite independent of and in a certain degree hostile towards the organisation from which they had broken away—the N.U.T. As the organisation which attempted to represent the views of all teachers, men and women, the N.U.T. was acutely embarrassed by the problems with which the equal pay issue confronted it. In the circumstances it is now clear that it was impossible for one association to hold the loyal and enthusiastic support both of those who strongly favoured equal pay and of those who were utterly opposed to it. But even if the most enthusiastic supporters and opponents were to join other organisations, the N.U.T. naturally remained anxious to keep as many as possible in membership. The position was especially difficult for the Union in the critical years immediately following the First World War when the membership seemed to be intent on mutual strife.

The more active women were still within the N.U.T., but the N.F.W.T. was on the way to becoming a rival union rather than just an internal pressure group. The adoption of equal pay as official policy after the referendum of members in 1919 was not enough to satisfy the N.F.W.T. supporters; to them the N.U.T.'s largely male leadership appeared to be playing the matter down in the face of mounting hostility from schoolmaster members, both centrally and in the localities. In London, for instance, it was announced at the conference of the London Teachers' Association (N.U.T.) in 1919 that the referendum had shown that 6,209 of the London Association's members favoured equal pay while only 3,595 opposed it. A month later a mass meeting was arranged at the Kingsway Hall by men opposed to the equal pay policy of the N.U.T. and its London Association. It was decided to form a London Schoolmasters' Association to support the newly formed National Association of Men Teachers. The men feared that the demand of the women for equal pay would prejudice their own chances of gaining improved salaries.[21] On 22nd September, 1919, *The Schoolmaster* published a letter from the secretary of the N.A.M.T. to N.U.T. representatives on Fisher's Joint Advisory Committee on Salaries reminding them of the 'irreconcilable antipathy' of the great bulk of men teachers to equal pay.

During 1920 the N.U.T. came under increasing pressure from schoolmasters opposed to equal pay. In July the executive received a deputation which referred to the possible secession of members from the N.U.T. who would not be satisfied unless the referendum vote on equal pay was rescinded, or they were granted the power to act separately on the salary question within the Union. An executive meeting in December discussed the question of equal pay at length and appointed a committee to go further into the matter. The possibility of seeking equal pay plus family allowances was considered as a possible way out of the difficult situation, but the general opinion was that the question of State family allowances was outside the province of the N.U.T., while if local authorities paid family allowances it was possible that the unmarried might be employed at the expense of the married.[22] Thus a policy favouring occupational family allowances seemed to the executive to offer no escape from the dissension and bitterness raised by the equal pay issue. The effect of this on membership figures in areas where feelings ran strongly may be seen from the position in London. At the end of 1919 N.U.T. membership there totalled 11,365; a year later it was down by 671 to 10,694, during a year when total Union membership had increased by approximately 3,000.[23]

Faced with difficulties from militant men and women, it was hardly surprising that a degree of bitterness grew up in the N.U.T. On 18th December, 1920, the leading article in *The Schoolmaster* wrote of the N.F.W.T.'s grievance at the failure to obtain equal pay. 'But behind the façade of that grievance there is an effort motivated by sex hatred, and the leading members of the Federation are probably not more anxious to exalt interests of women teachers than to depress the cause of men. The basis of the Schoolmasters' Association is to some extent the reverse of that; we hardly suppose there is much sex hatred in it, but probably some members of the Schoolmasters' Association were formerly opposed to women's suffrage.' To entirely reasonable persons it was obvious that 'as the number of women coming into the profession is not only much greater than the number of men, and the increasing supply of girl teachers is also greater than the increasing supply of boy teachers, to the unbiased mind it is clear that the cheaper the woman teacher can be had, the lower the rate of pay offered to a candidate who is a man'.

Bitterness between the N.U.T. and the N.A.S. intensified considerably in the next year or two, and in October, 1922 W. G. Cove, President of the N.U.T., wrote in an article on the London Schoolmasters' Association that the policy of the N.A.S. was being determined by 'disappointed post-hunters', 'by pseudo-socialists who desire to apply a socialist doctrine in a capitalist society, and by men abnormal in sex hatred'. The N.A.S. was a parasitic organisation. 'It waits and hopes for mistakes on the part of the N.U.T. It hopes to fatten itself on the ills that afflict us all.'[24]

Equal pay remained a part of the official salary policy of the N.U.T. in the inter-war years, but it was not a facet of policy which the Union chose to emphasise. Its attempt to steer a moderate course drew criticism from both sides. The N.A.S. and the N.U.W.T. were often more critical of the N.U.T., which they both—for different reasons—regarded as shifty and insincere, than they were of each other. The N.U.W.T. said that it much preferred to deal with an open enemy than an insincere friend and 'we are well aware that the N.A.S. can, and will, do more for our cause in a year than the N.U.T. could and would do in a whole life time'.[25]

The replies given by Sir Maurice Holmes, the Permanent Secretary of the Ministry of Education, in answer to questions from members of the Royal Commission on Equal Pay in 1945, probably indicated accurately the position of the N.U.T. in the previous quarter-century. When asked about the strength of feeling in the teaching profession on the question of equal pay, he replied, 'Of course the main Union of teachers, the National Union of Teachers, have all along stood for the doctrine of equal pay, but I think that they have regarded it hitherto as an unattainable ideal. I myself should not have said that there was this vast sense of injustice or grievance.'[26]

To the further question of whether failure to grant equal pay would result in any more than a temporary disturbance in the attitude of teachers towards the authorities, Holmes replied, 'You have this fact, the National Union of Teachers embraces the vast majority of teachers, and the majority of members of the Union are women. I think if the women felt as strongly as your question would lead me to think that they ought to have had equal pay, they would have said "This is a very nice Union and they have got us additional pay, but they have never looked like getting us equal pay; we had better start one of our own and go for it." There is the dissident Union, the National Union of Women Teachers, but that is relatively very small.'[27]

Between 1920 and 1945 the leadership of the N.U.T. gave the appearance of being satisfied with the four-fifths compromise. During much of this period it had been greatly concerned with defending the salary scales, but even had it been less pressed with this problem, it seems unlikely that it would have wished to give the appearance of vigorously advocating an equal pay policy. There was in the Union a considerable number of men who were not in favour of equal pay, but were content to remain members in the expectation and hope that its realisation would depend upon broad political factors, and that for financial, if not for other reasons, the local authorities were very unlikely to accept the principle. Moreover the N.U.W.T. was hardly a threat to the

N.U.T. for most of this time, because of the apathy of many women teachers, but the N.A.S. was a different proposition. Were the N.U.T. to appear to be enthusiastic in support of equal pay, it would risk losing male members to the N.A.S. and itself become increasingly vulnerable to the charge of being only a women's union. As late as 1954 the General Secretary spoke of the 'hostility' shown by some of the male members to the Union's support for the Equal Pay Coordinating Committee and described how 'a certain hesitancy' had been revealed.[28]

Over the quarter-century following the introduction of national salary scales for teachers the N.U.W.T. offered a marked contrast to the N.U.T. This never became a large organisation and never succeeded in attracting a numerically significant following in a profession where some 70 per cent of the members were women. It is impossible to give exact membership figures, for these the N.U.W.T. never published; in 1945 it refused even to supply figures to the Royal Commission on Equal Pay. It probably had fewer than 5,000 members, but it undoubtedly contained some of the most committed and active women teachers who were prepared to devote time and energy to activities designed to influence public opinion, M.P.s and the government on feminist questions. From one point of view it was not so much a teachers' association concerned with professional problems as an association of women teachers dedicated to the advancement of the feminist cause in society generally. This was certainly the sense in which the first of the N.U.W.T.'s stated aims was interpreted viz: 'to collect and express the opinions and wishes of women teachers and to secure their combined action' and lends significance to the Union's motto 'She who would be free herself must strike the blow'.

During the 'twenties the N.U.W.T. became deeply involved in pressing for the full extension of the franchise to women which was seen as the first step towards full equality. The Union's Annual Report for 1926 pointed out that if women teachers wanted equal pay, equal opportunities and equal consideration of their point of view on professional questions, the surest way was to get women enfranchised on the same terms as men so that they might use the political machinery to express their opinion 'of the legislation which governs their lives'.[29] The N.U.W.T. worked closely with other political organisations which sought to build up pressure for the widening of women's rights. Early in 1926 the Equal Political Rights Campaign Committee was formed and the General Secretary of the N.U.W.T. became its Vice-chairman. The next year the N.U.W.T. organised a deputation to the

Prime Minister on behalf of the Campaign Committee which was supported by 56 organisations.[30] The equal franchise was enacted in 1928 and it is interesting to notice that in a eulogistic passage about the work of Miss E. E. Froud, the General Secretary, Emily Phipps, editor of the *Woman Teacher*, claimed that the winning of equal franchise 'is the first great result of her work as leader of the N.U.W.T.'.[31]

The tactics used by the Union were those forged in these political battles. Members were active in lobbying M.P.s, taking part in demonstrations and mass meetings, poster-parades, writing to the press and the like. London members, in particular, appear to have been experienced campaigners. Following the suffrage movement, nearly every branch of the Union had provided itself with a banner. These were displayed at every N.U.W.T. procession, at every open-air meeting and public meeting in which the Union participated. Members believed that reasoning alone was inadequate as a means of altering the general opinion. 'It is an exceptional person who can be influenced by argument only; the imagination must first be roused. . . .'[32] After 1928 the N.U.W.T. turned its tactics to campaigning to create a public opinion favourable to equal pay. Shortly before the Equal Franchise Bill received the Royal Assent an editorial in the *Woman Teacher* urged women to use the new freedom they had attained to work for the removal of the payment of salaries according to sex. 'Our weapon is the vote. Every woman teacher who has sufficient clearness of vision to see that it is unfair to pay men a higher salary than women merely because of sex should make it her business to write to, or interview, her member of Parliament, or the candidates for Parliament in her constituency, and point out to him (or her) that her vote will be given to the candidate who is sound on the question of equal pay. Every woman teacher who is a member of a political party should raise the question at party meetings, and keep it to the front.'[33]

The N.U.W.T. not only saw equal pay for women teachers as a political issue but it also saw that the most likely route to this goal would be through the central government first accepting the principle in the case of civil servants. In 1927 the N.U.W.T. had supported the Federation of Women Civil Servants in their demand for the appointment of a select committee to inquire into the cost and method of the application of the principle of equal pay in the civil service. In 1936 there was a debate in the Commons on a motion from Ellen Wilkinson (which was carried) that women in the common classes of the civil service should be paid the same salary rates as men. The Speaker had not put the motion in the accepted form, and further debate on it took place the following week, when the Prime Minister made its defeat a matter of confidence. Members of the N.U.W.T. lobbied M.P.s on the day the vote of confidence was taken. The *Woman Teacher* left its readers in no doubt as to why the Union was involved, saying that it was 'in this campaign on behalf of women civil servants because of the justice of the case primarily, and because also the woman civil servant's case is the woman teacher's case. When once equal pay has been conceded in the civil service it will have to be conceded in the teaching service—Burnham or other committees will have no choice in the matter.'[34]

The N.U.W.T. had no representation on the Burnham Committee. When this was first established, Fisher, then President of the Board of Education, said that membership was not a matter for the Board since it was established by agreement between the local authority associations on the one hand and the N.U.T. on the other.[35] Between 1919 and 1931 there was no agreement between the President of the Board and the Burnham Committee as to which was responsible for determining the constitution of the Standing Joint Committee. In 1931 the President of the Board told the Commons that he had now agreed with the Committee that he was responsible for determining what bodies should be entitled to appoint representatives and their number.[36] This did not, however, lead to any widening of representation, and the N.U.T. continued to be the sole representative body for elementary school teachers in spite of repeated requests from the N.U.W.T. and the N.A.S. In May, 1931, for instance the N.U.W.T. held a mass meeting at the Central Hall, Westminster to protest against their exclusion. A resolution pointed out that while 70 per cent of teachers were women, the Standing Joint Committee consisted of 46 men and 4 women.[37] At its conference in December, 1932 the N.U.W.T. decided that in future no member should also be a member of the N.U.T. This step was taken in order to refute the suggestion that women teachers through dual membership might have some sort of representation on Burnham through the N.U.T.

Closely associated with the question of equal pay was that of equal opportunity. From the beginning of this century the tendency on the part of local authorities to develop their elementary systems on the basis of mixed rather than single sex schools raised the fears of women teachers that there would be a restriction of career opportunities since the headships of mixed schools usually went to men. The position was further exacerbated when in January, 1925 the Board of Education issued Circular 1350 commending to local authorities the virtues of Junior Mixed and Infants' departments. This often led to the mistress in charge of the infants being an assistant under a male head of the whole school, and no longer a head herself. The N.U.W.T. made vigorous representations to the Board on this point and in its Pamphlet No. 60 of 1928 the Board ceased to press this preference. Nevertheless, Infants' schools aside, the Board continued to advocate senior mixed and junior mixed in place of separate boys' and girls' elementary schools. The N.U.W.T. fought a continuous campaign to assert the claims of women to headships of mixed schools. In 1926 the Union forwarded a memorandum to local authorities urging them on the three grounds of educational efficiency, fairness to girl pupils and fairness to women teachers, to make appointments to the headships of all mixed schools on the basis of educational qualifications only, irrespective of the sex of the candidates. The Union also attacked the N.U.T. from time to time between the wars for carrying advertisements of vacancies for *headmasters* only of mixed and infant schools in *The Schoolmaster*, its official journal.[38]

The campaign for equal pay, equal opportunities and for women teachers' rights generally naturally stimulated opponents as well as supporters, and the continued growth of the National Association of Schoolmasters during the first 30 years or so of its existence owed a great deal to the vigour with which the women pursued their claims. After the National Association of Men Teachers had changed its name to the National Association of Schoolmasters in 1920, the movement towards complete separation from the N.U.T. gathered considerable impetus. At the Whitsun 1921 Conference of the N.A.S. compulsory secession from the N.U.T. was rejected by a large majority. But in 1922 a referendum of the members of the London Schoolmasters' Association, probably the most active and powerful of all the branches, showed an overwhelming majority in favour of secession. Accordingly it was agreed at a special conference of the N.A.S. held at Nottingham in 1922 that as from 1st January, 1923, no member of the N.A.S. could also be a member of the N.U.T. At the conference it was felt that salary efforts were being frustrated by dual membership, and that little progress could be made while the N.A.S. remained a 'ginger group' within the N.U.T. The N.A.S. was said to have lost 'some hundreds of members' but to have 'gained in strength' as a result of this decision.[39]

Having broken with the N.U.T., the N.A.S. wrote to the President of the Board of Education seeking membership of the Burnham elementary committee. The reply from the Board stated that 'if the committee does not agree to a modification in the constitution of the Teachers' Panel, and Mr. Wood (the President) is faced with the alternatives of a continuance of the committee as now constituted or the discontinuance of its work through the withdrawal of the largest and most representative association of teachers, he would feel bound in the interests of the public service of education and the teaching profession to choose the former alternative'. For nearly 40 years the N.A.S. was to seek entry to the Burnham machinery without success. Many members of the N.A.S. believed that the opposition of the N.U.T. to their representation lay in the acceptance of the N.U.T. of the principle of equal pay.[40]

The central argument of the N.A.S. over the years was that the cases of men and women called for separate consideration—as the Departmental Committee of the Board had indeed suggested in its Report in 1918. The Association maintained that there were two quite distinct markets, one for men and one for women teachers. In each there was a distinct market price determined by the forces for supply and demand. In its early years the Association was fighting against the 'dilution' of male staff that had arisen during the First World War. It claimed that this did not show that there was really only one market for teachers but that on the contrary it emphasised that a distinct men's market existed but had suffered from neglect and that 'strong economic justification exists for more exclusive treatment until equilibrium is established'.[41]

Since the N.A.S. believed that women should be paid less than men, it followed that a 'separate market' theory was essential so as to avoid reducing employment opportunities for men. If men and women teachers really were largely interchangeable, then the cheaper women would always undercut the men, and employers would naturally employ as many women as they could get in preference to men. Thus throughout these years the N.A.S. insisted that boys needed male teachers. The official favour shown towards mixed in place of single sex elementary schools in the inter-war years stimulated the N.A.S. as much as it did the N.U.W.T. to argue vigorously over senior posts in mixed elementary schools. In 1933, for instance, the annual conference of the N.A.S. passed a resolution strongly resenting any man being called upon to serve under a headmistress, insisting that all mixed schools should be under headmasters and that the staff should include as many male assistants as would ensure that the boys came predominantly under the influence of men. Another resolution in similar vein strongly disapproved of the use of women inspectors to assess the professional competence of men teachers.[42]

The steady increase in the proportion of mixed to single sex schools meant that employers, the parents and teachers themselves became increasingly familiar with a position where boys were taught by women with no apparent loss of efficiency and it could be argued that the public appeal of the 'separate market' argument was weakening considerably by the later 1930s. It is interesting to notice that in 1936 the National Association of Local Government Officers adopted the principle of equal pay for equal work at least partly because the markets for men and women could no longer be kept apart and there was some fear of women being used to replace the more expensive men. In his history of the National Association of Local Government Officers, A. Spoor suggested that in adopting the policy of equal pay, most members 'grounded their support on the fear that, with the increasing use of office machinery, in whose handling women were singularly apt, the continuance of unequal pay must close blocks of clerical work to male workers'. Only a minority—of both men and women—genuinely backed the principle.[43]

Wartime conditions after 1939 acted as a stimulant in this as in other fields of social reform. The greatly increased demand for female labour, which arose out of the introduction of women to work traditionally the preserve of men, resulted in agreements that where women were employed on work hitherto performed by men, they should receive the man's rate of pay. Women's organisations were particularly annoyed that the Personal Injuries (Emergency Provisions) Act provided that the weekly rates of pensions for totally disabled adult men should be 32s. 6d. and for women 22s. 6d. The N.U.W.T. was represented on a deputation to the Minister of Pensions in March 1940 which protested against these terms. A resolution at the N.U.W.T. conference in 1941 called for the granting of equal rates of compensation to men and women.[44] A Conservative M.P., Mrs. Mavis Tate, championed the cause of equal rates of compensation. On 25th November, 1942 she divided the Commons on an amendment to the Loyal Address in reply to the King's Speech. The amendment was defeated but the appointment of a Select Committee on equal compensation was agreed. The report of this Committee favoured the adoption of flat-rate compensation for all adult civilians, irrespective of sex or occupation. The Minister of Pensions accepted the recommendations on behalf of the government and from 19th April, 1943, the rates of compensation for women and non-gainfully occupied persons were increased to the rate paid to gainfully occupied men.[45]

Another and perhaps more far-reaching outcome of this successful wartime campaign for women's rights was that many of the groups or organisations and individuals involved in it went on to set up the Equal Pay Campaign Committee. This Committee was formally established in January, 1944, with Mrs. Tate as its chairman. On her death in 1947, Mrs. Cazalet Keir, another Conservative woman M.P., took over the Chairmanship until the Committee wound up its affairs in 1956, after it had become government policy to introduce equal pay.[46]

Wartime conditions led to the removal of a grievance which many women teachers had felt in the interwar years, when most local authorities were unwilling to employ married women as teachers and compelled single women to leave their posts on marriage. In 1942 the Board of Education issued a circular to authorities advising them that local regulations requiring the resignation of women teachers on marriage could not be justified in existing circumstances, and should be suspended at least for the duration of the war. Prior to this, whenever Presidents of the Board had been pressed on this question in the Commons they had expressed the view that they had no power to intervene with local authorities. The different social attitude of the war years brought permanent change here, for in 1944 it was enacted that 'No woman shall be disqualified for employment as a teacher in any county or voluntary school, or be dismissed from such employment, by reason only of marriage'.[47]

Even the atmosphere of war-time was not sufficient, however, to enable the N.U.W.T. and the N.A.S. to secure representation on the main Burnham committee. M.P.s anxious to secure representation for the N.A.S. moved an amendment to clause 82 of the Education Bill and a debate on this issue ensued. R. A. Butler took the same line as his predecessors at the Board. He was unwilling to grant representation to additional bodies without the agreement or on the request of the existing teachers' panel of the Burnham committee. While the President did not wish to offend the minority associations, the number of teachers' organisations was considerable, and if representation were granted to one it would have to be granted to all. 'We have a particular difficulty in the question of the National Association of Schoolmasters and the National Union of Women Teachers, to which no reference has been made hitherto. The National Association of Schoolmasters stands aloof from the N.U.T. on the ground that the N.U.T. has too many women members, and the National Union of Women Teachers stands aloof from the N.U.T. on the ground that the N.U.T. is not sufficiently feminine, so we find that the claims of these two organisations cancel each other out.'[48]

On March 28th, 1944, another amendment to the same Clause 82 was proposed, this time by Mrs. Cazalet Keir, to provide that in approving scales of salaries for teachers the President should 'not differentiate between men and women solely on the grounds of sex'. General speeches followed, supporting the principle of equal pay, and the N.U.W.T. later claimed that it had asked certain women M.P.s if they would take the opportunity of raising this question in discussing the Clause.[49] Butler explained that the object of the clause was only to secure that Burnham agreements should be mandatory on local authorities, and that it was not his practice to give directions to the Burnham panels before they came to decisions about salaries. He claimed that he had no evidence that the Burnham panels desired equal pay and that the question was linked up with the national position and could not be decided in isolation. Mrs. Keir's amendment was carried by 117 votes to 116. The next day the Prime Minister stated that the government proposed to delete clause 82 as amended from the bill, but on the report stage the clause would be reintroduced in its original form and the matter would be treated throughout as one of confidence. On 30th March Churchill secured his vote of confidence by 425 votes to 23. On 9th May he announced in the Commons that the government had decided to set up a Royal Commission to consider the question of equal pay for equal work.

The use made by advocates of equal pay of the opportunity which clause 82 gave them was a considerable embarrassment to the N.U.T., at whose request Butler had inserted the original clause. The Union's sole object had been to give the Minister power to compel local authorities to pay scales agreed upon by the Burnham committee. Following the events in the Commons, a leading article in *The Schoolmaster* explained why the N.U.T. executive was opposed to Mrs. Keir's equal pay amendment. It said that while the Union was in favour of equal pay it was also in favour of free negotiation in the Burnham committee, 'untrammelled by outside dictation on either principles or figures . . . the fact that the first expression of such dictation was to be along lines acceptable to the Union did not remove the possibility that later expressions might well prove unacceptable'. Members were advised that 'The Union stands for equal pay not in the narrow context of Mrs. Cazalet Keir's amendment, but in a much wider sense. The Union's objective is not a one dimensional but a three dimensional equality—equality between the sexes, equality between different areas, and equality between different types of school.'[50] There can be little doubt that pressures from different sections of the membership meant that the N.U.T. Executive had to tread warily, and it may be significant that it was only after the latter two objectives appeared to have been largely achieved in the 1944 Burnham negotiations that the Union turned with any appearance of enthusiasm to work for the achievement of equal pay.

The occasion of the hearings held by the Royal Commission on Equal Pay in 1945 gave the teachers' associations an opportunity to state their views publicly. The case for and the case against equal pay as advanced by the N.U.W.T. and the N.A.S. followed closely the arguments they had been advancing over the years. The N.A.S. based its case on the 'axiomatic truth' that 'there are two jobs, teaching boys and teaching girls. These jobs are not interchangeable and no individual can adequately perform both. There are limitations imposed by sex which no technical or professional competence can overcome.' If all boys over infant age were taught by men, as the N.A.S. desired, the proportion of men and women teachers would be 39 to 61, not the 29 to 71 which it actually was in 1938.[51] The real fears of many men teachers were no doubt expressed by Mr. J. Mason, Vice-president of the N.A.S., who told the Commission that the country couldn't afford to bring women's salaries up to the men's level, so that in actual practice equal pay would mean a dragging down of the whole rate of pay.[52]

Both of the associations for secondary school women teachers submitted evidence in favour of equal pay. The Assistant Mistresses Association stated that hitherto salaries had been negotiated mainly on a market test for men, the women's scale then being a fixed proportion of that decided for the men. The controlling market conditions in the secondary field were likely to remain unchanged, particularly so far as graduates were concerned, except that it was growing increasingly difficult to bring the graduate into teaching. For this reason the men's scale was unlikely to be reduced by the adoption of equal pay for women, particularly as the demand for women graduates was likely to continue to grow more quickly than the supply.[53] The Headmistresses'

Association considered that it was rather the differentiation of the teaching profession as a whole from others, not the differentiation between men and women within the profession which had had an unfortunate effect on its market value and for which another name was 'public esteem'.[54]

The N.U.T. in its evidence supported equal pay and pointed out that family men would in future receive free secondary education for their children, as well as children's allowances, under the government's social welfare scheme; moreover the additional burden involved in supporting a wife and children was largely offset by Income Tax relief. In any case, the Union believed that it was the actual rather than the relative level of his salary which would decide whether a man was likely to become a recruit to teaching, and it would be politically impossible for equal pay to be introduced except by the process of levelling up.[55]

The Royal Commission itself was not concerned with the principle of equal pay but with examining and considering the social, economic and financial implications of the claim for equal pay for equal work. So far as the teaching profession was concerned, the Commissioners were particularly anxious to reach some conclusions about the balance of men to women which would be likely to result from a levelling up of women's salaries to those of men. In their Report they pointed out the conflict in the evidence submitted by the different associations and the conclusions they themselves offered were vague. In general they thought there was some substance in the argument that if a uniform rate were established for men and women, this salary level would tend to fall below that obtaining for men in comparable employments outside teaching. It followed from this that a material drop in the number or quality of male teachers was a possibility which could not be ruled out.[56]

III A SUCCESSFUL CAMPAIGN

The period between the publication of the Report from the Royal Commission and the acceptance by the government of a scheme for the implementation of equal pay in the public services nine years later was marked by a steady increase in political pressure from women's organisations, often working together through the Equal Pay Campaign Committee. One of the most energetic supporting organisations was the N.U.W.T. On the day following the publication of the Royal

Commission's Report a letter was circulated to M.P.s urging them to take all possible steps to raise the question of implementing the Labour Party's stated policy of equal pay for equal work. The N.U.W.T. took a leading part in the organisation of an equal pay meeting convened by the Equal Pay Campaign Committee at the Central Hall, Westminster on 30th January, 1947, under the chairmanship of Mrs. Cazalet Keir. Women's organisations co-operated also at by-elections where they canvassed, issued handbills, held meetings and generally took all practical steps to put their case.

Apart from the N.U.W.T. other organisations which remained with the Equal Pay Campaign Committee until it was dissolved included the A.A.M., the British Federation of University Women, the Council of Women Civil Servants, the Fawcett Society, the L.C.C. Staff Association, the National Association of Women Civil Servants, the National Council of Women, the National Federation of Women's Institutes, the National Union of Bank Employees, the Royal College of Nursing, the Suffragette Fellowship, the Women's Engineering Society and the Women's Freedom League. In brief, the E.P.C.C. was composed mainly of smallish groups of professional women aiming to secure the immediate and full implementation of the principle of equal pay in the public services.[57]

Among the bigger unions of public employees, none of those represented on the National Whitley Council for the Civil Service was a member of the E.P.C.C.; the N.U.T. was a member only for two years and N.A.L.G.O. was a member from 1949 to 1954. The difficulty here was that relations between the Campaign Committee and the larger mixed unions were often vitiated by the suspicions and enmity between the large and small unions. In spite of the apparent weight attached to publicity efforts, political lobbying and the like, Allen Potter suggested in his study of the E.P.C.C. that the greater influence of the organisations of the Committee lay in this relationship. 'The existence of the women's trade unions as competitors to the large "mixed" unions of public employees made the large unions more responsive to the demand for equal pay than they would otherwise have been.'[58] The extent of any such responsiveness in the case of the N.U.T. had been limited between the wars by the opposite pressures from the existence of the N.A.S., but in the years immediately after the Second World War the strength of any influence from this source appears to have been lessening in the changed climate for social attitudes. The N.U.T. after withdrawing from the Campaign Committee, later gave its support to the Equal Pay Co-ordinating Committee, a body originating in the staff side of the National Whitley Council and expanded to include representatives of the N.U.T., N.A.L.G.O. and the L.C.C. Staff Association. The Co-ordinating Committee followed a more 'moderate' line than the Campaign Committee in that it pressed for equal pay by stages, whereas the latter pressed for full implementation of equal pay at once.

At the end of 1950 the N.U.T. Executive appointed a special sub-committee whose terms of reference were 'to consider the question of Equal Pay in all its implications'. The attitude of the authorities' panel of the Burnham Committee had been and remained that it was not prepared to consider the application of equal pay to the teaching profession until the government had given a lead by introducing it for their own employees, the civil servants. Throughout the year, close contact had been maintained with the staff side of the Whitley Council, who had renewed their approaches to the Chancellor of the Exchequer. The 1951 Conference of the N.U.T. passed a resolution demanding that the government should make equal pay 'a reality and not merely a principle', and instructed the Executive to launch a campaign in support of this demand. A deputation met the Minister of Education in May to press the claim for equal pay and the next month the Chancellor of the Exchequer rejected the actual implementation but accepted the principle. Correspondents of local associations were asked to raise the question when interviewing parliamentary candidates in the constituencies during the general election in October. By the election all political parties accepted the principle.[59]

Pressure on the government was increased during 1952 and 1953. In May 1952 the House of Commons, without a division accepted a motion which read: 'That this House re-affirms its belief in the principle of Equal Pay for equal work as between men and women; supports the doctrine universally accepted in the trade union movement of payment for all work at the rate for the job irrespective of sex; recognises, however, that the economic position of those with family responsibilities must be assured, which can be and is being progressively achieved by a combination of family allowances and other social services, and tax reliefs; that therefore in the opinion of this House, there is no justification for continuing the 32 years' delay in implementing the motion passed on 19th May, 1920, which declared that it was expedient that women in the public services should be given equal pay; and it now calls upon Her Majesty's Government to announce an early and definite date by which the application of equal pay for equal work in the civil service, the teaching profession, local government and the public services will begin.'

The campaigns conducted by all the organisations involved reached their greatest intensity in 1954. In March two huge petitions were presented to the Commons, one by the Campaign Committee and one by the Co-ordinating Committee. Answering questions on 9th March, Mr. Butler, now Chancellor of the Exchequer, repeated that the government intended to make a start on the introduction of equal pay as soon as the economic situation permitted. He still offered no date, but added in his reply that 'the general interest in the subject which has been evinced in the House today and the sincerity of the questions cannot but have their influence upon anybody in a position like myself'.[60] In May, Mr. Butler agreed that negotiations should begin in the Whitley Council with the object of evolving a scheme for the introduction of equal pay in the non-industrial civil service, and on 25th January, 1955, the Chancellor told the Commons that the government was prepared to accept the scheme agreed in the Whitley Council whereby equal pay would be achieved by means of seven equal annual increments.

Throughout its existence the N.U.W.T. had regarded equal pay as being as much a political issue to be attained by political ends as was equal suffrage. In 1953 the Labour Party Conference accepted a motion calling for the immediate implementation of equal pay under the next Labour government. The General Secretary of the N.U.W.T. commented that it would be the business of the rank and file to see that the undertaking was met when the next Labour government was returned, and added that 'in view of this pledge, the present government might deem it politic to steal a march on their opponents and implement equal pay now'.[61] The *Economist* commented that 'Doubtless Mr. Butler felt impelled to take the plunge by the Labour Party's pledge made a year ago, to "implement the policy of equal pay" immediately it was returned to power. Yet he can hardly be accused of direct electioneering. Although the women civil servants will get their first instalment immediately, there will probably have been at least two general elections before the seventh and last annual increase is paid—and equality is achieved—on 1st January, 1961.'[62]

During the negotiations preceding the salary scales adopted from April, 1954, the authorities' panel had said it would reconsider the position in relation to women teachers if and when government action was taken to operate equal pay in the civil service. Following the Chancellor's statement on 25th January, the teachers' panel accordingly asked for a meeting of the Burnham Committee. The meeting took place on 4th March and the teachers' panel sought that equal pay should be applied in full at once. The authorities insisted on following the Civil Service pattern of gradual application. Thus the first step was taken on 1st May, 1955, and the remaining six steps on 1st April of each succeeding year until 1961. There was something of a sense of anti-climax when equal pay was actually achieved. After the presentation of the two great petitions in March, 1954, there had been the wait from May to January while the Whitley Council negotiations proceeded to produce an agreement for the Civil Service. Indeed, in his speech to the 1955 Conference, the General Secretary of the N.U.T. commented on how quietly equal pay had eventually come. 'No one was chained to railings, no banners were carried, no police truncheons were used, and, when it was announced, no bonfires were lit.'[63]

Both the N.U.W.T. and the N.A.S. called upon the Minister to reject the settlement, the former because it did not give full equal pay immediately, the latter because its opposition remained as strong as ever. Early in February, 1955, the N.A.S. had sent a circular letter to all local education authorities expressing the view that the social and economic consequences of equal pay were 'both greater and more harmful than is realised and therefore urges that each local authority should give consideration to these consequences and, in particular, to the cost of the introduction of equal pay in its service'. The letter ended by appealing to local authorities to take such steps as they could to prevent the extension of equal pay 'which will not only cause grave economic difficulties but will undoubtedly have serious repercussions'.

The N.U.W.T.'s annoyance at securing the fulfilment of its aim only over a seven-year period was such that it declined to be associated with the Milestone Dinner held by the Equal Pay Campaign Committee with R. A. Butler as the chief guest. Miss Pierotti, the General Secretary, commented acidly that the N.U.W.T. saw no grounds for jubilation over a scheme which postponed the application of the principle for another six years, and considered that the time and money spent on the dinner would have been better employed in continuing to work for the implementation of equal pay at once.[64] However, the actual passage of time inevitably put a different complexion on matters and in 1961 the Union closed down, feeling its purpose had been accomplished. Miss Pierotti was said to have remarked, 'A general does not feel it wrong to disband his army when he has won his battle.'[65]

The achievement of equal pay did not lead, of course, to the winding up of the other association which had originally been the product of the equal pay issue. On the contrary, the N.A.S. has grown in size and influence since 1955. Its General Secretary was reported in March, 1955 to have said that even if the battle against equal pay was lost the Association would carry on with its work, since 'with equal pay, the schoolmaster will need more looking after than ever'.[66] Perhaps inevitably, within two years the President claimed that the cost of introducing equal pay was being met by a process of levelling down.[67] From one point of view the N.A.S. seems to have benefited from the granting of equal pay in that it has perforce been obliged to broaden its aims and to look further than the equal pay issue if it were to survive and flourish. The Association successfully sought membership of the Burnham Committee, developed wider aims and radical methods and built up its membership.

Admission to Burnham was eventually achieved in the face of stormy opposition from the N.U.T. after sufficient support had been built up in the Commons, mainly among Conservative members.[68] C. Fletcher-Cooke introduced an adjournment debate on the question of representation for the N.A.S. on Burnham on 14th April, 1960. Dr. H. King, a member of the N.U.T., opposed the claim strongly, arguing that the N.A.S. merely wanted to reopen in the Burnham Committee the equal pay issue. The Minister, Sir David Eccles, refused to move from the position taken up by his predecessors and claimed that once the existing basis was abandoned, claims to representation would be made by other sectional groups.[69] The Parliamentary pressure was maintained, questions were asked and in the following November Mr. Robert Jenkins tabled a motion that the N.A.S. should be represented. The motion attracted 88 signatories, the majority of them Conservative members.

At the same time the N.A.S. was refashioning its policies to enable it to work in the context of Burnham. The Association had come to recognise that it was a fact that Parliament had decided on equal pay in the teaching profession and, whilst retaining the democratic right of the Association's members to seek to change Parliamentary policy, the Association would work responsibly on the Burnham Committee.[70] The difficulty facing the leaders of the N.A.S. was neatly summarised in the comment of *The Times Educational Supplement*. 'The N.A.S.

seems to have found a formula sufficiently elastic to give them a chance of representation on Burnham with the least risk of being accused of betrayal by the diehards in the Association. It was clear from the annual conference last year that for some older members, if the Association abandoned its opposition to equal pay it would be Hamlet without the Prince of Denmark. At the same time there is a growing feeling among the younger members that the realities of power must be accepted, and power resides in Burnham.' The continued refusal of the Minister to grant representation led directly to strike action in 1961, when there were various short and local strikes in the summer followed by a one-day strike by all members on 20th September, which was a protest against the new Burnham salary proposals as well as against the exclusion of the N.A.S.

On 16th October, 1961, representatives of the N.A.S. and of the N.A.H.T. were invited to meet the Minister, and the discussions led to an exchange of letters and the granting of Burnham representation to the N.A.S. The letters set out the understanding on which the representation was given. The General Secretary of the N.A.S. accepted that equal pay was national policy, and would not allow opposition to that policy to obstruct the working of the Burnham Committee. The Minister replied that in the light of the assurance he could agree in principle to N.A.S. representation, adding that he was doing this on the understanding that the N.A.S. would cancel its campaign of militant action and instead work responsibly inside the salary negotiating machinery.[71] Some of the difficulties which arose over the conventions of confidentiality in the Burnham negotiations have been discussed above.[72]

NOTES

1. E. Phipps, *History of the N.U.W.T.* 1928, pp. 1–3.
2. Ibid., p. 7.
3. Ibid., p. 19.
4. Ibid., p. 33.
5. Memorandum submitted by N.U.W.T. to Royal Commission on Equal Pay, 1945, para. 13.
6. Report of the Departmental Committee of the Board of Education for Enquiring into the Principles which should determine the construction of scales of salary for teachers in Elementary Schools, Cd. 8939, 1918, Vol. I, p. 9.

7. *The Times*, 7th March, 1918, p. 7.
8. Departmental Committee Report, Cd. 8999, 1918, Vol. II, pp. 67–8.
9. Ibid., p. 70.
10. Ibid., Vol. I, p. 9.
11. Report of the War Cabinet Committee on Women in Industry, Cmd. 135, 1919, p. 194.
12. Ibid., pp. 167–8.
13. Ibid., p. 40.
14. *The Schoolmaster*, 31st May, 1919, p. 851.
15. Ibid., 3rd January, 1920, p. 12.
16. Phipps, op. cit., p. 86.
17. *The Schoolmaster*, 1st May, 1920, p. 894, letter from the Press Secretary of the N.A.S.
18. *Supra*, Chapter III.
19. *The Schoolmaster*, 3rd April, 1925, p. 567; Board of Education, Report for 1924–5, Cmd. 2695, 1926, p. 94.
20. H. Meigh, *Schoolmasters' Salaries since the Beginning of the Twentieth Century*, 1957, p. 19; E. Phipps, op. cit., p. 87.
21. *The Schoolmaster*, 7th June, 1919, p. 898.
22. *The Schoolmaster*, 11th December, 1920, pp. 1017–18.
23. Ibid.
24. *The Schoolmaster*, 27th October, 1922, p. 616.
25. *The Woman Teacher*, 16th February, 1923, p. 154.
26. Royal Commission on Equal Pay, Minutes of Evidence, 1945, p. 182, Q 2587.
27. Ibid., Q 2588.
28. *The Schoolmaster*, 23rd April, 1954, p. 649, Speech by Sir Ronald Gould to N.U.T. conference.
29. *The Woman Teacher*, 14th January, 1927, p. 110.
30. Ibid., 13th January, 1928, p. 110.
31. Phipps, op. cit., p. 89.
32. Ibid., p. 59.
33. *The Woman Teacher*, 29th June, 1928, p. 288.
34. Ibid., 10th April, 1936, p. 235.
35. *Hansard*, H. of C., 1st December, 1919, col. 66.
36. Ibid., 21st May, 1931, col. 2158.
37. *The Woman Teacher*, 22nd May, 1931, pp. 221–2.
38. E. Phipps, op. cit., pp. 75–6.
39. H. Meigh, op. cit., p. 27.

40. Ibid.
41. London Schoolmasters' Association, *Equal Pay and the Teaching Profession*, 1921, p. 45.
42. *T.E.S.*, 22nd April, 1933, p. 126.
43. A. Spoor, *White-Collar Union*, 1967, pp. 467-8.
44. *The Woman Teacher*, 2nd May, 1941, p. 190.
45. Hansard, H. of C., 7th April, 1943, cols. 624-26.
46. A Potter, 'The Equal Pay Campaign Committee: A Case-study of a pressure group', *Political Studies*, V, 1957, p. 49.
47. 7 & 8 Geo. 6, c. 31, S.24.
48. Hansard, H. of C., 9th May, 1944, col. 1773.
49. *The Woman Teacher*, 29th November, 1946, p. 25.
50. *The Schoolmaster*, 6th April, 1944, p. 213.
51. Royal Commission on Equal Pay, Minutes of Evidence, 16th February, 1945, evidence submitted by the N.A.S., pp. 21-2.
52. Ibid., evidence of J. Mason, p. 27, Q 404.
53. Ibid., 23rd March, 1945, evidence submitted by the A.A.M., p. 89.
54. Ibid., evidence submitted by the A.H.M., p. 86.
55. Ibid., 10th February, 1945, evidence submitted by the N.U.T., pp. 10-11.
56. Ibid., Report, 1946, pp. 148-51.
57. *Political Studies*, V, pp. 50-1.
58. Ibid., p. 60.
59. N.U.T. Annual Report, 1952, pp. lxxvi-lxxvii.
60. Hansard, H. of C., 9th March, 1954, col. 1917.
61. *The Woman Teacher*, October, 1953, p. 9.
62. *The Economist*, 29th January, 1955, p. 351.
63. *The Schoolmaster*, 15th April, 1955, p. 641.
64. *The Woman Teacher*, October, 1955, pp. 3-4.
65. *T.E.S.*, 29th April, 1960, p. 829.
66. Ibid., 11th March, 1955, p. 266.
67. Ibid., 26th April, 1957, p. 565.
68. R. A. Manzer, *Teachers and Politics*, 1970, footnote p. 34.
69. Hansard, H. of C., 14th April, 1960, cols. 1547-61.
70. *Education*, 12th February, 1960, p. 325.
71. *Education*, 27th October, 1961, pp. 669-70.
72. *Supra*, Chapter 4.

6
Superannuation

Apart from salaries, the achievement of a satisfactory scheme of pensions has occupied quite as much of the time and energy of teachers' associations as any other single objective. Adequate superannuation arrangements have been one of the attributes of salaried professional occupations throughout the period during which the teachers' associations have existed. Quite apart from the attraction of proper pension arrangements to the professional employee, recognition by his employer of the need to remove him from the sphere of active work at a set age was an indication of the need for a degree of discretion and judgement in the discharge of duties which in itself could be held to indicate a professional or semi-professional status. Moreover it has been pointed out elsewhere that the pensions issue has borne immediately on the relationship of the teaching profession with the state; the latter's withdrawal or lessening of the value of the superannuation arrangements in 1862, in the 1920s and in 1954-6 has contributed substantially to the 'ideology of betrayal' which the teaching profession exhibits from time to time.[1]

The first provision for pensions was offered by the state in the Code in 1846 when the Committee of Council, as part of the new grant arrangements designed to build up a body of trained teachers for elementary schools, spoke of its being 'expedient to make provision in certain cases by a retiring pension for schoolmasters and schoolmistresses who after a certain length of service may appear entitled to such provision'.[2] The conditions under which pensions might be awarded were set out more fully a few months later; these were both vague and discretionary. In fact few of these 'Code' pensions were granted. Lingen later explained to the Cross Commission that the aim in framing these minutes had been to facilitate the removal of inefficient teachers; it was simply a form of aiding schools, just as grants for training were meant to aid them in obtaining better teachers.[3]

Many teachers certainly interpreted the minutes as a promise of a general system of pensions, even though memoranda issued in the 1850s and a minute of 1851 indicated that this was far from being the case. The minute placed a ceiling of £6,500 on the pensions, which were to be distributed in the following way: 20 pensions of £30 each, 100 pensions of £25 each, 150 pensions of £20 each, the remaining sum to be in the form of donations or special gratuities. It warned teachers generally against 'calculating on the minutes as affording a substitute for the economy which is incumbent upon them, in common with all other workers, while their strength lasts'.[4] In 1862 the existing arrangements for granting pensions were abolished and no more were awarded until 1875. Lowe, as Vice-President, agreed with the advice of the Newcastle Commission; teachers were in no sense quasi-civil servants and must make independent provision for their old age. The teachers themselves, on the other hand, regarded the withdrawal of the 'right' to a pension as a 'cruel breach of faith'.

The annoyance and bitterness among elementary school teachers over the pensions issue was one of the main reasons for the foundation of the N.U.E.T. in 1870. An early result of the Union's activity was the appointment by the House of Commons of a Select Committee 'to inquire whether, by a deduction from the Parliamentary Grant in aid of public elementary schools, or by any other like means, a provision can be made for granting annuities to the certificated teachers of such schools upon their retirement by reason of age or infirmity'. The Committee became absorbed in the controversy over the suspension of Code pensions and the session ended before the members had come to a 'complete conclusion' on the issue referred to them. In general the members were not sympathetic to the claims of the teachers. In spite of their hope that they might be re-appointed at the beginning of the next session, the matter was not taken any further.

In 1875 the Committee of Council revived Code pensions subject to the pre-1862 limit of the total cost not exceeding £6,500 annually, only those teachers who had entered the profession before 1862 being eligible. In 1884 the limitation on the number of pensions which could be awarded was removed so far as entrants to the profession before 1851 were concerned and this led to an immediate increase in the number of pensions awarded. According to Kekewich, this 'conceded the contention of the teachers', and between 1884 and 1899 the maximum amount which could be spent annually on Code pensions was increased steadily so that by 1878 £36,000 was allowed for this purpose.[5] In some respects the claims advanced by the N.U.E.T. seemed modest indeed. At its conference in 1874 the Union resolved that 'all teachers who entered the profession previous to August, 1851, have a moral claim to pensions, pure and simple; and that those who entered between 1851 and the end of 1861 have a moral claim to pensions to the amount of £6,500 per annum, the sum fixed by the Minutes of 6th August, 1851'. For those who had entered the profession since 1861 the N.U.E.T. was willing to adopt some plan of annuities.[6]

With superannuation as with salaries the teachers' associations met with earliest success in the larger cities, and from 1885 London School Board was exploring ways and means of establishing a pension scheme for its own teachers. Teachers in voluntary schools in London were naturally opposed to any scheme which did not include them. Eventually the London School Board Superannuation Bill was introduced in the Commons and committed to a Select Committee which was instructed to review the whole problem and 'to consider the best scheme for providing for the superannuation of public elementary teachers in England and Wales'. The committee recommended the rejection of the London Bill in 1891 and went on to urge the adoption of a national scheme in 1892. A fund should be established by the state to which men teachers would contribute £3 and women £2 annually, interest at 3 per cent being guaranteed. In addition to the annuity purchased from these contributions, each teacher should on reaching retiring age also qualify for a pension at the rate of 10s. per annum for each year of service. Compulsory retirement was to be at the age of 60 for men and 55 for women. The committee was convinced that the scheme was necessary for the sake 'not only of the teachers, but the schools'. The question was one of 'educational policy as well as one of benevolence towards a body of public servants'.[7]

This scheme followed closely that suggested in evidence by N.U.T. representatives. Ernest Gray, a London head teacher and chairman of the Parliamentary Committee of the N.U.T., outlined its main features. He also told the Committee that there was no topic in which teachers were currently so interested 'as this one of the pension'.[8] J. H. Yoxall, President of the N.U.T., saw in a state-run superannuation scheme a way of checking what the Union believed to be the oversupply of teachers. The profession was too crowded to provide a fair salary for teachers because the Education Department 'manufactured' teachers at its own will regardless of the demand; 'if you establish a superannuation system for teachers the Education Department will take care, in justice to the interest of the Treasury, not to manufacture any more teachers than are absolutely necessary, because these teachers will have to be pensioned and partly subsidised'.[9]

The N.U.T. campaigned vigorously for the implementation of the Select Committee's recommendations and on 24th February, 1893, the Commons agreed without a division that 'it is desirable that a national state-aided system of superannuation for teachers in public elementary schools in England and Wales should be established at an early date'. The motion was introduced by Sir Richard Temple, chairman of the Select Committee, and his speech was addressed more to the Chancellor of the Exchequer than to Acland, Vice-President of the Committee of Council, who was already converted to the cause.[10] Acland also pointed to the consequences of the large increase in the number of certificated teachers after the 1870 Act. In 1870 there had been 12,000, by 1893 there were 50,000. 'In another 20 years it will be more pressing than now, and it is far wiser to grapple with it at present than leave it until it becomes more embarrassing.'[11] Shortly afterwards the government appointed a Departmental Committee to review the recommendations of the 1892 Select Committee. It reported in 1894, and the Elementary School Teachers' (Superannuation) Act 1898[12] was based on the reports of these two committees.

The Act came into force on 1st April, 1899. It applied to all who became certificated teachers thereafter and to all certificated teachers then in service who accepted it. Just over a quarter (17,660) did not do so.[13] While serving, teachers were to contribute to the Deferred Annuity Fund at the rate of £3 for a man and £2 for a woman. If the average salary increased by 10 per cent or more, the contributions were to be increased, and the contribution rate was increased in 1905 and in 1910. At the age of 65 the teacher was entitled to an annuity based on his contributions to this fund. In addition he received from the Treasury a superannuation allowance at the rate of 10s. for each complete year of recorded service. For existing teachers, who would have less time to build up an annuity, the superannuation allowance was larger, thus for a man who had served for 40 years before the Act the allowance was £40 per annum.[14] In the event of death during service, contributions paid were not returnable to the family of the deceased teacher, and the Teachers Provident Society, founded by the N.U.T. in 1876, offered a special insurance scheme to enable members to assure for the return of their annuity contributions in case of early death.

Although the benefits offered were comparatively meagre, the N.U.T. executive gave its support to the 1898 measure when it was before Parliament rather than imperil its enactment by pressing amendments. It did establish the principle that teachers were public servants entitled to superannuation, and the leaders of the Union believed that once this was established it would be much easier for them to achieve a more satisfactory system later on. The need to increase the size of the superannuation allowance was emphasised in the President's address to the 1903 conference. He suggested that the next step forward would be for the new local education authorities to be required to contribute towards teachers' pensions.[15]

The 1898 Act provided for septennial reviews of the Deferred Annuity Fund by the government actuary. His first report was published in 1908 and disclosed a large deficit due to the unexpected longevity of pensions. According to the mortality tables on which the fund was based, there should have been 2,963 male deaths in the seven years; there were in fact only 1,071. The actuary accordingly recommended a reduction in the size of the annuities. There was strong opposition from the N.U.T. and the scale of annuities remained unchanged.

The pressure brought by teachers' associations on local authorities first yielded benefit in London. Parliamentary action and influence used by the N.U.T. while the L.C.C.'s General Powers Bill was before the Commons in 1908 achieved the addition of a clause which gave power to that Council to provide superannuation for teachers. For elementary teachers this was to be through a complementary system in which the benefits, together with the benefits already provided for in the Teachers' Superannuation Act of 1898, would be brought up to the level of the benefits obtainable by any other officer of similar salary under the L.C.C.'s own scheme. In 1911 other complementary schemes were authorised in local acts concerning Newcastle, Halifax, St. Helens, Chiswick and Southport. In 1912 the N.U.T. estimated that a third of the certificated teachers in England and Wales were, or would shortly be, provided for in this respect by the operation of local acts, adding, 'it may be said that it is now impossible for officers of a local authority to obtain a local superannuation system unless the teachers are included too'.[16]

Pressure from the N.U.T. for an improvement in national provision led the Treasury to make more funds available, from which the existing superannuation allowance was doubled in 1912—from 10s. to £1 per annum for each year of service—and a Departmental Committee was set up to determine how much money would be available for other benefits and to recommend an order of priority. In 1914 the committee reported that there was in fact no surplus available for increasing the benefits for elementary school teachers. It had a second reference, however, which was to report on a possible scheme of superannuation for teachers in secondary, technical and art schools and training colleges; this was a group for whom there had hitherto been no national provision.

A report issued by the I.A.A.M. in 1910 stated that in the great majority of secondary schools regular pensions for the teachers were non-existent. Where there were schemes, the state made no contribution and the schemes themselves did little more than provide very small retiring allowances for which the teacher had borne half the cost.[17] In 1893 a scheme for schoolmasters to insure for an annuity had been launched after long discussion between the I.A.H.M. and the I.A.A.M. It was operated by the Imperial Life Office which was taken over by another company in 1902 that refused to take new business under the scheme. This had never attracted much support, for only 165 policies were taken out during the period 1893 to 1902.[18]

The I.A.A.M. urged local education authorities to provide schemes for the staffs in the secondary schools they were empowered to establish by the Education Act of 1902 and along with the other associations continued to press the Board of Education to make some national provision. The I.A.A.M. had an amendment moved in the Commons to exempt secondary school teachers from the National Insurance Bill of 1911, but this was defeated, although a government amendment then followed which made it possible to allow exemption to secondary teachers should they establish a Provident Society. Subsequent action by the I.A.A.M., the A.A.M. and other interested organisations led to the setting up of the Secondary, Technical and University Teachers Insurance Society in 1912 which was recognised by the Insurance Commissioners for the purpose of National Health Insurance. At the same time the four secondary associations, the A.T.T.I., the Art Teachers' Guild and other bodies agreed on a scheme which should be managed at the expense of the state by a council representing the teachers concerned, local authorities, governing bodies and the government. Discussions on these proposals were going on with the President of the Board of Education in 1912 and the Treasury's agreement to some form of state aid for a pension scheme was promised in May, when a deputation of secondary teachers met Lloyd George, Chancellor of the Exchequer. He promised Treasury support for the proposal by which each teacher would contribute £7 annually towards an annuity, while the state would add £1 per annum to the actual annuity for each year of recorded service. After 35 years of service it was estimated that a teacher would secure a pension of at least £100.[19] In July the Departmental Committee was set up to look into the elementary school teachers' scheme, and one month later the question of a superannuation scheme for grant-aided institutions other than universities and elementary schools was referred to the same committee.

In the report it made on its second reference the Departmental Committee described such schemes as existed in grant-aided secondary and technical schools and training colleges. These covered a total of 126 schools, divided between local authorities and foundations. Those authorities with schemes usually included secondary school teachers in their wider schemes for other officials and these arrangements were most common in the larger cities. It was found that among the wealthier endowed schools a movement had set in for having the governors' powers modified so that they might institute pension funds or contribute towards them. The committee found many schemes—although better than nothing—inadequate, and also defective in failing to provide for the circulation of teachers between school and school, and one part of the country and another.[20]

The committee recommended that a national system should be adopted, based on the Federated Universities Superannuation Scheme which had just been set up. Under this system the individual teacher would choose endowment or deferred annuity policies from an approved list into which his own and his employer's contribution would be paid; the policies maturing at retirement would provide the wherewithal for paying the pension. All grant-aided secondary schools would have to join the system, as would all the members of staff in the schools. The contribution suggested was 10 per cent of salary divided equally between employer and employee. The report from the Departmental Committee appeared in 1914 and was welcomed by the teachers' associations, but the First World War prevented any action being taken to implement it for the next four years.[21]

When he received a deputation from all the main teachers' associations, led by Sir Philip Magnus in December 1917, H. A. L. Fisher, President of the Board, then said that he was considering the proposal to set up a scheme similar to the F.S.S.U. for teachers in grant-aided secondary and technical schools in accordance with the recommendations of 1914.

The planning for the post-war expansion of the educational system necessarily raised in a more or less urgent form the problem of recruiting far more teachers after the end of the war, while the rapid inflation of the war years and the inadequate adjustment of teachers' salaries had made the profession extremely unattractive.[23] Since salary scales were still a matter for local arrangement, one of the few ways in which the central government could take direct action to make teaching more attractive was through offering a generous pension scheme. Fisher weighed up the relative attractions of an insurance scheme worked through insurance companies, of a contributory scheme with contributions funded by the state or of extending a non-contributory scheme—virtually that enjoyed by the civil service—to teachers. He argued that the first scheme involved the state in subsidising and virtually guaranteeing private companies. Of the second arrangement he pointed out that a state fund would always be credited with a lower rate of interest than an insurance company would in fact earn for the teacher-contributors, and that the latter—if compelled to contribute—would wish at least to be allowed to put their contributions where they would earn the best rate of profit. With the agreement of the Treasury the third course, the most generous, was chosen. Fisher believed that the arrangements embodied in the Teachers' Superannuation Act of 1918 would achieve 'three objects of great educational reform'. It would promote the unity of the teaching profession; it would improve the quality of the instruction given in the school; and it would 'secure for the great educational developments which are bound to ensue under the operations of the Education Act an army of men and women teachers who will be attracted to that calling not only by the additional material benefit which the bill will give them, but still more by the sense that for the first time the state has been giving adequate recognition to the teaching profession'.[24]

The scheme applied to all teachers in grant-aided schools, elementary and secondary; unlike earlier schemes it also applied to the 70,000 uncertificated elementary teachers. The non-contributory pension which made it available was calculated on the basis of $\frac{1}{80}$th of the average of the salary received during the last 5 years for each year of pensionable service in a recognised school, the maximum pension being $\frac{40}{80}$ths payable after 40 years of service. A lump sum calculated at the rate of $\frac{1}{30}$th for each year of service was also paid on retirement. The new arrangements were warmly welcomed by teachers' associations. Their attractiveness was perhaps illustrated by a resolution passed at a conference representative of university staffs with F.S.S.U. provision in April, 1919, 'That this conference wishes to urge strongly that the Teachers' (Superannuation) Act, 1918, be extended so as to include the staffs of universities and university colleges.'[25]

The national mood in which 'the genial rays of educational enthusiasm' had caused 'the flinty heart of the Treasury' to melt[26] soon changed and by 1922 the Superannuation Act was under attack. The Geddes Committee in its First Interim Report on National Expenditure recommended the abandonment of the 1918 scheme and a fully contributory superannuation system after a full inquiry. As an interim arrangement the Committee proposed a 5 per cent deduction from teachers' salaries to help meet the cost of pensions (December, 1921). The government accepted the proposal, and on 9th May, 1922, a bill to impose this levy on teachers' salaries was given a first reading in the Commons. The teachers' associations fought back and opposed with a vigorous campaign the imposition of the levy. The keynote of the associations' campaign was struck in a leading article which appeared in *The Schoolmaster* and touched on the main arguments which teachers used against the imposition of a charge for their pensions. The bill 'amounts to an income-tax of 6d. per £ of salary on teachers, and on teachers only. It is not introduced for the sake of efficiency or of equity, but to provide £2,300,000 this financial year towards the cost of reducing the general income-tax by one shilling.'

'It amounts to that breach of faith with the salary scales (based on a non-contributory system of pensions) which the government in March announced that they would not, could not, commit.'[27] Whatever its other consequences, the government's bill gave a powerful impetus to the idea of the betrayal of the teaching profession by the state. By public advertisements in the newspapers, by speeches, by lobbying M.P.s, the N.U.T. was especially active in getting across the message that since the current salary scales had been negotiated on the basis that superannuation was non-contributory, the deduction of a 5 per cent levy was in fact a reduction of salary and a breach of public faith. When the bill came for second reading in the Commons a motion moving the adjournment of the House in order that further time might be given for consideration of the question was carried by a majority of 3, the government was defeated and the House adjourned. A select committee was appointed 'to consider and report whether in fixing the present scales of salaries for teachers in grant-aided schools any understanding by the government or parliament was given or implied that the provisions of the Teachers' Superannuation Act, 1918, should not be altered while these scales remained in force'. The government had certainly pledged itself not to touch salaries, thus the answer to the question facing the select committee depended on whether salaries and superannuation were so closely allied that a pledge not to touch salaries involved a pledge not to put a charge on salaries for superannuation purposes. By a majority vote which disregarded the opinion of its chairman, the committee reported that the bill of 1922 involved the breach of no undertaking.

The report of the select committee proved to be crucial. The second reading of the bill was resumed on 3rd July, 1922, and passed by 210 votes to 54. Much of the heart went out of the teachers' resistance, but the associations gained a number of minor concessions through parliamentary action such as the substitution of 1st June for 1st April as the date from which contributions would be payable, and the provision in the Finance Act whereby income tax would not be charged on the amount represented by the contribution. Comment among the teachers was naturally bitter. *The Schoolmaster* claimed that the government had 'established a fatal precedent; it will be quoted against them and their successors; they have established that a tax may be levelled on one class of persons only'. It was a 'shameful bill to legalise a forced benevolence'.[28]

The 1922 measure was intended as a temporary arrangement while a Treasury departmental committee under Lord Emmott evolved proposals for a permanent settlement on lines more economical than those of 1918. The committee found that with the development of the national Burnham scales providing adequate salaries it was no longer important for the central government to use a generous pension system as a way of compensating teachers. Since teachers were not government employees there was no parallel with the position of civil servants; rather it was a matter of providing a scheme similar to that existing for other local authority employees—a scheme paid for by the contributions of both employers and employees.[29] The committee proposed the establishment of a fund to be built up by a contribution of 5 per cent of salary from teachers, $2\frac{1}{2}$ per cent from local authorities and $2\frac{1}{2}$ per cent from the state. The benefits were to remain similar to those of the 1918 Act, the sums payable being related to average salary during the last five years of service rather than to the fund built up on behalf of the individual contributor.

The N.U.T. gave evidence to the committee opposing a contributory scheme, but both the Union and the secondary associations thought the Emmott Report as a whole was not unsympathetic to the interests of teachers. *The Times Educational Supplement* described the proposals as 'extremely generous to the teachers, and not unfair to the local authorities'. Protracted salary negotiations were going on in 1924 and 1925 and opposition to superannuation contributions had, to some extent, become part of the salary negotiation strategy. The secondary associations were not opposed to a contributory scheme provided that it met certain conditions. One of these was that it should be extended to include teachers in non-grant-aided schools. The principle of the 1918 Act had been that the school, not the teacher, was the unit—hence teachers in secondary schools not under the direct purview of the state had been excluded. The free movement of staff between grant-aided and non-grant-aided schools would clearly be facilitated by common superannuation arrangements.[30] In the meantime the Burnham Committee had been told to conduct its negotiations on the understanding that some superannuation contributions would have to be paid by teachers.[31]

The new Superannuation Bill, based on the Emmott Report, was introduced in the Commons on 19th March, 1925. The local authorities strongly opposed the measure, which required them to find from their own resources $2\frac{1}{2}$ per cent of their salary bill while the state contributed $2\frac{1}{2}$ per cent. As a compromise this was changed so that the local authorities were to pay 5 per cent but were to receive the same central government grant on this as on teachers' salaries, viz. 60 per cent. Lord Eustace Percy, President of the Board of Education, conducted negotiations with the teachers' associations and managed to reach agreement on most points at issue. While the bill was before Parliament the N.U.T. and the Joint Four sought to improve the benefits it offered in two respects. They wished to see deleted a provision which declared that 'nothing in this Act shall give any person an absolute right to any superannuation allowance or gratuity'; they also wished to alter the permissive 'may' to the imperative 'shall' in section I so that it read 'superannuation allowances and gratuities shall be granted and in respect of all teachers who after the commencement of the Act are employed in contributory service'. At the committee stage of the Bill both of these objectives were accomplished.[32] After the enactment of the measure a leading article in *The Schoolmaster* commented that 'The history of teachers' superannuation is a history of broken promises on the part of many governments, but at last we have got on the statute book a scheme which grants superannuation as the absolute right of a teacher who has fulfilled the conditions'.[33]

The most important variation from the Emmott Committee's recommendations lay in the abandonment by the government of the proposal to invest the contributions in an actual fund. Instead the government actuary was to value at seven-yearly intervals an imaginary fund of contributions earning interest at a constant rate of only $3\frac{1}{2}$ per cent. The terms for contributors were to be revised if the valuations showed this to be necessary. The failure of the government to establish a fund was due to the opposition of the Treasury, which wanted to use current contributions to cover the cost of current pensions, meeting future costs as they arose. The short-term advantage to the Treasury was clear; as Lord Percy said, for the next thirty years at least the net charge to the Exchequer would be less if contributions were not funded.[34] When the measure was before the Lords, Lord Emmott referred to this as 'a legalised malversation of funds'—it was neither financially sound nor morally right.[35] The absence of a well-administered fund has combined with such other factors as inflation to ensure that with the passage of time valuations of the 'notional' assets invariably show deficits when related to the benefits offered. An article in *The Nineteenth Century* made what proved to be the most accurate comment when it spoke of the financial profligacy of the imaginary fund arrangement, adding that probably the only effect of the clause would be to produce a septennial and inconclusive wrangle as to the rate of contribution.[36]

The government actuary investigated the situation in 1935 and estimated that the notional fund would have a deficit of £10,000,000. An increase of 2 per cent was needed to liquidate this, 1 per cent of the increase being added to the teachers' contributions. The N.U.T. took the view that in making this proposal the actuary went beyond the scope of his obligations, which the Union claimed should be restricted to ascertaining the sufficiency or insufficiency of the contributions. Preparations were made for a full campaign to resist any increase should the Chancellor of the Exchequer proceed to adopt the recommendation.[37] The government did not in fact try to increase the contributions at this stage.

The outbreak of war in 1939 necessitated the passing of the Teachers' Superannuation (War Service) Act to safeguard the pension rights of teachers on war service. Where a teacher ceased his normal work in order to take this up it was to be regarded as contributory service; the contributions only became due where an authority supplemented a teacher's income up to its normal level or where his war service salary exceeded it.[38] Where contributions were due these were collected directly by the Board of Education from the teachers; 80 per cent of those eligible had paid up in 1944.[39] The cost of teachers' pensions fell, since some pensioners were re-employed and many continued in service over the age of 60. The second septennial valuation was due during the war but was postponed until conditions became more normal.

The increase in the cost of living rendered pensions calculated on the basis of pre-war salaries inadequate, and the question of pressing the government to grant increases engaged much attention from the salaries and pensions committee of the N.U.T. The difficulty was that legislation was required not only to provide for retired teachers but also for other public ex-employees—civil servants, local government officers, police and so forth. The matter was raised in the Commons from time to time but was resisted by the Treasury until December, 1943, when it pointed out that this was part of the problem of all those on small fixed incomes, and government subsidies and price controls 'had gone far to prevent extreme hardship'.[40] In May, 1943, a joint deputation which included representatives of the teachers met the Chancellor of the Exchequer to press for an increase for all public service pensioners. The strength of feeling grew during the rest of that year and in December the Chancellor announced that a small increase was to be given to those on the lowest pensions. So far as teachers were concerned the augmentation was confined to those whose pensions did not exceed £300 (married) or £225 (single). At its 1944 conference the N.U.T. expressed dissatisfaction with the Treasury's decision to confine the pension increase within its definition of 'hardship', and called on the government to grant to all pensioned teachers adequate allowances to meet the increased cost of living.[41] Nevertheless the Pensions Increase Act of May, 1944,[42] remained limited to the hardship categories.

The valuation of the assured assets and liabilities of the teachers' superannuation scheme which had been postponed during the war was carried out by the government actuary, and his report was issued in March, 1951. The report led to a prolonged period of dispute between teachers' associations and the government. It showed in terms of the actuary's definitions a capital deficiency of £102,000,000 which was mainly due to upward revisions of salaries which had taken place from time to time. The Minister, Miss Florence Horsburgh, decided she could not accept a situation in which any further upward revision of salaries would lead to an increased deficit and she informed teachers' associations that she was going to seek legislation amending the Act of 1925. The proposed changes included reviews by the actuary at five-year instead of seven-year intervals, and power for the Minister to vary rates of contribution by statutory instrument. When the legislation was passed, the contributions required from teachers and authorities would be increased immediately from 5 to 6 per cent. Other minor changes were proposed, such as an increase in the limit from 40 to 45 years in calculating the superannuation allowance and an increase from 65 to 70 in the age up to which contributions for pension might be counted, the aim of these minor changes being to induce teachers to remain in service until a later age.[43]

The proposed increase in the rate of contribution naturally met with strong opposition from the teachers' associations. *The Schoolmaster* commented that it knew of no other superannuation scheme applying to public employees where the beneficiaries were asked to make additional contributions to make good losses caused through no fault of their own but through the fall in the value of money.[44] The campaign which the N.U.T. was to mount against increased contributions concentrated on the unfairness of imposing this burden on teachers and no other public servants. The Union appointed a deputation to see the Minister to oppose the increases in contributions, to support the improvements for very long-serving teachers and to seek the Minister's views on a scheme of pensions for widows and dependants.[45] A working party was set up jointly with the local authorities to examine the question of benefits for widows and orphans, although the authorities made it clear that they were not prepared to commit themselves to any additional contribution for the purpose. The report of the working party was completed in July, 1953. The authorities agreed with the government that the rate of contribution should be increased to 6 per cent from teachers and employers. Both sides agreed in opposing the Minister's suggestions for more frequent valuations and for the use of statutory instruments for varying the rate of contribution.

The text of the bill giving effect to the Minister's proposals was published in January, 1954. The N.U.T. sent a letter to all M.P.s expressing its strong opposition, and among the membership throughout the country there was a welling-up of resentment against the government's proposals. Letters were written and deputations visited M.P.s. The Minister found herself unable to convince all the M.P.s of her own party of the wisdom of her proposals, and at a meeting of the

Conservative Parliamentary Party's education committee the government's scheme was voted down by a two-to-one majority.[46] The struggle between the Minister and the Union for the support of Conservative M.P.s continued through the spring.[47] In late May the cabinet decided not to proceed with the measure in the immediate future, the pressure of essential financial and other legislative business being given as the reason, but the press generally ascribed the decision to the successful campaign mounted by the teachers. The following October Sir David Eccles replaced Miss Horsburgh as Minister of Education.

The new Minister began by calling a meeting of representatives of teachers' associations and authorities in February, 1955. The government was now willing to bear the whole of the accumulated actuarial deficit but insisted that future contributions should be sufficient to cover future liabilities. Working parties were set up to ascertain the facts and to gather information concerning other pension schemes for public servants. The teachers' associations accepted the retention of the existing interest rate of $3\frac{1}{2}$ per cent and the proposal that future deficiencies be met by local authorities, but remained strongly opposed to the 1 per cent increase in teachers' contributions. They also made a strong plea for an adequate scheme for widows and orphans.[48] They did not want a scheme based merely on a reallocation of existing benefit but one based on the same criterion as that obtaining in the civil service, where the employers shared the cost on an equal footing with employees. The local authorities continued to refuse to meet any share of the cost. The bill containing the government's proposals had its second reading in the Commons in December, 1955, and the N.U.T. mounted a publicity campaign unequalled since the crisis of 1931. The N.U.T. executive asked members to withdraw from the collection of school savings for the spring term.[49] Seen in perspective, this was the first sanction taken by teachers' associations for many years and appears in the knowledge of subsequent events to have been very minor and tentative. Yet at the time it provoked a series of interesting reactions. The press criticised it widely and Eccles commented, 'The public will not like something so clearly against the character building of the children. It is an unwise thing to do . . . it seems a doubtful proposition that the teachers should think that by injuring school children they should advance their own cause'.[50] The Joint Four did not agree with the N.U.T. ban. On the other hand the more militant N.A.S. wanted the N.U.T. to join it in a ban on school meal duties, but the latter did not accept the invitation.

Superannuation

In January, 1956, the Council of the I.A.A.M. approved a 3-point plan of action by which the Minister would ask the Burnham committee to submit to him, as a matter of urgency, recommendations for 'professional' scales of salary, and would initiate further discussions on improving the superannuation bill—particularly in connection with widows' pensions—and no increased contribution would be paid until satisfaction had been obtained on these points. A deputation from the Joint Four discussed these proposals with the Minister on 12th January; it seems likely that this indicated to the Minister the direction in which he would need to move to avoid completely alienating moderate opinion. A fortnight later a letter was sent by the Joint Four to all M.P.s explaining the agreed policy and making detailed suggestions for improving the bill (that all service and not just completed years might count towards pension, that service in excess of 40 years given before the coming into operation of the bill might be permitted to count, that part-time service should be pensionable, that pensions should be paid monthly instead of quarterly, that the period of national service should be pensionable). On 26th January, the Burnham Committee agreed to negotiate for a new award to come into effect on or before 1st October, 1956.[51] Early in February the Minister tabled amendments to his bill designed (1) to bring the Act into force on 1st October instead of 1st April, (2) to include for pension calculation all service—not just completed years, (3) to include for pension calculation service in excess of 40 years given before the operation of the Act, (4) to enable pensions to be paid monthly instead of quarterly. The bill was passed with the amendments and from October, 1956, both teachers and their employers paid 6 per cent of salary in contributions.

The N.U.T. at its annual conference in 1956 passed a resolution censuring the executive for its vacillation and failure to implement successfully the policy laid down by the previous conference. In his address to the conference, Sir Ronald Gould attempted to draw up a profit and loss account. On the debit side there was the 6 per cent contribution. On the credit side the 4 major gains were:

(1) Teachers would not be responsible for any part of future deficiencies:

(2) Improved benefits:

(3) Delay in the payment of 6 per cent—the government's original intention had been to raise the contribution on 1st April, 1954:

(4) A new salaries agreement to operate from 1st October, 1956, although the existing Burnham agreement had not been due to expire

until 31st March, 1957.⁵² The vote of censure on the executive was indicative of the bitterness of feeling among teachers on the issue of the one per cent additional contribution. The bitterness was fed by apparent parallels with disputes over pensions in 1922–5 and earlier. The comment has been justly made on a number of occasions that the whole episode served to confirm the idea that teachers are members of an occupation which lacks public esteem and is shabbily treated. Given the persistence of the notional superannuation fund, the value of the Act of 1956 to teachers may be illustrated by the subsequent course of events. In 1966 the government actuary reported that a deficiency of £148,000,000 existed at 31st March, 1961, and that in order to make good this deficiency contributions had to be raised by $2\frac{1}{2}$ per cent. Under the terms of the Act the whole of this fell on the local authorities, who have had to contribute $8\frac{1}{2}$ per cent of their total teachers' salary bill since April, 1966.

BENEFITS FOR WIDOWS AND ORPHANS

The controversy over superannuation in the 1950s had the effect of sharpening the desire of the teachers' associations to achieve adequate provision for the widows and orphans of teachers. As a result of pressure from the associations the Teachers' (Superannuation) Act of 1937 had been passed, which enabled a teacher on retirement to ask that two-thirds of his lump payment be kept by the state as a single premium to meet the cost of provision for his wife should he predecease her. Neither state nor local authorities made any contribution towards this and there was no provision in the Act for the widow or dependants of a teacher who died before retirement. In 1949 the Treasury agreed to a scheme to cover the widows and dependants of civil servants, the cost being shared between the Exchequer and the employee. In reply to representations from the N.U.T. for a similar scheme for teachers, the Minister stated that the matter would have to await the government actuary's report on the general finances of teachers' superannuation. Following the publication of the report in 1951, the permanent secretary to the ministry of education informed the N.U.T. that there was no possibility of a widows' pension scheme to which the local authorities did not contribute and which would put a new burden on the Treasury. In spite of pressure from the teachers, the Act of 1956⁵³ did no more than enable the ministry to establish a scheme paid for by the teachers mainly by surrendering part of their lump sum benefits on the lines of the 1937 measure. A deputation of representatives from the N.U.T., the A.T.T.I. and the Joint Four met the Minister at the close of 1956 and reaffirmed their desire for a scheme in which employers shared the cost, but the Minister held out no hope of such a scheme. The teachers' organisations indicated that the financing arrangements incorporated in the 1956 measure was unacceptable to most teachers and no further progress was made for some years.

In 1962 a working party set up by the Secretary of State for Scotland adopted a new approach by suggesting that teachers should pay for widows' pensions by means of additional contributions, thereby attracting concessions under the Income Tax Acts which would reduce the net outlay on the basic additional contribution from 2 per cent of salary to an average level of 1·4 per cent. Representatives of the different teachers' organisations met to study the Scottish proposals and a deputation went to meet the Minister in October. The deputation was told that any scheme which involved sharing the cost with the employers would have to be ruled out because of its repercussions on other groups of employees. At a meeting with the local authorities in December the latter stated that they would be prepared to accept something on the lines of the Scottish scheme for teachers in England and Wales and that they would bear the cost of administering such a scheme. Both sides agreed to set up a working party representing associations of teachers and local authorities. This reached agreement on the main outlines of a scheme but asked that the Minister should establish an official working party which would have the services of the government actuary's department and of the ministry itself. This working party completed its task early in 1965, the scheme it proposed being broadly similar to that for Scotland.

The teachers' associations considered the report during the spring. The N.U.T. had pressed throughout for direct contributions from the Treasury and local authorities, but these would not contribute beyond giving tax allowances and meeting administrative costs.[54] Towards the end of March the N.U.T. executive voted to accept the scheme; although not as generous as had been hoped, it was felt to be much better than that rejected after the Act of 1956. The scheme was accepted by the Annual Conference of the Union, the impression being generally held that the trend of governmental policy was against special schemes for particular occupational groups and that if this scheme were rejected there would be no opportunity for any scheme at all.[55] The other teachers' associations also accepted the proposals, and they came into operation on 1st April, 1966.[56] Men teachers already in service had to exercise their option to enter the scheme by the end of July and by that time some 45,000 had decided to avail themselves of the opportunity.

In common with other organisations representing public servants, all the teachers' associations have devoted time and energy to the difficulties which their retired members have encountered in trying to cope with inflation since the Second World War, and they have been represented on the Public Services Pensioners' Council. The policy of the Council has been one of 'parity' or 'broad equivalence', i.e. that the pensions of the retired should be reviewed periodically and automatically to bring them more nearly into line with the pensions of those currently retiring from similar posts. In urging this policy the Council has met with little success and has been obliged to campaign from time to time for Pensions (Increase) Acts as temporary, alleviating measures. These campaigns have been largely responsible for the various measures of relief that have been enacted in 1956, 1959, 1963, 1966 and 1969. But the increases granted have failed entirely to keep up with the rising cost of living. Recent acts have given the largest increases to those who have been retired longest; that of 1969, for instance, granted an increase of 18 per cent to those who retired in or before 1954 but only 2 per cent to those who retired in 1966.[57] The unsatisfactory nature of these arrangements led the N.U.T. to examine the possibility of making more adequate provision for teachers by linking pensions to existing salary scales. The issue has occupied the Salaries and Superannuation Committee from time to time and in 1961 the Law Committee of the Union reported on it. It found that it would be impractical to attempt to gear pensions to future salary scales for various reasons, such as the unwillingness of governments to depart from the principle of basing pensions on length of service and terminal salary, the impossibility of calculating what contributions would be needed in times of inflation, and the impossibility of making accurate comparison between teachers who retired some time previously and currently retiring teachers, owing to changes in the structure of the Burnham scales. The committee concluded that the only practical method of dealing with the problem was through further Pensions (Increase) legislation and that approaches to secure this were best made through the Public Service Pensioners' Council.[58]

In November, 1970, the government announced new arrangements for reviewing all public service pensions. The main innovation was that there would in future be regular reviews every two years to ensure that the purchasing power of pensions is maintained.

NOTES

1. A. Tropp, *The School Teachers*, 1957, p. 123; R. A. Manzer, *Teachers and Politics*, 1970, p. 72.
2. Committee of Council on Education, Minute dated August, 1846.
3. Cross Cssn., Third Report, C5158, 1887, p. 537.
4. Committee of Council on Education, Minute 1851-2, pp. 25-7.
5. W. R. Barker, *The Superannuation of Teachers in England and Wales*, 1926, p. 15.
6. *The Schoolmaster*, 18th April, 1908, p. 776.
7. Report from the Select Committee on Elementary Education (Teachers' Superannuation), 1892, p. 176.
8. Ibid., pp. 215-16.
9. Ibid., pp. 224-5.
10. *Hansard*, H. of C., 24th February, 1893, cols. 368-9.
11. Ibid., col. 386.
12. 61 & 62 Vict. c. 57.
13. According to W. R. Barker, 'The general insufficiency of the allowances was no doubt one of the chief reasons why so many teachers refused to accept the Act. By accepting it they subjected themselves to a compulsory retirement at 65 and to the obligation to contribute to the deferred annuity fund, while if they did not accept it, they could remain in employment till death, or till their employers dispensed with their services.' (Op. cit., p. 22.)
14. Departmental Committee on the Superannuation of Teachers, Report of the Committee on the 2nd Reference, Cd. 7365, 1914, pp. 2-3.
15. N.U.T. Annual Report, 1903, pp. xxxiv-xxxv.
16. Ibid., 1912, p. lxxvii.
17. Report of an inquiry into the conditions of service of teachers in English and foreign secondary schools, presented to the Council of the I.A.A.M. on 6th January, 1910, p. 161.
18. I.A.A.M. Annual Report, 1902, p. 43.
19. *Journal of Education*, June, 1912, p. 369.

20. Departmental Committee on the Superannuation of Teachers, Report of the Committee on the 2nd Reference, Cd. 7365, 1914, p. 16.
21. Ibid., p. 19.
22. *Journal of Education*, January, 1918, p. 13.
23. *Supra.*, p. 36.
24. *Hansard*, H. of C., 21st October, 1918, col. 483.
25. H. Perkin, *Key Profession, the history of the Association of University Teachers*, 1969, p. 43.
26. *Hansard*, H. of C., 28th October, 1918, col. 1225. Fisher's comments to the House at the committee stage of the bill.
27. *The Schoolmaster*, 13th May, 1922, p. 823.
28. Ibid., 7th July, 1922, p. 7.
29. Report of the Departmental Committee on the Superannuation of School Teachers, Cmd. 1962, 1923, par. 48.
30. *T.E.S.*, 17th January, 1925, p. 33; 18th April, 1925, p. 166.
31. *The Schoolmaster*, 9th January, 1925, p. 40.
32. The desire of teachers' associations for these changes should be seen in the context of the consternation caused by a current Treasury decision to reduce the superannuation allowance of civil servants. The Treasury was exercising a right conferred in the Superannuation Act of 1834 which provided that 'nothing in this Act shall extend to giving any person an absolute right to compensation for past services or to any superannuation or retiring allowance under this Act.' *The Schoolmaster*, 10th April, 1925, p. 608.
33. Ibid., 7th August, 1925, p. 175.
34. Ibid., 24th April, 1925, p. 738, Lord Percy in a statement to a deputation from the N.U.T.
35. *Hansard*, H. of L., 20th July, 1925, cols. 192–3; J. Vaizey, 'Teachers' Superannuation in England and Wales', *B.J.E.S.*, vol. VI. No. 1, p. 19, wrote that 'The (Emmott) Committee recommended strongly, therefore, the establishment of a notional superannuation fund. . . .' This statement is repeated in J. Vaizey, *The Costs of Education*, 1958, p. 172. It hardly does justice to the expressed views of Lord Emmott.
36. *The Nineteenth Century*, June, 1925, p. 806.
37. N.U.T. Annual Report, 1936, p. liii.
38. Board of Education Circular No. 1476, 4th September, 1939.
39. 'The Superannuation of Teachers' by D. du D. Davidson, Board of Education, 2nd June, 1944.

40. Ibid.; N.U.T. Annual Report, 1943, p. lx.
41. N.U.T. Annual Report, 1944, pp. lii–liii.
42. 7 & 8 Geo. 6, c. 21.
43. Letter from the Deputy Secretary, Ministry of Education, to the General Secretary, N.U.T., 10th July, 1952, printed in *The Schoolmaster*, 18th July, 1952, p. 64.
44. *The Schoolmaster*, 26th September, 1952, p. 310.
45. Ibid., p. 313.
46. Ibid., 26th February, 1954, p. 325.
47. An account of this is given by R. A. Manzer, *Teachers and Politics*, 1970, pp. 58–60.
48. *The Schoolmaster*, 28th October, 1955, p. 591.
49. Ibid., 9th December, 1955, pp. 841 and 849; Manzer, op. cit., pp. 64–8 gives a very full description of the N.U.T.'s campaign against the 1955–6 Teachers' (Superannuation) Bill; S. E. Finer, *Anonymous Empire*, 1966 ed., p. 119 shows that the N.U.T. allocated £100,000 for the necessary publicity but spent only a fraction of it since it received a great deal of free publicity with extensive radio and television coverage as well as over 3,000 press references in ten weeks.
50. *The Schoolmaster*, 16th December, 1955, p. 883.
51. *Supra.*, p. 78, where other factors governing these salary negotiations are discussed.
52. *The Schoolmaster*, 6th April, 1956, p. 249.
53. 4 & 5 Eliz. 2, c. 53, S.8.
54. *The Teacher*, 12th February, 1965, pp. 4 5.
55. Ibid., 7th May, 1965, p. 22.
56. The scheme is fully set out in *Family Pension Benefits for Teachers in England and Wales*, D.E.S., 1965, p. 43.
57. For a summary table setting out the effects of the Pensions (Increase) Acts since 1956 see *The A.M.A.*, December, 1969, p. 200.
58. N.U.T. Annual Report, 1961, p. 96.

7

Security of Tenure, 1868–1939

Members of any self-respecting profession might be expected to seek not only reasonable salary and superannuation arrangements but also a considerable measure of security of tenure. The circumstances in which teachers' associations have sought to secure this have become more favourable over the last hundred years. In the 19th century the nation accepted security of tenure of office for such groups as civil servants and the clergy of the established church, but it was generally felt that there were strong grounds for not conceding it to those who taught in either the elementary or secondary schools. This widely-held view was expressed by the secretary of the Education Department, Cumin, to the Cross Commission in 1887. He was asked whether he saw any way of allowing teachers to appeal to the Department in cases of capricious dismissal. He replied 'That is a subject that I have a very strong opinion about, and I will explain why. When I was Secretary of the Scotch Education Commission, in Scotland the parochial schoolmaster had a freehold of his office; and the result was that an enormous number of most incompetent teachers continued in office, and you could not get them out. In the same way in the endowed schools one of the most crying evils was that masters had a freehold in their office, and that consequently the endowments were wasted, or at all events very inefficiently used. In consequence of that, with considerable difficulty the law was changed in order to leave it to the managers, or to the governing body, to make a bargain with their teachers as to the tenure of their office; and not only that, but in endowed schools this other security was taken, that the fixed salary was made so low that unless a teacher could attract pupils he would practically be starved out; and in all the schemes passed by the Endowed Schools Commissioners, from the beginning they laid down this principle: that there is a contract to be made with the master or mistress, and with him or her only, and that the sole judges of whether or not that contract has been fulfilled are to be the governors or the managers, subject of course to the opinion of a court of law.' He did not think that the Department would ever agree to hear appeals from teachers complaining of capricious dismissal.[1]

I ELEMENTARY SCHOOLS BEFORE 1944

In these circumstances it is hardly surprising that the gaining of security of tenure was one of the basic aims of the N.U.E.T. from its foundation. In reflecting the same line of thought that Cumin expressed, the Act of 1870 laid it down that teachers to be employed by the school boards were to only hold office 'during the pleasure of the board' and the N.U.E.T. sought to have this provision amended so as to ensure that a period of notice be given for dismissal and that there should be some body to which a teacher might appeal. Dismissal often hinged on failure to perform some extraneous duty and from its early days the Union linked freedom from extraneous duties with security of tenure. A survey which it carried out in 1891 showed that about 400 out of a sample of 1,200 teachers depended for tenure of their post on the performance of outside duties such as playing the organ, training a choir or some other parochial function.[2]

Tenure and extraneous duties were matters which had to be dealt with on a local basis in the 19th century. Elementary teachers sought to persuade the state to intervene and to give them safeguards, but without much success. At the local level in this as in other respects the teachers were happiest when dealing with the large school boards. They encountered most difficulty with small school boards and with managers of voluntary schools. The Union fought with such weapons as a register or black-list of schools to which members were advised not to apply for posts, legal advice and assistance to members who might have a case for wrongful dismissal, and electoral pressure in the case of recalcitrant school boards. Perhaps the best-known case of the latter form of pressure was at Brighton when the school board dismissed a teacher and the Union intervened in the next board election to get a majority returned pledged to his reappointment. The campaign was successful and the dismissed teacher himself became chairman of Brighton School Board.

The only responsibility which the Education Department took concerned the granting or suspension of teachers' certificates, and in the 1890s particularly the N.U.T. pressed strongly to get it to take a wider view of its duties. In the debate on the elementary education estimates in 1896, Yoxall put the Union's point of view. He claimed that the attitude of the Department was wrong in principle, and also cruel, for while it was prepared to test and issue a certificate to a teacher and by the inspection system ensure that he performed the functions assigned to him, yet the Department disclaimed all responsibility in the matter of the engagement of a teacher, it refused to be a court of appeal or even a moderator in regard to dismissals, 'it shuffled off responsibility'.[3] In replying to the debate the Vice-President, Gorst, indicated that he was prepared to compel school boards and managers to make contracts in writing with their teachers. Public money was spent on teachers' salaries and managers were really trustees of that public money, so that they could not really complain if obliged to put the contracts in question in writing. Consequently an addition to article 71 of the 1897 Code stated that any agreement entered into between managers and teachers must be in writing, and a model form of agreement was set out for the engagement of the principal teacher in a school.

The passing of the Superannuation Act in 1898 led to renewed efforts by the N.U.T. to secure 'the establishment of means whereby a teacher may be secured from dismissal, except for a reasonable assigned cause'. Future pension as well as present job might now be at stake, and the Union appointed a standing committee for the sole purpose of dealing with questions of tenure. Yoxall, General Secretary of the N.U.T., in a letter to Gorst pointed out that 'the loss which a teacher has hitherto sustained as the result of capricious dismissal from employment in a given school is considerably augmented by certain terms of that Act'. The letter also cited examples of recent unwarranted dismissals which included:

Head mistress of a voluntary school dismissed because she maintained friendly relations with the family of the squire of the parish, who was not on good terms with the vicar;

The master of a board school dismissed because he informed the local sanitary authority that the water supply for drinking purposes to the scholars was impure;

Head master of a board school dismissed because in the law courts he cleared his character from an aspersion of gross immorality cast upon it by the vice-chairman of the board;

Head mistress of a board school dismissed as a consequence of her admission to the Roman Catholic Church.

The letter suggested that a form of contract be made compulsory which would prevent a teacher from being removed from his office *except for assigned reasonable cause*.[4] The annual conference of 1899 followed this up by calling for 'active and unremitting efforts' to ensure that no certificated teacher be dismissed except by a meeting summoned by notice sent to each member of the school board or managers at least three weeks before the meeting and that the dismissal should only be effective if voted by two-thirds of the managers or board members.[5]

The pressure continued, and in the debate on the estimates in 1900 Gorst admitted that he now believed it inevitable 'after the passing of the act by which pensions are given to teachers, to bring in some measure to prevent their unreasonable and improper dismissal'. He thought the problem could best be dealt with through a Minute requiring managers whenever they dismissed a teacher to give a written statement of the grounds on which the dismissal had taken place, reserving to the Board of Education the right of saying whether that ground was reasonable or not.[6] The N.U.T. continued to press for legislation to protect its members, and in 1901 it succeeded in having a bill introduced into the Commons to give teachers a right to appeal against capricious dismissal. The bill was not enacted, but the Union regarded its introduction at all as something of an achievement.

The change in pattern of administration brought about by the Act of 1902 meant that the context of the tenure issue became fundamentally different. The responsibility of the new local education authorities for all elementary schools and the abolition of the school boards meant that the schools were controlled by larger and more balanced public authorities. The new authorities were themselves the direct employers of teachers in provided elementary schools, while the pressure built up by the N.U.T. from 1898 led to the inclusion of a clause to cover the position of teachers in non-provided (voluntary) elementary schools. Here the consent of the authority was to be required for the appointment of teachers, and this could only be withheld on educational grounds; equally 'the consent of the authority shall also be required to the dismissal of a teacher unless the dismissal be on grounds connected with the giving of religious instruction in the school'.[7] This was introduced by Balfour by way of amendment at the committee stage of the bill, and Macnamara, an N.U.T. spokesman in the Commons, accepted this as 'a simple act of justice to a very deserving body of public servants'. But he went on to inquire what would happen if there was a dismissal nominally on grounds of religious instruction but not actually so. Balfour replied that the local authority nominees on a body of voluntary school managers would be in a position to indicate to the authority that since religious grounds for the dismissal were only a pretence, the authority could then veto the dismissal. In any case of difference between the managers and the local authority under this section of the Act, power was conferred on the Board of Education to determine the matter. Macnamara accepted the amendment and explanation taken together as an entirely satisfactory settlement of the issue.[8]

The years following 1902 showed that now there were larger and responsible education authorities, the tenure committee of the N.U.T. was able to establish sound working relationships with the employers which enabled the great majority of cases to be amicably settled. Very seldom was it any longer necessary to make a public issue of a case. The tenure committee drew the attention of the Union to the new position in the 1903 Report: 'With the passing of the small school board and the one-man manager the problem of tenure assumes a different aspect', and it noted, 'with profound satisfaction', the provisions of the new Education Act. The following year the committee was again able to report with 'unfeigned pleasure' the results of the operation of the Act so far as the tenure of teachers was concerned; many cases were now being settled without the necessity even of making a formal appeal to the local authority. Where such appeals were made the great majority of authorities conducted inquiries on judicial and satisfactory lines.[9] There remained a few local authorities who exercised their powers of confirming dismissals by managers of non-provided schools without giving the dismissed person a hearing at an inquiry. One of these cases which received a good deal of publicity concerned the headmistress of a school in Berkshire where the county authority merely confirmed the actions of the managers of a denominational school and gave the headmistress no opportunity of putting her case.[10] But such cases became increasingly infrequent.

The Act of 1902 contained no provision dealing specifically with the problem of the extraneous duties which some managers still expected teachers to perform. Macnamara raised the issue in the Commons and in fact moved an amendment which would have made it illegal for any body of managers to make it a condition of appointment that a teacher should undertake to perform any duties outside school hours or unconnected with the ordinary work of the school. The emphasis which Macnamara—who was a Liberal member as well as a spokesman for the N.U.T.—laid on the iniquities of voluntary school managers and his use of this matter as a partisan stick with which to attack church schools made it very unlikely that the government would accept his amendment and so it proved. Instead Gorst undertook to consider the propriety of requiring that the engagement between a teacher and his employer should be made according to a specific form which would exclude extraneous tasks, the Board of Education not recognising any teacher who was engaged in any form other than that laid down in the Code.[11] The following year the Elementary Schools Code prohibited the imposition on teachers of extraneous tasks as a condition of employment. In spite of this provision in the Code for 1903 some complaints continued to be made, although they were far fewer in number.

The earliest legislation dealing directly with extraneous duties was the Education (provision of meals) Act, 1906. The N.U.T. submitted evidence to the select committee on this bill and secured the insertion of a clause protecting teachers in elementary schools. 'No teacher seeking employment or employed in a public elementary school shall be required as part of his duties to supervise or assist, or to abstain from supervising or assisting in the provision of meals, or in the collection of the cost thereof.'[12] While this afforded teachers protection against being required to prepare or provide school meals in a direct sense, it did not always appear to relieve them of being in charge of school children and premises during the dinner interval, and by 1908 the N.U.T. Conference was urging the Board of Education to declare that such work was no part of a teacher's duty.

The First World War and the accompanying inflation led to financial pressure on local authorities who sought economies in their schools. A number of L.E.A.s tried to lessen expenditure by closing small schools and by reducing the teaching staff at others to the minimum required by the Code. The tenure committee reported in 1916 that in all these cases prompt action had been taken through the local associations and through teacher-members of education committees, by direct negotiations and in other ways, with the result that the teachers concerned had almost invariably been retained in their posts or adequately provided for by transference to other appointments.[13] The machinery established in the years following 1902 was, in fact, continuing to work well, although it was reported in 1917 that at least one local authority denied teachers a hearing before passing judgement on dismissal questions.

Wartime economies proved to be only a forerunner to much more far-reaching economy campaigns in the post-war period. At the beginning of February, 1922, it became known that the government was considering excluding children below the age of 6 from elementary schools, thereby reducing the size of the teaching force required and saving public funds. The prospect of the exclusion of the 5-year old children from schools stirred much opposition in the country generally, and on 1st March the Chancellor of the Exchequer told the Commons that the government had decided to drop the idea, with the consequence that the much-feared wholesale dismissal of teachers did not ensue.[14] Even so, many local authorities came to regard the minimum staffing requirements laid down in the Code as a maximum beyond which no addition might be made. Authorities sought to economise by grouping small, non-provided schools, thereby abolishing the offices of the head and assistant teachers. One authority passed a resolution authorising the replacement of headmasters by relatively cheaper headmistresses in the case of its smaller schools. The N.U.T. usually succeeded in protecting the interests of individual members involved by obtaining their transfer to other schools. Even so, an increasing number of authorities were reducing the number of teachers they employed by dispensing with the services of married women and by insisting on retirement at the age of 60.

There was little the teachers' associations could do to prevent the compulsory retirement at 60 of those teaching in an authority's own provided schools. But in December, 1923, three legal actions against Sheffield Corporation were undertaken on behalf of 2 headmasters and 1 headmistress who were working in non-provided denominational schools maintained by Sheffield. This authority, in order to reduce its estimates by £20,000, decided to dismiss a number of its teachers who had reached the age of 60. The dismissal of those in the council's schools who held office at the pleasure of the city corporation could not be contested. The managers of 3 non-provided schools refused to dismiss their head teachers and the corporation thereupon dismissed the teachers on educational and financial grounds.[15] The N.U.T. sought a declaration in the Chancery Division of the High Court that their dismissal was invalid and inoperative. The legal questions involved in the litigation were (a) whether these teachers were in fact dismissed upon 'educational' grounds; (b) whether an L.E.A. in deciding upon dismissal on 'educational' grounds could take into account 'financial or other non-educational' grounds; whether, admitting that the teachers were efficient, it was an 'educational' ground merely to allege that there were other, younger teachers who would fill their positions more satisfactorily and (d) whether the mere fact that the teachers had reached 60 and were eligible for pension was an 'educational' ground. It was contended on behalf of the teachers that they had been dismissed on financial and not educational grounds, while the corporation's case was that they had been dismissed on educational grounds. The judgement was a vindication of the attitude of the N.U.T., for the court held that 'the real and only grounds for the dismissal of the plaintiffs were financial grounds and that the alleged educational grounds were merely colourable'.[16]

At one time it had been teachers in non-provided schools who had appeared to enjoy less security of tenure than those in an authority's provided schools, but now it appeared that in face of the wave of economy which was sweeping the country the reverse might be the case. Accordingly the executive of the N.U.T. instructed the law committee to report upon the feasibility of seeking to secure the establishment by the Board of Education of appeal tribunals before which teachers should have the right to appear accompanied by a friend. It had been thought that about 75 per cent of teachers in the non-provided schools were prepared to support the Union's policy of seeking to end the system of dual control, but they would clearly hesitate to do so if this would have the effect of lessening their security of tenure.

This demand for an appeal tribunal at the Board of Education was not new. The importance of the Board's right to suspend the certificate of a teacher or to order his total exclusion from schools in certain circumstances was more far-reaching than the power of an individual employing authority. The Superannuation Act of 1918 also gave the Board the power of suspending, diminishing or withholding a pension. Thus during the 1920s this question of appeal machinery became one of increasing importance. A dispute over reports on teachers by an H.M.I. in Northamptonshire in 1922 led the N.F.C.T. to pass a resolution—later endorsed by the N.U.T. and N.A.H.T.—asking that teachers reported upon should have the right to appear before appeal tribunals established by the Board of Education. The events following the cancellation of the teaching certificate of John Towers, head of Hedley Hill Council School, Durham, by the Board of Education served to draw attention to the Board's power.

Towers was fined £5 at petty sessions for punishing two children who had gone to a canteen for meals. The case against him was that he had given orders to the children as secretary to a canteen committee but had invoked his authority as head of the school to punish them. The

Board of Education informed him that it could no longer recognise him as a teacher in any school in respect of which it paid grant. The matter was discussed in the Commons where the President of the Board claimed that he paid no heed to the technical point; 'my argument, from first to last, is that this headmaster, in a mining village, at a time of great, acute and bitter feeling, dealt with these children throughout, stage by stage in such a way as to make them marked children among the whole of their schoolfellows'.[17] The N.U.T. annual conference in 1927 resolved that the punishment was 'harsh and unwarrantable' and instructed the executive to take all necessary steps to secure the restoration of Towers' certificate. In spite of bringing pressure to bear, the Board refused to relent and at its 1928 conference the N.U.T. instructed the executive to press for a judicial inquiry into the facts. The Union was eventually successful, for in July, 1929, the President restored Towers' certificate without any restriction. The N.U.T. had paid Towers his former salary throughout the period during which recognition as a teacher had been denied him.

Against the background of this case the N.F.C.T. annual conference in September, 1927, resolved that teachers should be given a statutory right to a hearing by an independent tribunal before the Board of Education took any action to refuse recognition. The N.U.T. annual conference passed the same motion unanimously the next year. In the following months the Union's law committee visited the Board on three occasions to discuss the matter with the President and senior officials. The committee came to the conclusion that it might happen that under a tribunal the position of teachers would be worsened rather than improved. A compromise was reached and a new form of procedure agreed. After the official letter had been sent to the person whose certificate was in danger of cancellation, asking for his or her statement upon the facts on which the accusation was made, and a letter had been sent back to the Board, the Board would then notify the person that they took a serious view of the case, but that the teacher would have the option of attending at the Board with his or her legal adviser.[18]

In the remaining years before the Second World War individual cases concerning tenure continued to arise and were usually satisfactorily dealt with. Indeed, in the course of a debate in 1936 the chairman of the tenure committee said that as a result of years of effort they had at last gained for teachers in elementary schools what was practically security of tenure, as far as members of the Union was concerned.[19]

II SECONDARY SCHOOLS BEFORE 1944

Security of tenure remained a more critical problem for longer in the secondary than in the elementary field, for three reasons. In the first place the teachers' associations themselves were more divided, weaker and unable to exert as much effective pressure as the N.U.T. exerted in the elementary schools. Secondly, the employing bodies remained much more fragmented in the twentieth century and were thus less susceptible to the sort of pressure that could be brought to bear on the large public authorities who employed the great majority of elementary school teachers. Finally, historical factors made the original situation in the third quarter of the nineteenth century extremely unfavourable to the great mass of assistant teachers in secondary schools.

The condition of extreme inefficiency of most of the secondary schools which has been documented in the reports of the Public Schools Commission in 1864 and of the Schools Inquiry Commission in 1868 was held by those Commissions to be due in no small degree to the system of tenure of office then existing in many schools. The message of the Commissioners was that if the schools were ever to become more efficient the virtual life tenancy of many head and assistant masters must be ended. The headmaster must be appointed and dismissed by the governors and he must be entirely responsible to them. The headmaster in his turn must be given power to appoint and to dismiss the assistants at pleasure, 'for if the (head) master has not the appointment and control of his assistants, it is impossible to hold him responsible for the good conduct and teaching of the school'.[20] The recommendations were fully accepted and incorporated by Parliament in both relevant measures. The Public Schools Act of 1868 provided that 'The headmaster of every school to which this Act applies shall be appointed by and hold office at the pleasure of the new governing body. All other masters shall be appointed by and hold their offices at the pleasure of the headmaster.'[21] The Endowed Schools Act of the following year stated that 'In every scheme the Commissioner shall provide for the dismissal at pleasure of every teacher and officer in the endowed school to which the scheme relates . . . with or without a power of appeal in such cases and under such circumstances as to the Commissioners may seem expedient.'[22]

The absence of effective opposition to provisions of this sort which left assistant teachers in such a weak position may be ascribed in part to the circumstances that many schools were small, with simply a master and possibly two or three assistants, sometimes known as ushers, and often poorly qualified. In the few schools where there were larger staffs of well qualified assistants the reaction was one of protest, as at Harrow, where the assistant masters sent a strongly-worded memorandum to the governors. They pointed out that the staff included twenty-five graduates holding 'positions of important responsibility'. 'The internal arrangement of the several boarding-houses is, as you are aware, confided almost entirely to the assistant masters in charge, and on them falls the entire pecuniary risk of building or renting, as well as furnishing, these houses; a risk which in some cases amounts to many thousand pounds.' Hitherto appointment had been permanent, with removal only for misconduct, ill-health or inefficiency. In future, apparently, the legal status of the assistant master was to be destroyed and his prospects to be entirely at the mercy of any future headmaster. 'The latter will often be young, he may possibly be inexperienced; but he would thus be invested with a power almost without example in the English Public Service, a power exceeding that of a Commander-in-Chief of the Army—that of summary dismissal, on his own authority, of any member of a large and educated staff, while the governing body are precluded from hearing in his defence, or supporting by remonstrance, an old, it may be a valued, servant.'[23] Trouble over this issue at Rugby and at Eton in the early 1870s gave the matter some publicity and a parliamentary bill was prepared to meet the assistants' grievance, but it never got as far as a second reading.

In the schemes produced by the Endowed Schools Commissioners a clause was included which stated that the 'headmaster should have the sole power of appointing and dismissing all assistant masters'. Between 300 and 400 assistant masters sent a memorial to the Commissioners in 1872 urging that in case of dismissal the schemes should always provide for a right of appeal to the governors. In their reply the Commissioners stated that in future in all schemes which gave the headmaster power of dismissing assistant masters they proposed 'to make such dismissal subject to an appeal to the governors.' The Endowed Schools Commission was soon to be abolished and this ruling was only followed by its successor, the Charity Commission, in the case of schools described as third grade where both appointment and dismissal of assistants was usually placed in the hands of the governors.[24]

The Charity Commission defended its policy of refusing the right of

Table 7.1. *Analysis of the Approved Schemes of the Charity Commission for the administration of Secondary Schools for boys to October, 1894*[25]

Dismissal of assistant masters: number of cases in which the power is given to:

the governors	50
the headmaster, subject to an appeal to the governors	42
the headmaster, subject to an appeal to the governors if expense has been incurred in setting up a boarding-house	4
the headmaster, subject to the approval of the governors	4
the headmaster	309

appeal by invoking 'the importance of keeping in view, above all, the interests of the scholars; and next of securing the headmaster from a too great weakening of his position, such as would follow if he were himself dismissable at pleasure without assignment of cause and had not an equivalent power over his assistants, upon whose co-operation his own success must in large measure depend.'[26] The I.A.H.M. submitted a memorandum to the Bryce Commission arguing strongly for the retention of the right to dismiss staff at pleasure and without appeal, arguing that the public had more reason to deprecate the continued employment of an incompetent assistant master than the unjust dismissal of an efficient one.[27] The Bryce Commission itself recommended that the power of headmasters to dismiss their assistants should be made subject to the approval of the governing body.[28]

The problem was not of the same magnitude in girls' schools. For one thing there were fewer endowed schools for girls to be pressed into this pattern by the Commissioners, and those established in the late nineteenth century usually avoided this arrangement. The headmistresses of Girls' Public Day Schools were obliged to refer any question involving possible dismissal of an assistant to their governing body, and this practice was usual in other secondary schools for girls.[29]

Right at the end of the nineteenth and at the beginning of the present century a number of cases of dismissal which the I.A.A.M. fought brought the question of security of tenure to the notice of the public and eventually obliged a reluctant secondary branch of the Board of Education to face the need for change and even for legislation in 1908. A further factor in bringing this change about was the steady increase in the involvement of local authorities with their own code of practice as employers in secondary school affairs under the Welsh Intermediate

Education Act of 1889, the Technical Instruction Act of 1889 and the Education Act of 1902. The action of the I.A.A.M. over the matter of tenure in the years around 1900 won it a good deal of publicity and served as a powerful aid to the recruitment of new members; it was after all the need to secure a more assured tenure that was one of the main reasons for the foundation of the Association in 1891.

The first case to draw nationwide attention occurred at King's School, Grantham, an endowed grammar school, in 1898, when a new headmaster was appointed. The assistant masters were dismissed so that he might have men of his own choice. The assistants protested to the governors and acting on legal advice from the I.A.A.M. presented themselves on the first day of the new term, but the new head refused to continue their employment. Both the I.A.A.M. and the I.A.H.M. accepted this as a test case of 'the legal change if any affecting the tenure of assistant masters upon the appointment of a new headmaster' and asked the Charity Commission to hold a public inquiry. Selby-Bigge, then an Assistant Commissioner, held the inquiry at Grantham on 30th May, 1899. It was found that there was no ground for the assumption that the appointments of assistant masters were, *ipso facto*, terminated by a vacancy in the headmastership. The Charity Commissioners in their letter giving their findings also stated that 'under the terms of their engagements the assistant masters became by custom of the profession entitled to one term's salary in lieu of notice, and that these sums are payable out of the funds of the charity'.

'In order to avoid any further misapprehension I am to add that the provisions of the scheme do not appear to impose any personal liability on a headmaster vacating his office by reason of his omitting to give notice to terminate the engagements of the assistant masters, a step which is neither customary, nor in the interests of the school desirable.' The I.A.A.M. felt that the holding of the inquiry and the judgement was something of an achievement for the Association and its secretary used the occasion to send a circular letter to schools giving the verdict at length and urging those members of staff who were not already members to join.[30]

In the Grantham case the Charity Commission took no steps to enforce its verdict and the I.A.A.M. decided to take the matter to court by having a writ issued against the governors on behalf of one of the assistants for the recovery of a term's salary. Counsel advised the Association to drop the legal proceedings, since there was a possibility of losing the case and the I.A.A.M. was not strong enough financially to risk failure. While these repercussions from the Grantham affair were still occurring, further cases involving similar questions of the security of the assistant master's tenure arose at Alleyn's School, Dulwich (1899), and at the Merchant Taylors' School (1901). One early consequence of the Grantham case was that the Headmasters' Association set up a special committee to reconsider the position and while it maintained that headmasters should continue to have the power to appoint and dismiss assistants, it added that dismissed assistants should have the right to submit a written statement of their case to the governors within six months of receiving notice.[31]

When the educational powers of the Charity Commissioners were transferred to the Board of Education[32] some county councils wanted to see a right of appeal to governing bodies against dismissal written into the schemes of government of the endowed schools they were assisting with scholarships and grants. The L.C.C. wrote to the Board suggesting this in October, 1901. In a minute he wrote to Kekewich, the Secretary of the Board, W. N. Bruce of the secondary branch related the history of the matter and pointed out that under the Welsh Intermediate Education Act there was no appeal from the headmaster's decision in eleven authorities, but appeal was allowed under the other five. He thought this showed that opinion was beginning to flow in favour of allowing a right of appeal. He added 'Nor do I think the other view, though I prefer it on the whole for the higher secondary schools, worth a great fight. Both plans will work well with reasonable people to work them.' It was best to avoid a sudden change of policy such as the Assistant Masters' Association was seeking and to take each case on its merits so far as possible. Kekewich agreed that the aim of the Board must be to avoid committing themselves to any general rule.[33]

The headmasters were well aware of the attitude of the local authorities, and sought to come to an agreement with the I.A.A.M. and to persuade the Board to act sufficiently to take the heat out of the issue lest local authorities should eventually try to limit the powers of heads of secondary schools much more severely. Towards the close of 1901 the I.A.H.M. wrote to the Board asking that it should receive a deputation and that the question of tenure be referred to the Consultative Committee; the letter pointed out that some local authorities had already passed resolutions on this issue. The I.A.A.M. asked that its representatives might join the deputation and cited in its letter of 22nd December many cases of unjust dismissal. The deputation was received in January, 1902. The headmasters urged the Board to hear all sides and then lay down a national policy on tenure so as to avoid letting the various local authorities each go their own way, for the authorities were much less competent to consider the matter. Representatives of the I.A.A.M. sought a right of appeal to the Board, with the Board having power to order reinstatement in case of wrongful dismissal. The deputation led to no action, the final comment on the matter being from Gorst, then Vice-President, to the Lord President, recommending that the matter be not referred to the Consultative Committee since 'the Board of Education by such action would give a kind of pledge to deal with the matter.

'The only possible appeal seems to me to be one to the governing body of the school. There are, however, strong objections to this and on the whole the question might rest at present. There is no difficulty in getting plenty of assistant masters on present terms.'[34]

In these circumstances it was hardly surprising that the attempt made by the Bishop of Hereford to move an amendment to the Education Bill of 1902 in the Lords was negatived, for this would have provided that the consent of the local authority should be required in all secondary schools either to be aided or provided under the Bill and that any dismissed teacher should have a right to appeal to the Board. The question was also raised in the course of the debate on the Bill in the Commons but, again, no progress was made, since Gorst claimed that while he was prepared to consider 'any practical plan' he did not consider that the idea of an appeal to the Board was a practical plan, as the Board was neither qualified nor able to undertake such a task.[35]

By the close of 1903 the I.A.H.M. and the I.A.A.M. at a joint conference were able to agree on a common policy statement on security of tenure which the respective associations endorsed early in 1904. The headmaster was to retain the power of dismissal but if he exercised this he was to notify the governing body who might inquire into the matter. The assistant would have a right of appeal to the Board against his dismissal, the decision of the Board being accepted as final by all the parties concerned.[36] The parties reported their agreement to the Board and asked it to receive a deputation, which it declined to do, Bruce minuting that there was not much point in doing so unless the government was prepared to amend the Endowed Schools Act of 1869. The essence of this Act was that the teacher must be subject to dismissal without being able to call on anyone to state to him the grounds for the action. This might be so even where there was an appeal, because the governors or the Board could hear both sides and give a decision without ever stating to the applicant the grounds for his dismissal. Morant added his opposition 'on all grounds' to the Board's having the duty of hearing appeals, and a negative reply was given to the associations.[37] In the autumn the I.A.H.M. repeated its request that the associations might send a deputation pointing out in its letter that if a settlement was delayed the assistant masters of locally-aided endowed schools might appeal to local authorities: the result would be to diminish 'the freedom and authority which the Board wisely desire to maintain for headmasters'. This time the deputation was seen largely because Sir William Anson, Gorst's successor, took the hint and feared that to do otherwise would be 'to throw the Assistant Masters into the arms of the local authority'.[38] Even so, the Board remained unwilling to accept the duty the schoolmasters wished to give it and it continued to enforce what was essentially the Charity Commission's policy whenever it could. The governors of Bradford Grammar School wished to make a slight modification in the power of the headmaster to dismiss his assistants and this proved to be enough to make the Board throw back the whole scheme for the reorganisation of the school. A letter to the press from C. Norwood, then Secretary of the West Riding Branch of the I.A.A.M., gave publicity to the matter.[39]

By 1905, although the Board showed no signs of wavering in the matter of an appeal to itself, it was having to give way to the local authorities when these insisted strongly enough on taking upon themselves responsibility for the appointment and dismissal of assistant masters in the new secondary schools which they were now providing under the Act of 1902. The actual conditions of tenure varied a good deal from one local authority to another. In London the question of tenure was settled in practice in many endowed schools by the L.C.C. The Council resolved that governors of all schools receiving any aid be informed that it was the wish of the Council 'that they shall exercise control and responsibility in the appointment, dismissal and payment of all teachers employed in their schools'. Governors of schools where trust schemes prevented them from discharging these functions were asked to apply to the Board of Education to have them modified.[40] Middlesex County Council took a similar line. At the 1905 general meeting of the Association of Directors and Secretaries for Education the president spoke on this topic. Until recently, he said, the Board's secondary branch had been asking that the headmasters of the new maintained secondary schools should be given the same powers to appoint and dismiss at will as the endowed school heads had possessed under the Act of 1869. 'County and county borough authorities are asked at this time of day to give to one class of servant autocratic powers which they deny to every other chief officer in their employ. Surely the assistants in our secondary schools have their rights as to tenure as well as the headmaster... I sincerely hope that the authorities of this country will protest in the very strongest possible manner against this modern recrudescence of despotism.'[41]

It really became impossible for the Board to refuse all change any longer and in answer to a question in the Commons, Birrell, the new President, said that where schemes came up for reconsideration and in all new schemes the Board's present practice was to insert provisions requiring the approval of the governing body in all cases where the approval or dismissal was vested in the headmaster.[42] Meanwhile the case of Richmond Grammar School served to drive the Board further in the direction of change. Here a new headmaster was appointed who wrote to the existing staff in the summer holiday stating that he required their services no longer as he proposed to engage a new staff for the September term. Supported by the I.A.A.M., one of the dismissed men sued the governors for a term's salary. The case eventually went to the Court of Appeal where the judge confirmed the earlier judgement that the action must fail since the governors were not the right body to be sued. Clause 40 of the Richmond Grammar School scheme gave the usual powers of appointing and dismissing to the head. The decision implied, therefore, that the assistant masters in this and many other endowed schools were the servants of the headmaster and that he might dismiss them at any time without notice.[43]

There was a very sharp reaction to this verdict, the existing state of tenure of secondary assistants being universally condemned. The I.A.H.M. and I.A.A.M. sent a further deputation to the Board to press for legislation, and at last the Board gave serious consideration to changing the law. The Endowed Schools (Masters) Act[44] was passed by Parliament in 1908 to prevent any more cases as scandalous as that of Richmond. This enacted that assistants were employed by the governing body and not by the headmaster, that they could only be dismissed at the end of a term and after at least two months' notice.[45] That legislation should at last have been enacted was largely due to the persistence of the I.A.A.M., which, weak as it was, succeeded in bringing various cases to wide public and professional notice and, in the more immediate sense, by raising a guarantee fund of £900, made a test case of the Richmond scandal. Many felt the Act did not go far enough. There was still no right of appeal to the Board even though the Education (Scotland) Act of the same year gave the Scottish Education Department the power to hear such appeals and to compel re-instatement or compensation of a teacher unfairly dismissed. Nor did the Act secure for a dismissed master the right to a personal hearing before the governors.[46] The Act of 1908 marked a notable victory for secondary school teachers, but events were soon to show that there were plenty of difficulties still to be overcome before reasonable security of tenure could be assured.

In order to try to prevent potential cases of security of tenure arising from personal incompatibility between a headmaster and one or more of his staff, an arbitration court was established by the I.A.H.M. and the I.A.A.M. in 1910 with three members from each association and an independent chairman. Within the first year of its existence three cases of difficulty were settled by it and recourse to tenure proceedings before governing bodies had been avoided. Although the machinery continued to exist, little use appears to have been made of it after the first few years.[47]

Tenure cases continued to occupy a good deal of the time and energy of the I.A.A.M., one of the more blatant being that which arose at Dorking High School, where an assistant being paid a salary of £210 was dismissed and replaced by another master at a salary of only £120. The Association protested to both the governors and to the county education committee, but without effect.[48] It was this as much as any other single case which led the I.A.A.M. to adopt the policy in 1912 of drawing up a black list—the practice of naming unsatisfactory schools and retrograde authorities in *The A.M.A.* and warning candidates for posts against going to work in such places.

As with teachers in the elementary schools, various 'economy' measures during the First World War itself and in the period between the wars led to the disappearance of posts and to problems of tenure. In 1915 a deputation went to the Board of Education to make representations on the general question of reduction of school staffs on grounds of economy. The war also produced a number of cases where men who joined the armed services returned to find that their school posts had not been kept open for them. The outcome of these tenure problems was that the I.A.A.M. Council in 1921 decided that a Sustentation Fund should be established, and after the appearance of the Geddes Report calling for widespread public economies, it was decided to make a levy of 10s. 6d. on members for the Fund in order to strengthen the position of the Association. An I.A.A.M. deputation went to see the President of the Board in June, 1922, to urge him to take all possible steps to prevent the dismissal of members on grounds of economy, and, where this could not be avoided, to mitigate the resulting hardship. The President, Fisher, thought that it would be impossible to avoid causing hardship to individuals but that the Board would naturally seek to avoid unnecessary hardship. H.M.I.s would be asked to assist local authorities in any economy steps they might take to ensure that staffing economies should be made in such a way as to minimise possibly harmful effects on the educational efficiency of schools.[49]

The official policy of economy affected tenure in two ways, both of which could lead to the displacement of teachers, namely by lowering the standard of staffing and by raising fees in secondary schools, thereby reducing the number of pupils. The policy imposed serious hardship on the individuals selected for dismissal although it is impossible to give a figure for the total number of teachers from secondary schools actually involved. But it was said that the Executive Committee and the officers of the I.A.A.M. were constantly preoccupied with cases of this nature. Such cases tended not to result in actual dismissal but were dealt with by transfer in schools controlled by the larger local authorities such as London or Birmingham. Overstaffing due to any cause, whether it arose from a policy of economy or from a decline in the local population and a consequent fall in the number of pupils, was most difficult to deal with in the smaller endowed schools, possibly aided, particularly in rural areas. A master given notice in such a school which had come to be overstaffed and who could not obtain another post on the open market must inevitably have been faced with unemployment, and the prospects of his pension would also have been imperilled.[50]

Apart from the effects of economy drives, the position of teachers in secondary schools was improved when the Board of Education made it obligatory for them to be employed under written agreements, or, in the case of schools provided by a local authority, under a minute of the authority. Moreover, standard forms of agreement were worked out between a committee of the Joint Four and the Association of Education Committees for the first time in 1923 and, although not compulsory, these soon came into general use. The agreement provided for the same notice as was required under the Endowed Schools Act of 1908 (two months expiring at the end of a term), and made provision for a right of appeal against dismissal.[51] There were two main weaknesses of the right of appeal, firstly the fact that the appeal was itself to the body which had often already decided on the dismissal, having heard only the headmaster's side of the case; in these circumstances hearing an appeal might be little more than a farcical formality. Secondly, it was legally possible to refuse to state to the dismissed assistant the grounds on which his dismissal was based. A case of this type occurred in a grammar school in 1930 where a master and his representatives appeared before the governors not knowing what charges they had to answer. The I.A.A.M. in consequence black-listed the school.[52]

The most notorious tenure case in the inter-war years was that at Haverfordwest Grammar School. This was an aided endowed school receiving £600 from its endowments and £6,000 annually from Pembrokeshire County Council. The governors gave notice to five of the staff in order to change the curriculum of the school. There was fierce public controversy. Both the I.A.A.M. and the N.U.T. made representations to the governors, but they remained unmoved. The local authority was in the position of giving financial aid without imposing control, thus the governing body was supreme although its actions were condemned by Pembrokeshire education committee. The Board of Education was asked in the Commons to inquire into the administration of the school, but the Parliamentary Secretary stated that the school was regulated by a scheme framed under the Endowed Schools Acts which gave the governors of the school absolute control over the appointment and dismissal of masters. 'Consequently the Board have no power to intervene. If there is a remedy it would appear to be a legal one.'[53] There appeared, in fact, to be no remedy for the dismissal of a third of the total staff. At its council meeting in 1934 the I.A.A.M. demanded the right to a full hearing before an impartial tribunal before any dismissal took effect. Haverfordwest Grammar School was black-listed by the I.A.A.M. from 1934 until 1947, when it accepted the national agreement on tenure. During those years this notice regularly appeared in *The A.M.A.*, 'Any member thinking of applying for a post in this school is earnestly requested to write to the Secretary of the Association for information.'

The legal position of the tenure of assistants in secondary schools remained unchanged down to the Second World War in spite of the efforts of the I.A.A.M., which annually passed resolutions seeking reform, and despite the discussions among other Joint Four members and in the N.U.T., which had an increasing interest in the secondary field. Many members of the N.U.T., with their wide experience of the elementary schools, felt that security of tenure was weaker in the secondary schools. In 1936 the N.U.T. conference passed a resolution expressing the view that there was urgent need for improvement in conditions of tenure for teachers in secondary schools, that teachers in all schools, whether aided or maintained, should be servants of the L.E.A., and that transfer schemes for redundant teachers in all such schools—including direct grant—should be instituted.[54] Certainly it appeared that the greatest security of tenure was enjoyed by the staffs of those county boroughs which had no governing bodies but which administered their secondary schools through the higher education sub-committee. Where there were governing bodies they were usually too apt to be influenced by the head and to adopt his views for it to be possible for them to be able to adjudicate on an appeal in a thoroughly impartial manner. But where the schools were directly administered by the local authority few heads would bring forward a proposal for dismissal unless certain of a very strong case that would stand any amount of cross-examination and inquiry. In the many schools financed and controlled by local authorities with governing bodies of their own, tenure difficulties were rare where the authority maintained adequate control by not permitting a dismissal to take effect until it had given approval. Where the governors' decision was subject to confirmation, it meant that there was in effect a further court of appeal. It was in schools where the local authority gave aid without imposing control that the worst cases of insecurity of tenure arose—as at Haverfordwest —and in schools independent of a local authority, for there the governing body remained supreme.

Whatever machinery was evolved, the supply position was also bound to have its effect on conditions of tenure and of service generally. When there are plenty of recruits to a profession there is little incentive for employers to improve conditions. After, as before, the First World War there were plenty of well-qualified persons seeking posts in the secondary schools. It was reckoned in the 1930s that for approximately 300 posts available in secondary schools each year there were about 900 newly trained men seeking appointments. Most heads of grammar schools in those days could tell stories of receiving as many as 100 applications for one post. The following table summarises the position and shows clearly enough that a situation of chronic over-supply existed. In view of these figures it says much for the teachers' associations that they achieved what they did.

Table 7.2. *Employment in grant-aided schools of graduates completing courses of training in university training departments in July, 1936, 1937 and 1938*[55]

Qualified leavers (England and Wales)			Grant-aided secondary schools —appointments obtained
1936	Men	933	269
	Women	688	245
1937	Men	888	236
	Women	662	232
1938	Men	860	152
	Women	682	172

NOTES

1. Cross Cssn. Third Report, 1887, p. 682, q. 59, 453, evidence of P. Cumin.
2. A. Tropp, *The School Teachers*, 1957, p. 132.
3. *Hansard*, H. of C., 10th July, 1896, col. 1245.
4. N.U.T. Annual Report, 1899, pp. xxxvii–xl, Letter to the Vice-President, 13th December, 1898.
5. Ibid., p. lxxxi.
6. *Hansard*, H. of C., 14th June, 1900, cols. 123–4.
7. 2 Edw. VII, c. 42, S7 (1(c)).
8. *Hansard*, H. of C., 27th October, 1902, cols. 886–88.
9. N.U.T. Annual Reports, 1903, pp. lv–lvi, and 1904, pp. lvii–lviii.
10. *The Schoolmaster*, 10th February, 1906, pp. 273–75.
11. *Hansard*, H. of C., 27th and 28th October, 1902, cols. 873, 998–9, 1007.
12. 6 Edw. VII, c. 57, S6.
13. N.U.T. Annual Report, 1916, pp. lviii–lix.
14. *The Schoolmaster*, 11th March, 1922, p. 406.
15. Under the terms of the 1902 settlement an L.E.A. could only dismiss on educational grounds teachers employed by managers of a non-provided school which it maintained.
16. N.U.T. Annual Report, 1924, pp. lv–lvi (Report of Law Committee); *The Schoolmaster*, 11th January, 1924, pp. 50–2; ibid., 1st February, 1924, p. 186.
17. *Hansard*, H. of C., 17th February, 1927, col. 1262.

18. *The Schoolmaster*, 11th April, 1929, p. 764.
19. Ibid., 17th April, 1936, p. 694.
20. S.I.C., vol. I, Report, p. 238.
21. 31 & 32 Vict., c. 118, S.13. This Act applied only to the seven 'great' public schools named therein.
22. 32 & 33 Vict., c. 56, S. 22.
23. Memorandum to the Governors of Harrow School from the Assistant Masters printed in W. E. Bowen, *Edward Bowen: a Memoir*, 1902, pp. 135–6.
24. Bryce Cssn., 1895, vol. IV, pp. 76–7.
25. Ibid., Appendix No. 3A., p. 534.
26. Charity Commission, 42nd Report, 1894, p. 41; J. Montgomery, *The Tenure of Assistant Masters in Secondary Schools administered under the Schemes of the Charity Commission*, 1895, is a pamphlet giving a useful survey of this issue by the honorary secretary of the I.A.A.M.
27. Bryce Cssn., 1895, vol. V, pp. 317–20.
28. Ibid., vol. I, pp. 316–17.
29. Ibid., vol. IV, pp. 41–2, 55–6.
30. *Journal of Education*, September, 1899, pp. 549–51; I.A.A.M. Annual Report, 1899, pp. 18–19.
31. *Journal of Education*, February, 1901, pp. 147–8.
32. The transfer of this work began in May, 1900, and was not completed until April, 1903—P.R.O. Ed. 24/63, Memorandum by D. R. Fearon; P. H. J. H. Gosden, *The Development of Educational Administration in England and Wales*, 1966, pp. 96–7.
33. P.R.O., Ed. 17/178, Minute of 21st October, 1901, from W. N. Bruce to G. Kekewich.
34. P.R.O., Ed. 17/178, Note of 15th January, 1902; Minute 24th January, 1902, J. E. Gorst to Lord President.
35. *Hansard*, H. of C., 26th May, 1902, cols. 611–2.
36. I.A.A.M. Annual Report, 1903, p. 13.
37. P.R.O., Ed. 17/178, Minutes of 19th April, 1904, and 15th July, 1904, by W. N. Bruce and 16th July, 1904, by R. L. Morant.
38. I.A.A.M. Annual Report, 1904, p. 9; P.R.O., Ed. 17/178, Minute of 27th October, 1904, by W. Anson.
39. *Yorkshire Daily Observer*, 1st July, 1904, p. 4.
40. *Journal of Education*, April, 1905, p. 255.
41. *Education*, 27th January, 1905, Supplement, p. 6.
42. *Hansard*, H. of C., 5th December, 1906, cols. 936–7.

43. *The Times*, 6th and 7th November, 1907, Court of Appeal, Wright *v.* Zetland and others.
44. 8 Edw. VII, c. 39. In spite of its description, the Act applied equally to women assistants in any girls' schools working under Endowed Schools Act type of schemes.
45. One immediate consequence was apparently a change in the model 'Articles of Government for a Secondary School provided by a County Council' (Form 24 S) which were being drafted in the Board of Education in the course of 1908. The first draft gave as clause 18, 'The Headmaster/Headmistress shall, subject to the approval of the Governors, have the sole power of appointing, and may, subject to the like approval, at pleasure dismiss all Assistant Masters/Mistresses in the School'. This was deleted and a footnote added that 'The Board of Education will require that all assistant masters should be employed under a contract determinable by a notice'—P.R.O., Ed. 12/137.
46. C. Norwood and A. H. Hope, *The Higher Education of Boys in England*, 1909, p. 265.
47. A. Gray Jones, 'Tenure in Secondary Schools', *Journal of Education*, November, 1934, p. 691.
48. I.A.A.M. Annual Report, 1911, p. 7.
49. *The A.M.A.*, July, 1922, p. 118; A. Sinclair, 'The Problem of Tenure of Assistant Masters in Secondary Schools', unpublished M.Ed. thesis, Manchester, 1940, p. 193.

    Expenditure on teachers' salaries accounted for 70 per cent of the gross cost of maintaining secondary schools in the inter-war years —Board of Education Circular No. 1428, 1933.
50. *Journal of Education*, November, 1934, p. 690; *The Assistant Masters' Year Book*, 1924, p. 37.
51. S.R.O. No. 214, 1924; *T.E.S.*, 16th November, 1929, p. 509.
52. *Journal of Education*, October, 1934, p. 656.
53. *Hansard*, H. of C., 22nd February, 1934, cols. 492–4.
54. *The Schoolmaster*, 17th April, 1936, p. 694.
55. *Hansard*, H. of C., 23rd November, 1938, cols. 1765–68.

8

Tenure and Conditions of Service since 1939

In the early months of the war difficult problems of tenure were encountered by staffs of some independent and endowed grant-aided schools. On the outbreak of war all schools in evacuation areas were closed and the buildings of some were requisitioned. The schools themselves were evacuated, although not all of their pupils were prepared to go, and many schools became much reduced in size. The considerable expense involved in the evacuation fell upon the schools if these were not local authority financed institutions. This increase in expenditure came at a time when income from fees was dropping along with the fall in the number of pupils. At the end of October, 1939, a deputation from the Joint Four and the Headmasters' Conference went to the Board of Education to press the case for generous treatment for direct grant schools in these difficulties. With fewer pupils and inadequate finance, the only answer appeared to be to discharge staff, and towards the middle of the autumn term many direct grant and independent schools gave provisional notice to members of their staffs to take effect from 31st December. The Board announced its intention to help such direct grant schools as had suffered financial losses, and the grant earned by the reduced number of pupils at the standard rate of £8 13s. p.a. was to be increased by a proportion equivalent to the drop in numbers as compared with the last school year.[1] This went a considerable way in easing the situation and, to judge from the experience of the I.A.A.M., most of the notices of dismissal were withdrawn.

Difficulties of this order did not arise in local authority schools, partly because of the greater resources available and partly because teachers could be transferred from one school to another if necessary. The circumstances of the war years, especially the call-up of many schoolmasters to the armed services, turned a situation of over-supply of teachers to one of shortage, so that tenure cases were soon greatly reduced in number.

During the period of reconstruction in the last phase of the war and in the immediate post-war years, the teachers' associations were specially alert to try to have incorporated in the regulations issued by the central government and local authorities provisions which would guard against unjust dismissals. In 1944 the Ministry of Education issued a White Paper on the principles of government in maintained secondary schools which set out proposed procedures to be followed for the dismissal of teachers. For heads a resolution of dismissal would need to be passed at two meetings of the governing body with an interval of at least fourteen days between them and with not less than two-thirds of the governors being present and voting. The resolution could not take effect until it had been accepted by the L.E.A. (or until the authority had given its consent in the case of aided schools). There should be a right of appeal to the L.E.A. for the person to whom notice was being given. L.E.A.s would also have power to initiate the proceedings for dismissal themselves. The head should be entitled to appear accompanied by a friend at any meeting of the governing body or the L.E.A. at which his dismissal was to be considered and should be given full notice of such meetings. The white paper added that the procedure would be similar in the case of assistant teachers, but it need not necessarily be so elaborate, provided that opportunity was given for the assistant to appear before a meeting of the governors accompanied by a friend and to appeal to the L.E.A. This apparent difference of treatment between heads and assistants caused some alarm among the latter and it was pointed out that it could be interpreted to mean that a head would be entitled to a hearing before his dismissal was decided upon, whereas an assistant could only be heard afterwards.[2] This difficulty was in fact disposed of in the course of negotiations between local authorities and teachers' associations. The creation of divisional executives raised some doubts among teachers' associations; the N.U.T. was particularly anxious to ensure that they would not supplant the county authorities as employers where they were set up. Before issuing its circular on schemes of divisional administration, the Ministry received a deputation consisting of Sir Frederick Mander and two other representatives from the Union, and one consequence of this was that matters such as the termination of tenure and the employers' functions generally were to remain with the county authorities.[3]

The negotiations between the teachers' and the local authorities' associations resulted in a set of joint recommendations relating to tenure in county and voluntary schools whether they were primary or secondary. These recommendations were ratified by the N.U.T., the Joint Four and the various local authority associations. They amplified the general points set out by the Ministry in its White Paper of 1944 and have governed the situation in the great majority of schools since the war. The recommendations recognised that it should be a condition of service of every teacher that before any decision relating to dismissal was taken he should have the right to be heard and be represented before the L.E.A. which was employing him or whose consent was required to his dismissal. The regulations of each authority should provide for this. The actual hearing was to be before a sub-committee of the education committee appointed for the purpose and when notice of the hearing was given to the teacher he was to be given a copy of any charge, complaint or adverse report on which the proposal for his dismissal was based.[4]

Since the shortage of teachers which appeared during the war has persisted in some form or other ever since, tenure troubles in the sense in which they were a feature of the 1920s and 1930s have virtually disappeared. The machinery carefully devised in 1946 has not been much used. Indeed, in one sense the very existence of the machinery to ensure a fair hearing for teachers has itself ensured that only in the most extreme circumstances when the evidence was very clear would any attempt be made to dismiss someone holding a permanent appointment. From this point of view it may be said that the machinery has worked well and has prevented tenure cases from arising. The greater strength and more widely acknowledged influence of the teachers' associations themselves has also served to make the position easier than it was before the Second World War. Many of these factors have carried over into and influenced the independent sector also. The independent schools sub-committee of the I.A.A.M. was set up in 1919. During the 1930s there was scarcely a meeting at which there were no tenure cases to be considered; by contrast, such cases no longer occupied much of the sub-committee's time in the 1950s.[5]

The growth of comprehensive secondary reorganisation has obviously necessitated the creation of new posts and the disappearance of others, and this could have led to a good deal of trouble over tenure had not authorities generally taken steps to try to ensure that the interests of individual teachers should be safeguarded so far as possible. A joint policy statement agreed upon by the N.U.T. and the four secondary associations emphasised the need to safeguard the salary and, wherever possible, the status of teachers affected by reorganisation. Any form of reorganisation of schools such as has been taking place must lead to some individuals having their professional prospects diminished—just as the prospects of others may be enhanced by the new arrangements—but at least dismissals and redundancies have been avoided.

If a teacher is convicted of a criminal offence or if he commits some grave act of misconduct or professional default, the Ministry of Education has continued to expect to be informed, so that a judgement may be made as to whether the individual should be disqualified from continuing to teach. If the central authority declares a teacher to be unsuitable for employment on grounds of misconduct, then the teacher must not be employed. This over-riding power is exercised rarely and for the obvious purpose of keeping persons of possibly undesirable influence away from children. Teachers' associations have a clear interest in maintaining the reputation of the profession for a high standard of conduct. Consequently they have not sought to abolish this power of exclusion, but they have naturally endeavoured to ensure that it is used justly and that every opportunity is given to the teacher of clearing his name. The Ministry before taking any action is careful to inform the teacher of the charges against him and to give him an opportunity for explanation. If school teachers possessed their own professional governing council, this sort of function might well be discharged more appropriately by it than by a central government agency.

THE 'CLOSED SHOP' ISSUE AND POLITICAL TESTS

Since the Second World War teachers' associations have found themselves confronted by threats to the security of tenure of their members which have arisen from political and social issues. Foremost among these was the issue of the 'closed shop'. The repeal of the Trade Disputes Act (1927) in 1946 meant that local authorities could then, if they wished, require union membership as a condition of employment. A number of local authorities did then resolve that their employees must belong to an appropriate trade union. These resolutions were in accord with the wishes of many of the trade unions, and caused little or no difficulty so far as the skilled, semi-skilled and unskilled grades were concerned. Difficulties arose, however, when authorities attempted to apply such rules to their professional employees. One of the earliest instances of this was at Gateshead in 1947. Teachers were asked to state what trade union or professional association they belonged to. The teachers' associations advised their members not to reply to such communications. The associations were anxious that all those eligible for membership should join, but they preferred to 'rely on our record of service to the profession to attract members, and we refuse to exercise, or to allow anybody else to exercise, the slightest compulsion in the matter'.[6] Generally speaking those local authorities which enforced a 'closed shop' policy among their employees were prepared to exempt such professional grades as teachers, doctors and dentists from the requirement. One authority, however, which made strenuous attempts to enforce a 'closed shop' among its professional employees was the Durham County Council.

In November, 1950, Durham County Council resolved that all of its employees be required to be members of an appropriate union and that 'notice be given to all those persons in the employment of the County Council who are not members of a trade union and, at the same time, the persons concerned will be offered re-employment on their existing terms with an over-riding condition that they become members of an appropriate trade union before being re-engaged.'[7] Teachers were not only strongly opposed to the 'closed shop' as such but saw in this an involvement in party politics which their associations had always assiduously avoided. The N.U.T. in Durham made its opposition clear and succeeded in getting its policy statement to the schools on the same morning as the Council's circular arrived. The Ministers of Education and of Health wrote to the Council expressing the government's disapproval. The former wrote on 22nd November, 1950, 'The Minister is in favour of teachers joining a union or professional association, but he considers that they should not be coerced into membership. If the Council were to persist in the line of action proposed, they might find themselves, as a result, unable to discharge their statutory obligations under Section 8 of the Education Act, 1944. The Minister wishes the Council to know that he could not remain indifferent to this threat to the educational service, and that, if it materialised, or seemed likely to do so, he would be compelled to take action. . . .'[8] There was some hope that the authority would allow the matter to blow over. If it did not, the threat to security of tenure contained in the resolution made it quite clear that teachers would have to fight. The British Medical Association, the British Dental Association and the Royal College of Nursing all made their resistance clear too, and the solidarity among professional employees was an important factor in the dispute.

Although the county council did not implement its policy in the way outlined in its November resolution, it did institute a system of questioning candidates for headships as to whether they were members of a union. The teachers' associations advised their members not to answer this question but to reply, 'I consider that this is an improper question and must decline to answer it.' It has been said that a study of the Durham files shows that many teachers followed this advice, with the consequence that they were not promoted.[9] At the end of March representatives of the N.U.T., the A.T.T.I. and of the Joint Four met an emergency committee of Durham County Council and asked that candidates for promotion should not be requested to give details of their union membership. The county council refused to give any such assurance. The teachers' organisations then called on their members in selected areas of the county to let them have notices to terminate their appointments. On 3rd April the Minister of Education issued a direction to Durham County Council under Section 68 of the Act of 1944 instructing it to refrain from taking any steps to ascertain whether applicants for teaching posts were or intended to become members of a union or association. In view of this the teachers' associations suspended the collection of notices. At a joint meeting of representatives of the council and of the teachers' associations under the chairmanship of the Minister, the council's representatives gave assurances that they would comply with the letter and spirit of the Minister's directive.[10]

The teachers' associations thought the matter was now closed, but within a few months Durham was making yet another attempt to enforce a 'closed shop', and issued regulations stating that future applications for the extension of sick payments would only be considered if made by or through a union or association, applications for leave of absence to be made in similar manner. This seemed to many teachers to be a particularly odious way of trying to force the 'closed shop' on them. The N.U.T., A.T.T.I. and Joint Four asked the Minister to intervene at the earliest possible moment. The N.U.T. Executive called on members in the county to place their resignations in the hands of the Union and made it clear that unless the council put forward proposals for a satisfactory settlement before 30th May it would tender such resignations as it deemed necessary to achieve its purpose. On 31st May, 1952, notices terminating the engagements of 3,790 teachers were handed in to take effect from 31st August. 4,700 out of 4,900 members of the N.U.T. in Durham placed their resignations in the hands of the Union and only those of teachers in denominational voluntary schools and in the excepted district of Stockton-on-Tees were not handed in to the council. The other teachers' associations which were members of the joint action committee did likewise. A joint emergency committee of the professions was also established, which included the B.M.A., the B.D.A., the Royal College of Nursing and the Engineers' Guild.[11]

Durham was faced with the breakdown of its education service from 1st September and the possible breakdown of other professional services at a later stage. The county council accordingly decided to report to the Ministry of Labour that a dispute existed between itself and those of its employees represented by the joint emergency committee of the professions. Representatives of the two sides were called to a meeting at the Ministry of Labour and were able to agree on the terms of reference under which the dispute should be submitted to arbitration, viz.:

> It being accepted by the parties that the professional employees of the County Council represented by the Joint Emergency Committee of the Professions, namely dentists, doctors, professional engineers, midwives, nurses and teachers, should not, as a condition of employment be required to belong to a trade union or professional organisation, the Board are asked to determine:
>
> (i) whether the present regulations of the Council governing the making of applications for extended sick pay are in conflict with the principle of voluntary membership of a trade union or professional organisation and should therefore be withdrawn, or
>
> (ii) whether the regulations are made in the present exercise of the discretion vested in the Council in the granting of extended sick pay and are not in conflict with the principle of voluntary membership of a trade union or professional organisation.[12]

Both sides undertook to accept and implement any Board of Arbitration award. In the meantime the teachers' organisations withdrew the notices of resignation and the council suspended immediately the operation of the offending regulation. At the end of July the arbitrators made known their findings that the county council's regulation about extended sick leave conflicted with the principle of voluntary membership of a trade union or professional organisation and should be withdrawn. The findings were accepted by the local authority, the regulations were withdrawn and the teachers' organisations had succeeded in preventing union or association membership from becoming a condition of tenure.

A novel tenure issue arose when official political tests were imposed as a condition of appointment to the headships of schools, to lectureships in training colleges and to some posts in further education by the Middlesex County Council in 1950, and were maintained for a period of eight years. In 1949 and 1950 there was a fairly widespread outcry against the possibly insidious danger to the country from members of the Communist Party, and some alarm at the dangers of political indoctrination by communist teachers in the schools. The issue was especially acute in Middlesex, where a number of communists had been elected to official positions in the local associations of the N.U.T. and a communist ex-President of the Union was headmaster of one of the authority's secondary schools. The authority decided to ban both communists and fascists from its more senior teaching appointments, and to enforce the ban by asking candidates being interviewed for appointment whether they were members of the communist or fascist parties or whether they had ever been associated with such parties and, if so, in what capacity. The county council also agreed that 'where the information given by the candidate is not precise or appears incomplete the Chief Education Officer will make such inquiries as instructed by the interviewing committee or the Chairman of the Education Committee'.[13]

Teachers' associations were very strongly opposed in principle to any form of political test. They have always laid stress upon freedom of religious and political beliefs for teachers on the understanding that, whatever their personal tenets might be, teachers did not propagate them in the classroom. An inquiry held by the Middlesex authority into a school whose headmaster was a communist, and which had a number of communists on the staff, did not show that any teacher had misused his position by spreading party-political ideas.

The I.A.A.M. Council repeatedly condemned the imposition of political tests by Middlesex. The Executive of the N.U.T. protested to the local authority and to the Minister. The Minister regretted the action of the county council and hoped that it would desist from carrying out its declared policy. The Middlesex County Association of the N.U.T. called on the Union nationally to support the protest by strike action if necessary. But calls for strike action are only likely to be effective if there is unanimity among teachers on an issue. It was apparent from the feelings expressed at branch meetings of the Union in different parts of Middlesex that the necessary unity was lacking. After more than a year of discussion and protest, the N.U.T. came to the conclusion that there was no substantial move which it could take that would get rid of the ban.[14] Thus the ban continued and so did the resolutions against it. On 17th February, 1955, the Minister said in the Commons that although he did not like the policy Middlesex had been following, he would only be justified in interfering if the education service was being seriously and adversely affected.

A letter which was published in *The Schoolmaster* brought out the reasons why the teachers' associations were able to deal successfully with the contravention of their principles by Durham, yet were unable to change the policy of Middlesex. The Durham policy could potentially have affected every teacher in the county and as a result the Durham teachers were united in asking for support from their associations and in backing the action taken. By contrast the Middlesex ban affected only a comparatively small number of Middlesex teachers. Its imposition had split them into four main groups: (1) communist and fascist teachers who opposed it for obvious reasons; (2) non-communists and non-fascists who opposed it on purely professional grounds; (3) teachers who were in favour of it on religious or political grounds; (4) a large group who were comparatively indifferent to its existence, perhaps because most of them were unlikely to apply for a headship anyway.[15]

This analysis was certainly not contradicted by the outcome of a referendum of its members in Middlesex held by the N.U.T. in 1956. The referendum was not conducted through the branches but directly by post from headquarters to the individual teachers. The members were asked whether they were prepared to lodge their notices of resignation with the General Secretary for use in the struggle to get Middlesex to change its policy. 54 per cent of the N.U.T. members in Middlesex returned the form, and by a majority of 3 to 1 those voting declared themselves not to be in favour of taking strike action to remove the ban.[16] This result made it quite clear that argument, the passage of time and possibly local political party manoeuvring were likely to be the only means of getting rid of the political test.

The end of the policy of maintaining a political test came in May, 1958, when the local elections returned the opposite party to power on the county council, eager to reverse the more controversial of its rival's policies. By this time the strong feeling against individual communists as possible sources of indoctrination among the young had lessened somewhat. The years of difficulty in Middlesex, as in Durham, had given the N.U.T., the A.T.T.I. and the Joint Four secondary associations useful experience in working together to safeguard interests common to all teachers, regardless of the type of school in which they were serving.

EXTRANEOUS DUTIES

Teachers have always undertaken on a voluntary basis a wide variety of non-teaching, extraneous duties in the interests of their pupils. They have also resisted any attempt to make the performance of these duties a condition of tenure. Considerable difficulty therefore arose over the attempt by the government to make the duty of supervising school meals a compulsory condition of service following the Act of 1944.

The Second World War produced something approaching a change in the very concept of the school in this country. The evacuation of children from the cities in 1939 meant that the schools had to do far more for their pupils than they were expected to undertake when children were living at home. The teachers who accompanied their pupils were well aware of this and were very willing to devote far more time than usual to the performance of these voluntary duties which they knew someone must undertake. There was, however, a tendency on the part of some persons in authority to impose upon the goodwill of school staffs. This led to the inevitable reaction among teachers' organisations when, for example, the I.A.A.M. executive committee at a meeting in November, 1939, resolved that no staff should be required compulsorily to discharge the extra duties consequent upon evacuation, and that when such duties must be performed their scope and extent should be agreed at common-room meetings.[17]

As the war proceeded it brought about changes in the pattern of life of all schools, whether evacuated or not, and the extraneous duties discharged by teachers multiplied in number. Sometimes the initiative and enthusiasm of the teachers was largely responsible for the introduction of these, at other times the duties arose out of pressure from civil defence authorities, the Ministry of Food or the Board of Trade. The accumulation of duties became so considerable that in the autumn of 1941 the N.U.T. sent a deputation to the Board of Education to discuss the problem. The discussion ranged over the duties associated with the provision of meals and milk on the greatly increased scale, the demands made by the activities of other government departments including the

Ministries of Health, Supply, Agriculture, Food, Home Office, Board of Trade and the War Savings organisation. Attention was also drawn to the action of representatives of the Ministry of Labour and National Service in approaching individual teachers to assume responsibility for children of women factory-workers during the hours before and after school. The deputation stressed the lack of consultation which often characterised the procedure when teachers were expected to accept these duties.[18]

The Board of Education had already become increasingly concerned at the extent to which the demands of wartime activities such as the needs of agriculture for child labour had been impinging upon the educational work of the schools, and received the deputation sympathetically. It consulted with other government departments and indicated its concern that the schools should be given every opportunity of getting on with their primary task, and that they should not be diverted from this because they happened to be convenient organisations through which, for example, to distribute clothing coupons. A joint circular issued by the Board and the Ministry of Health on 5th December dealt with the position of the young children of working women and suggested that it should not be taken for granted that teachers should undertake the supervision of these children. The Board also issued an Administrative Memorandum to local authorities which warned them of the need to see that teachers were not so overburdened with other tasks that their teaching was impaired. 'The war has inevitably involved teachers in a number of extraneous duties, and their participation in these duties has been of the greatest help in forwarding the war effort. The incidence of these extra duties is naturally uneven but there is evidence that in some cases they have reached a volume which seriously interferes with the teachers' primary duty of teaching.' It went on to point out that under the Education Act of 1921[19] teachers could not be required to participate in arrangements for the provision of meals, and in making arrangements for this or other purposes extraneous to those for which teachers were appointed local authorities should undertake prior consultation with teachers' representatives.[20] Until the Second World War, meals in elementary schools had been for needy children only. During the war the school dinner was seen as a way of supplementing the meagre food ration available, and the school meals service was developed on a huge scale with this end in view. This transformation meant that by 1944 $1\frac{1}{2}$ million children, or 33 per cent of those in maintained schools, were taking school dinner.[21]

During the war years schools came to be seen as social institutions of the first order, with activities of an enormous variety to meet the needs of national life. It was against this background that the Education Act of 1944 was planned. It made a fundamental change in the teachers' conditions of service so far as school meals were concerned. The 1921 provisions were replaced by a provision that 'Regulations made by the Minister shall impose upon local education authorities the duty of providing meals ... for pupils in attendance at schools ... and such regulations shall make provision ... as to the services to be rendered by ... teachers in respect of the provision of such meals ... as the Minister considers expedient, so, however, that such regulations shall not impose upon teachers at any school ... duties in respect of meals other than the supervision of pupils'.[22] The regulation which the Minister issued under this section stated that 'The authority shall ensure that suitable arrangements are made for the supervision and social training of pupils during meals and may require teachers of any school to supervise pupils....'[23]

The Board of Education had judged that the enormous growth in school meals made it necessary to introduce compulsion to ensure that the service could be staffed; it was no longer prepared to rely on the voluntary co-operation of teachers. At this time most of the N.U.T. executive supported the involvement of teachers in meals supervision, but many of the rank and file of the Union were opposed to the position set out in the 1944 Bill. In a debate on the issue at the annual conference of 1944, Mr. G. Thomas, a member of the executive, accused the Board of Education and the local authorities of exploiting the patriotism of teachers. There were bitter debates around this issue at the Union's annual conferences in 1945 and 1946, but the executive's policy was not defeated. In 1948 the conference passed a resolution urging the Minister to relieve teachers of the burden of school meals duties, and from that time it became the policy of the N.U.T. to try to remove the liability to supervise school meals from being a condition of tenure for teachers.[24] The increasing amount of agitation among teachers over this issue owed something to the continuing growth in the number of children taking meals at school. Whereas at the end of 1944 about $1\frac{1}{2}$ million were having school dinner daily, by October 1947 more than $2\frac{1}{2}$ million, or nearly 50 per cent of the children in attendance, were doing so. During these years representations made to the Ministry about the burden on teachers of the supervision of increasing numbers of diners led to an investigation of the problem by representatives of the Ministry, the local authorities and the teachers. The outcome of the review was a circular which recommended the appointment of persons to assist teachers with mid-day supervision; no change was made in the compulsory nature of the duty for teachers themselves.[25]

Increased feeling against compulsion became more evident from 1956. In that year there was much discontent over the new Teachers' Superannuation Bill, and by way of protest some members of the National Association of Schoolmasters decided to discontinue the collection of school dinner money. In 1956 also the I.A.A.M. Council resolved that the school meals service should be a fully staffed ancillary service and that it should be no part of a teacher's duty to supervise school meals. The Association called for an amendment of the Act of 1944 and for the removal of school meals from the education estimates.[26] All of the teachers' organisations in their resolutions on this topic in the 1950s implied that legislation would be required to release teachers from the statutory obligation to participate in the supervision of pupils taking school meals. After the 1962 conference the N.U.T. executive appointed a special *ad hoc* committee on school meals. This committee concluded that the Act left the Minister with a discretion as to whether regulations issued by him should require any service to be rendered by teachers in respect of meals. Accordingly suitable arrangements could be made even under existing legislation for a fully-staffed ancillary service under the direction of the head teacher of a school if the Ministry and local authorities would agree.[27]

At a meeting between representatives of the local authorities and the teachers' associations (N.U.T., Joint Four, N.A.H.T. and N.A.S.) in November 1962, the case was argued that teacher participation in the school meals service should not rest on compulsion and that supervision should be the task of ancillary staff appointed for the purpose and controlled by the head teacher as part of his general responsibility for the conduct of the school. The local authorities admitted that more supervisory assistance was needed, but did not agree, on grounds of practicability and of educational principle, that arrangements should be envisaged in which teachers took no part in the supervision of school meals. The Ministry shared the view of the local authorities and did not see how the meals service could be run without the participation of teachers.[28] The outcome was that local authorities were enabled to take on additional ancillary staff but no change was made in the position of teachers.

The increasing difficulty over salaries in the 1960s, the growth in the influence of the N.A.S. and of militancy generally, increased the determination of the teachers' organisations to end compulsion for 'the unprofessional task of dinner-duty'.[29] The unsatisfactory progress of the Burnham negotiations led to an emergency N.U.T. conference in May, 1967, when it was decided that should the result of salary negotiations prove unsatisfactory, selective sanctions should begin in September with a triple aim in view, viz. improved salaries, the ending of school meals duties and an end to the employment of unqualified staff. The annual conference had already agreed that unless satisfaction over school meals could be assured within the life of 'the present parliament' all teachers would be withdrawn from school meals by 1st April, 1968.

'Sanctions' were, in fact, undertaken by the N.U.T. in the autumn term of 1967 and continued for some weeks. As part of the settlement of the three matters of contention a joint working party of representatives of the teachers and of the authorities was set up on the school meals issue, 'with the primary aim of achieving a position in which the regulation empowering authorities to compel teachers to assist in the supervision of the midday meal could be withdrawn'.[30] It was hoped that the working party would report within a month, but in fact it was March of the next year before its report appeared. The main recommendations were that the regulations should be changed so that school meals supervision duties ceased to be compulsory for teachers. Teachers who agreed to supervise school meals should be entitled to a free school dinner, while other teachers remaining in school should be able to get a meal on payment. The authorities were to revise their arrangements for supervisory and clerical assistance to ensure that it was adequate, and certain guide-lines were suggested.[31] The N.U.T. conference overwhelmingly endorsed the executive's decision approving the tentative agreement. There was some criticism that teachers were exchanging legal compulsion for a form of professional obligation, yet the outcome of the negotiations was that compulsory supervision of school meals ceased to be a condition of tenure for teachers in maintained schools. It remained the overall responsibility of the head teacher to see that arrangements for the midday break and meal worked smoothly, even though he could no longer compel his assistant teachers to help.

NOTES

1. *The A.M.A.*, November, 1939, p. 294; Board of Education Circular No. 1491, 1939.
2. Ministry of Education, Principles of Government in Maintained Secondary Schools, Cmd. 6523, 1944, p. 7; *The A.M.A.*, June–July, 1944, p. 126.
3. P.R.O., Ed. 136/588, Notes from meeting with N.U.T. deputation 23/8/44 and letter from R. S. Wood (Deputy Secretary) to F. Mander dated 1/9/44; Ministry of Education Circular No. 5, 1944, paras. 57–60.
4. Recommendations of Joint Conference of the A.E.C., C.C.A., N.U.T., Joint Four Secondary Associations relating to conditions of tenure in county and voluntary schools—primary and secondary and day special schools and nursery schools maintained by local education authorities, 1949.
5. *The A.M.A.*, September, 1960, p. 209; June, 1958, p. 179.
6. Ibid., January, 1947, p. 1.
7. Durham County Council Education Department Circular 58, 10th November, 1950, quoted by W. Roy, *The Teachers' Union*, 1969, p. 131, where a full account of the Durham Dispute is given.
8. *Hansard*, H. of C., 13th March, 1951, col. 1409.
9. Roy, op. cit., p. 136. 'At interviews for a number of headships, e.g. the Deaf Hill Girls' School, Spennymoor Infants' School, the Blackhall Secondary Modern and the Aycliffe Primary School, the offending question was asked, and none of the candidates who refused to reply was offered the appointment.'
10. *The Schoolmaster*, 29th March, 1951, pp. 413–14; 5th April, p. 463; 12th April, p. 506; 3rd May, p. 605; *T.E.S.*, 4th May, 1951, p. 352.
11. *T.E.S.*, 23rd May, 1952, p. 455; *The Schoolmaster*, 6th June, 1952, p. 840.
12. The items of reference were reprinted in *The Schoolmaster*, 4th July, 1952, p. 5.
13. A Tropp, *The School Teachers*, 1957; *The Schoolmaster*, 7th October, 1955, p. 490.
14. N.U.T. Annual Report, 1952, p. lxxxii.
15. *The Schoolmaster*, 30th September, 1955, p. 452.
16. *T.E.S.*, 24th February, 1956, p. 221.

17. *The A.M.A.*, November, 1939, p. 289.
18. N.U.T. Annual Report, 1942, pp. xlvii–xlix.
19. 11 & 12 Geo. 5, c. 39, S.85.
20. Board of Education, Administrative Memorandum No. 336, 8th December, 1941.
21. Ministry of Education, Report of the Chief Medical Officer for 1939 to 1945, chapter II, where a full account is given of this transformation in policy and scope during the war years.
22. 7 & 8 Geo. 6, c. 31, S.49.
23. S.R.O. No. 698, 1945.
24. N.U.T. Annual Reports from 1948; similar sentiments were expressed at the conferences of other teachers' organisations, e.g. *The A.M.A.*, January–February, 1946, pp. 7 and 38 and subsequent reports of meetings of the I.A.A.M. Council.
25. Ministry of Education, Education in 1947, Cmd. 7426, pp. 56–7; Ministry of Education Circular No. 97, 1946.
26. *The A.M.A.*, February, 1956, pp. 79–80.
27. N.U.T. Annual Report, 1963, pp. 60–61.
28. Ibid., pp. 62–63.
29. The phrase used in the resolution on school meals supervision at the N.U.T. Conference in 1967.
30. *Education*, 1st December, 1967, p. 876.
31. *The Teacher*, 22nd March, 1968, p. 1.

9
The Training of Teachers for Elementary Schools before 1914

Those who follow certain occupations, such as those of solicitor or general practitioner, have for many years succeeded in maintaining a measure of control over entry into and training for their professions. This control they have been licensed by the state to enforce. Teachers' associations have sought a similarly favoured position for their own occupation with more or less vigour at different times since the late nineteenth century, but have not met with as much success. Their failure to achieve this is probably due to a number of factors, the most important of which are the nature of the occupation itself, the fact that the great majority of teachers have always been employees and have not enjoyed the independence of the professional man—client relationship, and the interest of the state as the monopolistic buyer of their services through the financial relationship it has established with the local authorities and voluntary bodies actually employing them. Thus in the case of elementary schoolteachers, the state has traditionally prescribed in some detail the conditions of entry to the occupation and has determined the training required. This was not the position with regard to secondary school teachers in the nineteenth century, but their position has been assimilated ever more closely to that of the elementary school teachers in the last seventy years.

I NINETEENTH-CENTURY DEVELOPMENTS

One of the earlier manifestations of the State's concern for elementary education took the form of seeking to secure a supply of properly qualified teachers. The inadequacies of the monitorial system on which schools under the aegis of both the National and British and Foreign

Societies operated led to the early experiments undertaken by Kay-Shuttleworth with the pupil-teacher system from 1839. The Minutes of the Committee of Council for that year described a pupil teacher in these words:[1]

> A young teacher, in the first instance introduced to the notice of the Master by his good qualities, as one of the best instructed and most intelligent of the children; whose attainments and skill are full of promise; and who, having consented to remain at a low rate of remuneration in the school, is further rewarded by being enabled to avail himself of the opportunities afforded him for attaining practical skill in the art of teaching, by daily practice in the school, and by the gratuitous superintendence of his reading and studies by the Master, from whom he receives lessons on technical subjects of school instruction every evening.

The importance attached by Kay-Shuttleworth to training teachers came to be shared much more widely in the 1840s, and by 1846 fifteen training colleges had been established. It was essential that a supply of good entrants should be secured for these colleges and this was one of the aims of the system of grants offered by the State for pupil-teachers from 1846. Under these arrangements pupil teachers were appointed at the age of 13 to an apprenticeship lasting 5 years; they were selected on grounds of both attainment and character and on the recommendation of the inspector. They were paid salaries on a scale rising from £10 in the first year to £20 in the fifth, while the head teacher to whom the pupil teacher was apprenticed was paid £3 annually in respect of the instruction which he was supposed to give for $1\frac{1}{2}$ hours daily. The head teacher was also expected to arrange for his apprentice to observe and to practice teaching. Pupil teachers seem to have spent about 5 hours a day working in the school, another $1\frac{1}{2}$ hours being instructed and about $1\frac{1}{2}$ hours preparing their work. In this way it was hoped to supply the elementary schools with a reasonably skilled body of assistant teachers; the intention was that the best of the pupil teachers should pass into the training colleges at the end of their apprenticeship, and to achieve this a system of 'Queen's Scholarships' was provided which enabled the able but impecunious student to meet the cost of a training college course.

With some modifications the system continued as the principal mode of training future elementary school teachers for the remainder of the nineteenth century, even though it was modified in its details as circumstances changed. The direct grants from the Education Department to pupil teachers were abolished by the Revised Code of 1862, when the cost of employing these young assistants fell upon the managers of schools. The establishment of school boards from 1870 had an important consequence, for under their influence it became usual in the larger cities to provide special centres to which pupil teachers were sent to be instructed in groups, instead of continuing to rely on each individual head teacher to undertake the entire responsibility for instructing his own apprentices outside normal class hours. Moreover, the spreading custom of employing assistant teachers led to an important change in the manner of conducting schools. When the pupil-teacher system was introduced it had been customary for most of the school to be housed in one large schoolroom where the head teacher could constantly supervise all that was going on and keep an eye on his pupil-teachers. The increasing employment of adequate assistant teachers made it possible to build separate classrooms and to get away from the confusion and hubbub of all the classes being in one large room, for it was naturally possible for assistant teachers to conduct classes without being continually under the supervision of the head teacher. This new physical arrangement led to pupil-teachers also being withdrawn from constant contact with the head teacher as they came to be put to work in classrooms, and in this way an essential feature of the system as originally conceived was brought to an end. In spite of these changes, the Majority Report of the Cross Commission, issued in 1888, stated that there was no source from which an adequate supply of teachers would be forthcoming other than the pupil-teachers, and the existing arrangements for the apprenticeship of pupil teachers, with certain modifications, ought to be maintained. A minority of members of the Commission took a very different view and considered that the pupil-teacher system had become the weakest part of the educational machinery, needing drastic reform if it were to continue. 'The complaint is general that the pupil-teachers teach badly, and are badly taught. The wretched state of their preparation when they enter the training colleges will be dwelt on when that part of our educational system is dealt with, and the remarkable thing is that the witnesses, while complaining generally of the backwardness and ignorance of pupil-teachers, lay special stress on their ability to teach, and on their ignorance of school management.' They added later that the fact that the defenders of the system based their arguments on the value of early familiarity with school management, and to this end were willing to sacrifice the general education of the pupil teacher, made particularly grave the evidence which showed that the bulk of pupil teachers ended up both poorly instructed and bad teachers.

The general drift of educational opinion in the next few years in the direction of the conclusions of the Minority Report of the Cross Commission culminated in the appointment of the Departmental Committee to inquire into the working of the system and the supply of teachers in 1896. The Committee reported early in 1898, and the view which it took of desirable future developments in training elementary school teachers is particularly important, since in the long term it was this view which prevailed.[2] It was also a view which, in some of its premises, was to cause the National Union of Teachers considerable offence. The primary schools had been regarded hitherto as the main and most natural recruiting area for elementary school teachers; the knowledge of school routine, familiarity with its methods and discipline, all made it easy for those accustomed to the elementary school 'to fall into its ways and associations and to look for a career within its walls'. The committee felt it desirable that all intending teachers should pass through a secondary school for the completion of their personal education. 'The traditions of primary teaching are still, through no fault of the teachers, narrower than is consistent with sound education; and we believe that better methods, greater spontaneity, a wider outlook ... would result from the more frequent employment in primary schools of persons whose experience has not been exclusively or chiefly primary. ...' The Committee considered it essential that pupil teachers should be offered instruction over and beyond what a head teacher could offer outside school hours. Pupil teacher centres were costly attempts to fulfil a task impossible under existing conditions, they produced professional and social narrowness of aim, their staffs were imperfectly qualified and themselves narrowly trained. 'We look forward to the ultimate conversion of those centres which are well staffed and properly equipped into real secondary schools, where, although perhaps intending teachers may be in the majority, they will have ampler time for their studies and will be instructed side by side with pupils who have other careers in mind.' The Education Act of 1902 made the same local education authorities responsible for the maintenance of both elementary and secondary schools, and paved the way administratively for the implementation of the suggestions of the Departmental Committee.

Until 1889 the training colleges to which the most successful products of the pupil teacher system went were all governed by private bodies, being nearly always denominational and residential. The weaknesses of the colleges in the nineteenth century have been described frequently.

Table 9.1. *Training College Provision, 1850–1910*[3]

Year	Number of Colleges	Number of student places provided
1850	16	991
1870	34	2,495
1890	49	3,679
1910	85	12,625

The fact that they were residential led them too often into being little worlds of their own—at no time did their average size reach 100 students—almost completely cut off from outside educational thought and activity. The main cause of their weaknesses was probably the staffing difficulties they encountered. The principal was normally a clerk in holy orders, who might sometimes lecture but quite often confined himself to general supervision and religious instruction. It was customary, especially in the women's colleges, to appoint promising students as junior lecturers and to promote them in due course to be senior lecturers, so that the colleges produced their own staffs. Such teachers were no doubt well able to ensure continuity in the ideals and traditions of their college, but lack of acquaintance with any form of education other than that given in the elementary schools produced a narrow, mechanical and illiberal approach. By the 1890s there were signs of change. The Cross Commission recommended the foundation of day training colleges associated with university colleges. The pressure for such non-residential colleges came largely from the school boards in the bigger cities who found the supply of trained teachers from the existing colleges inadequate. Nonconformists also sought some such widening non-confessional training facilities for their students, who were finding it difficult to secure places in the colleges since so many of them belonged to the Church of England.

Some of the larger school boards had earlier sought to extend their powers so as to enable them to establish and maintain training colleges, and they pressed their case before the Cross Commission. Dr. Boddington, Principal of the Yorkshire College, Leeds, submitted an elaborate scheme for the establishment of a university day training college in that city. Official influence showed itself clearly in support of arrangements on the lines of this second scheme which would avoid awkward problems concerning denominational difficulties and the extension of the power of school boards. In his evidence, Cumin, Secretary to the Education Department strongly supported the establishment of day training colleges under the direction of local university colleges. He did not propose to 'interfere in the slightest degree with the existing training colleges. They are to remain as they are. One of the objects is to make the position of the denominational colleges more secure by opening a new entrance for teachers as to which the question of denomination would not arise.'[4] Thus it was not surprising when the Education Department accepted the recommendation and issued regulations in 1890 permitting the establishment of day training colleges by the existing universities and university colleges, and extending from 2 to 3 years the maximum permitted length of the course so as to enable those who sought to do so to read for a degree. The actual regulations introduced a much more liberal approach to teacher training, for while day students were required to pass the examination prescribed in the Department's training syllabus in reading and recitation, teaching a class and school management, in the normal academic subjects the Department was prepared to accept the course and examination operated by the university to which the day college was attached. Two conditions were attached to this concession initially; firstly the course of instruction had to correspond with the official syllabus in extent and difficulty and, secondly, the question paper and scripts had to be sent to the Department with the marks awarded in order that there might be an adjustment to the common standard adopted for the national classification applying to students at other colleges.[5] By 1900 the new day training colleges had over 2,000 student places.

The impact of these new colleges on the existing colleges was considerable. The students in the new colleges came into contact with teachers who were eminent in their own subjects and were able to follow their own inclinations in studying under such teachers. The number of alternative courses from which to choose provided a markedly liberal alternative to the fare provided in the traditional colleges. The residential colleges, faced with this competition, sought to improve the quality of their own teaching and began to seek to appoint to their staffs men and women of wider experience. The change was noted by H.M. Inspector of training colleges in 1896 when he wrote, 'The tide is now setting steadily, if not with any great strength, in the direction of introducing into the staffs of the colleges teachers of higher intellectual qualifications. Persons with university degrees, or holding certificates of examining bodies recognised as vouchers of efficiency, and ladies trained in the Cambridge Training College for Secondary Teachers, are being introduced into the colleges, who amalgamate with the teachers, and are importing into the teaching broader views and a stronger impulse.'[6]

Down to the end of the nineteenth century the attitude of the elementary school teachers to these changes had been largely favourable. The general improvement in the traditional training colleges, the establishment of day colleges, the involvement of the universities in teacher training and the possibility of a three-year course leading to a degree as well as the teaching qualification—all of these changes were attractive to the organised elementary school teachers, all could be viewed as ways of enhancing the standing of the occupation. Even on the issue of secondary schooling for future recruits, which was to cause much vexation in the first decade of the twentieth century, the future troubles had not so far appeared. As early as 1878 T. E. Heller, then Secretary of the N.U.E.T., read a paper to the National Association for the Promotion of Social Science in which he suggested that the education of elementary teachers was exclusive and narrow and too separated from the influences of a liberal general education. The existing training colleges should be affiliated to the universities and the course of study so altered as to lead to a university degree.[7] In 1896 the President of the National Federation of Assistant Teachers, A. A. Thomas, was also a member of the N.U.T. executive when he prepared the policy document on the pupil teacher system which was adopted by the N.U.T. Executive. This recommended that probationers should be engaged at the age of 13 and that they should attend a secondary school until they became pupil teachers at the age of 15.[8] The apparently changed attitude in the years following 1902 arose partly from the more systematic organisation of secondary education, and the increasingly sharp administrative distinction made between elementary and secondary schools, following the period of haphazard expansion and blurring of such distinctions in the 1890s. The completely different conceptions of 'secondary' and 'elementary' schools and teachers which obtained in official circles in the early 20th century seemed to emphasise the cultural poverty of the training which elementary teachers had received and, as a consequence, to sharpen feelings.

II RECRUITMENT AND TRAINING AFTER 1902

The general strategy of the Board of Education after 1902 was to build up a secondary education system and to recruit from its products the future teachers for the elementary schools. The first steps in this direction were taken in the Pupil-Teacher Regulations of 1903. These regulations contained two important principles, firstly, to postpone employment in elementary schools so as to ensure the continued full-time education of the future teachers themselves and, secondly, to continue such personal education so far as possible during the actual period of pupil teachership. The first of these aims was to be achieved by raising the minimum age for the recognition of pupil teachers to 16 (save in rural areas); the second by insisting on at least 300 hours of instruction in approved centres or classes of pupil teachers. Many secondary schools were recognised for this latter purpose, and a circular issued at the end of 1903 spelt out more fully the Board of Education's intentions.[9] The importance of drawing candidates for the elementary teaching profession from among secondary pupils was stressed, as was the aim of utilising the secondary schools 'to the fullest possible extent' for preliminary training purposes. It was hoped 'that the result may be to bring the Pupil-Teachers under the influence of a wider outlook and a more humane ideal of education than have been possible under the difficult conditions generally prevalent in the past'. An increasing number of secondary schools became involved in this work, so that by the year 1906-7, out of 694 secondary schools recognised for grant under the Secondary School Regulations, 357 were also recognised as pupil-teacher centres; at this time there remained 179 independent pupil-teacher centres in receipt of grant.

In its General Report on the pupil-teacher system of 1907,[10] the Board argued that the normal education of a future teacher should involve secondary school from 12 to 16 or so and no commitment to teaching as a career before 16 or 17. The practice of introducing prospective teachers into secondary schools on bursaries at the age of 14 for 2 years was condemned as a survival from the days when they were selected directly from the older scholars in elementary schools at about that age. The difficulty of choosing which children to send to secondary schools with a view to their becoming teachers at the age of 12 was to be solved by making an education in secondary schools freely available for all such children from elementary schools as would be capable of profiting from it. It was suggested that until this could be achieved 'the provision of a good and steady supply of elementary school teachers will continue to present the gravest difficulties'. In reply to the claim that students needed early experience in elementary school management and discipline, it was pointed out that inexperience in enforcing discipline was capable of remedy, whereas it was beyond remedy when teachers were brought into the schools 'without the trained intelligence and the refinement of character which are alone able to make their work permanent and effective'. It was precisely this argument which lay behind the new regulations issued in 1907. The part-time nature of the attendance of pupil-teachers in secondary schools from the age of 16 (when their pupil-teachership began) led to disorganisation of work in the secondary schools. The new regulations made it possible for full-time secondary education to continue until the age of 18 and any attempt at gaining practical experience in an elementary school to be deferred until the training college had been entered. Where there was still an inadequate supply of secondary schools 'the ancient resource of Pupil-Teachership must continue to be available'.

The move towards utilising the growing secondary school system for educating future elementary school teachers meant that the number of pupil-teacher centres declined rapidly in these years. Their demise was in one sense a consequence of the unified local administration of elementary and higher education; no longer were there boards charged with providing only elementary schools and teachers for them. Moreover Morant was not slow to observe that the centres' position had become anomalous—as anomalous as that of the higher grade schools. He had written in a memorandum as early as 1901 that 'The whole arrangement of the pupil-teacher centres has grown up, as it were, haphazard and unobserved, developed by the school boards without any direct approval of the Education Department, just as was the case with the higher grade schools'.[11] The abolition of many pupil-teacher centres either by converting them into secondary schools or by simply closing them down became one of the matters of controversy between the N.U.T. and the Board of Education, as relations between the elementary teachers and Morant worsened for a variety of reasons, and suspicion and mistrust replaced any sort of confidence, this situation culminating in the affair of the Holmes circular in 1911. Undoubtedly many elementary school teachers felt some sentimental attachment to the type of institution in which they themselves had been educated; its replacement because of its inefficiency might be thought to reflect on their own qualifications. Moreover, the teachers in these centres, through the Federation of Teachers in Central Classes, naturally opposed strongly the attack on their centres, their opposition being sharpened by their frequent inability to match the qualifications required for posts in the secondary schools which were replacing them. In the circumstances a considerable campaign was mounted by the N.U.T. to save the centres and the pupil-teacher system itself—at least in some form. Questions were asked in Parliament by M.P.s sympathetic to the Union when the closure of individual pupil-teacher centres was proposed. In answer to a question from P. Snowden in 1906, A. Birrell, then President of the Board of Education, justified his department's policy in these words: 'a good general education for these young persons between the ages of 16 and 20 seems to me, and I believe to all educational experts, a matter of far greater importance than any attempt to develop in them at so early an age any special technical dexterity in handling large classes or other professional specialities, which can only be achieved by stunting their intellectual development at what is perhaps the most important stage of their mental growth'.[12]

The dissatisfaction of the N.U.T. showed clearly at annual conferences and in the columns of *The Schoolmaster*. In his presidential address to the 1907 Conference, A. R. Pickles argued strongly the case against the Board's policy and saw in it an attempt to push up the number of pupils in secondary schools and thus to bolster them up.* The Board was making use of 'whatever audacity can dare and subtilty contrive to close down pupil teacher centres, transferring the boys to the more cultured atmosphere of the grammar school, and the girls to the more refining influence of the girls' high school. I speak of audacity and subtilty because, in order to effect its purpose, the Board has attacked a centre here, and another there, working beneath the surface like a mole, putting pressure upon the local authorities to close down admirable centres through its inspectors, and avoiding a frank and open

---

* That such an incidental purpose could be served had been pointed out as early as 1903: 'It is difficult enough for a secondary school in a small town to get a sufficient number of boys to make its classification efficient. And there is still greater difficulty in girls' schools. Some small towns have built or are building schools suitable for the coeducation of boys and girls—a plan which has much in its favour. But where there are already separate schools established, the addition of some twenty or thirty children from the pupil teacher centre might be a real boon'. *Jnl. of Educn.*, June, 1903, pp. 380–1.

declaration of policy.' The president urged that the old system and the new should be permitted for a time to continue side by side.[13] A few weeks earlier *The Schoolmaster* complained that, following the closure of pupil-teacher centres, inspectors of the secondary school branch were suggesting that the teachers from them should not be appointed to the staffs of municipal secondary schools.

There can be no doubt but that the impression was becoming widespread among elementary teachers that they were regarded by the administrators of the Board and by the secondary teachers as socially inferior beings. In the presidential address referred to above, Pickles complained that in many secondary schools holders of bursaries intending to become teachers were taught in separate classes and not permitted to mix with the other pupils in the schools. In some secondary schools this seems to have been the consequence of the need to release pupil teachers for service in elementary schools for part of the week. In such cases schools might have found that separate classes and groupings were the most convenient way of overcoming the organisational problems which arose out of having full-time and part-time pupils in the same school. In other schools there can be little doubt that local snobbery played its part, for traditionally elementary school teachers had been drawn from those classes of society which had generally to content themselves with elementary education, while those who passed through the secondary schools would not normally have considered elementary school teaching as a possible career. *The Schoolmaster* thought it worthwhile to publish an article from the *Sunday Chronicle* entitled 'A Stolen Profession', alleging that the teaching profession was gradually becoming the preserve of children of middle-class parents. It claimed that the evidence for this was to be found in the regulations of the Board of Education relating to pupil-teachers which had been issued in the last five or six years. Ten years ago it was possible for a boy or girl from a working-class family to become an apprentice from the higher forms of an elementary school and eventually to gain the certificate by part-time study and part-time teaching, receiving some salary—albeit a small one—throughout. The scholarships which came to be given to carry the future teacher through the secondary school and training college meant that artisan parents would have to sacrifice their children's earning capacity for a number of years. The position was even worse, however, because many of these scholarships were being won by middle-class children, so that 'we had the public scandal of . . . children for whom the scholarships were clearly intended, . . . beaten to the wall'. 'A useful profession is being stolen from the child of the working man, and while he sleepeth an enemy hath removed his landmark.'[14] But the idea that the closure of pupil-teacher centres and the despatch of intending teachers to grammar schools was a deliberate attack by the authorities on attempts by working class children to advance themselves and to keep them in their place can hardly be substantiated. Indeed, in circular 494 of December, 1903, the Board, in commending the use of secondary schools, suggested that even where a secondary school offered no direct gain so far as instruction was concerned, 'there will be a social gain if candidates are drawn from homes of more than one class and if something is thus done to break down the existing and undesirable barrier between Elementary and Secondary School Teachers'.

The general worsening in relations between the N.U.T. and the Board of Education in the years before 1911 also led the Union to criticise severely certain aspects of official policy concerning the training colleges. At the time when the Education Act of 1902 was before Parliament the N.U.T. had mounted pressure on the government to make better provision for training future teachers who were not of the same religious persuasion as the bodies controlling most of the training colleges. One consequence of the pressure was that the Act authorised local education authorities to spend their funds on training teachers, and this was to put them in a position to establish and maintain training colleges. The Training College Regulations of 1904 were the first to be issued by the Board of Education as a separate volume and no longer as part of the Elementary Code. In some ways this symbolised important developments in teacher training. One of the most significant new provisions was the recognition of a new type of training college which need neither be residential nor in connection with a university; these were to be maintained by local education authorities. The growth of the new municipal colleges, as they were called, was encouraged by the provision of building grants in 1905. By the beginning of the First World War there were 20 of these colleges in England and Wales with accommodation for nearly 4,000 students. Although most of these were intended as day colleges, the authorities soon found that under such conditions their choice of students was greatly restricted by comparison with the field of applicants from which the residential colleges might select. Consequently they soon began to provide hostels for women and, to a lesser extent, for men.[15]

Another direction in which the Regulations of 1904 were important was in the much closer control which the Board assumed over appointments to the staffs of colleges, with the aim of improving their quality. Two-thirds of the teaching staff of colleges applying for recognition had in future to hold academic qualifications approved by the Board. From 1st August, 1904, in the existing colleges alternate vacancies among the non-graduate staff had to be filled with academically qualified persons until the prescribed proportion was attained. A little later the Board issued this regulation: 'A man proposed as Principal of a College who does not hold a degree in honours of a British University will not, save in exceptional circumstances, be recognised for this purpose by the Board.'

While in one sense the N.U.T. welcomed measures which would improve the quality of the future teachers' education and therefore was in favour of many of these post-1902 developments, in so far as the measures involved raising standards through enforcing demarcation between the well and less well qualified, the Union took a different attitude and showed a considerable degree of sensitivity. From the 1890s it had been possible for students in training colleges to prepare for university degree examinations if suitably qualified in the eyes of the university to embark upon such a course. They were then excused the academic part of the normal Board of Education final examinations required of training college students. Those who failed their degree examinations had been permitted to obtain their certificate on passing a more or less formal examination set by the college authorities. In the years following 1902 successive steps were taken by the Board to discourage students from trying to read for degrees in the colleges unless they stood a good chance of succeeding in gaining them. Much closer scrutiny was undertaken of the fitness of students to embark on degree courses, and the degree course actually selected had in every case to be submitted to the Board for approval. Students who failed their degree examinations were obliged in future to enter for the Board's Final Examination. The effect of these regulations was to reduce the number of candidates taking degree courses and to increase the percentage of successes in degree examinations from 61·5 in 1900 to 75·5 in 1906.

Complaints about the new policy appeared in *The Schoolmaster* from time to time and were most numerous in the period following July, 1905, when the Board issued Circular 530 which announced the abolition of the King's Scholarship examination for college entry and replaced it by the Preliminary Examination for the Certificate. The new regulations to be issued would require a college student to have obtained in the Preliminary Examination passes in 7 subjects, including 2 languages, before permitting him to enter on a degree course. *The Schoolmaster* complained that 'Such erudition on the part of budding teachers is only comparable with that of Gargantua'; it continued, 'to put the matter bluntly the Board is producing the impression that it does not wish the primary teacher to read for a degree whatever his qualifications and ability may be, that it is desirous to limit his outlook and his ambitions'. The general condition of resentment felt by some of the more militant of the N.U.T. membership was expressed in an article entitled 'The Degradation of the Elementary School Teacher' and written by a certificated teacher who was a London graduate. He claimed that degree work had been carefully fostered and built up in the colleges, where highly qualified staff had been appointed. 'Recently, however, article by article, and regulation by regulation, the Board of Education has placed such serious discouragement in the paths of teachers and students that we fear some of the colleges will be driven in sheer desperation to abandon their higher work'. This official action was akin to the attack on higher grade schools and pupil teacher centres. It was not really so much a question of preventing waste and overlapping, but rather 'these movements are inspired by one unworthy and sinister purpose, which is to confine the elementary teacher, trained or untrained, graduate or non-graduate, to work of a purely elementary kind, and to bring in persons of other antecedents for every kind of higher work and for every office of substantial emolument'.[16]

In defence of its policy generally and in reply to resolutions against Circular 530 forwarded by Principal Headlam of King's College, London, the Board pointed out that it fully realised the stimulus that the presence of graduates could be to the work of an elementary school and that it had no intention of departing from the policy of recent years. But it also pointed out the dangers that tended to arise, namely, that students who were not sufficiently well prepared embarked on degree courses; it was hoped that the regulations would reduce in future years the number 'not of those who are successful in University exams., but of those who fail in such exams'. It was also explained that training college students differed from ordinary university students in that immediately they finished their course they would have to teach a range of subjects to children in elementary schools. Their course must, therefore, ensure sufficient competence in each of these subjects to enable them to be in a real sense teachers of them. The Board added that 'it cannot be too clearly stated that the large Exchequer Grants made in aid of the training of teachers are voted by Parliament with the definite intention of providing thoroughly qualified teachers for children in public elementary schools. They are not made primarily for the purpose of enabling as many elementary teachers as possible to obtain degrees'. Having thus justified its policy, the Board conceded that it would be willing to accept a pass in one of the matriculation examinations as evidence of fitness to proceed to a degree course in 1907 and undertook to consider permanent provisions on these lines for 1908 and subsequent years. In answer to a question in the Commons at this time, Birrell, President of the Board of Education, stressed that the Board did not wish to discourage those students who would certainly benefit from degree courses, but that the grants for these students came from monies voted by Parliament to secure the regular supply of competent teachers for the elementary schools and that it was his duty to see that other objects, however desirable in themselves, did not supersede this primary purpose.[17]

A change in the regulations governing training colleges in 1907 which was welcomed by the leaders of the N.U.T. was that which forbade the colleges to reject candidates for admission on the grounds of religious faith. The previous year the N.U.T. Conference had passed a resolution opposing religious tests for training college candidates and urging that admission should be dependent solely on personal character and educational fitness. Similar resolutions had been passed before, but circumstances had now made the demand timely. The Liberal government was then making attempts to deprive the denominational schools of the position they achieved under the 1902 Act. Both Catholics and Anglicans saw in the action of the government a move designed ultimately to destroy denominational instruction in the schools following the failure of Birrell's Bill in the Lords.[18] It was a highly political move with little educational motive. The Archbishop of Canterbury led a deputation organised by the National Society to see the Prime Minister to protest against the new regulations. T. H. Yoxall, the General Secretary of the N.U.T. and a member of the Commons, welcomed the new regulations on the grounds that they would remove 'a standing source of injustice and irritation, whereby a teacher, high up on the list of merits, had been unable to obtain admission, because his place was filled by a candidate low on the list of merits who happened to fulfil a denominational test which the higher candidate did not fill'.[19] A compromise was eventually reached on this highly political issue by which a half of the places in denominational colleges might be reserved to members of the denomination, while the other half were to be filled without denominational tests.

The drastic re-organisation of teacher training in the first decade of the twentieth century by which the normal mode of entry—except in rural areas—became a full secondary schooling followed by 2 years in a college contributed to some difficulties over the supply of new entrants. The number of pupil-teachers commencing their apprenticeship naturally diminished as had been intended, but the total number of entrants through the secondary schools failed to expand to the extent expected and after 1909 there was a marked diminution in the number of boys coming forward. In order to supplement the general system of scholarships to secondary schools, from 1907, bursaries were offered to secondary school pupils of 16 to afford them financial assistance in staying at school until they entered a a training college. The failure of these to attract a sufficient number of young people, especially boys, may be judged from the table.

Table 9.2. *Number of Pupil-teachers and Bursars recognised for the first time in England*[20]

Year	Pupil-teachers commencing	BURSARS Boys	Girls
1906/7	11,018	—	—
1907/8	10,297	637	1,406
1908/9	5,209	1,112	2,393
1909/10	3,850	1,090	2,251
1910/11	2,612	723	2,041
1911/12	1,955	723	2,135
1912/13	1,469	614	2,225
1913/14	1,454	598	2,434

One reason for the diminution in the number of entrants was the extent to which the Board of Education left matters in the hands of local authorities. Some of these offered scholarships to secondary pupils of 12 to 16 on condition that they intended to become teachers—but many others made no provision for this, so that some children who would have sought to become teachers were undoubtedly prevented from doing so for financial reasons, whereas they would not have encountered this difficulty had the pupil-teacher system continued to flourish or if earlier financial assistance had been offered on a national basis.* The recruitment to the occupation of certificated teacher was left increasingly to whatever attraction it might offer to secondary school leavers by way of 'emoluments, immediate and prospective, status and security.' That the expectations of those leaving secondary schools would be greater than those of elementary school leavers was obvious. Although the average salaries of certificated teachers had risen to some extent under the new local authorities, there was also a marked rise in the cost of living in these years.

The expansion of the number of places in training colleges also affected the position, for while there had been a shortage of places the students were able to obtain posts with little difficulty immediately their training ended; after the number of college places had been increased, the newly-trained teachers were not absorbed so rapidly as before. This unemployment, although possibly of a temporary nature, was sufficiently alarming to discourage many would-be entrants. This was particularly noticeable in 1909 and 1910. Thus there was concern over both a shortage of entrants to teaching and over unemployment of trained teachers in these years. Certainly the unemployment of trained teachers, both actual and feared, played its part in leading the N.U.T. to oppose aspects of the Board's policy on the recruitment, training and employment of teachers, and in mounting pressure for such reforms as the reduction in the size of classes and an end to the recruitment of untrained teachers to the elementary schools.

At the time of its Buxton conference in 1903 the Union put forward

---

* According to the Board itself 'The postponement of the time of wage-earning involved in the "Bursar" system has to some extent affected recruiting for the teaching profession. Under that system, it will be remembered, the intending teacher must attend a secondary school for at least 3 years before the age of 16 or 17, when he is recognised as a bursar. He spends the years of bursarship also in the secondary school and then either proceeds direct to a training college for a two-year, three-year or four-year course, or becomes a Student-teacher. He receives a small salary while a student-teacher and after a year spent in that capacity may either go to a training college or become an uncertificated teacher for an indefinite period. He does not become a certificated teacher until he has either completed a training college course, or has passed the Acting-teacher's Certificate Examination after a certain period of service as an uncertificated teacher; and if he hopes to rise to the highest posts in his profession, a training college course is essential. Thus, it will be seen that the ambitious boy or girl who enters by what is now the commonest avenue to the profession, cannot begin full wage earning before, at earliest, the age of 19, and must often postpone it till later.'

Report of the Board of Education for 1912–13, 1914, p. 150.

a plan for the improvement of elementary school staffing on the grounds that since elementary schools were no longer dependent for their maintenance on voluntary contributions, the former financial stringencies of the voluntary schools could no longer be accepted as a reason for inadequate staffing. The attempts being made by the Board after 1902 to build up the secondary schools led elementary teachers to compare their own staffing ratios with those of some of the grammar schools. In his presidential address to the N.U.T. Conference in 1906, J. P. Sykes claimed that the staff of 28 at Bradford Grammar School would have had to take 1,680 children under the elementary regulations, instead of the 538 boys they actually taught.[21] In 1907 a deputation from the Union went to see the President, McKenna, and Morant to urge that the maximum size of class should be reduced from 60 to 50 pupils and that pupil-teachers should not be counted in calculating the minimum staff required in a school under the code.

In the following year complaints of unemployment and of difficulty in finding work became increasingly frequent among elementary school teachers. It was reported that some young teachers from the training colleges were offering to take posts at less than the scales offered by local authorities, and that some were even expressing willingness to take posts at the salaries appropriate to uncertificated staff.[22] That there was some truth in this last claim may be borne out by the staffing returns made in the next few years by local authorities. The figures returned for 31st January, 1913, showed that there were then over 400 men and over 2,000 women certificated teachers in England employed at salaries below those ordinarily paid by authorities to teachers so qualified. The Board's explanation of these figures was that some teachers preferred to take employment within reach of their present home rather than move to another area. In June, 1908, Yoxall questioned Runciman, the President of the Board, in the Commons as to whether he was aware of the difficulties the newly trained teachers were having in finding employment, and the steps he proposed to take to secure that all certificated teachers should be college trained.*[23] The pressure that the N.U.T. has consistently maintained to lessen the size of classes and to eliminate 'untrained', 'uncertificated' or 'unqualified' teachers has often been at its strongest when unemployment threatened. Indeed, the situation in 1909 led to a deputation to W. Runciman

---

* It was still possible for teachers who had not been to a training college to sit the certificate examination; more than 5,000 had done so and passed it in 1907.

which set out a series of demands concerned with training and admission to the profession which serves to summarise the N.U.T.'s aims in this field for some years to come. These were:

—no further recognition of additional supplementary teachers

—the continued recognition of existing supplementary teachers to depend (after a certain date) upon the production of satisfactory educational qualifications

—pupil-teachers and student-teachers should not be counted as effective members of the school staff

—the standard of examination qualifying for recognition as an uncertificated teacher should, if possible, be raised

—that a date should be fixed after which no more uncertificated teachers should be recognised

—that a date should be fixed after which no teacher should be certificated who had not been trained in a training college or other collegiate institution

—that only certificated teachers should be eligible for recognition as head teachers

—that certificated teachers should be trained for service in any state- or rate-aided school, and the issue of separate regulations for the training of teachers for elementary and secondary schools should be discontinued.

In one sense it can be said that the N.U.T. sought to ensure the scarcity value of its members by excluding the competition of the untrained who would sell their services more cheaply; at the same time the Union was anxious to prevent the secondary school teachers from becoming an exclusive group of more highly qualified persons, whose status the non-graduate certificated teacher could not really hope to enjoy. The superior status of the secondary teacher was another issue around which a great deal of ill-feeling was stirred in the early years of this century by efforts to set up separate registers of elementary and secondary teachers.[24]

NOTES

1. Minutes of the Committee of Council for 1839–40, 1840, p. 33.
2. Departmental Committee on the Pupil Teacher System, 1898, Report and Minutes of Evidence.

3. Report of the Board of Education for 1912–13, 1914, p. 5.
4. Cross Cssn., 1888, vol. III, p. 653.
5. Report of the Committee of Council for 1889–90, 1890, pp. 205–7.
6. Report of the Committee of Council for 1895–6, 1896, p. 173.
7. T. E. Heller, 'On the Registration, Certification and Training of Teachers', a paper read to the Education Section, *Transactions of the National Association for the Promotion of Social Science*, 1878, p. 437.
8. Departmental Committee, 1898, vol. II, evidence.
9. Board of Education, Circular 494, 1903.
10. Board of Education, General Report on the Instruction and Training of Pupil-Teachers, 1903–7, with Historical Introduction, 1907, pp. 22–3.
11. Quoted by A. Shakoor, *The Training of Teachers in England and Wales, 1900–39*, unpublished Ph.D. thesis, 1964, Leicester University, p. 36.
12. Hansard, H. of C., 18th July, 1966, cols. 197–98.
13. *The Schoolmaster*, 6th April, 1907, p. 691.
14. Ibid., 5th September, 1908, p. 358, quoting from the *Sunday Chronicle*.
15. Report of the Board of Education for 1912–13, 1914, pp. 39–40.
16. *The Schoolmaster*, 12th August, 1905, p. 315.
17. Hansard, H. of C., 1st March, 1906, cols. 1317–18.
18. In his Bill of 1906 Birrell had sought to send the 1902 system of rate support for voluntary schools.
19. Hansard, H. of C., 11th July, 1907, cols. 140–3.
20. Report of the Board of Education for 1912–13, 1914, p. 149.
21. *The Schoolmaster*, 21st April, 1906, p. 838.
22. Ibid., 11th July, 1908, p. 77.
23. Hansard, H. of C., 11th June, 1908, col. 844.
24. *Infra.*, Chapter 11.

10
The Training of Teachers for Secondary Schools before 1914

The attitude to training teachers for secondary schools has differed greatly from the position in the elementary field. Even in 1970 considerable numbers of untrained graduates are still being recruited for service in both maintained and independent secondary schools. In 1914 many headmasters of secondary schools remained unconvinced of the need for training, even if the headmistresses generally appreciated the value of professional preparation. The paucity of provision for secondary training in the years immediately before the First World War may be seen from the official figures of students who completed a course of training for work in secondary schools (Table 10.1). The figures are for the years following 1908, since it was only in that year that the Board of Education first issued a set of regulations for secondary training.[1]

Table 10.1

Year	Men Trained	Women Trained	Total
1909–10	35	139	174
1910–11	30	133	163
1911–12	43	156	199
1912–13	38	178	216
1913–14	38	167	205

The point may also be illustrated by analysing the training of teachers in post in grant-aided secondary schools in 1913. Of a total of more than 5,000 men, only 180 had been trained for secondary school work, while 1,970 had been trained for elementary work and most had not been trained at all. The large number of elementary trained men in grant-aided secondary schools was partly due to the number of such schools which had been higher grade elementary schools before the

1902 Act and which became secondary under the post-1902 local education authorities; they kept their former staffs for the most part. Many other men had, no doubt, trained in elementary institutions simply because facilities for secondary training had not been available. The percentage of men who had been trained was 37·5 while the proportion of trained women teachers in secondary schools was 47·4. The actual numbers trained and untrained were as follows:[2]

Table 10.2

		Graduates	Non-Graduates	Totals Men	Women
Trained	Men	1,466	504	1,970	
	Women	1,534	915		2,449
Untrained	Men	2,257	1,019	3,276	
	Women	1,186	1,523		2,709
				5,246	5,158

There were many reasons why comparatively little progress had been made in training secondary teachers in the nineteenth century. In terms of absolute numbers, the total of secondary teachers required, even in 1900, was very small by comparison with the total number of elementary teachers. Perhaps the divided nature of secondary education was an even more important factor, for the various types of secondary schools were far removed from each other; their heads and staffs—as well as parents—appeared to think that they had little in common. There were three main groupings in the later nineteenth century. The most influential consisted of the more famous public schools and those grammar schools which were profoundly affected by them. Secondly there was a group consisting of the great mass of middle-class schools for boys. Thirdly, there was the expanding group of secondary schools for girls.

The first of the groups was, of course, by far the most influential. The staffs of the big public schools were regarded as the aristocracy of secondary school teachers; they were the best educated, the best paid, teaching under the best conditions and in some ways embodying much of what was regarded as best in English education. Lecturing at the Cambridge summer meeting for university extension students in 1900, Miss E. P. Hughes spoke of the schoolmasters as 'the only possible leaders of an united profession of teachers in England.' She added, '... we still wait for our leaders'.³ During the nineteenth century most of the masters in these schools were themselves drawn from Oxford and Cambridge, where they would have followed highly traditional courses. They would certainly never have come into contact with those who could not afford the relatively expensive university life and this would have included most elementary and middle class schoolmasters. For most of the century they would also not have come into contact with the other great excluded class, women. In many ways public school masters had little need of 'training' in the formal sense, but their disregard of it and the low opinion they showed for it was certainly one of the main obstacles to the creation of a system of training for secondary school teachers. The attitude of leading masters from the well-known schools may be illustrated from an episode recorded by R. H. Quick. In the Spring of 1875 Kay-Shuttleworth got together a committee of persons interested in establishing a training college for secondary masters. On 1st May it held a meeting with a group of headmasters; 'What we wanted was an expression of opinion from the H.M.'s that something ought to be done for training men before they were entrusted with a form in school, but bodies won't move without a leader, and somehow no headmaster there took a very keen interest in the matter.... The Masters said they had considered the thing over and over before, and had come to the conclusion that nothing could be done. On the whole they seemed rather bored, and were simply obstructive.'⁴

The very fact that training was widely introduced for elementary school teachers made it more difficult to introduce secondary training. The professional and social gap between public school and elementary school teachers made training for teaching itself seem to involve some loss of status for public school men. According to a letter from the Rev. Dr. E. Abbott, headmaster of the City of London School, which appeared in the *Spectator* in 1877, whenever he tried to advocate training for public school masters the question continually put to him was, 'Do you want to degrade the teachers of our public schools to the level of certificated masters?'⁵ The opposition was not always expressed in such crude social terms but more often seems to have taken the form of criticising the type of training given in the colleges and the professional competence of their products. F. W. Walker, once head of Manchester Grammar School and later of St. Paul's, was a very influential figure among the schoolmasters. He frequently expressed scepticism of any benefits claimed for training and believed positive harm resulted from training in teaching. On one such occasion in 1877 he explained that 'At Manchester I had among my assistants some first-rate trained masters, but there was a mechanical completeness about their teaching which was very deadening. Whatever was the subject, they had the whole thing completely at their fingers' ends, and when they had gone through it one felt the thing was done with, and one never wanted to hear of it again so long as they lived. There was no growth in the knowledge they implanted. It did not in the least inspire the desire for further knowledge. An intellectual man from the University might seem very inferior in teaching power, but the boys' minds were in the end more awakened by him, and there was endless power of growth in the man himself: he was not finished off like other men. Then as to class drill, we may have a great deal too much of it. Really good, inspiriting teaching is perhaps impossible with what is called by trained schoolmasters perfect order. I have found a good deal of seeming laxity of discipline in the forms of the very best teachers. I think, therefore, that a man who has the activity of mind and the general interests which our best University men have will do better in the schools themselves without any artificial system of training.'[6] Criticism of the allegedly narrow and mechanical training of the training colleges and their products came to be widely accepted by influential persons in the late nineteenth and early twentieth centuries; perhaps the best known expression of the view is to be found in the 'Holmes-Morant' circular of 1910.[7]

Dorothea Beale, a strong advocate of training for secondary teachers, countered such arguments as were advanced by F. W. Walker and those who were like-minded, by pointing out that the mechanical nature of the teaching in elementary schools was not because the teachers had been trained but rather because of the acute pressures set up by the impoverished circumstances surrounding elementary education; it 'was due, perhaps, to the fact that so few entered training colleges with a wide culture or habit of philosophic thought. There was, however, an equal loss when teachers with the necessary intellectual and moral qualifications lacked the power of maintaining order and adapting their knowledge to the minds of the children.'[8]

Miss Beale herself established a training department at Cheltenham Ladies' College, and from 1885 this department operated a full course in secondary school teaching for future mistresses. The very rapid growth of secondary and higher education for girls and women from the 1860s led to a demand for teachers which could not be met by any traditional means. It was only in 1879 that women were first admitted to degrees in the University of London, and Cambridge decided to admit them to the tripos examinations in 1881. The work of the National Union for Improving the Education of Women of all Classes was significant in the field of establishing girls' high schools, both through the part it played in setting up the Girls' Public Day School Company and through actively seeking to divert endowed funds to the support of girls' schools. One of the leading members of the National Union, Mrs. W. Grey, emphasised the need for professional as well as academic preparation for the mistresses. Miss Buss, at the North London Collegiate School, recruited her staff largely from among those who had learned something of teaching in the Governess Class of the Home and Colonial Training College.[9] The influence of these pioneers of women's education was considerable, and the obvious importance which they attached to training meant that girls' schools generally tended to attach some importance to evidence of professional qualification in their mistresses. Women found it advantageous, therefore, to submit to training. While the cause of professional training thus drew strength from the serious regard in which it was held in many of the girls' secondary schools, this proved in another way to be disadvantageous. If many of the public and secondary schoolmasters were liable to spurn training because the first class of teachers to be trained were *elementary* teachers, their prejudices tended to be confirmed by the fact that the second class were *women* secondary teachers.[10]

Against this background, the establishment and growth before 1890 of institutions for training secondary teachers made slow progress. The earliest significant institutional development was probably the foundation of the College of Preceptors in 1846. Its beginning lay in a group of teachers in Brighton getting together to help one another and to offer help to others in the field of professional practice. The new organisation soon moved to London and obtained a charter in 1849. It was especially designed for those teaching in private schools and the founders sought to improve the status of such teachers by improving their efficiency and qualifications and by establishing a register of qualified practitioners. From the earliest days, the College had organised lecture courses on various aspects of education. At a time when the English universities remained indifferent, the first professorship of education was established at the College, although it lapsed after a few years. After years of endeavour, enough money was accumulated by

1894 to start a training college for secondary teachers and this was set up, but the scheme failed and was abandoned in 1897. The increasing concern of the state with secondary education has effectively prevented most of those who teach in this field from becoming independent practitioners, not salaried but charging fees as with lawyers or medical practitioners. Consequently, although the College did useful work as a training institution, the hopes of its early members could hardly be fulfilled.[11]

From 1871 to 1877, in the wake of the Endowed Schools Commission, the Headmasters' Conference discussed the question of professional training at its annual meetings. While as individuals running schools and recruiting staff, the headmasters clearly attached virtually no importance to training, yet the Conference did in 1877 forward memorials to Oxford and Cambridge asking them to give consideration to this matter, to provide the kind of training required and to establish an examination leading to a certificate in education.[12] Schemes were drawn up by both universities in 1878. Oxford University rejected the scheme put forward. At Cambridge a committee which included Henry Sidgwick and Oscar Browning was set up by the University. It recommended that the University should take action with regard to theoretical training but it did not recommend it to undertake training in practical teaching.[13] Accordingly the Senate appointed a Teacher Training Syndicate in 1879 and authorised it to arrange for the delivery of certain courses of lectures and for the establishment of an examination in the theory, history and practice of education. The Syndicate was empowered to award certificates of practical efficiency to candidates who had already gained the certificate of theoretical efficiency and had taught for a year in schools approved by the Syndicate. The examinations proved to be a good deal more lasting than the lecture courses. Some idea of the difficulties into which the lectures ran may be obtained from the notebooks kept by R. H. Quick, the first to lecture for the Syndicate. '18 Oct. '79. First lecture on Education in University of Cambridge. This may prove an event in the history of the University, but no beginning could be less promising. There has been a notion in the minds of a few leading men, that the University should do something for the training of teachers. Nobody thought the opposite and so the scheme was allowed to pass. But who cares about the subject? The dons don't, and if they did they would naturally read about it rather than come to lectures. Undergraduates don't care about it . . . Today I found that my audience was composed almost entirely of young ladies from Newnham and Girton. There were from eighty to ninety of them and from ten to fifteen men. Besides Oscar Browning, who came officially, there were I think two dons and eight or ten young men. . . .'

'24 Oct '79 I gave my second lecture the day before yesterday. There was a falling-off from 100 to 68, but I believe some came to the first lecture who did not intend coming any more. There were about ten men at the second lecture. I am somewhat vexed that not a single one of my personal acquaintance, old or young, should have come, but this is a trifle. What is of much more moment is that the subject is utterly despised by the University public.'[14]

The lectures were soon abandoned, the examination was also largely ignored by men few of whose names were to be found in the examination lists. By the end of the century there had been some 1,500 successful candidates in the examination for teachers, only 60 of whom were men.[15] In 1881 the question of training was again discussed by the Headmasters' Conference and a further inquiry was sent round to the members in 1882. The response was so poor that the matter was dropped. The headmasters were very critical of the lack of organised school practice in the Cambridge scheme. They had themselves placed little emphasis on the need for this in their suggestions to the two Universities in 1877, but the fact that they had made such a suggestion —albeit a somewhat shadowy one—and that it had not been acted upon provided them with some sort of an excuse for failing to support that for which they were virtually responsible. Their standard of value in training became henceforth practice to the exclusion of theory.[16]

A further venture to provide training for men intending to teach in secondary schools was launched in 1882. Largely on the initiative of a small group of heads of middle-class schools for boys the Finsbury Training College was set up. It opened in January, 1883, in rooms lent to it at Cowper Street School by the corporation for middle-class education in London. The College never seems to have attracted more than about fifteen students and they were said to be 'men who had tried to teach, and had failed, or men who had not the confidence in their own powers'. The main difficulty was, of course, that 'it was not clear that it was to a young man's advantage to spend time and money, and to submit himself to training; it was not clear that it would secure him a higher salary afterwards. So that there was no evidence afforded by the College that it was to the man's advantage to go through the training, or rather, what I mean is, that it was not clear to the men who, it was hoped, would submit themselves to training, that the headmasters of schools would prefer a trained teacher to an untrained teacher.'[17] Thus in October, 1886, the College was closed, partly for want of support from headmasters and partly from want of funds.

The sad experience of the Finsbury Training College affair served merely to illustrate further the lessons which the history of the Cambridge Syndicate itself illustrated. In a letter to *The Times* in 1887, Oscar Browning, Secretary of the Syndicate, pointed out that while the Cambridge examinations were becoming more important every year to women teachers, they had almost ceased by this time to have any effect upon the supply of qualified men. In 1884 only 3 out of 29 candidates were men, in 1885 only 7 out of 35, and in 1886 only 3 out of 56. 'This is due', he wrote, 'to one cause, and to one cause only—the indifference of the headmasters of our public schools. Cambridge sends out every year a large number of young men anxious to adopt the teaching profession. The competition is very keen. Men wishing to be schoolmasters would be ready to do anything to improve their chance of gaining a post. If it were felt that the headmasters set the slightest value on the possession of the University certificate, or on evidence of attendance at lectures, such as the University supplies on the theory and practice of education, our class and examination rooms would be crowded. At present this is by no means the case. While distinction in athletics is known to be a very marketable commodity, a teacher's training is considered to be of no value. The few male students who come to us are drawn, not by any prospect of gain, but by a desire to know something of the theory of the profession to which they intend to dedicate their lives. . . . All professions, learned and unlearned, are nowadays guarded by examinations. The teacher, or, I should say in fairness, the male teacher alone is supposed to know his arduous duties by intuition.'[18]

A few days later a further letter on this subject appeared in *The Times* in reply to Browning. It was written by H. Kynaston, headmaster of Cheltenham College, and part of it is, perhaps, worth quoting, since it sets out the sort of argument which was to be used on countless occasions in the years to come by headmasters of famous schools and others against the training of secondary school teachers. It spoke of 'a certificate which gives no real guarantee that its holder will not fail when he comes to meet his class and to deal by the application of lecture-taught rules with the manifold temperaments which are there placed under his control. He will have to face numberless problems, for any solution of which he will ransack in vain the pigeon-holes of his stored pedagogik. It is surely impossible to certify by examination that any man is a practically efficient teacher, and if he is not his theory is worthless. The subtle influence over boys which characterizes a "good disciplinarian" is a quality which cannot be imparted by lectures. We cannot tell how it is acquired. . . . Anyone who has been educated at a public school has had a previous training which, if he is a man of intelligence and sound common sense, must be of service to him as a teacher in a public school. For he has vivid recollection of the methods of his former teachers—of the reason why this one failed and that one succeeded; and he knows what are the difficulties of public school boys and why they can get on with one master and not with another.'[19]

In these circumstances it is not surprising that progress in the 1880s and 1890s continued to be mainly confined to the training of women, and one of the earliest successful foundations for training secondary teachers was the Cambridge Training College for Women, founded in 1885 and later to be known as Hughes Hall. It was the first residential secondary training college and the first to utilise lectures on education given at a university. It was also the first to have a large proportion of graduates among its students. The College might indeed have begun 'under the beneficent shadow' of the University of Cambridge as Miss Hughes later put it,[20] but the University was far from being its founder. It began in two small cottages, virtually without funds and it owed much of its success to the energy shown by Miss Hughes as its first principal. A few friends guaranteed the working expenses of the first year and four schools allowed the students facilities for school practice. During the first six years of its existence the College struggled on with inadequate accommodation. In 1893 a grant of £3,000 from the Pfieffer Trustees and additional subscriptions of £2,000 made it possible to erect a college building to accommodate 50 students, which was formally opened in 1895.[21]

As early as 1877 the Teachers Training and Registration Society had been established. Under its auspices a college was opened in Bishopsgate in 1878 to provide systematic training for young women intending to take up secondary teaching. The institution flourished and moved to larger premises in 1885 taking the title of Maria Grey Training College to commemorate the part played by Mrs. William Grey in its foundation. The College moved again in 1892 to Brondesbury, where a new building made more adequate provision both for the college itself and for an associated high school. The students were prepared for the teachers' certificate examination which Cambridge had begun to offer in 1880. Apart from regular school practice, the Brondesbury and Kilburn High School was handed over for two days at the end of the autumn and spring terms to the students, one of whom was appointed as 'head mistress' by the principal. The main education courses were in logic, methods, theory and history of education; there were also lessons in physiology and hygiene, in voice production and in Swedish drill.[22]

The strongly contrasting views held by leading figures in the fields of boys' and girls' secondary education which had produced this wide disparity in the training undertaken by men and women in the late nineteenth century found expression both in the evidence offered to the Select Committee on the Teachers' Registration and Organisation Bill of 1891, and to the Bryce Commission.

When the Select Committee of 1891 examined G. C. Bell, headmaster of Marlborough and Chairman of the H.M.C.'s Committee on Registration, he was asked whether he could tell the Committee if headmasters as represented at the Conference were in favour of a system of training teachers. He replied accurately enough, 'Well, they are, and they are not; that is to say, by their resolutions and their votes they seem to be in favour of urging a system of training teachers... but there seems to be a want of some impulse to bring them into connection with the schemes when actually formulated with the universities.'[23] The memorandum which the Conference submitted to the Bryce Commission in response to a set of questions agreed very briefly that it was desirable that persons wishing to teach in secondary schools should receive some professional training and that this 'should include arrangements suitable to persons actually engaged in school work'.[24]

The two representatives of the Association of Headmistresses who appeared before the Bryce Commission made it clear that they believed it to be 'most essential' that training in teaching should be made a necessary qualification for those seeking to work in secondary schools. The Association felt that it was not yet clear which was the best way of organising the training. Training colleges for secondary teaching such as the Maria Grey—a day college—or the Cambridge college—residential—which made use of local schools for practice purposes, had much to offer. So too had training colleges attached to large secondary schools, such as that attached to Cheltenham Ladies' College. The third approach to secondary training the witnesses considered to have been much less successful. It involved attaching student teachers to schools which undertook to make adequate provision for theoretical and practical training. This system, which some headmasters came to advocate in the next century, one of the witnesses, Miss Day who was headmistress of Manchester High School, had operated in her school. She had abandoned it because she felt the professional training which one school could offer was narrow and constricting by comparison with what a college could give its students. The headmistresses also attacked the idea of a two-year period of probation as a substitute for training—an idea which received some support in the 1890s. Such probation would be a 'sham altogether and an evasion of principle' since no training was involved and the probationer was to be paid a salary and regarded as a member of the school staff. Moreover, the system of probation would be injurious to the pupils on whom the probationers in their ignorance would be free to experiment.[25]

The Assistant Mistresses' Association agreed with the Headmistresses in condemning the proposed system of probation on the grounds that there was no guarantee that such probationers would ever get any systematic training in teaching. Miss Lumby of Cheltenham Ladies' College, who was president of the Association of Assistant Mistresses, told the Bryce Commission that her Association was anxious to see courses in professional training for teachers following on from what she called the 'knowledge qualification'. Such courses should not be more than a year in length so that they could follow a University degree without making the total amount of time spent in preparing to teach inordinately long. The necessary financial support for students during the period of training should come through scholarships, either awarded by the central government or by the technical instruction Committees.[26]

The evidence offered by representatives of the Association of Assistant Masters agreed broadly with that of the mistresses. Their witnesses hoped that the normal pattern of qualification for those entering secondary school teaching would be a university degree followed by professional training. Too often what happened in fact was that a young graduate came directly from getting his degree and found himself set to teach the lowest forms in a school 'where the greatest amount of skill and the most patience and the greatest experience are required'. The professional training ought to include the mental and moral sciences so far as they related to the work of the teacher, the organisation and management of secondary schools, the methods of teaching the main school subjects, the educational systems of other countries and the history of education.[27]

In one sense the strongest advocate of professional training as a compulsory requirement before appointing teachers in secondary schools was the N.U.T. In its memorandum to the Bryce Commission it urged that no teacher should be recognised in any school which received public money who did not hold a certificate of proficiency in the art of teaching which had been 'issued or approved by the Education Department'. But even the secondary associations most enthusiastic for a teaching qualification would certainly not have agreed with the N.U.T. that 'the provision to be made for training in the profession of teaching should be the same for teachers in all classes of schools'.[28] One of the witnesses from the Association of Assistant Masters pointed out that the organisation and management of a secondary school was very different from that of an elementary school and was likely to remain so, indeed, the witness could not 'conceive that a secondary school could be cast on the same model as an elementary school'.

The Bryce Commission itself went no further than to suggest it was 'generally desirable' that those who intended to enter secondary teaching should take a course of special preparation for it. The Commissioners explained that while some persons were natural teachers and while others would never be any good, no matter how much training they were given, between these extremes there were many 'whose natural capacities, be they greater or smaller, may be substantially improved by the special preparation which is contemplated: and even persons whose natural gift is unmistakable may have something to learn from the accumulated experience of those who have studied the subject and become practical experts in it.' The actual courses of training should include the theoretical study of the branches of learning which underlie education as well as subject teaching methods. The practical side should include observation of experienced teachers at work as well as actually giving lessons. The theoretical and practical sides ought to be carried forward concurrently, since the more closely they could be associated, the more they would support each other.[29]

The Commission found a consensus of opinion in favour of associating the professional training of teachers as closely as possible with the universities. In 1876 J. G. Fitch, H.M. Inspector of Training Colleges, in what proved to be an almost prophetic article, had advocated training courses for secondary teachers and suggested that the universities should assume responsibility for this. He looked forward to chairs being established in education and the institution of the necessary courses and diplomas. He did not favour either the setting up of separate training colleges or the establishment of a form of quasi-apprenticeship, although he recognised that both could be of some value. The secondary teacher ought to receive his general education in the company of students intending to enter other professions. 'The truth is that special isolated training for any profession is justifiable within very narrow limits, and for certain distinctly defined purposes. . . . Theological colleges, medical schools, legal universities, are defensible only on the supposition that they supplement, not supersede, other places of instruction, and that their students have first received in the midst of other and broader associations, that general knowledge and discipline which are common to all professions. Otherwise all such institutions have a fatal tendency to obscure in the mind of the student the true relations between his own professional employment and the larger world of duty and of mental activity in which those employments are to find a place.' Fitch had hoped for the recognition of teaching as a learned profession for which it was the business of universities to furnish definite preparation. 'Side by side with schools of medicine, of divinity and of law, it is expedient that a faculty of education should find a distinct and honoured place, so that the man who proposes to devote his life to tuition may find in the quarter in which he is best entitled to look for it —in his own university—the help and guidance needed to equip him for the task, and may obtain from that university an appropriate diploma which may serve as a passport to professional success.'[30] Fitch continued to campaign on these lines for the next twenty years. When day training colleges came to be set up by university colleges for elementary teachers, he drew attention to the advantages that would accrue if they were also used for training secondary teachers. He pointed out in 1893 how few were the institutions offering secondary training and how great the need for trained persons; the newly-founded university day training departments were ideally suited to meet the need and they should expand into the secondary field.[31]

The Bryce Commission reported that the experience of Cambridge University showed the need for theory and practice to be regarded as a single whole, to be undertaken by one body. The Commission drew attention to Arthur Sidgwick's proposals. He divided the training process into three parts, the study of the theory and history of education, school practice and finally 'a prolonged period of trial where the student is teaching largely by himself but under the general supervision of an experienced person'. The first two stages might well form part of the training organised by a university, the third stage really amounted to a period of probation in a school. But the Commission found itself unable really to define the most desirable or suitable way of organising training and concluded that there would 'no doubt be room and need for other experiments'.[32]

Following the Report of the Bryce Commission, the Summer meeting of the I.A.H.M. in 1896 resolved to appoint a committee and report on the best practical method of training teachers for secondary schools. This led to a wide approach and in 1897 the Training of Teachers Joint Committee was appointed, which also included representatives of the headmistresses, the assistant masters and mistresses, the College of Preceptors, the Teachers' Guild, and the Preparatory Schools Association. It issued a report in 1897 which was important, for it summarised for the first time the agreed opinions of the organised secondary school teachers on preparation for their calling.[33] This preparation for teaching they saw as falling into two phases, the first the continuation of general education up to at least the pass degree standard, the second a period of professional training. The teaching diploma itself should certify proficiency in both the theory and practice of education. The theoretical studies should include elementary psychology, ethics, logic, physiology, school hygiene, school administration, history of education and the study of teaching methods. Under practice were included model lessons, criticism lessons and actual practice in teaching. The shortest period of professional training which ought to be contemplated was a year. Institutions in which professional training was given should, if possible, be organically connected with universities or university colleges; if connected with a school, as at Cheltenham Ladies' College, the training department should be separately staffed and organised. Full responsibility should lie with the institution for all aspects of training, practical as well as theoretical. It was felt to be inadvisable that the work of secondary training should be tacked on to a training college for elementary teachers, since the general attainments of the two classes of teachers differed so widely. The staff of a training institution should consist of lecturers of university standing who had also had experience as teachers in secondary schools and who had made a study of some aspect of education.

The Headmasters' Conference was not represented on the Joint Committee, although many of its members were, through their overlapping membership of the I.A.H.M. The absence of the H.M.C. from the Joint Committee was commented on by the *Journal of Education*, which felt it a pity that the headmasters of the H.M.C. did not cooperate more readily in this field, but, it claimed, the reasons for this were obvious. 'Dr. James and Dr. Warre (two leading members) are a dead weight, and a very heavy dead weight, in the balance opposed to professional training. And, secondly, the large public schools are able to get the pick of schoolmasters, and therefore the need of training is not so directly felt.'[34]

The increasing concern shown by most of the secondary teachers' organisations was partly due to changes in the curriculum in the schools themselves. These changes increasingly led to the recognition of teaching particular subjects as an art requiring special preparation. An increasing amount of time was given to the newer subjects such as history, science and modern languages. The new methods advocated for teaching some of these subjects could clearly not be taught by teachers simply on the basis of their own experiences as pupils. Particularly influential in this respect was the introduction of direct methods of language teaching and of heuristic methods of teaching science. A further significant influence was the application of a more scientific attitude of mind to the study of education itself.

Against this background of increasing interest in training among the secondary teachers themselves, one of the most interesting and successful school-based training schemes was established. The originator of the scheme was Mrs. Sophie Bryant, headmistress of the North London Collegiate School. The essential feature of her scheme was that the school took ultimate responsibility for the students' training while the university was to provide the broad principles.[35] This scheme, confined to graduates, was operated by the North London Collegiate School itself and by a group of high schools of the G.P.D.S.C., including Blackheath, Croydon and Notting Hill. Each School was allowed to take one student teacher to every fifty pupils and charged a fee of £8 for a term of training. The student was to take between three and ten lessons each week. Arrangements were made with the London Day Training College for students to attend lectures in the afternoon. Senior staff of the school supervised practice and were paid a fee for so doing.[36]

The making available of public money from local sources for the aiding and later for the foundation of secondary schools, through the operation of the technical instruction legislation of 1889-91 and the Education Act of 1902, led to a rapid expansion in the size of the secondary school teaching force. The growth of the municipal secondary schools created a demand for secondary teachers among a group of employers who also employed large numbers of trained elementary teachers. These developments added to the urgency of the need for a more systematic provision of secondary training. In 1908 Morant stated quite bluntly that the existing sources of supply of teachers had not been adequate to meet the needs of the greatly increased number of secondary schools which had come under the cognisance of the Board of Education. He claimed also that inspection by H.M.I.s had disclosed faults in many schools which systematic training would have done much to avoid, and went on to express the hope that 'so real a growth of opinion has taken place in favour of giving to teachers destined for secondary schools a technical preparation for their profession, that there may be some likelihood that the wider opportunities for training now provided will in future be utilised.'[37]

These were the factors which led the Board of Education to issue the first set of Regulations for the Training of Teachers for Secondary Schools in 1908. As well as recognising existing secondary training colleges or departments for grant purposes, the Regulations also offered recognition and grant-aid to the few specially organised secondary schools where 'a great deal of excellent training work is being carried on', although grant was only payable in cases where a minimum of ten students could be trained in this way. The Board sought to ensure an adequate academic standard by refusing to pay grant unless entry to the one-year course was restricted to graduates, and the course itself had to be confined to purely professional work. The course had to include a reasonable balance of school observation and practice as well as the lectures on the theoretical studies. At least half of the staff of a college or training department were required to have had experience in teaching in secondary schools. In justifying this requirement the Board appeared to accept the arguments put forward to the Bryce Commission by the secondary teachers' associations and to reject the view of the N.U.T., for while it agreed that there was a great deal that was common to the needs of all kinds of teachers, it explained that the effective handling of the subjects and the pupils of the different types of secondary schools called for familiarity with the conditions of teaching peculiar to such schools, as distinguished from teaching in elementary schools or in universities. Grant was offered at the rate of £100 in respect of every five students, provided that it should not exceed one half of the sum paid for salaries for work in the secondary training department. Morant explained that the intention of this condition was to encourage the payment of higher salaries to staff and the recruitment of better qualified teaching staff since 'It is certain that, while the work of most of the training colleges for secondary school teachers has been well done, yet they have often been unable to supply themselves with staffs of sufficiently high standing and experience to command general respect.'[38] The total sum of money available for paying grants was limited to £5,000. It should, perhaps, be added at this point that the Regulations for Secondary Schools for 1907 and for 1908 contained a paragraph suggesting that the Board might require a certain proportion of all new appointments to consist of persons who had taken an approved course of training.

The first inspections of institutions applying for grant under these regulations resulted in 17 being recognised, and 171 students, 156 women and 15 men, were regarded by the Board as having completed a period of training during the year. Grants totalling £1,900 were paid to 10 institutions, of which 5 formed part of a University. The institutions giving training were said to contrast strongly between those which pivoted upon a university and those centred on the schools in which the practice was undertaken. The universities were said to be severely handicapped by not having their own demonstration schools, whereas students who were school-based could more easily be placed under the care of specialists and could more certainly derive profit from their practice than if they were based on a university or college and attended a school from time to time.[39]

The main effort to provide training was in secondary training colleges or departments, often forming part of university day training colleges—or departments of education as they were coming to be known—but there was no marked increase in the number of graduate students coming forward to be trained in them. In its Report for 1911–12, the Board remarked that the number of students trained was far from sufficient to fill the vacancies in the secondary schools and that the existing institutions seemed unlikely to cover the whole field. Certainly by the end of the first decade of this century there was evidence of a great deal of feeling among secondary school teachers against the amount of 'theory' in training courses and in favour of more 'practice'.[40] Some evidence of this feeling may be seen in the number of schemes suggested for school-based training—though few of them were ever established. At their annual Conference of 1912, the Headmistresses passed a resolution reaffirming the need for teachers to take a course of professional training following their academic course and welcoming experimentation in different types of professional training. One scheme was put forward for the consideration of the A.H.M. Committee whereby a graduate would serve two years in an approved school as a 'teacher in training'. An approved school was one where at least half the staff were graduates and the headmistress was to guarantee an adequate amount of efficient supervision and facilities for observing lessons. The teacher in training was to be required to write a thesis on a subject approved by a university examiner. During training the teacher would be paid a salary to cover living costs.[41]

The Board of Education undertook a series of somewhat protracted negotiations with the H.M.C. and other teachers' associations about schemes of this sort, and in 1913 the secondary training Regulations provided that any school on the recognised list of secondary schools might apply to the Board of Education for leave to receive one, two or three teachers in training. The Board required proof that the head teacher or some other senior member of staff was specially qualified and had the time and interest to supervise the training. A course of study in the practice and principles of teaching, extending over a full school year, was to be submitted for the approval of the Board. The student teachers had to be graduates of not less than 21 years. Grants were offered to schools at the rate of £40 for the first, £30 for the second and £20 for the third student in training. At the end of the year the Board would endorse the certificate issued by the school. In the first draft of these regulations, circulated for discussion, only boys' schools were to be included, apparently on the grounds that the existing training institutions already attracted future women teachers, and the problem lay in attracting men. This led to strong protests from the headmistresses, and girls' schools were then included.

According to the *Journal of Education* the scheme was no more than a 'pill against the earthquake'. 'The Board has for years been proclaiming that the chief blot on our secondary education is that the teachers are untrained, and its main object in reconstituting the Registration Council was to promote training. But how can the Council insist on training as a qualification till there is sufficient provision of normal schools or colleges?'[42] G. E. Hodgson, head of the secondary training department at Bristol University, expressed the resentment felt by those already in this field when she pointed out that a university department could only qualify for grant at the rate of £10 per student and then only if it had at least 10 students. She feared that teachers might tend increasingly to be trained in the schools in which they had been pupils and thought that the new regulations were designed to reduce the number of students training in universities.[43]

In fact the Report of the Board for the year 1913-14 showed that the new regulations had achieved very little impact. Few applications for the recognition of arrangements for training in approved secondary schools had been received. At Rugby and at Exeter Girls' School teachers in training had been recognised conditionally on their completing a year of training satisfactorily. The Board's recognition of a school for training was limited to certain subjects, at the Exeter Girls' School, for instance, the approved subjects were English, history, modern languages and science.[44]

Thus at the outbreak of the First World War the problem of training for secondary school teachers had not been settled. The teachers' associations themselves had perhaps been more concerned with the issue of registration in the early years of this century. The question of training is, of course, very closely related to that of registration, but much of the time and energy of the secondary associations was directed more urgently to such issues as the form that registration should take and how much influence the different groups of teachers were to have over the machinery established.

NOTES

1. Annual Reports of the Board of Education for 1909–10 to 1913–14.
2. Statistics of Public Education, 1912–13, Part I, Table 38.
3. E. P. Hughes, 'The Training of Teachers', a lecture published in R. D. Roberts (ed.), *Education in the Nineteenth Century*, 1901, p. 176.
4. F. Storr (ed.), *Life and Remains of the Rev. R. H. Quick*, 1899, p. 352.
5. Letter from Rev. Dr. Abbott in *The Spectator*, 24/2/77, quoted by M. G. Fitch, *The History of the Training of Teachers for Secondary Schools in England*, unpublished London M.A. thesis, 1931, p. 281.
6. Storr (ed), op. cit., p. 357.
7. *Infra.*, pp. 333–4.
8. Dorothea Beale, 'On the Training of Teachers for High Schools', paper read to the Education Section, *Transactions of the National Association for the Promotion of Social Science*, 1878, p. 432.
9. *The Training of Women Teachers for Secondary Schools*. Board of Education Pamphlet No. 23, 1912, p. 4.
10. Hughes, op. cit., p. 184.
11. For the part played by the College of Preceptors in the Teachers' Registration Movement, see chapter 11.

12. Board of Education, Pamphlet No. 23, 1912, pp. 4–5.
13. *Cambridge University Reporter*, June, 1878, p. 626.
14. Storr (ed), op. cit., pp. 75–7.
15. E. P. Hughes, op. cit., p. 181.
16. M. G. Fitch, 'The History of the Training of Teachers for Secondary Schools in England', unpublished thesis, London M.A., 1931, p. 252.
17. Select Committee on the Teachers' Registration and Organisation Bill, Report and Evidence, 1891, p. 28, evidence of Dr. R. Wormell, headmaster of the City Middle Class Schools, Cowper Street.
18. *The Times*, 2nd April, 1887.
19. Ibid., 8th April, 1887.
20. Hughes, op. cit., p. 182.
21. Board of Education, Pamphlet No. 23, 1912, pp. 29–30.
22. Ibid., pp. 43–45.
23. Select Committee of 1891, p. 60.
24. Bryce Cssn., 1895, vol. V, p. 314.
25. Ibid., vol. IV, pp. 28–30.
26. Ibid., pp. 49–51.
27. Ibid., p. 150.
28. Ibid., vol. V, p. 325.
29. Ibid., vol. I, pp. 322–3.
30. J. G. Fitch, 'The Universities and the Training of Teachers', *Contemporary Review*, December, 1876, pp. 108–10.
31. Report of the Committee of Council on Education for 1892–3, 1893, p. 159.
32. Bryce Cssn., 1895, vol. I, p. 207.
33. Training of Teachers Joint Committee, Summary of Report and proceedings, 1897.
34. *Journal of Education*, April, 1897, p. 216.
35. J. Adams, 'Work for the Training of Teachers in London', in the private memorial publication *Sophie Bryant, D.Sc., Litt.D., 1850–1922*, 1922, p. 47.
36. Girls' Public Day School Company Ltd., *Provisional Scheme for Training Graduate Teachers*, 1902.
37. Board of Education, Regulations for the Training of Teachers for Secondary Schools, 1908. Preparatory Memorandum by R. L. Morant, p. iii.
38. Ibid., p. v.
39. Report of the Board of Education for 1908–9, 1909, pp. 166–7.

40. G. E. Hodgson, 'The Training of Secondary Teachers', *Journal of Education*, November, 1910, pp. 719–20.
41. *Journal of Education*, July, 1912, p. 496.
42. Ibid., August, 1913, pp. 553–4.
43. Ibid., September, 1913, p. 627.
44. Report of the Board of Education for 1913–14, 1914, p. 172.

11
The Teachers' Registration Issue

Closely linked to the question of requiring training of those who intended to teach was the issue of registration.

Pressure for a register of teachers was associated from the first with the College of Preceptors (1846). In one sense the College was an expression among schoolmasters of the widespread movement in the professions during the second quarter of the nineteenth century to set up organisations to represent their group interests. The earliest of these seems to have been the Law Society (1825). A few years later the Royal Institute of British Architects and the Provincial Medical and Surgical Association were set up (1832); the latter became the British Medical Association in 1856. The General Medical Council was established by Act of Parliament in 1858. It consisted entirely of members of the medical profession, had power to maintain a register of qualified medical practitioners, to lay down qualifications for admission to the register and to strike off the register any person deemed guilty of 'infamous conduct'—a term which the Council itself interpreted. The success of the medical practitioners in gaining a council and register encouraged the College of Preceptors in its attempt to achieve comparable legislation. Commenting on the Medical Act in 1862 the Journal of the College stated that 'it is obvious that the object of the Act is simply to exclude incompetent men from the practice of Medicine, and to enable the public to distinguish qualified from unqualified practitioners. . . . A Scholastic Council, formed on a plan analogous to the constitution of the General Medical Council, would represent the interests of education and of educators without favour or partiality towards any particular college, society, or system of education; while teachers would be as free and independent in the management of their schools, and in their methods of teaching as at present. Qualified educators would be registered irrespectively of their religious opinions or denominations, the only conditions being competency to instruct and good moral character.'[1]

In 1864 an attempt was made to widen the support for a council and register by setting up the General Committee of the Association for promoting Scholastic Registration. The membership included schoolmasters from endowed schools, proprietary schools, private schools, and schools for the 'industrial classes'. The secretary to this body, B. Rule, Principal of Aldershot Classical and Mathematical School, explained to the Taunton Commission the view of his association 'that a Scholastic Registration Act, analogous in its main provisions to the Medical Act of 1858, might be passed; that at the time of its passing all *bona fide* schoolmasters in the country should be entitled to be registered; that after some given date only those should be registered who had one or more of the qualifications stated in the Act; that no name should be struck off the register except for offences specified in the Act, or in case of death; and that any unregistered person assuming any title or designation mentioned in the Act as being restricted to duly registered persons, should be liable to a penalty.'[2] In answer to questions, Rule explained that it was not intended to forbid the unregistered to teach but it was expected that parents would, in fact, discriminate in favour of those schoolmasters who were on the register. He implied that there was a further parallel here with the medical register, for those not on the register could still practise, they were merely unable to sue for payment of fees.

The Commission was not entirely convinced by the arguments put before it. But it did suggest a system of certificates and examinations for those who intended to be teachers, the system to be operated by a central council of examinations on which the universities were to be represented; there were to be 6 Crown and 6 university nominees. A system of examination and certificates 'would meet without further difficulty the chief desire of those, who are seeking for a Scholastic Registration Act. The Register of those, who had obtained such certificates, as we describe, would be precisely such a register, as these witnesses appear to desire; and we do not see the need of any further legislation for the purpose, than would be necessary to work out what we now propose. For although there were some, who spoke of disallowing the recovery of school fees, except by teachers who had been registered, and some even proposed, that teachers, who had not been registered, should be altogether prohibited from keeping private schools, we are not of opinion that it would be expedient to go beyond permitting all teachers to be candidates for certificates, and requiring all masters of endowed schools to have obtained them.'³

The general state of inefficiency in the secondary schools revealed by the report of the Taunton Commission led to the Endowed Schools Bill which was introduced in the Commons by W. E. Forster in 1869. A second part of this, known at the time as 'Mr. Forster's Bill No. 2', made certain provisions for the organisation of secondary education and for the examination and registration of teachers, other than elementary. An educational council was to be set up, consisting half of members nominated by the Crown and half of those nominated by the Universities, whose duties were to include:

(1) Drawing up rules and making arrangements for the examination of persons who were teachers or wished to become teachers and applied to be so examined;
(2) Granting certificates to teachers who had passed their examinations and keeping a register of persons having such certificates;
(3) Examining annually the pupils in endowed schools.⁴

The private schools were also to be encouraged to reform themselves voluntarily by taking advantage of this machinery. Forster explained to the Commons that while the government was naturally anxious to avoid any interference with the right of private schoolmasters, it felt 'it would be nothing less than a boon to private schoolmasters to offer them the same examination as was made compulsory in the case of masters of endowed schools.'⁵

Forster's proposals for the certification and registration of teachers by a state body which would also examine the pupils in middle-class schools was not really the sort of professional self-government sought by the Scholastic Registration Association. The scheme for an educational council examining pupils annually in order to test the efficiency of middle-class schools met with much opposition from the heads of endowed and proprietary schools. The exclusion of teachers in the elementary schools from the proposed scheme of certification and registration aroused the hostility of the organised elementary school teachers, while even some members of the Liberal Party in the Commons suspected Mr. Forster's No. 2 Bill to be an unwarrantable interference with the liberty of the subject.⁶ The Bill was dropped before it could secure a second reading, and the attention of politicians and administrators was turned to the Elementary Education Act of 1870 and the problems which flowed from it for some years. The episode of the dropped bill was important for a number of reasons; some of the ideas it contained were to be revived from time to time in the next half-century and the varying and opposed attitudes taken up by different groups of teachers were indicative of the attitudes which the same groups would assume on occasion in the years to come.

The question of a register continued to occupy much of the energy of the College of Preceptors in the years following 1870, and the call for action was made repeatedly.[7] In 1879 Lyon Playfair introduced a Teachers' Registration Bill on behalf of the College of Preceptors. This reproduced Forster's educational council with the modification that a quarter of its members were to be elected by the general body of registered teachers, so that the Council would no longer be a State body with university representation, but would be at least partly representative and would be more akin to the body sought by those who hoped to see a self-governing profession.[8] This measure would again have applied only to secondary schools and excluded elementary teachers. The N.U.E.T. opposed the Bill on the grounds that it 'set up a distinct line of separation between the certificated teachers and all other parts of the scholastic profession'. Local associations of the Union brought pressure to bear upon their M.P.s to oppose the measure and the promoters finally withdrew it.[9] With certain modifications the Bill was reintroduced in 1881 by Sir John Lubbock, but again it failed to make any progress.

The general notion of registration for teachers was supported by the N.U.E.T. as early as the 1870s; it was the exclusion of certificated elementary teachers which occasioned their opposition. In a paper to the education section of the National Association for the Promotion of Social Science in 1878, T. E. Heller, secretary of the N.U.E.T., urged that legislation should be enacted to enforce registration. The public needed to be protected from 'educational pretenders' and incompetent teachers, while qualified and capable teachers themselves deserved some protection from 'educational quackery', and some means of being distinguished from the impostors and charlatans who infested the private schools. The law did not permit unqualified persons to practise as doctors or lawyers, and it was quite as important that the public should be protected from the danger of employing unqualified and incompetent teachers. There should be a scholastic register for all kinds of teacher, and entry to it should eventually depend upon scholarship, professional skill and practical experience. The proposal of the

N.U.E.T. for a Representative Educational Council including elementary teachers would furnish the requisite machinery to operate such a register. As well as its certification and registration functions, such a Council would fulfil a useful consultative role alongside a remodelled Ministry of Education.[10]

I THE SELECT COMMITTEE OF 1891

The question of whether a register should be confined to secondary school teachers or whether it should include all school teachers became acute again in 1890 and was the main reason for the setting up of a Select Committee in 1891. In 1890 there were two registration bills before the House of Commons. The first was introduced by Sir Richard Temple and was a College of Preceptors measure confined to the registration of secondary teachers in England and Wales, excluding from its scope the seven schools to which the Public Schools Act of 1868 applied as well as all elementary schools. It sought to set up an educational council of 16; the Education Department, the Universities of Oxford, Cambridge and London and the College of Preceptors would each appoint two members; initially the Crown would nominate the other 6, but 4 of these would subsequently be elected by the registered teachers. The council was to administer a register of those teaching in schools under the bill, the qualifications for admission to this to include possession of a degree, or membership by examination of the College of Preceptors, but there was no insistence on training as such as an essential qualification for registration. The second bill was introduced by Arthur Acland with the support of the Teachers' Guild, and there were three main points of difference. It was not confined to secondary teachers but included all school teachers in the British Isles. Secondly, it insisted on training as the essential qualification for registration. Finally, it proposed the double sanction of excluding unregistered teachers from appointments in endowed schools and excluding them from using the law courts to recover tuition fees, by analogy with the Medical Registration Act of 1858.[11] In these circumstances Acland's educational council was also more widely based among teachers, since it sought to add to Temple's council one member from each of the other universities of the United Kingdom and 2 from each of the N.U.T., the Teachers' Guild, the Irish National Teachers' Association and the

Educational Institute of Scotland, and one member each from the Headmasters' Conference and the Association of Headmistresses. Both the Temple and Acland Bills reached a second reading in the Commons and were then referred to the Select Committee which was appointed on 5th March, 1891, and reported four months later.

During the course of its inquiry the Select Committee heard the opinions of a large number of educational witnesses, some of whom gave evidence simply as individuals and some of whom represented the views of teachers' organisations. On the general question of registration the great majority of witnesses favoured it in some form or other. One of the few to be opposed to it was Miss Collett, President of the Association of Assistant Mistresses, who gave evidence against both Bills, largely on the grounds that they were premature. The extent to which her views represented those of the A.A.M. is not clear, since she stated that the association had not been thoroughly sounded on this matter. Sir Arthur Sullivan, as a member of the Council of the Royal College of Music and former Principal of the National Training School for Music, protested on behalf of his Council against the inclusion of music teachers in any scheme of registration for teachers. He admitted, however, that if the Royal College and Royal Academy of Music were alone recognised by the proposed council as competent to give certificates to music teachers, then much of the objection to registration would be removed.

Most of the teachers' associations followed a predictable line in their evidence. The Association of Head Masters favoured compulsory registration on the lines suggested by the Temple bill, that is to say to the exclusion of elementary teachers. According to the Rev. R. B. Poole, Chairman of the Committee of the Association, 'We consider that they are sufficiently organised already by the Education Department; that any further organisation in the way of registration with them is therefore unnecessary; and we also consider that, unless some arrangements could be made for obviating it, they, in electing members to serve on the Council, would completely swamp all the masters of the secondary schools, their numbers being, of course, very considerably greater.'[12] Poole was asked what advantage registration would be to masters in public schools. He replied that 'from our own point of view, we care for registration a great deal more for the sake of the profession, as a profession, than for any advantage that we shall gain ourselves by it.'[13]

C. R. Hodgson, secretary to the College of Preceptors, naturally defended Temple's Bill. He gave three reasons for excluding elementary teachers from the register. In the first place, they were already registered by the Education Department; secondly, if they were registered under the Bill they would have to be represented in proportion to their numbers, but one of the chief functions of the council would be the inspection of examinations, so that necessarily the examinations of the Education Department would come under purview and it was extremely probable that elementary teachers on the Council might like to exercise their rights and criticise the position of the Education Department with regard to their certificates; and finally the elementary teachers would have a 'preponderating influence' on the educational council by virtue of their numbers.[14]

Those witnesses who hoped to see a General Council and a Register for Secondary Teachers feared that the inclusion of elementary teachers would undermine their aim of making secondary school teaching a self-governing profession on the lines of medicine. The large number of elementary school teachers by comparison with secondary school teachers meant that under any sort of democratic, representative, system, the elementary teachers would probably predominate in any general council. Moreover, the graduate masters teaching in an established public school or endowed grammar school were held in considerably greater public esteem than were elementary school teachers, and while it might be possible to persuade the public and their parliamentary representatives to treat the former with much the same sort of regard as medical practitioners, they would certainly not extend such regard and professional self-government to an occupational group dominated by elementary teachers.

The elementary teachers were determined not to be excluded from any organisation of the teaching profession which might be set up. Their view was put to the Select Committee by G. Girling, a London School Board inspector, representative of the N.U.T. and an ex-President of the Union. He spoke strongly in favour of Acland's Bill, 'I believe it is a bad thing for any country to have very sharp lines between the teachers of the country. There have been such lines in this country, and, I think, that a Bill of the kind of one of those before the Committee today would accentuate that. . . . Again, the elementary teachers of the country, so called, are the only ones in the country who have been specially trained for their work. . . .'[15]

What might be described as an official's view was put by J. G. Fitch, H.M. Inspector of Training Colleges, who dwelt on the dangers of teachers becoming a self-governing corporation. The Medical and Dental Acts, the regulations of the Inns of Court and of the Society or British Architects and of the Civil Engineers, had all been formed with a view to the interests of a profession and he would be sorry to see the same thing happen in a field of such public interest as teaching. 'The public interests are the chief interests to be conserved and very important as the interests of teachers are, yet we all know that what are felt to be corporate and professional interests are not always absolutely identical with the public interests, the interests of parents and children.' He would prefer to see no more than an advisory council with the minister of public instruction as its chairman.[16]

The Select Committee had great difficulty with its report and produced only a brief and inconclusive document. It was based upon a draft report drawn up by the chairman, Sir William Hart-Dyke, from which some sections were struck out by the committee and other parts were amended. The committee found a general consensus among witnesses in favour of the principle of registration. It recommended that registration of teachers in secondary schools was in principle desirable and that such registration should be based upon four suggestions, one of which was 'that teachers certified by the Education Department should be placed on the register'. Thus the report finally tried to deal with the most divisive issue before it by suggesting that elementary teachers should be registered as 'Teachers in Secondary Schools'. On this anomaly the committee was evenly divided and reported both bills back to the House without amendment.[17] The House took no further action on these bills. In 1894 the Royal Commission on Secondary Education was set up, with James Bryce as chairman, and the issue came to wait upon the Commission's recommendations.

Most of the teachers' associations in their evidence supported the early creation of a register, but the sharp difference of opinion between those who would open it to all teachers and those who would confine it to secondary teachers remained and the arguments in favour of the one course or the other were rehearsed again. The Commissioners suggested that this difference 'has become almost a traditional dispute. It has helped to delay registration and has prevented the teaching profession from realising what seems—this one point apart—to be its undivided aim.'[18] The Commission believed that since the idea of a register for secondary teachers only was first adumbrated about 1860 circumstances had changed materially and what would have been most suitable at that time was no longer so. It therefore proposed one register for all teachers who fulfilled certain prescribed conditions, regardless of the class of school in which they were engaged. The register ought to be based not on occupational divisions, but simply on qualification and ability. Any criterion but that of merit would shut out many persons who had a just claim to a place on a register of qualified teachers, and their exclusion would bring the register itself into discredit. Moreover an exclusive register, or a register based on occupational divisions, would hinder what was most desirable for all branches of the profession, the free passage of teachers from one type of school to another. The Commission left the detailed definition of conditions for admission to the register for the Educational Council to define, but since it was important that admission to the register should be regarded from the beginning as 'an enviable distinction', no one should be registered who did not possess:

(1) a degree, or a certificate of general attainments, granted by some university or body recognised for that purpose by the registration authority, and accepted as satisfactory by that authority; and
(2) a certificate or diploma of adequate knowledge of the theory and practice of education, granted by a university or body recognised as above.

Those who were already teaching but lacked these qualifications were to be admitted after three years of successful experience in secondary schools. The only actual sanction proposed was that after two years of grace the unregistered should be disqualified for appointments in endowed schools.[19]

The management of the register was to be one of the functions of the Educational Council to which the Bryce Commission assigned a number of important functions in the central administration. This Council was to have not more than twelve members, of whom one-third should be nominated by the Crown, one-third by the four universities of Oxford, Cambridge, London and Victoria (one member by each), and one-third might be selected by the rest of the Council from among experienced members of the teaching profession. In the matter of instituting and keeping a register of teachers it should act quite independently of the minister and his department.[20]

The administrative recommendations of the Bryce Commission cut across a wide variety of interests; they stirred a good deal of opposition in some political and local government circles and, in spite of a number of attempts, many were never enacted. A bill to bring about registration on the lines of the Bryce recommendations was introduced in 1896. The register was to be kept by a council appointed for this purpose, to which the Crown, the Universities and the registered teachers were to appoint six members each.[21] This bill met with the same fate as Gorst's Education Bill of 1896 and was dropped in favour of more pressing matters.

In the interval that followed and before the Board of Education Act of 1899 paved the way for a Consultative Committee and a register, the headmasters again put forward their argument for separate treatment for secondary teachers. If elementary teachers were also to be registered, at least this should be on a different register. The I.A.H.M. argued that the minimum requirement for the registration of persons qualified to teach in secondary schools must be higher than the minimum requirement for those qualified to teach in elementary schools. 'The registers for elementary and secondary teachers must therefore be separate, though some names would appear on both registers.'[22] At its meeting in December, 1898, the Headmasters' Conference resolved unanimously 'that in the registration of teachers a distinction should be clearly drawn between persons qualified to teach in (1) secondary and (2) elementary schools.' It was also agreed, however, that admission to one register should not of itself disqualify a person from being admitted to the other.[23]

II THE FIRST TEACHERS' REGISTER

The Board of Education Act of 1899 provided for a Consultative Committee to frame regulations for a register of teachers, and to advise the Board on the inspection of secondary schools and on any matter which the Department referred to it.[24] The Consultative Committee arrangement was held by some to be promising; the *Journal of Education* went so far as to describe the Bill itself as 'the Magna Charta of education', although it did go on to express some concern over the membership of the Consultative Committee.[25] *The Educational Times*, the publication of the College of Preceptors, felt that the new Act had brought about a fundamental change in the situation, for now that all grades of school were to be under one governing body, it followed that all classes of teacher must have a common register. This was a very desirable result; it was, in fact, the beginning of the unification of the teaching profession.[26] At the same time the Consultative Committee really did not look like a professional council suitable for the leadership of the teaching profession which many advocates of a register had been seeking, nor did its composition resemble very closely the Educational Council recommended by the Bryce Commission. It was to be entirely nominated by the Board of Education and to consist in 'not less than two-thirds of persons qualified to represent the views of universities and other bodies interested in education.' In fact the eighteen members of the Committee included three ministers or ex-ministers, seven M.P.s, four ministers of religion, representatives of the universities and secondary school headmasters. There were no representatives of assistant masters or mistresses in secondary schools and the only conceivable representative of the elementary teachers was an M.P. who happened to be an ex-elementary teacher. Mrs. Sydney Webb described the Committee, not entirely unfairly, as 'weird' and as 'an almost comical travesty of a Professional Council'.[27]

For the first two years of its existence the Consultative Committee devoted itself to the task of framing the regulations required for a teachers' register. It reported its proposals to the Board of Education in June, 1901. There were to be two columns to the register, column A for teachers qualified solely as holders of the government certificate, i.e. the certificated elementary teachers, and column B for teachers who possessed a university degree or equivalent qualification and, after an initial period of grace, a teacher's diploma as well. These proposals were accepted by the Board of Education, and an order in council was issued at the beginning of 1902 bringing the register into force along with a registration authority called the Teachers' Registration Council of twelve members, six of them nominees of the President of the Board of Education and one each to be nominated by the Headmasters' Conference, the Incorporated Association of Headmasters, the Association of Headmistresses, the College of Preceptors, the Teachers' Guild, and the National Union of Teachers.[28]

The *Journal of Education* commented that the proposals for one register in two columns, one for elementary teachers and one for secondary, was 'a happy solution of a much vexed question which should satisfy all but the Intransigeants'.[29] This hope was not fulfilled. Both the arrangement of the register itself and the managing body were seen by the great majority of qualified teachers in the elementary schools as weighted against them. While the register conformed to the requirement of a single alphabetical list, the two columns proved highly objectionable.[30] Certificated teachers were to be inscribed *en bloc* in Column A, without individual application and without payment of fee. During the initial period of grace requirements for registration in column B were such that virtually any secondary school teacher, including non-graduates as long as they had passed such examinations as the Higher Locals of Oxford and Cambridge and could show three years of teaching could be admitted. For the first four years from 1902, the Teachers' Registration Council could admit anyone to column B who had taught for at least ten years in any school other than an elementary one. Individual application and a fee were required for admission to column B. It was intended to introduce the full requirement of a degree and training diploma as soon as possible, but the lack of training particularly among male graduates at this time made it unlikely that it would in fact prove to be possible to enforce these full requirements for some years.[31] Many hoped that the Board of Education would move in the direction of refusing to recognise a secondary school in which the head and a good proportion of the assistants were not registered, and that this would, in its turn, greatly encourage training. This did not happen and the Board seemed to regard registration as unsuitable to form the basis for a business-like criterion for classifying schools as efficient or otherwise. Some indication of the lack of importance attached to the registration scheme by the state may, perhaps, be seen in the way in which the post of Registrar was handled. This post was advertised at a salary of no more than £500 to £600. This was about the salary normally paid to a junior examiner (scale maximum £600) or a first-class clerk (scale maximum £500) at the turn of the century.[32] There had been pressure for a salary in the region of £1,000 to obtain someone of the 'right calibre'; assistant secretaries at this time were paid on a scale rising from £900 to £1,200.

There was no rush to seek entry to the register. By the end of 1902, 1,637 applications had been received for column B and 461 had been registered. Early in 1902 the I.A.A.M. had attempted to discover how many competent teachers in London schools would not be able to gain admittance to the register, but the circular it sent out met with little response and a good deal of indifference. The first chairman of the Teachers' Registration Council, Professor Withers of Manchester, died soon after the Council was established, and Dr. R. P. Scott, a representative of the Headmasters' Association, became chairman in his place. By the end of the next year, 1903, the largely formal column A contained the names of about 80,000 certificated elementary school teachers, while there had been 6,866 applications for registration in column B. Of these 4,506 had been registered, 1,212 rejected and 1,148 remained to be dealt with.[33] Financial difficulties had complicated the Council's work, for the Treasury refused to find the £3,000 required for the initial printing of the Register and the £1,000 needed to print an annual revision. The only income was the fee of one guinea paid by applicants for column B registration, since the Board of Education made no payment for its certificated teachers in column A. The Treasury maintained that the Register should be self-supporting, but in the circumstances of course it was not. The Council itself stated that 'The publication of the Register is virtually complied with by declaring it open to the public, but it is submitted that publication by means of printing is the only effective publication, and was contemplated both in the Board of Education Act and in the Registration Order itself.'[34]

The difficulties confronting the Teachers' Registration Council showed no sign of diminishing during 1905. By 31st December of that year, 10,459 teachers were registered in column B, but only 230 of these satisfied the conditions of registration (i.e. both a degree and training) that were intended as the permanent conditions to be required for registration. All that registration implied so far as the great majority of column B were concerned was that they had been teachers for three years in a recognised secondary school or that they had served for at least 10 years in any secondary or private school. In its Report for 1905, the Council commented that the financial prospects of men who were proposing to become secondary schoolmasters were so poor that most of them could not afford both to take a degree and to train. For lack of finance the register could still not be printed. It was becoming clear that the register as conceived in 1902 could hardly continue much longer. Although the temporary provisions for registration in column B were extended until 31st July, 1906, the *Journal of Education* commented, 'It is highly questionable whether the movement towards Registration will become general until the Board (of Education) is prepared to state that no secondary school in which the headmaster and a fair proportion of the staff are not registered will be eligible as a grant earning institution.'[35]

Apart from the sheer ineffectiveness of the whole registration exercise so far as secondary school teachers were concerned, the fate of the 1902 scheme was really sealed by the active hostility of the National

Union of Teachers. From the beginning the N.U.T. had not accepted the 'compromise' of one alphabetically arranged register with two columns. As early as its 1902 conference the N.U.T. resolved 'That Conference, having considered the Order in Council regulating the registration of teachers, protests in the most emphatic manner, against the injustice which will be inflicted on the primary teachers of the country by the introduction of the Register in two lists.'[36] This strong opposition to the form of the register was maintained, indeed, many elementary school teachers believed the two column arrangement to be a contravention of the Act of Parliament requiring the register to consist of a simple alphabetical list. Moreover, they also considered the representation of the primary teachers on the Registration Council (one nominee of the N.U.T. in a Council of twelve) to be inadequate and unjust.[37]

The change of government in December, 1905, when the Liberal party won a large majority in the Commons and Birrell became President of the Board of Education, made action against the existing register more likely. In fact a clause was included in the Education (Administrative Provisions) Bill to relieve the Board of Education of the responsibility which the 1899 Act had placed upon it of operating a register. In proposing abolition Birrell was probably influenced by two main factors, the dissatisfaction which the existing register had excited among the primary school teachers, and the views of the permanent officials of the Board who could not get on with the Consultative Committee and who desired a free hand to deal with all teachers and their training in the same way as they had customarily dealt with the elementary school teachers.[38] A memorandum on the registration of teachers by Morant and dated 8th June, 1906, was issued to explain the decision.[39] He pointed out that while registration had been sought by one set of people as a way of devising an organised profession for secondary teachers and to encourage professional training, another group sought it as a way of promoting unification of the whole profession. Column A of the existing register was clearly serving no useful purpose, while the effect of Column B on encouraging secondary teachers to train was clearly negligible. Moreover, 'the Act of 1899 laid down that there should be a "Register of Teachers", not a Register (a) of some out of the many teachers approved by the Board for service in public elementary schools, and of (b) teachers for service in secondary schools (as Column B had administratively though not explicitly been interpreted to be) but "of teachers".' The Board had come to believe that a register as contemplated in the 1899 Act was 'not practicable'; the existing regulations for registration clearly failed to carry out the intentions of Parliament and there was no prospect of amending them in such a way as to do so. Suitable alterations in the official Regulations for Secondary Schools would do as much to encourage the training of teachers as any scheme of registration. In a supplementary note Morant stated that the Board intended to change its Regulations for Secondary Schools to make it possible to require that a proportion of new appointments to school staffs should be of trained persons, and that they intended to issue supplementary regulations in 1906 instituting grants in aid of courses of training specifically designed for secondary school teaching.

The abolition of the register met with a great deal of hostility from teachers' associations. The A.H.M., the I.A.H.M., the I.A.A.M., the Teachers' Guild and the College of Preceptors all passed resolutions of opposition to the proposed discontinuance of the register. A conference convened by the University of Oxford and attended by representatives of universities and teachers' associations passed a resolution demanding the withdrawal of the offensive clause from the 1906 Education Bill. The conference also criticised the main contention of Morant's Memorandum that the register had failed to promote the training of men teachers, claiming that at Cambridge since 1902 the number of candidates examined in the Theory of Education had risen significantly. The Federal Council of the Secondary Associations protested against the abolition of the register in a memorandum which pointed out that training was not the only aim of the register. The first objective was rather the formation of an official list of efficient teachers which would be a guide to appointing authorities and protection for the public against incompetence.[40]

The N.U.T. welcomed the abolition of the 1902 form of register. In his address to the Easter Conference of 1906, the President of the Union said that 'it was planned by a consultative committee acting *ultra vires* in distinct contravention of the Act. It was built upon a foundation of exclusiveness and invidiousness. It did not obtain the support of teachers generally and consequently has been toppled down.' He reiterated the view that if there was to be a register of teachers it must be comprehensive, free from class prejudice, efficient and fair.[41] The N.U.T. was particularly annoyed by the reaction of some members of the Consultative Committee who seemed to be trying to justify and continue the existing two column arrangement. Two members of the Committee, Sophie Bryant and Mrs. Henry Sidgwick, wrote to *The*

Times to correct the widespread misunderstanding that the Consultative Committee had been consulted by the Board on the abolition of the register. They went on to put their view that its abolition would do harm to secondary education, check the progress of the professional training of teachers and diminish seriously the confidence of secondary teachers in the Board of Education.[42] The Association of Head Mistresses at its conference in June, 1906, deplored the abolition of the existing register and passed a resolution which indicated that the A.H.M. contemplated any future register as one confined to secondary teachers, as the minimum academic qualification recommended was a university degree or its equivalent.[43] In a leading article *The Schoolmaster* felt obliged to warn its readers that 'a very carefully engineered agitation' was being got up to continue the register in the form of an official list for secondary teachers, and to point out that the N.U.T. had been campaigning for thirty-six years for a truly comprehensive professional register.[44]

III OPPOSITION FROM THE BOARD OF EDUCATION

For a while it looked as though the abolition of the 1902 register was to be the occasion for another major outbreak of inter-association strife among teachers. But resentment at the way in which the Board of Education had made it clear that it would have no more to do with any sort of register played a considerable part in softening attitudes among teachers' organisations and enabling some measure of agreement to emerge. In June, 1906, representatives of the H.M.C., the I.A.H.M. and the A.H.M. met and referred the duty of maintaining a register to a professional council of representatives of the three associations who should have power to co-opt. A university degree and training were to be the requirements for admission. In October there was a meeting between these representatives and the representatives of the N.U.T., and it was agreed that any teacher registered in column A and who apart from the requirement of service in a secondary school would have been entitled to register in column B would be admitted to the new register. The representatives of the teachers' organisations were able to get sufficient sympathetic support in the House of Lords for that House to amend the Education Bill, so that while the Board itself was still relieved of responsibility for keeping a register, nevertheless it provided for the creation of a Registration Council representative of the teaching profession which should frame and keep a register of one column of such teachers as should satisfy the conditions of registration.[45]

Thus the growth since 1902 under Morant of a much better organised and much stronger bureaucracy at both central and local levels created a common sense of danger and in this way a greater measure of unity among teachers on the issue of registration than had existed before. At the I.A.A.M. annual conference in January, 1907, the President seems to have expressed the feelings of many teachers when he saw in the proposed representative council and the register that it was to maintain bulwarks against the threatened danger of bureaucratic tyranny from local education authorities.[46] In these circumstances it was only to be expected that the Board of Education would show not so much indifference as hostility to the implementation of the amendment in the Education Act inserted in the Lords. The Board did nothing to enable the teachers' associations to come together to form the Registration Council that the Act called for, and when the leading organisations came together to work out proposals, Morant did all he could to impair their unity and to play off one group of teachers against another in order to prevent progress from being made. A series of papers published by the Board of Education in these years bears witness to the mixture of hostility and contempt which the Permanent Secretary felt towards the teachers' associations.[47]

On 29th February, 1908, representatives of the H.M.C., the I.A.H.M., the A.H.M., the I.A.A.M., the A.A.M., the N.U.T., the Preparatory Schools Association, the Teachers' Guild, the Association of Technical Institutes, the College of Preceptors and the A.T.T.I. met together and produced a scheme for a Registration Council. The membership of this Council was very widely representative and was agreed by all the organisations at the meeting. The Chairman, Dr. James Gow, headmaster of Westminster School, sent the proposals to Morant. He replied inquiring about the representation of kindergarten teachers, cookery teachers, music teachers and so forth. A deputation led by Gow went to see Morant to discuss the various points arising in an informal manner. They got a hostile reception and Morant seems to have had little difficulty in ensuring that no progress was made. He issued a statement purporting to give an account of the meeting two months later without even showing a prior draft of it to the members of the deputation or even advising them that he intended to issue any statement. According to the Morant statement, 'no representation at all had been contemplated for such important sectors of the teaching profession as teachers in kindergartens, none to teachers of art of either sex . . . none to one of the most important branches of teaching, viz. the teaching staffs of training colleges. . . . It appeared that no provision had been made for the representation of teachers of music.'[48] Morant himself declined to offer any solutions to the problems he had raised, claiming that the purpose of the clause in the Act of 1907 was that teachers themselves should settle the issues. The Board was simply waiting for them to come up with an agreed scheme so that it could be put into effect. Yet it apparently did not contravene the intentions of the Act of 1907 for Morant to write round to a number of minor subject associations, inviting them to comment on the Gow scheme, and giving maximum publicity to any reply he received saying that they would like representation on the new Registration Council. The main advocates of the new Registration Council had already pointed out by letter as well as at the interview that the many small subject associations could hardly be incorporated, but that most of their members were also heads or assistants in elementary, secondary or technical schools 'and might, if they chose, belong to one of their existing organisations'. The residuum was eligible for the Teachers' Guild, which would be represented on the Council.[49] Morant replied raising further issues such as representation for university teachers and asking for a further reply 'without delay'.[50]

The Committee representing the main associations met in the early autumn and decided that they could not incorporate all the associations which Morant had stirred into requesting representation—which included the Royal College of Organists and the Incorporated Phonographic Society—and resolved that 'the plan of the Registration Council already recommended be further pressed upon the Board of Education'. The reply from the Board of Education to the committee's further representation was predictably unhelpful. It included: 'The President of this Board greatly regrets the delay that has occurred in this matter since the passing of the Act, in consequence of the ineffectual nature of the proceedings of your conference since that date, resulting it would seem, from their insufficiently representative character.'[51] Morant published the series of letters he had received in response to his circular to various educational bodies which had not been represented. These included the London Association of Art Masters, the Royal Drawing Society, the Society of Art Masters, the Art Teachers' Guild, the Union of Graduates in Music Incorporated, the Incorporated

Society of Musicians, the Society of Certificated Teachers of Shorthand, the Association of Book-keeping Teachers, the Union of Teachers of the Deaf on the Pure Oral System, and the National Association of Teachers of the Deaf. However miscellaneous or peripheral such a group might appear to be, the Board seems to have regarded it as an adequate defence, for when asked in the House what the reasons were for the delay in giving effect to the provisions of the 1907 Act for the constitution of a registration council, the President replied, 'The proposals for the constitution of a registration council, which were submitted to the Board by a committee comprising delegates from twelve educational associations, and have since been published, have elicited protests from various important sections of the teaching profession. The weight attaching to these objections makes it difficult to regard a council so constituted as representative of the profession as required by the Statute.'[52] A further Parliamentary encounter early in 1909 added to the impression that the Board had turned its back on any register. Sir Philip Magnus asked whether Runciman, the President, would take steps to accelerate the formation of a registration council so that it might continue to encourage the training of teachers for secondary schools. The Board's Report for 1908 had contained a statement that the old Register had encouraged women to train. Runciman replied that the stimulus had occurred when the registration of secondary was separate from that of elementary teachers. He doubted whether the same stimulus would be supplied by any register in which the names of all registered teachers must be 'in alphabetical order in one column. . . . I am informed that some people, whose opinion is entitled to respect, think that a more effective stimulus for the training of secondary teachers, men as well as women, will be derived from Section 15 of the Board's Regulations for Secondary Schools.'[53]

The implacable hostility shown by the permanent officials of the Board to a register had the effect of driving the teachers' associations more closely together than at any time before. The I.A.H.M., for example, invited J. H. Yoxall, currently General Secretary of the N.U.T., to speak at its conference in 1909. He claimed that behind the registration issue there lay the whole question of whether there could be such a thing as teaching as a profession or whether the administrators would succeed in the efforts they were making to reduce teaching to a state function and teachers to state functionaries.[54] Yoxall was not alone in taking this view of the significance of the Board's resistance to a register; it was coming to be quite widely held at the time. According to an editorial in the *Journal of Education*, there were 'unmistakable signs that the policy of the Board of Education—or, rather, of its permanent officials—is to make teachers a branch of the Civil Service and to prevent them from organising themselves as a profession. We cannot otherwise explain the autocratic and, we venture to say, illegal opposition of the Board to the formation of a Teachers' Register.'[55]

The members of Dr. Gow's committee agreed to dissolve their existing committee, and to the proposal of the Federal Council of Secondary School Associations to try to break the deadlock by summoning a conference of representatives of as many associations as possible to discuss the principles on which the Teachers' Registration Council should be constituted. James Easterbrook, Chairman of the Federal Council and headmaster of Owen's School, was chiefly responsible for this new initiative. The conference took place at the Clothworkers' Hall on 13th November, 1909. 147 representatives from 37 associations attended the meeting. They agreed on a scheme for a Registration Council the basis of which should be a tripartite division of the profession into three branches, primary, secondary and technical, with nine members assigned to each. In addition there were to be three members representing other associations such as the Froebel Society, which was to have one representative. The seven associations of musicians were left to decide among themselves whence should come the one representative allocated to them. There were also to be a certain number of Crown nominees. The measure of agreement might appear to have been such that the Board would have to recognise it, but in fact Morant sheltered for a further year behind a protest from the Association of Teachers in Technical Institutions that the number of representatives offered to them was inadequate.

The further delay continued to force together the teachers' associations and M. P. Wood, in his Presidential address to the I.A.H.M. in 1910, remarking on this, suggested that there were two other factors which were bringing elementary and secondary teachers together. The first of these was the growth of municipal secondary schools whose heads attended I.A.H.M. meetings but which 'by reason of the lowness of the fee charged, or by the entire absence of fee, lean more closely to the elementary school.' The second factor seemed to him to be the great increase in the number of elementary teachers who received much of their education in secondary schools.[56] The combined pressures of virtually all the teachers' associations in seeking the carrying out of what was, after all, an Act of Parliament, meant that by the early part of 1911 apparent grounds for delay were exhausted and in March of that year Morant had a series of three meetings. The first was with representatives of the secondary associations, the second was also attended by N.U.T. representatives and at the third these two groups were joined by representatives of technical and other specialised teaching groups.[57] In his Report, Morant made a good deal of the difficulties, of questions remaining unresolved and so forth. While this series of meetings was being held, the affair of the Holmes-Morant circular blew up. Extracts from this document had begun to leak out at the beginning of 1911 and the matter was first raised in Parliament on 14th March. The storm that arose first removed Runciman, then in November Morant himself resigned. Thus during the crucial period of 1911, when the Board of Education was changing its attitude to the teachers' registration issue, Morant was under very strong attack on this other matter. The developments between March and July were not, therefore, surprising.

What was possibly more surprising was the way in which Morant, having for three years insisted that the Board could take no part in evolving a scheme for a register, himself rewrote some of the important features in the scheme which emerged from the meeting at the Clothworkers' Hall. Having by this time developed a bureaucratic system of branches within the Board to deal with university, technical, secondary and elementary education, the Secretary now re-wrote the teachers' proposals for a Registration Council to conform to this pattern. He claimed that since the Council must be truly representative of the whole profession there must be a representation of university teachers as well as of the other three branches, 'a Council composed of these four elements would, in fact, be *representative of the whole Teaching Profession*, which otherwise would not be the case'. Since the number of universities was eleven and since each must be represented, the university group would have eleven members. Since the Clothworkers' Hall meeting had proposed that all groups should be the same size (with nine members), it would now be necessary for them all to have eleven members.[58] The Chairman of the Council should be chosen by the Council itself from candidates outside. This would give a Council of 45, 'a large body, but by no means too large to represent adequately the whole of so vast and important a profession as the Teaching Profession'.

In spite of these fine words, Morant rejected the suggestion that the Board should recognise the register in its grant and training regulations. Representatives of teachers that he met urged that such recognition would be essential to its prestige and success, and that without it the register would lack any pressure or sanction and would fail to win its way. 'To this I replied that I could hardly believe a register established by a really representative professional council would be so wholly deficient in prestige and vitality as this view would suggest; and I then added that it must be clearly understood that, by the holding of these conferences and even also (I believed) by taking steps to bring the new Council into existence, the Board must not be regarded as in any way committed to any attitude, whether of active support or of passive recognition, or otherwise, towards such register as might subsequently be established by the Council.'[59] It was quite clear that Morant never contemplated conceding any real powers to the new council to determine the qualifications of teachers for certain types of school. The emphasis of the Board seemed to be on the efficiency of the school as a unit and this the Board intended to keep firmly in its own hands. The list itself would be of little use to appointing authorities, it would simply be a sort of London Directory, a lengthly alphabetical list which would do little or nothing to encourage greater efficiency within the teaching profession.[60] The teachers wanted a list and a council, their demands could no longer be resisted, but there was no necessity that the Board should attach meaning or significance to either of these. While it might have been premature for the Board to pledge itself to tie grants in aid of schools to the register beforehand, for the Board to announce in advance that it would neither give advice nor co-operate was 'to frustrate the clear intention of Parliament'.[61]

IV THE SECOND TEACHERS' REGISTER

After another eight months of negotiation, an Order in Council was issued on 29th February, 1912, establishing the Teachers' Registration Council of 44 members, divided into 4 groups with a co-opted chairman, as Morant had proposed. In the absence of any sort of electoral roll, the members of each group were appointed by the organisations agreed at the Clothworkers' Hall meeting with the subsequent additions suggested by Morant. The first chairman was A. H. D. Acland, and the second was Michael Sadler. The only power given to this body from which so much was expected was the duty of 'forming and keeping a Register of such teachers as satisfy the conditions of registration established by the Council.' The first meeting of the new Teachers' Registration Council was held on 23rd July, 1912. The Board subsequently transferred to it the funds of the old Teachers' Registration Council.[62] Thus, although Morant had now left, the Board's attitude remained unchanged. The new Council could not control admission to the profession but only to its own register, and since that register had no official standing, membership of it could never be effective in conferring status, nor would non-membership penalise those outside.

That these difficulties would eventually lead to the demise of the Teachers' Registration Council was by no means clear in 1912. All of the main teachers' associations rejoiced in what had been gained even though they had hoped for more.[63] The polite and professional words of J. A. Pease, the new President of the Board at the first meeting of the Council, were felt to indicate a significant step forward when he said that he was sure that the Board of Education would be glad to co-operate with the Council as representative of the teaching profession and would attach weight to its views.[64] Writing in 1915, Mrs. Webb recorded that the new Council had begun its work in a fine spirit of enthusiasm which was worthy of the highest promise.[65] Others, however, dwelt rather on some of the practical problems which even the drawing up of a list of teachers would involve. The term 'teacher' was itself so extraordinarily wide that the problem of discriminating would be very difficult, wrote J. L. Paton in 1912, yet members of a single profession must presumably have some common occupation and a common end in view. 'There are teachers of every mortal thing in the World—cookery and conjuring, elocution and swimming, Sanskrit and sausage-making, teachers of mothers and teachers of musketry, scoutmasters, Sunday schoolteachers, and drill sergeants.' Secondly, an organised profession regulated its own membership by fixing and enforcing the standard of qualification, but there were no real standards in teaching, even in state schools the lowest qualification required was to attain the age of 18 and to be vaccinated. In a profession the corporate body had control of the course of training and the admission of new entrants: 'Here the teachers come up against a hard fact. . . . This matter of selection and apprenticeship has been taken out of our hands, it has been done for us by administrative bodies, governmental, local and religious.'[66] It was problems such as these which could only be dealt with by a body with far-reaching powers which the new Council lacked completely.

The Council issued conditions of registration in 1913, the permanent requirements being enforced after a period of grace during which the register would also be open to persons who were without qualifications if they had taught for at least five years and were over twenty-five years of age. This temporary expedient, which was originally to be available until the end of 1918, helped to undermine further the standing of the register in the eyes of well-qualified teachers. The permanent conditions contemplated were:

(1) Attainments: a university degree, a teacher's certificate or the equivalent.
(2) Experience: at least one year of full-time or 3 years of part-time teaching;
(3) Training in teaching:
    A. General Requirement, to have completed an approved course of training (or to have taught in a university for a year for teachers in universities);
    B. Alternative Temporary Requirement (available until 1930), to have taught for 3 years, if the General Requirement could not be complied with.[67]

The Council was to be self-financing, that is to say it was obliged to charge a fee of all applicants for registration. The Treasury guaranteed the expenses of the Council up to £3,000 a year for the first three years, to be repaid out of registration fees.

The War naturally caused some delay in the formation of the register. By 1922 the register contained 73,359 names; further increase in the total number was steady rather than spectacular. The Constitution of the Council was changed by an Order-in-Council issued on 14th December, 1926. The aim was to bring the constitution into line with changes in the teaching profession since 1912. The grant of a Charter to the University of Reading meant that the universities group now had 12 members instead of 11. Teachers registered in the various groups were now given direct representation instead of indirect representation through nomination by their professional associations. This latter had been impossible in 1912, before there had been a register and when there had, therefore, been no electoral roll.

The changes made by this Order-in-Council did little to help the cause of an effective register as such. In spite of the words of J. A. Pease in 1912, the Board of Education had sought the Councils' views only on such comparatively minor matters as changes to be made in its publication *Suggestions to Teachers*, which it issued for the guidance of teachers in elementary schools. *The Times Educational Supplement* suggested at the time of the Order-in-Council that far more use should be made of the Teachers' Registration Council by those responsible for education. In spite of the evidence, it commented that 'it cannot be believed that the Council was established by Parliament with no further purpose in view than the formation of a register'. There should be some advantage secured to the registered teacher which the unregistered did not enjoy.[68] In fact this never happened. In 1929, in response to pressure from the Council, the title 'Royal Society of Teachers' was conferred on the body of registered teachers, but the pressure mounted at the same time failed to make it impossible for an unregistered teacher to open a private school or to occupy any post in the publicly supported schools which involved the direction of other teachers. Thus once again that which was without significance was conceded by authority but that which would have involved some sharing of power with the Registration Council was refused. By the Second World War the register and the Council had obviously failed to acquire any significance, so that the new arrangements made in the Act of 1944 for the Minister of Education to have power to grant qualified teacher status met with no resistance from this quarter. The Teachers' Registration Council was formally abolished by Order-in-Council in 1949.

Thus while the objectives of those groups of teachers seeking registration and a registration council had varied, none had achieved its aim. The College of Preceptors in the 1860s saw in such a register a ready means of enabling the public to recognise skilled practitioners and to avoid unqualified quacks. This analogy with the medical profession was certainly out of date by the twentieth century, when publicly responsible authorities in some form or other had come to shoulder the task of choosing teachers—quite unlike medicine, where individuals still chose the particular practitioner to whom they would go and where a register was needed to protect the public. A slightly later aim was to use the 'privilege' of registration as a way of encouraging teachers to improve their qualifications, but adjustments to grants for training and of salary and opportunities by the employing bodies have proved more effective means of achieving this end. Groups of secondary teachers had sought a register in the late nineteenth century as a way both of avoiding the form of close control that the state had imposed on elementary teachers and of maintaining the separate and superior status of the secondary teacher. The opposition of the N.U.T. had eventually broken this attempt by 1906.

The N.U.T. and most of the other associations saw in the movement for a register a step towards professional self-government.[69] This must involve controlling entry to the profession and deciding on minimum acceptable qualifications. The N.U.T. attached particular importance to this as a way of counteracting the manipulation of entry requirements by the Education Department in its efforts to maintain the supply of teachers by lowering standards. The achievement of this objective could not be attained unless the scheme of registration also brought with it a legal monopoly of the right to practice. Yet even if doctors or lawyers managed to create strong professional monopolistic corporations there was very little chance of teachers following in the same path, for the great majority of them were engaged on an employee-employer basis and their employer was a public authority. As Morant made perfectly clear, the government could never consent to allow the Teachers' Registration Council to fix the qualifications on which alone persons might be permitted to enter the profession, for this would give teachers power to limit their numbers and thus eventually to control salaries and the terms of service according to their own discretion. In fact, teachers' associations have come to exercise increasing influence through negotiating and consultative machinery, but they have never achieved and are unlikely to achieve the measure of monopolistic power and control which the legal and medical professions enjoy.

Recently the proposal for a Teachers' General Council has been given another airing, largely as a result of the personal interest of Mr. Edward Short when he was Secretary of State for Education and Science. Memories of the difficulties which had arisen over the operation of a register at earlier periods had, perhaps, begun to grow less vivid with the passage of time. In 1959, for example, a proposal for a Teachers' General Council which would regulate entry and qualification standards, establish a register of teachers and have disciplinary powers was put forward to the Minister, who rejected it, arguing that such a Council was unnecessary.

In 1960 a working party was set up representing the main teachers' associations which produced, four years later, a scheme for a Teachers' General Council with powers to determine entry qualifications, to keep a register and to administer professional discipline. The working party also recommended that the Minister be asked to set up an official working party to consider and report upon the scheme for a General

Council. At the end of 1965 the Secretary of State declined to pursue the suggestion, since he could not agree to changing the control over standards of entry and associated matters, especially during a period of teacher shortage.

The teachers' associations continued to press their views and in 1969 Mr. Short set up an official working party including representatives of teachers' associations and local authorities to draw up proposals. This group's report went to the Secretary of State early in 1970. It recommended both a Teachers' Council and a separate body to advise on training and supply. Registration, at a fee of £2, would be compulsory for all who intended to teach in maintained schools and the Council would be empowered to discipline teachers by striking them off the register. There were to be 40 members, 25 of them representatives of the teachers' associations (including 10 from the N.U.T.), the other 15 being appointed by the Secretary of State. It was felt that the actual register should be that already kept by the D.E.S. and that the Council itself did not need to prepare another. The advisory council for the supply and training of teachers was to have 29 members and was to replace the now defunct National Advisory Council on the Training and Supply of Teachers. This new advisory council was to play a part in ensuring that teachers did not raise standards of admission so high that the number of recruits fell below the number needed for the schools. Finally, the Secretary of State would have the right to accept or reject recommendations from the Teachers' General Council with regard to qualifications and entry.

The new proposals, therefore, still fell far short of the traditional desires of the teachers' associations. The powers reserved to the Secretary of State would have effectively preserved the position which the Board of Education had always sought to guard. It was argued that a profession should not be given a right which would enable it to control admission by raising the standards in a way judged by the D.E.S. to be contrary to the public interest. The General Secretary of the N.U.T. believed, in April 1970, that Mr. Short was anxious to go ahead with legislation, and warned the Executive that the political niceties of the timing of the next general election would not wait on the needs of teachers. Some members certainly found the proposals disappointing and the Executive decided to consult local associations before taking a decision on its attitude. When the general election followed in June, the issue was still undecided.

NOTES

1. *The Educational Times*, January, 1862, p. 219.
2. S.I.C., 1868, vol. V, pp. 203–4.
3. S.I.C., 1868, vol. I, 615.
4. A. E. Fletcher (ed.), *Sonnenschein's Cyclopaedia of Education*, 1889, p. 326; L. Magnus (ed.), *National Education*, 1901, essay by Francis Storr, 'Registration and Training of Secondary Teachers', p. 58.
5. *Hansard*, H. of C., 18th February, 1869, col. 115.
6. Fletcher, op. cit., p. 326; A. Tropp, *The School Teachers*, 1957, p. 111; Mrs. S. Webb, *New Statesman*, Special Supplement, 'English Teachers and their Professional Organisations', 2nd October, 1915, p. 15.
7. Cf. *The Educational Times*, March, 1877, p. 294.
8. Fletcher, op. cit., p. 326.
9. Tropp, op. cit., p. 116.
10. T. E. Heller, *Transactions of the National Association for the Promotion of Social Sciences* (1878), 1879, pp. 434–6.
11. Magnus, op. cit., p. 59.
12. Select Committee on Teachers' Registration and Organisation Bill, 1891, Evidence, p. 218.
13. Ibid., p. 229.
14. Ibid., pp. 2–3.
15. Ibid., p. 194.
16. Ibid., pp. 175–6.
17. *The Educational Times*, September, 1891, p. 397.
18. Bryce Cssn., 1895, vol. I, pp. 194–5.
19. Ibid., pp. 318–20.
20. Ibid., pp. 258–65.
21. G. Balfour, *The Educational System of Great Britain and Ireland*, 1898, p. 195.
22. I.A.H.M., *The Organisation of Secondary Education* (pamphlet), 1897.
23. *Journal of Education*, January, 1899, p. 69.
24. P. H. J. H. Gosden, *The Development of Educational Administration in England and Wales*, 1966, p. 116.
25. *Journal of Education*, June, 1899, p. 357.

26. *The Educational Times*, October, 1899, p. 407.
27. Webb, op. cit., p. 16.
28. Board of Education, S.R. and O. No. 206, 6th March, 1902.
29. *Journal of Education*, February, 1902, p. 101.
30. The Board of Education Act provided that the register 'shall contain the names of the registered teachers arranged in alphabetical order, with an entry in respect to each showing the date of his registration and giving a brief record of his qualifications and experience'.
31. *Supra*, chapter 10.
32. Gosden, op. cit., p. 30.
33. Teachers' Registration Council, Report for 1903, p. 4.
34. Ibid., p. 5.
35. *Journal of Education*, April, 1906, p. 252.
36. N.U.T. Annual Report, 1902, p. lxx.
37. G. Baron, 'The Teachers' Registration Movement', *B.J.E.S.*, vol. II, No. 2., p. 137; D. F. Thompson, *Professional Solidarity among the Teachers of England*, 1927, p. 276; Webb, op. cit., p. 17; *The Educational Times*, July, 1905, p. 283.
38. *Journal of Education*, June, 1906, p. 387.
39. Board of Education, R. L. Morant, Memorandum on the Registration of Teachers, Cd. 3017, 1906.
40. I.A.A.M. Annual Report, 1906.
41. *The Schoolmaster*, 21st April, 1906, p. 838.
42. *The Times*, 28th May, 1906, p. 9.
43. *Journal of Education*, July, 1906, p. 499.
44. *The Schoolmaster*, 9th June, 1906, p. 1189.
45. 7 Edw. VII, c. 43, S. 16; Thompson, op. cit., p. 276; *Journal of Education*, January, 1907, p. 71.
46. Webb, op. cit., p. 18; *Journal of Education*, February, 1907, p. 153.
47. Cd. 4185, 1908; Cd. 4402, 1908; Cd. 5726, 1911.
48. Board of Education, Scheme for a new Teachers' Registration Council proposed to the Board of Education by the Representatives of Certain Educational Authorities, Cd. 4185, 1908.
49. Ibid., letter of 27th June, 1908.
50. Ibid., letter of 8th July, 1908.
51. Board of Education, Correspondence concerning Cd. 4185, 1908, Cd. 4402, letter of 17th November, 1908.
52. *Hansard*, H. of C., 19th October, 1908, col. 713–14.

53. *Hansard*, H. of C., 23rd March, 1909, col. 1469–70. The reference to the lack of value of a register on which all the elementary teachers were included alphabetically might be interpreted as some evidence that it was this aspect of a register with its apparent consequence of a registration council dominated by elementary teachers rather than a register as such which the Board under Morant feared. Cf. A. Tropp, op. cit., p. 198.
54. Baron, op. cit., p. 140; I.A.H.M. Review, March, 1909, p. 32; *Journal of Education*, February, 1909, Conference Supplement, pp. 144–45.
55. *Journal of Education*, March, 1911, p. 212.
56. Ibid., February, 1910, p. 139.
57. A description of these meetings was given by Morant in the 'Report by the Secretary of the Board of Education to the President of that Board, upon Three Informal Conferences concerning the proposed Teachers' Registration Council and the proposed Teachers' Register', Board of Education, Further Papers relating to the Registration of Teachers and the Proposed Registration Council, Cd. 5726, 1911, pp. 31–42.
58. Ibid., p. 43.
59. Ibid., p. 40.
60. *Journal of Education*, May, 1911, pp. 319–20.
61. Ibid., July, 1911, pp. 467–68.
62. Board of Education, Report for 1911–12, 1913, p. 147.
63. Cf. *The Schoolmaster*, 1st July, 1911, p. 10.
64. Thompson, op. cit., p. 278.
65. Webb, op. cit., p. 19.
66. J. L. Paton, 'The Teachers' Register and Its Possibilities', *Contemporary Review*, August, 1912, pp. 239–46.
67. Teachers' Registration Council, *Conditions of Registration* (pamphlet), n.d.
68. T.E.S., 1st January, 1927, p. 8.
69. Cf. N.U.T. Annual Report, 1913, where the following passage occurs in the report from the executive, 'In accordance with the undertaking given by the President of the Hull conference the question of teaching as an independent profession has been carefully considered by the education (and a special) committee during the past year. Fully recognising the point of view of those members of the union who desire immediately to see the profession self-regulated and self-governed . . . the education (and special) com-

mittee have decided unanimously that the course will be to watch the development of the work of the Teachers' Registration Council and ultimately through its agency and influence to introduce the reforms demanded by practically every section of the teaching profession.'

12

Training of Teachers for Elementary and Secondary Schools, 1914–1939

Seen in retrospect, the most important single development in the training of teachers between the two World Wars was probably the establishment of machinery linking the training colleges with the universities. Although this did not amount at the time to much more than making arrangements to involve the universities in examining college students, it may now be seen as the formal beginning of a relationship which has become a good deal closer since the Second World War, firstly when Area Training Organisations were set up and ater with the establishment of the B.Ed. degree.

Although prominent members of the N.U.T. had from time to time spoken of the need to concern the universities more with training teachers, the immediate cause of the sequence of events which led to this development lay in finance. The financial problems of those local authorities which had set up training colleges reached crisis proportions in the years after 1918.

Following the Education Act of 1902, local authorities had been encouraged to set up colleges by being offered generous capital and maintenance grants for the purpose and 16 L.E.A.s had responded to the offer. Under this system the national exchequer had met about 90 per cent of the net cost of operating the colleges. An incidental effect of the attempt made to simplify the whole grant system in the Education Act of 1918 was to abolish payment of this special grant to L.E.A. training colleges. The Act provided for a 50 per cent deficiency grant[1] to be payable for higher education,[2] and the Board of Education Regulations issued under the Act in 1919 quite naturally included L.E.A. training colleges in the calculations for this deficiency grant. Thus the government grant to these institutions was cut from about 90 per cent to 50 per cent of the net cost (after fees) of the colleges, and the ratepayers were required to find the other 50 per cent.

The local authorities felt particularly incensed because the voluntary colleges continued to receive direct grant from the Board of Education on a capitation basis and were, therefore, not included in the scope of the new regulations. This meant that if local authority colleges met the situation by increasing their fees they would simply ensure that most students began by applying for admission to the lower fee voluntary colleges; these colleges would no doubt take their pick so that the L.E.A. colleges would be left with the less attractive students.

The local authorities found it very difficult to justify the use of the rates to subsidise the cost of their training colleges, since only a small proportion of the students were drawn from the local area and only 10 per cent to 20 per cent were absorbed in the area on completion of their training.³ Apart from closing the colleges down, the only solution to the problem appeared to be to persuade the government to pay additional grant and this the local authorities attempted to do, on the grounds that they were not providing a local but a national service. In the era of the 'Geddes axe' the government was hardly likely to welcome the solution advocated by the authorities, but after meeting a deputation at the beginning of 1923 the President of the Board of Education agreed to set up a departmental committee to review the position.

A departmental committee, however, would clearly need time to deliberate and to come to conclusions, and the local authorities were anxious to obtain a measure of immediate relief. In the *Memorandum* which they published in February, 1923, they took by way of illustration the position of the City of Leeds Training College. In 1919 the local ratepayers found £4,103 or 15 per cent of the net cost and the government grant amounted to £22,654 or 85 per cent. Since that year the ratepayers had to find 50 per cent, i.e. a 2½d. rate; the city was therefore putting a sum of £55 behind each student, but of the 494 students at the college only 28 were from Leeds itself. Various local authorities had had to increase fees for students from outside areas to £80, £85, £90, £105 and £120, while the denominational voluntary colleges were only charging £20 to £30 per annum. 'Preferential treatment of one type of training college cannot be justified and should cease. All training colleges are doing work similar in character and of equal national importance, and equivalent grants must be paid to all colleges.'⁴ Thus under pressure the Board of Education announced in April that an interim grant of about £70,000 would be paid to the authorities to enable them to avoid the sharp increases in the fees charged at colleges, until the departmental committee had time to report and a more permanent solution could be found to the problem.

The report of the departmental committee went much wider than financial matters and led to the colleges' link with the universities, although its actual terms of reference gave pride of place to the financial issue, being:

> To review the arrangements for the Training of Teachers for Public Elementary Schools, and to consider what changes, if any, in the organisation or finance of the existing system are desirable in order that a supply of well qualified teachers adjustable to the demands of the schools may be secured, regard being had to
> (a) the economy of public funds;
> (b) the attractions offered to young persons by the teaching profession as compared with other professions and occupations;
> (c) the facilities afforded by secondary schools and universities for acquiring academic qualifications.[5]

Lord Burnham was chairman of the committee whose 18 members were drawn from various parts of the world of education including the National Union of Teachers, the local authorities, the inspectorate and the universities. The committee dealt with the grants issue which had occasioned its appointment by recommending that the Treasury grants for L.E.A. colleges should be on the same basis as those for voluntary colleges. The additional expenditure which the Exchequer would thereby incur should be recovered 'by equitable apportionment among the Local Education Authorities for higher education which do not provide training colleges'.[6] This recommendation was incorporated in the Economy (Miscellaneous Provisions) Act of 1926 which enabled the Treasury to collect from L.E.A.s without training colleges the £70,000 p.a. or so which it had begun to pay to local authority colleges in 1923.

In the recommendations the Committee made on the wider issue of the changes desirable in the organisation of the system, there may be seen a number of the ideas then being advocated by teachers' organisations. In 1919 the Council of Principals of training colleges resolved that any scheme for the improvement of the general and professional education of teachers should secure that the work of the training colleges should be brought into close touch with that of the universities and should provide for a course extending over not less than three years. It also resolved that the education of those students who did not qualify for degree courses should be conducted by the training colleges under University recognition, and that the colleges should be organically connected with universities and be so organised that their teaching might receive university recognition for degree or diploma purposes.[7] At a conference held in the following year with representatives of the Board of Education and the universities, their chairman made it quite clear that the Council of Principals did not seek degrees for all teachers, since that would lower the standard of degrees, but that non-degree students should receive university recognition in the form of a diploma.

One of the most influential training college teachers was Winifred Mercier, principal of Whitelands College and president of the Training College Association in 1918-19. She voiced the aims of many of her colleagues and to some extent prophesied the future course of events in seeking a connection with universities through the reform of examination arrangements. She opposed any idea of incorporating the colleges in the universities, for that would flood the universities with boys and girls below the academic level of the degree student. The training colleges must develop and 'provide a higher education for such students which is neither school work nor university'.[8] Both at a conference for members of the Labour Party at Whitelands in 1923, and in evidence to the Committee, she stressed the importance of having different forms of training. The two-year college course was better suited to the majority of those who were going to teach children under eleven than a degree course. Moreover, the majority would not achieve matriculation, and if the universities lowered their entrance qualifications they would also have to lower the standards of their final examinations; there would also be twice as many teachers in training as there were students at the universities.[9]

The N.U.T. saw in a closer association of the training colleges with the universities a way of raising the status of primary school teachers. Indeed, the President of the Union argued in 1920 that its most pressing task was to secure free promotion for the primary teacher throughout the whole education service. This fluidity could only be achieved by revising the training system so that all should obtain a degree or its equivalent. At the Annual Conference of that year the training of teachers was discussed at length and a policy was adopted which fell under four headings.

1. *General Education*

All intending candidates should be required to have completed satisfactorily a course of higher (i.e. secondary) education and no person should be recognised as a candidate before giving evidence that he possessed qualifications justifying admission.

2. *Test of general aptitude for the work of teaching*

Courses of higher (secondary) education, whether normal or extended with the aid of a bursary, should be followed by a test of general aptitude which should only be applied in schools where the buildings were satisfactory, the staff suitable and the general organisation such as to provide for suitable teaching.

3. *The graduate course*

To be entered at matriculation level and to last for three years, at a university where intending teachers would associate with those intending to enter other professions. The course of study should include education, which should rank as the principal subject for the degree.

4. *Professional Training*

This was to be a year devoted to the acquisition of 'teaching craftsmanship'. The training colleges were to be used for this purpose, part of the time being spent in lectures and part in demonstration schools. The colleges should be recognised as colleges of the university. On completion of both academic course and professional training the teachers should be eligible for recognition by the Board of Education for service in any school.[10]

Thus elementary and secondary school teachers would be trained side by side and the status of the former raised to that of the latter.

The evidence submitted by the N.U.T. in 1923 to the Departmental Committee on the Training of Teachers for Elementary Schools followed quite closely the policy adopted in 1920. Any person seeking admission to teaching was to satisfy the Teachers' Registration Council that he had an appropriate degree from a recognised university and had secured a diploma in the theory, history and practice of education. The training colleges, as centres for professional work, would operate under university direction; their expenses would be met in the same way as university costs and the university would conduct the examination for the professional diploma. The scheme did not deal in detail with the preliminary education of teachers beyond stating that free secondary education should be provided for all who desired and would profit by it.

On the closely related question of the supply of teachers the Union suggested that an adequate supply should be secured by virtue of (a) the character of the work, (b) the salaries offered, (c) the assurance of pensions, (d) freedom from unnecessary and irksome school conditions, (e) public recognition of the teaching profession. The tactic of varying the regulations for training which had been used by the Board of Education and the local authorities as a way of controlling the supply was condemned. It should be made unlawful for either the Board or the L.E.A.s to impose regulations which would substantially modify the demand for teachers without giving adequate notice of such proposed changes.[11]

The implications of the N.U.T.'s proposals were examined further by M. Merrick, a member of the Union's executive, in a paper at the North of England Conference in 1924. He explained that the Union believed the right type of teacher was more likely to come from the secondary schools and universities than from other sources. While degrees and diplomas were not necessarily signs of future success in teaching, the universities were better staffed and equipped on the academic side than the colleges, and university education was seen as the best antidote to the narrowing influences that beset the teacher's life. But the question of status was ever an important factor, and Merrick added also that the teachers felt the status of the profession would be raised by its direct association with the university, and, accordingly, desired that teaching would rank with law, medicine and divinity as a profession normally involving a university training.

In its Report the Departmental Committee did not follow the suggestion that teachers should normally graduate before going to training colleges, but did emphasise the professional training aspect of work in the colleges. It held that the lengthening of secondary school courses and the consequent higher standard of general education reached before training began implied that training colleges need devote less time and effort to supplementing general education, and might therefore be expected to devote more of their energies to professional training. In spite of this improved level of achievement among entrants the Committee rejected the notion of cutting the college course to one year and concluded that it should extend over not less than two years.[12]

The most significant recommendations of the Committee were those which bore upon the relationship between the training colleges and the universities. The arrangements in a few colleges permitting a four-year course consisting of a degree followed by training might well be permitted to continue and develop where circumstances were favourable. On the other hand the existing two- or three-year courses which attempted to combine both degree and professional training on a concurrent basis into this shorter period were found to be undesirable.

The Committee suggested the involvement of universities in the examination arrangements for teachers' certificates through the setting up of examining boards representative of universities and colleges to examine students of a college or group of colleges for the purpose of recognition by the Board as certificated teachers. In addition to joint examining boards, the Committee suggested that there might be closer contact between universities and colleges through lectures in the colleges by university teachers, university representation on college governing bodies, and occasional conferences between universities, the L.E.A.s and training colleges.[13]

Not surprisingly, the N.U.T. found a Report which fell so far short of its own ideas on the future of the training colleges 'utterly disappointing'. *The Schoolmaster* complained that the Report attempted the impossible both by suggesting that the individual teacher could attain a higher standard of professional skill on a substratum of academic attainment 'of a lower standard than at present obtains', and by retaining, despite the logic of its own arguments, the dual function of the training college as a place of academic education (although to a lower standard) and professional training. The Committee's solution to the problem of the dual function of the training college lay in a 'feeble compromise which renders the academic side anaemic and the professional side no more robust. In this way it lowers the status of the normal training college and reduces the standard of qualification of the teachers'.

The Memorandum of Dissent which was signed by four of the Committee was welcomed as a solid contribution to the attainment of the Union's programme for the training of teachers. This Memorandum made eight recommendations, the main ones being:

> that all training college courses should be post-academic;
> that all entrants should be persons who had completed their academic education, to an increasing extent in the universities;
> that the content of training college courses should be strictly professional;

that the courses should be of one-year's duration;

that there should be no ear-marked scholarships for intending teachers as an inducement to recruiting.

The dissenting quartet added that their recommendations were intended to take into account the 'cumulative changes in universities, secondary schools and elementary schools during the last half-century (which) have in aggregate amounted to a revolution; and the training colleges, which after all are only a subsidiary machinery ... have not as yet been adjusted to the new conditions'.[14]

The Schoolmaster commented that the Memorandum marked a substantial step forward to the attainment of university status by all teachers so far as their academic subjects were concerned, since it envisaged training colleges with purely professional functions. The fundamental distinction between the main Report and the Memorandum was that the former was concerned only with the present and the immediate future while the latter had 'the faith that will remove mountains'.

The four dissenting members of the Departmental Committee were E. K. Chambers, a senior official of the Board who wrote the memorandum on the pupil-teacher system that was to lead to the advent of secondary schools as the chief avenue of recruitment, F. Roscoe, secretary to the Teachers' Registration Council, E. J. Sainsbury and Miss E. R. Conway, both former presidents of the N.U.T. and members of its executive. *The Times Educational Supplement* commented that in their Memorandum these four carried to a logical conclusion the principles which the majority of the Committee had approved but had felt unable to press home in view of the restricting terms of reference.

The Training Colleges Association and Council of Principals expressed their support for the idea of a closer connection between the universities and the training colleges in a letter to the Board of Education in October, 1925. In December they sent a deputation to meet the Committee of Vice-Chancellors which stressed that any connection should not be limited to examining alone; there was a need for personal contact between staffs to engender intellectual stimulus and to establish a truly internal form of examination. They were particularly concerned to ensure that the colleges were free to experiment in the choice of curriculum and methods of work.

It became clear in March of the next year that the Board of Education meant business when the President, Lord Eustace Percy, told a conference representative of all the interests involved that the Board intended to discontinue its own examination for the teachers' certificate. University representatives expressed the view that if universities were being expected to take responsibility for examination, they must have some influence on the courses of study and training in the colleges. The college representatives opposed any new forms of inspection, arguing that universities should not be given sole responsibility for examinations but that joint examining bodies should be formed with the training college authorities.

In June a draft of new regulations for teacher training was circulated. It proposed that the normal period of training for students who had passed the first school examination should remain at two years, but it would have permitted a course of only one year of professional training for those who had passed the second school examination (Higher School Certificate). The aim of this was 'to encourage pupils to stay at a secondary school long enough to prepare for and pass this examination without delaying their entrance into the teaching service'. *The Times Educational Supplement* welcomed the proposal as a way of raising the whole standard of secondary education, since the second school examination was essentially an examination of university standard, and teachers holding this certificate 'coupled with a year's professional training, will bring into the schools a university outlook'.[16]

The N.U.T. welcomed the attempt the Board was making to encourage future teachers to extend their general secondary education to the age of 18, but opposed the consequent shortening of the training college course, on the grounds that neither the academic qualification nor the increased maturity of the student provided adequate compensation for the loss of a year's training.[17] The training college staffs themselves were very strongly opposed to the shortening of their course.

In the debate on the education estimates the following month, the President of the Board said that he hoped the new regulations in their final form would meet most of the criticisms levelled against them in draft. He outlined the Board's policy as being increasingly 'to enable training colleges to take their proper place in the general educational provision of this country in cooperation with the universities and to give them the freedom and the right to exercise their academic judgement in regard to the education they give to candidates for the teaching profession'. He pointed out that he was proposing to devolve the Board's examining functions on bodies representing universities and training colleges, and to them he would refer the whole question of the length of the training college course.[18] In fact it was very unlikely that these bodies would ever agree to a course of only one year and this proved to be the case.

Under pressure from the Board of Education, which was determined to withdraw from examining training college students as soon as possible, rapid progress was made in setting up joint examining boards. The Committee on Universities and Training Colleges, as it came to be known, was set up, with R. G. Mayor, who had just retired from the post of principal assistant secretary of the universities and training of teachers branch, as its secretary. The Committee consisted of 6 members from universities, 4 from local authorities, 2 governors of voluntary colleges and 6 teachers from training colleges. It divided the country into 11 geographical areas, each centred on a university or university college. The negotiations leading to the setting up of joint boards were then conducted on a local basis. In 1929 the examination for the teachers' certificate was conducted by the Board for the last time, but in five areas students were examined under the new arrangements. The two ruling principles in drawing up local regulations were the desirability of allowing individual colleges to prescribe the content of their own syllabuses of study within limits imposed by the general regulations, and the inclusion among the examiners of the staffs of the training colleges.[19] In 1930 the Central Advisory Committee for the Certification of Teachers was appointed to maintain a general view over the final examinations conducted by the joint boards and to advise the Board of Education on these. The Committee had 24 members including 8 representatives of universities, 4 of local authorities, 4 of training college governing bodies and 4 of the teaching profession.[20] In the years before the Second World War only one major change was made in this structure and that was in 1937, when the three joint boards centred on Exeter, Southampton and Bristol agreed to amalgamate to form the Western Joint Board, thus reducing the total number of boards to nine.

The Board of Education also accepted the recommendation of the 1925 Report that pupil teachership should be replaced by the fuller period of secondary education. In spite of the opposition to this from some local authorities, but not by this time from teachers' associations, the Board maintained this policy, so that from 1927 any local authorities wishing to have any pupil teachers had to apply for special permission and 'state fully the reasons for which they desire a continuation of the present arrangements'. The virtual ending of this system of training in the inter-war years under steady pressure from the Board may be seen in this table.

Table 12.1. *Pupil-teachers appointed for the first time during the following years in England and Wales*

Year beginning 1st August	Boys	Girls
1917–1918	297	1,985
1918–1919	255	1,833
1919–1920	300	1,675
1920–1921	381	1,983
1921–1922	417	2,011
1922–1923	384	1,571
1923–1924	282	1,138
1924–1925	311	1,111
1925–1926	(no figures issued)	
1926–1927	267	821
1927–1928	120	412
1928–1929	123	300
1929–1930	127	293
1930–1931	128	257
1931–1932	90	183
1932–1933	97	149
1933–1934	72	108
1934–1935	43	132
1935–1936	40	98
1936–1937	25	86
1937–1938	18	77

Source: Board of Education, Statistics of Public Education and Annual Reports for relevant years.

The strong support which the N.U.T. gave to improving the general level of attainment of entrants to teacher-training reflected among other things a surplus of teachers for much of the period 1919 to 1939. No doubt this surplus could have been absorbed without difficulty if classes had been reduced in size and if the school leaving age had been raised, but the general economic situation seemed to dictate retrenchment rather than the expansion of publicly supported services, and in this sense the apparent oversupply of teachers was associated with these wider national problem of unemployment. Quite naturally the circumstances stimulated the N.U.T. to seek to end the entry of uncertificated and supplementary teachers to the profession. The objections to employing the untrained became most vigorous when the economy campaigns were at their height. In 1922 the Board of Education pressed L.E.A.s to exercise economies in staffing, as a consequence of which the L.C.C., for instance, proposed to bring the number of unqualified teachers in infant schools up to 600 over a period of three years. The President of the N.U.T. described this as 'deliberate dilution of the teaching profession' and a 'definite degradation of the status of the qualified teacher'. The 1923 Conference condemned the 'retrograde policy' the Board of Education was pursuing in trying to introduce teachers of lower qualifications, in attempting to increase the number of pupils per teacher and in withdrawing or reducing government grants to secondary schools.[21]

As a result of appeals for action from unemployed certificated teachers in 1923, the Executive of the N.U.T. issued a warning to parents who might be thinking of teaching as a career for their children. The Union pointed out that large numbers of qualified teachers were unemployed as a result of economy measures, and this despite the fact that when students began to train for the profession they were obliged to sign a declaration that they intended to teach. 'Yet the schools are understaffed, the classes are too large, the continuation schools promised by the Education Act are not in being, and unqualified teachers are taking the place of the qualified.'[22] Inevitably, the N.U.T. returned to the problem of the unqualified frequently. The Conference of 1930 resolved that no uncertificated teachers should be appointed after 1st April 1932 and that after 20 years of approved service such existing teachers should be recognised by the Board as certificated teachers.

The Board tried to deal with the problem of over-supply of teachers by regulating the flow of new entrants to the training colleges. These efforts were of little use, since neither the Board nor anyone else could forecast the demand for teachers with any reliability. Educational and social aspirations which seemed capable of achievement at one moment produced higher estimates of future requirements than were, in fact, justified, since when the time came to fulfil the aspirations another dose of economies had become necessary. In 1929 the government decided to raise the school leaving age to 15 from 1st April, 1931, and the training colleges were invited to expand. 1,000 more students were admitted that autumn than in the previous year, 1928. In November, 1929, the Board invited colleges to expand their intake further in 1930, and undertakings were given that the expansion would be maintained, since colleges were naturally unwilling to expand for only 2 years on a temporary basis. In September, 1931, 1,200 more students were admitted than in 1928, even though the financial crisis had led to the indefinite postponement of the raising of the school leaving age. The Board ordered a cut of $2\frac{1}{2}$ per cent in the number of admissions to colleges in September, 1932, a cut of 10 per cent for September, 1933, and eventually a further cut of 8 per cent for 1934. The fee grant to colleges was reduced and the closure of some colleges became inevitable. The Report of the Board of Education for 1934 perhaps put the best face it could on the matter when it suggested that the year concluded 'the period of gradual reduction in numbers' which when completed would result in a total reduction of 20 per cent in the total number of student places when compared with 1929.

The reaction of the teachers to these changes in government policy was hardly surprising. A delegation from the N.U.T. was received by the President of the Board of Education on 13th October, 1932, and made the point 'that the government was not free from responsibility towards the teachers who only 3 years ago were encouraged to enter the service in order to prepare for the raising of the school leaving age to 15. The government having thus deliberately accelerated the rate of recruitment, it was inconceivable that those additional teachers should now be left stranded.'[23] The period of training meant that estimates of the size of the supply of teachers likely to be needed had to be made up to three years in advance and could really be no more than guesswork. The supply of trained teachers coming forward could not be switched off or even turned down fairly rapidly to match sudden reductions in the number of posts in the schools. The following table shows how gradual were modifications in the supply of new entrants to elementary school teaching.

The position in the early 1930s was made worse by the actions of the Treasury and the local authority associations which set up a committee under Sir William Roy to find economies. The committee reported in November, 1932, and proposed a cut of 7,500 in elementary school staffs, to be carried through within three years. If the proposed reduction was thus spread over a period it should not be necessary to actually dismiss any teachers in service, although it would be even more difficult to absorb newly trained teachers from the colleges. The committee also proposed that for the first ten years of service the salary increments of teachers should be biennial instead of annual. This report led to another

Table 12.2. *Teachers recognised for the first time in the following years ending 31st December: England and Wales*

Year	Certificated		Uncertificated		Teachers of Special Subjects	
	Men	Women	Men	Women	Men	Women
1924	1,723	4,781	451	3,285	91	489
1925	1,963	5,429	507	3,116	95	417
1926	1,848	4,877	446	2,529	84	291
1927	2,223	5,952	439	2,118	159	282
1928	1,920	5,166	424	1,740	268	322
1929	1,852	4,934	378	1,334	273	355
1930	2,054	5,054	521	1,455	315	401
1931	2,438	5,420	456	1,371	384	401
1932	2,614	5,173	476	1,397	486	450
1933	2,789	5,313	373	1,235	400	465
1934	2,325	4,854	268	1,139	346	447
1935	2,336	4,721	241	976	350	497
1936	2,010	4,332	136	824	302	485
1937	2,097	4,541	140	795	340	497
1938	2,060	4,288	115	765	299	522

Source: Annual Reports of the Board of Education for the relevant years.

N.U.T. deputation to the Board of Education which again emphasised that since the government had so recently accelerated the supply of teachers it could not now repudiate its obligation to them. A further deputation in March, 1933, suggested that no new recognition in the Code should be accorded to supplementary teachers and that no more uncertificated teachers should be appointed.

Unemployment among teachers between the wars increased the efforts made by the N.U.T. to raise the standards required for entry to training and to exclude from the elementary schools those who were not certificated. This pressure certainly played an important part in bringing about the improvement in the level of qualification which is shown in table 12.3.

While secondary school teachers' associations were concerned about unemployment during these years, their reactions were muted by comparison with those of the N.U.T., and the rather different attitude taken by some of them, particularly the headmasters, to training meant

Table 12.3. *Numbers and percentages of different grades of recognised teachers in public elementary schools: England and Wales*

Grade of Teacher	1921		1931		1938	
	Number	%	Number	%	Number	%
Certificated	118,071	71·5	126,245	77·0	131,941	81·9
Uncertificated	35,178	21·2	30,632	18·6	24,058	14·9
Supplementary	12,898	7·3	7,270	4·4	4,905	3·2
	166,147		164,147		160,904	

Source: Annual Reports of the Board of Education for the relevant years.

that they did not look to an increased emphasis on improved professional qualifications as offering any alleviation of the position. The proportion of graduate assistant schoolmasters in secondary schools who were trained was little different in 1938 from what it was in 1927; about 60 per cent of such men were trained and 40 per cent remained untrained. There had long been a greater tendency among schoolmistresses to take training seriously and the corresponding figures for women in 1938 were 69 per cent trained against 31 per cent untrained. The actual figures are shown in table 12.4.

Table 12.4. *Secondary Schools on the grant list; teachers by sex and qualifications on 31st March, England and Wales*

Full time Graduates	1927	1930	1933	1936	1938
Men assistants					
(i) Trained	5,314	5,226	5,014	5,785	6,271
(ii) Not trained	3,433	3,720	3,929	4,036	4,071
Women assistants					
(i) Trained	3,022	3,836	4,534	5,120	5,487
(ii) Not trained	2,508	2,594	2,552	2,409	2,370

Throughout the 1920s and 1930s there continued to be a good deal of criticism of training courses and—especially from members of the Headmasters' Conference—demands for school-based training or 'apprenticeship' as it was sometimes called. One headmaster who expounded these ideas in an article entitled 'The Training of Teachers', was V. T. Saunders of Uppingham. Graduates should be trained by an apprenticeship system in which a light initial timetable for the newly recruited and raw graduate would enable him to 'attend in rooms where other journeymen of the craft are working'. He claimed that young teachers would not merely pick up the same old unimproved teaching methods from stale practitioners because they would attend in a 'constructively critical frame of mind', drawing the best from each one, afterwards moulding it for their own purposes. In this way the new teacher would learn his work 'not at the feet of the university professor of the science of education, but by daily contact with those who have trod the path before him and are treading it still'.[24]

The educational section of the British Association was told by the headmaster of Wellington at its 1925 meeting that most members of the Headmaster's Conference did not require training. He thought this was because 'In all schools the personality of the teacher is more valuable than his scholarship, his method or his equipment'.

Similar scepticism was shown by members of the larger I.A.H.M. This Association passed a motion in favour of a course of post-graduate training for secondary teachers in 1934, but only after a debate characterised by doubts as to the value of such training.[25] The I.A.A.M. also continued to show from time to time that it shared similar doubts. At the annual general meeting in 1938 a resolution was passed instructing the executive to report and make recommendations on the training of teachers, the existing system for a student being criticised as lacking 'real experience in an ordinary school'.[26] The education sub-committee of the Association thought that the problems involved in the question of the training of teachers were too complex for the I.A.A.M. to undertake by itself and suggested that the Board of Education should institute an inquiry. Pressure for such an inquiry mounted from different quarters, and a formal investigation was due to be undertaken when the outbreak of war in 1939 caused it to be postponed.

NOTES

1. 8 and 9 Geo. 5, c. 39, S.44 (2).
2. The term 'Higher education' covered virtually all education more advanced than 'elementary' at this time including secondary (i.e. grammar) schools.
3. *Memorandum on Training Colleges provided by Local Education Authorities*, by a special joint committee of the A.M.C., C.C.A., and A.E.C., 1923.
4. Ibid.
5. Board of Education, Report of the Departmental Committee on the Training of Teachers for Public Elementary Schools, Cmd. 2409, 1925, p. 9.
6. Ibid., p. 168.
7. *The Training of Teachers*, Memorandum of Joint Standing Committee of the Training Colleges Association and the Council of Principals, 1937, p. 45.
8. 'President's Address to Training College Association' in *Journal of Experimental Pedagogy*, vol. V, 1919–20, p. 4.
9. L. Grier, *The Life of Winifred Mercier*, 1937, pp. 179–81.
10. *The Schoolmaster*, 10th April, 1920, pp. 720–4.
11. Ibid., 17th August, 1923, p. 227.
12. Board of Education, Report of the Departmental Committee on the Training of Teachers for Public Elementary Schools, Cmd. 2409, 1925, pp. 84–6.
13. Ibid., pp. 107–11.
14. Ibid., p. 183.
15. *The Schoolmaster*, 22nd May, 1925, pp. 918–20.
16. *T.E.S.*, 12th June, 1926, p. 247.
17. *The Schoolmaster*, 11th June, 1926, p. 948.
18. *Hansard*, H. of C., 22nd July, 1926, col. 1449.
19. Board of Education, Annual Report for 1929, p. 54.
20. Board of Education, Annual Report for 1930, p. 61.
21. N.U.T. Annual Report, 1923, p. ci.
22. *The Schoolmaster*, 20th July, 1923, p. 87.
23. Ibid., 20th October, 1932, p. 543.
24. *Journal of Education*, January, 1925, pp. 20–22.
25. Ibid., February, 1934, p. 112.
26. *The A.M.A.*, January, 1938, pp. 37–8.

13
The Training and Supply of Teachers since the Second World War

Immediately before the Second World War the training colleges and university departments of education taken together were producing slightly fewer than 7,000 trained teachers annually. The total number of qualified teachers from the colleges and departments of education in 1969 was more than four times greater. This enormous growth in numbers is one of the more tangible features of post-war development and it has been the product of a number of factors, including both the immediate post-war need to make good the dearth of newly-qualified teachers during the war years themselves and, over the longer term, the rising standard of living of the community, bringing with it an ever-growing demand for more professional services, including education. This longer-term rise in the standard of living has also produced an effective demand not merely for more schooling in the pre-war sense but for more education of a higher quality. The provision of teachers fitted to provide this has led to a general up-grading of teacher training itself, so that the colleges of education have in recent years come to be acknowledged in their own right as an important sector of higher education.

These developments have enabled the teachers' associations to realise some part of their aims in connection with the training and status of the profession. For many years the N.U.T. has sought a lengthening of the minimum period of training. This would ensure that pupils had better qualified teachers. It would also improve the status of the teachers, bring them nearer to the much desired parity with better established professions and improve their financial rewards. The period which the Union has sought has been four years and it has asserted that the teaching profession 'will not achieve its rightful status until the college courses on education and training are of four years' duration and until the normal qualification for recognition as a teacher

Table 13.1. *Total number of students who satisfactorily completed initial training courses (excluding Emergency Training Scheme)*

Year	Number of Students
1939	6,121
1948	9,029
1949	9,735
1950	11,393
1951	13,379
1952	14,008
1953	14,096
1954	13,812
1955	14,003
1956	14,165
1957	14,554
1958	15,231
1959	16,034
1960	17,622
1961	18,500
1962	7,657
1963	17,997
1964	19,842
1965	21,688
1966	24,313
1967	27,634

Source: Ministry of Education and Department of Education and Science, Official Reports

includes a university degree' or the equivalent.[1] The fully qualified graduate has had a four-year period of training for a long time; if all teachers trained for the same length of time, then, it is argued, the unity of the profession would be achieved. It follows that the N.U.T. has opposed any lowering of the standard of entry to training colleges partly because that would widen the gap between college and university entrance requirements. It also follows that it has been strongly opposed to the idea of a shorter period of training for infants' teachers. Both the N.U.T. and the A.T.C.D.E. have been advocates of compulsory training for graduates, have sought a closer association between the colleges and universities and have become increasingly anxious to broaden the function of the colleges so as to include work other than teacher training. Many of these aims have been achieved wholly or in part.

During this period teachers' associations have been faced from time to time with quite acute dilemmas when apparently equally desirable aims appeared to come into conflict with each other. The lengthening of the period of training and the maintenance of entry requirements for college admission appeared to work against the achievement of such other aims as the raising of the school leaving age, the establishment of more nursery schools and, above all, the reduction in the size of classes —all requiring more teachers. Indeed, it is significant that it was not until the middle years of the 1950s, when problems of supply seemed to be easing, that the N.U.T. turned its full attention to the achievement of the three-year course of training. It can also be argued that while the abhorrence shown by teachers to the employment of auxiliaries is entirely understandable, it has in practice led to the lot of many junior school teachers being made more onerous.

I THE EMERGENCY TRAINING SCHEME AND PROFESSIONAL STATUS

Planning for the new Educational Bill which was to become law in 1944 focused attention on the likely shortage of teachers immediately after the war. In July, 1943, an office committee was set up in the Board of Education under the chairmanship of Sir Robert Wood, Deputy Secretary, to report on the emergency problems which would arise in the recruitment and training of teachers, on the passing of the bill. The committee found that the drop in the number of teachers between 1938 and 1942 was balanced by a drop in the number of pupils. There was an annual loss in the war years through non-recruitment of 3,250, while some 20,000 teachers had left the schools for various forms of war service. There had been an influx of 37,000 stop-gap staff, mainly retired teachers or married women who, it was thought, would probably leave after the war. Thus the problem was to recruit 40,000 new teachers as quickly as possible at the end of the war to replace the ravages of the war itself and to provide for the raising of the school leaving age to 15. The committee expressly excepted from its calculations the consequence of raising the leaving age to 16 and the reduction of class sizes.

The solution to the problem which the committee advanced was to set up some 50 training colleges, quite separate from the existing colleges, each having about 200 students, financed entirely by the Exchequer and operated on behalf of the Board of Education by local education authorities. The courses offered were to be of one year's duration, two-thirds of the time being spent in training and one-third in school practice. Special emphasis during the course ought to be laid upon the teacher's use of English. The committee suggested that an imaginative campaign should be undertaken to 'sell' the scheme to teachers' organisations and local education authorities. It was thought that the selection of candidates should be through personal interview and that every effort should be made 'to work new seams in our society', which had not been accustomed to contemplating teaching as a profession.[2] Sir Robert Wood addressed teachers' meetings in different parts of the country in the autumn and winter of 1943 and aroused sympathetic interest in the scheme, although there was opposition from some groups of trained teachers.

In October, 1943, the N.U.T. issued a memorandum stating its short-term policy for increasing the supply of teachers in an emergency. Among other factors thought to be likely to produce an urgent need for more teachers immediately after the war were the need to reduce the size of classes, to raise the school leaving age and to introduce both day continuation and nursery schools. The memorandum emphasised that the long-term policy must be to make the teaching profession more attractive. In the meantime, emergency training might consist of an initial period of training for 12 months followed by further training after 4 years of teaching. The whole of that time was to be regarded as part of the preparation for full professional status.[3]

Two months later Mr. Butler appointed an advisory committee on the emergency recruitment and training of teachers with G. N. Flemming (Permanent Assistant Secretary of the Board) as chairman, and including representatives of the teachers, local authorities and training institutions as well as officials of the Board and H.M.I.s. This committee's recommendations were set out in Circular 1652 in May, 1944, and followed closely the suggestions made by the office committee under Sir Richard Wood. Teachers trained under this scheme were to be recognised as fully qualified. The training year was to include 4 weeks of vacation, a preparatory stage of 6 weeks, 2 main courses totalling 30 weeks and 2 periods of teaching practice amounting to 12 weeks. As much of the work as possible was to be on a tutorial basis and at the end the students were to be assessed on their overall performance; they could pass, fail or be referred for more training. The first two years of actual service were to be probationary and to include a course of part-time study. The whole scheme was to be financed by the Treasury, the students selected being given free tuition and maintenance grants on the same lines as in the Further Education and Training Scheme for demobilised men and women.

The N.U.T. took a cautious attitude towards the proposals. In general it felt that the report showed the desire on the part of the committee's members to do everything possible to maintain the standards and traditions of the profession while securing the recruits necessary to make educational advance possible. The fears of some teachers were reflected in their letters to journals. One correspondent wrote to *The Schoolmaster* that 'so long as "teachers" can be raised like mushrooms, wholly at the expense of the state, their value in public estimation must be two a penny'.

Some of the smaller associations of teachers expressed misgivings fairly frankly. The President of the National Federation of Class Teachers pointed out the possible dangers to his conference in September 1944. 'If the selection is made with care then the leeway can be made up by private study, but it would be disastrous if the large number of new entrants required should lack the standard of culture and knowledge which is regarded as an essential part of a teacher's equipment. The proposal that these men and women should be regarded as qualified teachers at the end of a twelve-months' course, with no examination, subject only to the completion of a probationary period, is fraught with great risks, and every encouragement should be given to them to secure satisfactory evidence of academic proficiency after they have qualified.'[4] The N.U.W.T. told the Board of Education that it considered the scheme was as good as could be achieved with so short a course but added that to suggest that teachers trained in this way could adequately take their place as equals beside teachers who had entered the profession through other and more usual channels was to cast grievous doubt on the value of training and 'dangerously to undermine the professional status of the teacher'.[5]

The acceptance of the Emergency Training Scheme by the N.U.T. should be viewed against the Union's success in persuading the Board of Education to meet it at least half-way over the question of uncertificated teachers. A deputation to the Board in 1943 raised the issue of the situation which would be created by the anticipated proposals for the emergency training of recruits from the Forces in relation to the position of the uncertificated. The question was studied by a special committee established by the Board for the purpose of considering the status of uncertificated teachers. The President and General Secretary of the N.U.T. were members, and the committee's report was accepted. Mr. Butler told the House of Commons that from 1st April, 1945, uncertificated teachers who had served for more than twenty years would be graded as qualified teachers. Those with between five and twenty years of service would be eligible as soon as they could be spared and training facilities were available, to take a special one-year course which would entitle them to be graded as qualified teachers.[6] There would be no recognition of new uncertificated teachers. As far back as 1929 the Union had sought to resolve the problems of recognised uncertificated teachers by getting the Board to cease giving its recognition to future appointments and by granting a certificate to those already recognised on completion of twenty years' service.

The Emergency Training Scheme itself proved to have a very strong appeal to would-be teachers. During the latter part of 1946 and early 1947 applications were being received at a rate of more than 5,000 a month. The interviewing panels had difficulty in coping with the numbers, and admissions to colleges lagged far behind what was required, so that some successful candidates had to wait as long as two years before starting their courses. In a sense the sudden and unexpected end of the war in the Far East concentrated the rush of applications into a much shorter period of time than had been envisaged by the Ministry. There was much criticism of what turned out to be the inadequacy of the arrangements. At the 1946 Conference the President of the N.U.T. drew attention to the failure of emergency training college accommodation to keep pace with the number of applicants selected and urged the Ministry to requisition the necessary premises and to insist that its claims must override those of other ministries. If the teachers were not obtained the Act would not be implemented and high hopes would fade into 'cynicism and apathy'.

Criticism of the scheme itself began to increase among teachers from about 1948. Dissatisfaction generally was growing in the profession, and an intensive Ministry recruitment campaign in the press and by means of film to try to secure additional women teachers through the emergency scheme produced concern in the N.U.T. about methods of selection. The films and pamphlets seemed to suggest that anyone could teach, and the Union made representation to the Minister about the standards of selection of candidates under the scheme. In the following couple of years the feeling grew among teachers that doctors and dentists, who were also in short supply, had not relaxed their standards of entry and had reaped greater financial rewards and improved their status. Immediately after the war certificated teachers appeared to have done quite well financially, but by 1949 their position had worsened by comparison not only with other professional groups but also with semi-skilled and unskilled industrial employees. In November, 1949, a claim for an interim increase on the basic scale was refused. The leadership of the N.U.T. found the position to some extent embarrassing. In his address to the 1950 Conference the President referred to criticism of the emergency trained teachers and suggested 'Above all, let us acknowledge that they came in response to a national appeal to which this Union, rightly or wrongly, had given its approval.'

This particular sore continued to fester and towards the end of 1951 *The Schoolmaster*'s columnist 'Peter Quince' came back to it and, in effect, summarised the position as the leadership of the N.U.T. saw it. It was wrong for teachers to attribute the present ills of the profession to the emergency training scheme; that scheme should be seen as an integral part of a series of events which in total marked a great advance in the status of teachers as members of a trained and qualified profession. Before 1945 the door had been open to the unqualified, and these supplementary and uncertificated grades were a source of weakness to the profession as a whole. 'Indeed, the better they taught, the greater the source of weakness they became, for they were a living argument that teaching was a job that required neither qualifications nor training.' The real choice before the teaching profession never was, 'Shall we have an emergency training scheme or not?'; it was, 'Shall we have an emergency scheme or shall we continue to permit the entrance of unqualified people?' Subsequent events, it was claimed, had shown that the correct decision was taken.

By the time the emergency training scheme was terminated in 1951 it had produced more than 23,000 men and nearly 12,000 qualified women teachers. Thus by 1951 something like 15 per cent of the teachers serving in primary and secondary schools had been produced by this scheme. In secondary modern schools the proportion of emergency trained teachers was at its highest. Many of these schools were being set up or reorganised at this time, while 75 per cent of male students in the emergency colleges trained to teach pupils at the upper end of the age range, i.e. to fifteen years of age. As may be seen from Table 13.2 the great majority of candidates accepted under the scheme had had some secondary education.

Table 13.2. *Candidates accepted for training under the emergency training scheme (less withdrawals); analysis of previous education*[7]

Type of education	Men	Women
Elementary	2,981	1,119
Senior non-selective	793	352
Selective Control without School Certificate	1,815	687
Selective Control with School Certificate	334	99
Secondary without School Certificate	5,235	3,653
Secondary with School Certificate	9,558	4,726
Secondary with Higher Certificate	645	289
Technical without National Certificate	1,455	564
Technical with Ordinary National Certificate	131	54
Technical with Higher National Certificate	13	2
University without degree	311	84
University with pass degree	144	53
University with honours degree	12	2
Private tuition	42	39
Overseas	339	197
	23,808	11,920

II AREA TRAINING ORGANISATIONS

The first steps to adapt the permanent arrangements for the training of teachers to post-war conditions were taken during the war, the most significant being the setting up by the Board of Education in 1942 of a committee 'To investigate the present sources of supply and the methods of recruitment and training of teachers and youth leaders and to report what principles should guide the Board in these matters in the future'. Sir Arnold McNair, Vice-Chancellor of Liverpool University, was chairman of the committee, and its report was published in 1944. This recommended much of the structure of the present organisation of teacher training. The committee was divided over the most far-reaching of the recommendations, that for university schools of education. While agreed on the nature of the problem, namely the need to integrate on an area basis the institutions involved in teacher training, some members felt that the existing joint examining board arrangements should continue, with modifications designed to strengthen them. Others found that joint examining board arrangements had failed to bring about any constitutional relationship between the colleges and the universities as such, had failed to bring university education departments into relationship with the colleges, and had failed to bring the colleges themselves together. The schools and local authorities also needed to be involved much more closely in the task of training teachers.

The Universities, it was argued, should accept new responsibilities for the education and training of teachers. University schools of education would be responsible for the training of graduates and non-graduates alike, and institutions approved for the training of qualified teachers of all kinds would become integral parts of the schools. The idea that universities should concern themselves only with the training of teachers of older children was rejected, largely on the grounds that at a time when the education service was being unified, it would be doing a disservice to education to take a step which divided the teaching profession. Moreover the fundamental studies of all teachers such as psychology and sociology were, 'at their apex', the concern of the universities. The school itself would be governed by a delegacy subject to the ultimate control of the university and consisting of representatives of the university, of training institutions and of the local education authorities. It would be directed by a director appointed by the university, and by a professional board consisting mainly of teachers from the university itself and from the training colleges. The school would absorb the existing university department of education and the professional board would replace the existing joint examination board. It would offer a common professional qualification to graduate and non-graduate students alike. It would also foster educational research, organise refresher and advanced courses and offer such amenities as library and conference rooms, so that it would become the centre of the professional interests of practising teachers in the area, and the place to which local education authorities and other bodies concerned with education would look for accommodation and guidance in the matter of public lectures, conferences, discussion groups, exhibitions and other means of promoting the interests of education. While training colleges might continue to be financed in the existing manner for the present, the possibility should not be excluded of a block grant to the school to cover the costs of all the member institutions in future.[8]

The recommendation for the establishment of university schools of education (which came to be known as Scheme 'A', while reformed joint boards were known as Scheme 'B') met with a favourable response from most teachers' organisations. It was, perhaps, not surprising that the executive of the N.U.T. welcomed Scheme A, since its general secretary had been one of those members of the McNair Committee who had put it forward. The Union's leadership believed that this scheme would contribute to the establishment of a united teaching profession. The Association of University Teachers accepted the principle of Scheme A and urged the universities to accept responsibility for the education and training of teachers. One of the reasons it gave was that this could help to unite school teachers, raise their status and make possible a wider variety of training.[9]

Various local education authorities supported the scheme, among them the education committee of the L.C.C., which resolved that the universities should have the general responsibility for the training of teachers. Some of the existing joint examining boards also gave support to Scheme A. The Yorkshire Training Colleges Examination Board issued a memorandum in July 1944 which contained a powerful plea for university schools of education. This urged that a unified system of education required a unified teaching profession, which could only be achieved when all training had been brought within one system. 'Teachers will tend to remain a race apart so long as their training is kept separate from that of the other learned professions. The first scheme would bring them directly within the sphere of university influence during their training, the second would perpetuate the evil tradition of separate training and examination.'

The outcome of the discussions following the McNair report was that not all universities welcomed the responsibilities implicit in Scheme A, and a third scheme, 'C', was proposed under which the school of education would be an autonomous entity established by a declaration of trust and financed wholly by the Ministry of Education. In fact, most universities accepted Scheme A, often with some local variations and usually describing the new organisations as 'institutes' not 'schools'. Four area training organisations were constituted in 1947 (Bristol, Birmingham, Nottingham and Southampton) and ten more had been set up by the end of 1948. Eventually all but three were constituted on the lines of Scheme A, the three which followed the Scheme C pattern being Cambridge, Liverpool and Reading.

In 1952 the Institutes of Education were everywhere operational, carrying out the functions outlined for them in the McNair Report, growing rapidly in the number and variety of their activities. From the beginning most of them went beyond the basic function of supervising initial courses of training and recommending to the Minister for recognition as qualified teachers students who had been successful in the training colleges. Libraries and other facilities were provided, short courses and refresher courses were organised, and very soon advanced diploma courses for experienced teachers requiring a year of full-time study came to be offered by many institutes. While the area training organisations have served teachers from all types of school and background, they were probably most welcomed by the college-trained non-graduates. Such suspicion of them as there was initially came from the secondary teachers, more particularly from secondary school head teachers. The president of the I.A.H.M., in his address to the Association at the beginning of 1952, complained that the institutes had been set up without consultation with those most concerned, and without any effective participation by the I.A.H.M. or any other teachers' organisation. As the institutes have grown in function and in stature, so such suspicions as might have existed seem to have been dispersed.

III RECRUITMENT, SUPPLY AND THE 3-YEAR COURSE

The need was apparent for some central advisory body to keep the national demand for and supply of teachers under review, and in 1947 the Minister appointed an Interim Committee for Teachers consisting of teachers', training college, university and local authority representatives. This body considered current problems of teacher training and supply and agreed to the introduction of a scheme to secure the fair distribution of women teachers. The committee was replaced by the National Advisory Council on the Training and Supply of Teachers in 1949. The Council's task was to keep under review national policy on the training and conditions of qualification of teachers and on their recruitment and distribution. It had 40 members who represented the various teachers' associations (6 from N.U.T., 2 from the Joint Four, 4 from the A.T.C.D.E., 1 from the A.T.T.I. and 1 from the A.P.T.I.), as well as members from the local authority associations, area training organisations, the universities and the ministry. The Council set up two standing committees, one concerned with the training and qualification of teachers, on which all area training organisations were represented, and the other with recruitment and distribution.

During the first ten years or so of its existence there was sufficient harmony of view between the various partners of the education service for the Council to function smoothly and to achieve useful reforms by agreement. It pressed in 1950 for the abolition of the four-year grant system by which undergraduates who 'pledged' themselves to teach in grant-aided schools were given grants to go to university, and urged an increase in the number of state scholarships to 2,000, to help replace them. The abolition of these tied grants had long been an aim of the teachers' associations, and in March, 1951, the Ministry announced that the number of state scholarships was to be increased to 2,000 and that the four-year grant system was abolished for new entrants from the autumn of 1951.[10] The minimum entry requirements for admission to training colleges in terms of the newly introduced G.C.E. were suggested by the Council and accepted by the Ministry.[11] The need to increase the number of graduate teachers and the need to overcome the shortage of applications from women for admission to training colleges also attracted the attention of the Council. In the early 1950s nearly two-thirds of the girls who stayed at school until the age of 18 and who did not go to university went to training colleges. The Council suggested that special efforts should be made to attract girls who had already left school, with the result that in the autumn of 1951 only 250 out of the 8,000 places in the women's colleges were empty. Against this background the dilemma facing teachers' organisations of either insisting on high entry qualifications and tolerating large classes, or lowering the qualifications and shortening the period of large classes may be seen in a resolution passed by the N.U.T. Conference in 1951, viz., 'that the reduction to a maximum of 30 in all classes be the immediate and most pressing concern of our Union, but that this reduction be not effected by any lowering of the professional qualifications and standard of teachers'.

In spite of its representation on the Council, the N.U.T. was, in fact, disappointed by its First Report. The Union expected much bolder measures to be devised to meet the shortage of teachers. The Council did not seem to be prepared to state why so many pupils failed to complete the grammar school course nor why so few, comparatively, were prepared to train for teaching. Nor was it willing to advance long-term cures for the problem. The N.U.T. hoped that the next National Advisory Council statement would show 'more ruthlessness and a willingness to risk more'. From the Report the reader might conclude that the field of teacher training had become the happy hunting-ground of a posse of statisticians.[12]

The questions of standards of admission and of increasing recruitment continued to be a live issue for some years. In 1952 the local authorities suggested various schemes to meet the shortage of recruits, whereby young people were to be enabled to pursue preparatory courses at the end of which they might be eligible for admission to colleges even though they did not possess a qualification as laid down in the regulations. The N.U.T.'s policy was that the existing minimum qualifications of 5 'O' level passes should be maintained, and it was hoped that all future candidates would have at least one pass at 'A' level. The Union's 1952 Conference concerned itself with the danger of dilution of standards of entry and opposed strongly suggestions that lower standards might be acceptable for candidates proposing to teach infants. Existing minimum standards for admission were re-affirmed at the 1953 Conference, when the mover of the motion explained that their ultimate aim was that teaching should be a graduate profession and that as a first step there should be equivalence between the minimum standards for admission to training colleges and universities. At the end of 1953, a former member of the N.U.T. executive, Mr. G. Thomas, opened an adjournment debate on the supply and training of teachers and on the maintenance of the standards required for admission. He claimed that in 1950 216 students were admitted without the minimum academic requirements, in 1951 454, in 1952 775, in 1953 624. In replying to the debate the Parliamentary Secretary analysed the 624 of 1953. 124 of these students possessed Irish, Scottish, army or other academic qualifications, another 241 had some G.C.E. or School Certificate qualifications although they were not within the regulations. The remainder had been admitted by area training organisations after interviews or examinations.[13]

The other association the majority of whose members were non-graduate qualified assistant teachers, the N.A.S., showed similar alarm in the early 1950s. The N.A.S. annual conference in April, 1954, debated this problem and called for the maintenance of minimum academic and personal standards for entrants to the colleges. A deputation from the Association went to the Ministry to express concern at any attempts to lower the standard of entry to teaching and to urge the protection of the professional status of teachers.

The pressure to lower standards of admission was replaced in the later years of the decade by the real possibility of lengthening and improving the minimum training period. The shortage of teachers eased, partly because recruitment began to improve, but, more important, wastage among serving teachers fell; in particular more married women continued teaching than had been expected and more married women also returned to teaching.[14] The first official change in policy arising out of this change in the supply position was the omission from the training regulations which came into force on 1st January, 1956 of the requirement that students sign an undertaking to teach in a state-aided school as a prior requirement to receiving a grant while at training college. The abolition of this 'pledge' had long been sought by teachers and was welcomed by the N.U.T. which had particularly disliked it as it distinguished intending teachers from would-be entrants to other professions.

A minimum period of 3 years for the training of non-graduate teachers had been an objective of the N.U.T. for many years and the McNair Report had recommended 'that the normal period of education and training provided by area training authorities for those entering upon preparation for the teaching profession at about 18 years of age should be 3 years'.[15] It has been shown that the teachers' associations were concerned particularly with the shortage of entrants to the profession and the need to reduce large classes in the years immediately after the war, and the longer period of training was not, therefore, given priority. At its conference in 1949, for instance, while the N.U.T. reaffirmed the 3-year course as an objective, it rejected an amendment which tried to fix a definite date after which newly appointed teachers must have three years of training. In 1950 the A.T.C.D.E. put a plan to the National Advisory Council for the introduction of the three-year period by instalments, autumn 1952 for secondary teachers, 1955 for infant teachers, 1958 for teachers of juniors. The Council felt obliged to rule out any scheme which might reduce the number of teachers in the circumstances then prevailing, but by 1955 the supply situation had changed sufficiently for the Council to consider the question again. At the same time the Minister asked the Council for a statement of the educational advantages of the three-year course, the form it should take, the method by which it should be introduced and the factors of which account should be taken in considering the date of introduction. The Council gave its advice on all these points and suggested that the choice of date for the introduction of the three-year course lay between 1959 and 1960.[16] The very great change in the supply situation as the Council saw it led to a warning in its Fifth Report that without the introduction of the longer course or some equivalent restriction there might be difficulty in the early 1960s in maintaining full employment among teachers.

Although this latter point may well have played some part in the thinking of teachers, the general secretary of the N.U.T. warned against putting it forward as any part of the case for a three-year course. 'To ensure quality in the teaching profession, therefore, we must extend the minimum course to three years. That is a perfectly logical case. It is intelligible and it carries conviction to the general public.

'I have often heard it argued, however, that we must increase the length of the course to avoid unemployment among teachers when the bulge has passed through the schools. I personally do not regard the passing of the bulge as a valid reason for increasing the length of the course; it is only a reason for lengthening it at a particular time. Bulge or no bulge, there is a sound educational reason for a three-year course, and this is the reason we must stress.'[17]

At conference after conference of teachers the extension of the minimum training period was seen as a way of improving the status of the profession. The doctors and lawyers appeared to enjoy a higher status and the higher income that this attracted. The reason for their higher status was said to be their longer period of training. Moreover, a longer basic course for the non-graduate teacher would have the effect of 'unifying' and 'integrating' the teaching profession itself, and would pull the graduate and non-graduate elements more closely together.

The argument that a longer training period would unify the profession did not seem so strong outside the N.U.T. as within it. *The Times Educational Supplement* pointed out that although there was some truth in this argument, the training colleges could not expect to compete with the universities any more in the future than they had done in the past. 'The universities will still take the best academic brains. The training colleges will still recruit from the rest. . . . The chief value of the third year should be in the chance it will give them to get their students better grounded in the subjects they are to teach.'[18]

Successive governments since the McNair Report had spoken of welcoming an additional year's training for teachers when the supply position eased. Now that it appeared to be easing, the government of the day had little room left for manoeuvre—even supposing it had wished to do so—and in June, 1957, Lord Hailsham told the House of Lords that the three-year course would be introduced in September, 1960. The announcement was naturally welcomed by the N.U.T. A leading article in *The Schoolmaster* declared that there was no other reform which could ultimately do more to improve the quality of the teaching profession and raise its status; moreover, in welcoming the reform teachers were neither selfish nor lacking in concern for the public welfare, 'because better qualified teachers must inevitably produce better opportunities for the nation's children'.[19]

Within a few months of the decision being announced it became apparent that the National Advisory Council's assumptions about the supply position were much too optimistic. In a debate in the Commons in February, 1958, on the recruitment, supply and training of teachers it was shown that wastage had begun to grow much more rapidly. In the seven years ending in 1956 there was an annual average net increase of 6,500 in the number of teachers; in 1957 this dropped to 5,000. Although there was an arguable case for reversing the 1957 decision, Sir Edward Boyle undertook that the government would not change its mind. It regarded itself as being absolutely committed 'to this great forward project'.

There was certainly a degree of public controversy in 1958. *The Times* suggested that the three-year training scheme should be postponed until classes had been reduced to 40 and 30, and suggested that most people would agree with this priority. In the N.U.T. there were fears that if the supply situation deteriorated further the government might yet retreat, and there was some criticism of the utterances of the training college interest, the 'more politically innocent' of whom were said to have been talking in terms of doing in three years what they used to do in two, while even 'the politically adept' had fought hard to avoid giving demonstrable proof that standards would be raised. Teachers themselves had concentrated upon the benefit they expected in terms of better salaries and improved status. But the only argument likely to carry weight with the public was that the two-year trained teacher was insufficiently educated to do the job properly.[20] Even so, existing teachers no doubt found this a difficult argument to advance, since they would seem to be criticising themselves as insufficiently educated. *The Economist* wondered whether the longer period really would be rewarding. Some people regarded the whole affair 'as the manifestation of the non-graduate teachers' chip on the shoulder itch for "parity of esteem" with graduates'. The general, compulsory three-year training course was likely to worsen the supply of teachers without doing much to improve quality. *The Economist* concluded by wondering whether the politicians could reverse in the name of commonsense a decision they had already announced as a concession to special interests.[21]

Had readers of *The Economist* read the leading article in the N.U.T.'s journal eighteen months' later, some might have taken it as confirmation of the allegation that the longer course was a concession to special interests. The article complained that it was not widely enough known among teachers how directly the reform was due to steady pressure from the N.U.T. For years it had maintained the pressure, at one stage it had met opposition within the National Advisory Council itself. 'The Union can rightly claim this successful campaign as a major contribution to the advancement of professional status.'[22]

Faced with criticisms on these lines, the N.U.T. moved to the position of calling for an expansion of training college places of more than 50 per cent, so as both to provide for the three-year course and to increase the supply of teachers. The introduction of the longer minimum training course did in fact bring with it the commencement of the rapid expansion of the training colleges that was to be a marked feature of teacher training in the 1960s. In August, 1958, the National Advisory Council wrote to the Minister recommending that 16,000 additional places be provided in colleges by 1962. The Minister accepted a programme to provide 12,000 new places by 1962 and announced at the A.E.C. Conference in 1959 his intention of adding a further 4,000 or more by 1964. The expansion of the number of places in the training colleges was to make them one of the most rapidly expanding sectors of education over the next decade. The growth in the student entry for the ten years from 1959 is shown on page 300.

IV THE BALANCE OF TRAINING AND THREATS OF 'DILUTION'

The last decade had seen the growth within the educational system of much sharper conflicts which directly reflect the increasing pressure of social and economic issues in the nation generally. The associations representing non-graduate teachers—and particularly the N.U.T., of course—have found themselves much concerned to defend the position they have achieved in the face of outside pressures. One of the first instances of this arose in 1960. The Ministry of Education then sought to change the balance between primary and secondary training. The colleges were currently preparing 63 per cent of their students for primary work and 37 per cent for secondary. The ministry wanted to change the balance so as to fit 85 per cent for primary teaching and only 15 per cent for secondary. The colleges were asked to produce plans indicating how they would achieve this new balance, which was to be

Table 13.3. *Students admitted to initial teacher training courses at colleges (excluding university departments), 1959–68*[23]

Year of admission	Students admitted
1959	15,700
1960	16,600
1961	17,000
1962	17,700
1963	21,500
1964	25,100
1965	30,000
1966	34,000
1967	37,300
1968	39,000

attained within 3 years starting with the 1961 intake. Three reasons were given by the ministry for seeking this change; the expected substantial rise in numbers in the primary schools owing to the renewed increase in the number of births, the increased rate of wastage among women teachers, who constituted some two-thirds of teachers in infant and junior schools, and the increase in the number of graduate teachers which was expected as a consequence of the expansion of universities. It was expected that three-quarters of these graduates would be needed by the selective secondary schools and to teach those staying on in other schools, but the remaining 10,000, together with the non-graduates already in schools, would serve the needs of the secondary modern schools in the arts subjects 'without further re-inforcement from the training colleges'.[24]

The N.A.S., the N.U.T. and the A.T.C.D.E. were all critical of the ministry's suggestions. The N.A.S. in a statement criticised the implication that untrained graduates would be satisfactory teachers for the modern schools and that the value of professional training was, therefore, secondary to that of academic attainment. It reiterated that 'An essential step towards the establishment of true professional status for teachers is that all should be trained graduates'.[25] There was great consternation at the meeting of the executive of the A.T.C.D.E. on 28th and 29th October,[26] and the secretary, Miss Helen Simpson, in an article on 'The Balance of Training' pointed out that the severance of primary from secondary training contained 'the certain threat of a dichotomy, not only in the profession, but in the whole educational system as we know it. If this dichotomy were allowed to develop, the growing move towards a united profession would be halted. . . .'[27] This point had already been made elsewhere and it was one which particularly disturbed the N.U.T. The general secretary told the executive at its October meeting that this policy would have a disastrous effect on the profession if it were made permanent, for in due course the secondary schools would be staffed almost entirely by university graduates while primary schools were staffed by college trainees. This would drive a wedge between primary and secondary teachers and would mean that many secondary teachers would be untrained. There was certainly cause for these teachers' associations to fear that much of the ground they had apparently won since 1944 was in danger of being lost. Before the Education Act of that year the colleges had produced staff for the elementary schools while the universities had looked after the grammar schools. Once again the colleges were to be largely confined to the first stage and this would be bound to emphasise the division of the teaching profession.

In spite of the protests of the teachers' organisations, the ministry persevered with its policy. In its Report for 1961 it spoke of the 'great sense of duty' shown by colleges in carrying out the adjustments, and suggested that the changes might need to go further the following year, since the paramount need remained for teachers for the primary schools. In the first year of the new policy some 80 per cent of students entering general colleges were destined for courses which would prepare them for primary work. To some extent the worries of the A.T.C.D.E. and the other associations were assuaged by the development in the colleges of courses designed to fit students for more than one phase of schooling, e.g. for infant/junior or junior/secondary teaching.[28]

The lengthening of the course of basic training for teachers has had a particularly sharp impact on the supply of women teachers, since a considerable number leave full-time service to start families in their twenties. Thus a reduction of a year in the amount of service they could give represented a considerable proportionate shortening of their total career—disregarding their possible later return to the classroom. The lengthening of the course also meant that each trained teacher represented a considerably larger investment of public money, and the rapidly increasing cost of the expanding educational system has forced the government—whichever party happened to be in office—to seek ways of increasing the return from this public investment by trying to make fuller use of the existing resources, particularly of trained manpower. Any attempt to achieve this was likely to bring a clash between the government and the teachers' organisations. The most obvious way of trying to make trained manpower go further would be to increase the size of classes, but a reduction of these has long been a publicly asserted aim not only of the teachers but of successive ministers and for very sound educational reasons. The clash between the professional aims of teachers and the needs of the national economy became increasingly apparent in the National Advisory Council on the Training and Supply of Teachers in the years following 1960, and can also be seen in the skirmishes which have occurred over the possible use of auxiliaries in the classroom.

The most controversial of the government's proposals put before the House of Commons in May, 1962, in the course of a debate on the teacher shortage, was that there might be some form of auxiliary teaching service. After a short, practical training of 12 to 16 weeks, these assistants might work under the supervision of fully qualified teachers. The government also aired the suggestion that short service commissions might be introduced under which girls might be trained for two years with a further year of training at a later stage, giving a limited period of service in the schools after the first period of training before getting married. The next day the N.A.S. stated that the minister, 'having failed to obtain a supply of teachers large enough to provide adequate full-time education, shows his readiness to adopt dilutionary devices to mask the teacher shortage'. Parents were urged to protest as strongly against handing the education of their young children to unqualified persons as they would against the employment of unqualified doctors and dentists. The N.U.T. decided to oppose vigorously any attempt to introduce a new category of teacher with less than three years' service, and any move to use auxiliary helpers for teaching purposes.

In spite of the firm opposition of the teachers' associations, the minister had a fair amount of public support. *The Times Educational Supplement* urged him to go ahead 'Then, of course, we shall get the cry "No dilution!" Is there really anything in it? Would the two-year trained teachers of the future be worse than the two-year trained teachers of the past? We might go further. Extreme measures had to be taken once before. There was Emergency Training. Will the N.U.T. tell us now that this was a mistake? Have no teachers so trained proved their worth?'[29] The controversy remained bitter but out of the public eye for much of the time. Occasionally it flared publicly, as in 1964 when *The Economist* commented that the N.U.T.'s evidence to the Plowden Committee was confined to 'bland aspirations for the best'. The journal itself proposed that for children under six schooling could be carried out under the direct personal supervision of a highly trained teacher's auxiliary. Fully trained teachers would be in charge of these auxiliaries but would not have to be personally present for each moment of every class period. But it concluded that there was no chance that the official channels which governed educational policy would seriously consider this proposal, because 'like a lump of green and growing weed across these channels, lies the National Union of Teachers'.[30] At about the same time and at the other end of the political spectrum the Fabian Society submitted its evidence to the Plowden Committee (*New Patterns for Primary Schools*), suggesting that there should be something like a teacher hierarchy along the lines of master-teacher, teacher, assistant teacher, teacher-aide (technical) and teacher-aide (administrative).

In 1965 the then Secretary of State, Mr. Anthony Crosland, took as his theme in addressing the N.U.T. conference the teacher shortage and presented an emergency plan for overcoming this. This 14-point plan included measures to improve productivity. This was to be achieved partly by employing more ancillary help outside the classroom—clerical help, library assistants and the like—and partly by employing teaching auxiliaries. This latter was a thorny problem which he believed was provoking unnecessary anxiety. What was needed was an agreed uniform pattern for the qualifications, training and conditions of service of such auxiliary help. 'I ask you to help me by giving up *some* traditional attitudes.... I ask you to relax your traditional opposition to help inside the classroom.' The conference later (but not as a direct response to the Secretary of State's speech) carried a motion resisting the introduction of auxiliary teachers as a measure to meet the teacher shortage, and reaffirmed the policy laid down in 1962.[31]

Mr. Crosland returned to the theme at the N.U.T. conference the next year, this time envisaging the teacher enjoying a higher professional status in the role of manager. The teacher would need to call upon a growing variety of ancillary staff and would be more involved in technological developments such as television, tape-recorders and programmed learning. The Secretary of State invoked the example of the surgeon in his operating theatre 'in control of the total situation', and spoke of highly trained teachers more and more concentrating on professional tasks, while routine tasks were carried out by human and mechanical assistance.[32] Many of his listeners remained unimpressed, and early in 1967 the N.U.T. submitted a memorandum to the Secretary of State on the Plowden Report in which it regretted that the Plowden Committee had suggested that aides should be placed in charge of groups of children in circumstances that would almost certainly involve actual teaching. In his address a few weeks later to the annual conference the President was more blunt in his criticisms of the way in which the Plowden Committee saw aides being used, for they might result in one trained teacher being responsible for a group of up to 80 children. These were, he said, 'monstrous proposals'.

Throughout this controversy the teachers' associations had made it clear that they would welcome the employment of ancillaries, which the N.U.T. defined as falling into four categories, viz. those engaged in clerical duties, in school meals duties, welfare assistants and such grades as laboratory assistants.[33] The N.A.S. took the opportunity to issue a Report on *Ancillary Assistance in Schools* which set out minimum standards of ancillary assistance said to be required in schools of various sizes. Among associations with a predominantly graduate membership, the I.A.A.M. Council in January, 1966, welcomed the possibility of appointing more technicians and ancillaries in schools provided that they did not take over the educational work of trained teachers. Although there are no national sets of figures which make it possible to illustrate the point, the impression created by such figures as there are is that the schools have obtained the assistance of an increased number of ancillary staff during the 1960s. The teachers' associations have also fought a successful defensive action in preventing the introduction of auxiliaries, and now that the rise in the birthrate has been checked there is likely to be less pressure for the employment of teaching auxiliaries.

The conflict between long-standing educational aims and social and economic conditions which has become so marked since 1960 has had a victim in the National Advisory Council on the Training and Supply of Teachers. The divisions of opinion within this body between the groups representing different interests could no longer be reconciled as in the 1950s. Some members refused to go along with the majority in the Eighth Report, published in 1962, which recommended that the minimum period of training be increased eventually to four years. The minority felt unconvinced by the arguments advanced in favour of this recommendation, namely, the need for greater parity with other professions and for professional unity among teachers themselves. The Ninth Report, issued in 1965, indicated differences which could not be reconciled concerning both the employment of auxiliaries and the introduction of the four-term year in colleges of education. The chairman of the Council resigned after the Ninth Report had been published, this offering a convenient opportunity to do so. On resigning he told the Secretary of State that the divisions which had become apparent within the Council were not simply differences of opinion which an independent chairman might hope to reconcile, but were the outcome of fundamental conflicts of interest about issues of national policy which required decision at the political level. No successor has been appointed and the Council has not functioned since 1965, in spite of calls from some of the teachers' associations represented on it for a chairman to be appointed and for meetings to be held.

Apart from its irreconcilable internal divisions, the Council in its later Reports showed a lack of awareness of those external political and economic factors which govern the pace of educational development, and its recommendations had the appearance of being increasingly remote from reality. In these circumstances it has been criticised as offering advice that was largely irrelevant where its political assumptions were unjustified, or, at most, it provided some support for the Secretary of State in the shape of special pleading by a vested interest when he was engaged in the contest for funds from the Treasury.[34]

V TOWARDS A TRAINED GRADUATE PROFESSION

In spite of the difficulties which arose over the supply of teachers in the 1960s, there was progress in some directions in improving the quality of the training available and in raising the status of the training colleges themselves, these improvements being associated with the Report of the Robbins Committee on Higher Education. The evidence submitted to this Committee by the different teachers' organisations concerning teacher training naturally reflected their long-standing policies and contained few surprises. The N.U.T. and the A.T.C.D.E. recommended that degrees should be made available to students from training colleges. The N.U.T. urged four years of training for all teachers as the ultimate aim. The Joint Four Secondary Associations, while arguing that the training of graduate teachers should in general take place in

University Departments of Education, believed that the courses would be more effective if the schools shared a greater responsibility for the training. This, again, was an argument which some of these associations had advanced from time to time; the headmasters' association, for instance, had shown a particular keenness for what it called school based training for more than half a century. The secondary teachers' associations suggested that if links between the universities and the training colleges could be strengthened this would help to lessen the isolation of these colleges and to bring their students into closer contact with students intending to enter other professions.

The Robbins Committee's recommendations for teacher training were far-reaching. The Institutes of Education should give way to university Schools of Education which would take over administrative and financial responsibility for the colleges. Only in this way did the Committee believe that the colleges would achieve the standing they should have as part of higher education. Academic and administrative responsibility should go hand in hand. A university degree, to be known as a B.Ed., should be available in the colleges on the basis of a four-year course. To emphasise the enhanced position of the training colleges, they should be known in future as colleges of education.[35]

The recommendations were widely welcomed by the teachers' organisations. *The Teacher* commented that the establishment of the B.Ed. and the closer liaison proposed between universities and colleges were well in line with the N.U.T.'s own aims. At the beginning of 1964 the N.U.T. issued a statement accepting 'unequivocally' the Robbins Report's proposals to turn teachers' training colleges into colleges of education and to integrate them fully with university schools of education. The A.T.C.D.E., in a letter to the Permanent Secretary of the Ministry of Education, welcomed and entirely accepted the recommendations of the Robbins Report on the colleges. The secondary teachers' associations also welcomed the recommendations from their slightly different standpoint; the Vice-Chairman of the I.A.A.M., for instance, remarked that the opportunity for the colleges to develop degree courses in association with the universities was an improvement on the rather doubtful suggestion made by the N.A.C.T.S.T. that the colleges themselves should be given the opportunity to become degree-awarding institutions.[36] Lord Eccles, no longer in office as Minister of Education, perhaps expressed most clearly the reactions of non-graduate teachers when he said, 'There are more than a quarter of a million of these men and women to whom we entrust nine out of ten of all the nation's children, and I know that many of them suffer from being something more than a white-collar worker and something less than a professional man or woman.... The Robbins proposal to upgrade the training colleges and include them in the promise of higher education is, therefore, a chance not to be missed.'[37]

The government accepted the new name of 'colleges of education', it accepted the proposals for a B.Ed. degree, but under pressure from the local authorities, who were anxious to maintain their position in teacher training, it rejected the administrative and financial recommendations which would have made the colleges constituent parts of university schools of education. The Secretary of State told the Commons that the colleges 'should continue to be administered by the existing maintaining bodies under the present system of overall supervision.'[38] Arrangements for the internal government of the colleges were to be reviewed, however, and a departmental committee was set up to do that in due course. There was a good deal of anxiety that the failure to adopt the Robbins recommendations in full might undermine the effectiveness of those proposals that were accepted. The exclusion of the colleges from the university system has been a setback from the teachers' point of view, but the institution of the B.Ed. degree has inevitably led to much closer contact between colleges and universities than has ever existed before. At the same time the work of the departmental committee has been reflected in a measure of reform in the internal government of the colleges. Thus the outcome of the Robbins Report has been to enhance the status of the colleges by making them institutions where a student can work for a degree and by bringing them into greater contact with the universities. On the other hand not as much progress has been made as the Robbins Committee itself had hoped to achieve.

Recently two more professional objectives associated particularly with the associations representing a majority of non-graduate teachers have been achieved. The D.E.S. has announced an end to the employment of unqualified persons even as temporary teachers, and it has also announced that all persons graduating after the end of 1973 will be required to take a course of training before being allowed to teach. No more than a trickle of unqualified persons had been entering teaching and taking posts as temporary teachers. Although from the Second World War both the uncertificated and the supplementary categories had been eliminated, the entry of any unqualified persons to the classroom awakened to some extent fears of dilution among teachers but, perhaps more significantly, if untrained persons managed to teach competently, this might arouse doubts in some minds of the value of the training received by the qualified teachers themselves. The employment of any untrained persons devalues the currency of qualifications. The objective of the N.U.T. was set by its General Secretary in 1950 when he explained that before the war the door was wide open to the untrained; it was now only slightly ajar. 'Our task is now to slam the door and bar it and bolt it against the entrance of any more unqualified teachers. This would be a real service to children and to the teaching profession.'[39]

Many of the arguments against the employment of unqualified temporary teachers applied also to the employment of untrained graduates, and Sir Ronald Gould linked the two in his General Secretary's report to the 1954 conference when he said the Union must face three tasks; 'first, the complete elimination of the category of temporary teachers, secondly insistence on training for all graduates, and thirdly, an embargo on even the temporary employment of the untrained.'[40] Pressure to achieve these aims was maintained, but their achievement was made more difficult by the lengthening of the basic training to three years and the consequent sharpening of supply problems. In moving an amendment to a resolution at the 1960 conference which would have urged N.U.T. members to refuse to work with temporary teachers after 1st September that year, the Executive argued that the resolution stood no chance of success, since they had been told by the minister that they could have a three-year period of training or they could have the sort of thing this resolution sought, but they could not at that time have both.

It was not until December, 1967, that the Secretary of State felt able to set up a working party of local authority and teachers' association representatives to consider the position of the unqualified. The working party reported in the following May, and proposed that no unqualified temporary teachers should be appointed after September, 1968, and that no person already employed as a temporary or occasional teacher should be allowed to continue in employment after 1st September, 1970. Mr. Edward Short, a member of the N.U.T. of many years' standing, was Secretary of State, and it must, presumably, have given him much pleasure to accept these proposals and bring them into effect. Persons qualified for and awaiting entry to a course of teacher training may be still taken into employment by a school for a limited period, but such employment of this kind should be in the nature of training and is not in any way equivalent to the employment of a qualified teacher. It is also possible for schools still to employ certain classes of specialist instructors who are not trained teachers for 'office arts and skills' or 'the playing of musical instruments'. The President of the N.U.T. commented, 'We may regard the terms of the working party recommendation as a victory for the Union, for we were responsible for the setting up of the working party and for making the claims we did. I think it marks an historical achievement in the history of the Union.'[41]

By way of footnote, the working party recorded its full support for the long-declared intention of the Secretary of State to introduce a training requirement for graduates as soon as practicable. Before education ranked a Secretary of State, various ministers had made similar declarations from time to time since 1945;[42] they had also usually added that it would be unwise to fix a date for this reform at the time of speaking.[43] While the N.U.T., the N.A.S. and the A.T.C.D.E. have attached great importance to training graduates, the secondary teachers' associations have not all placed the same emphasis on the need for it. In 1959 the council of the I.A.A.M. resolved by a large majority 'that in order to establish a proper professional status, Council instructs the Executive Committee to take immediate steps to ensure that after 1961 at the latest all new entrants to the teaching profession be required to furnish evidence that they have successfully completed a recognised course of teacher training.'[44]

Yet towards the end of the next year, at a meeting of representatives of the A.T.C.D.E. and of the Joint Four, the latter were not prepared to endorse the policy of the A.T.C.D.E. that all graduates entering maintained primary and secondary schools in and after 1965 should be trained. The representatives of the headmasters had particular difficulty in accepting this.[45] In 1958 the I.A.H.M. had suggested that the introduction of compulsory training for graduates should be deferred for a further ten years, in view of the inadequate supply of teachers for grammar schools.[46] The headmasters have brought forward schemes at different times for 'school-based apprenticeship', and for various other forms of apprenticeship rather than training, which would make the schools primarily responsible for the training of teachers.[47] But none of these schemes has been accepted and none of them has looked any more viable than a similar scheme for which special regulations were issued by the Board of Education early in the century and which, although backed by the headmasters, failed to attract support.[48] The very severe criticism of existing training courses shown for many years by the I.A.H.M. and repeated in evidence to the Select Committee on Education as recently as April, 1970, seems to spring as much from a desire by headmasters to control the training themselves as from any appraisal of the actual training given. In the words of the report of the I.A.H.M. working party on the training of teachers in 1965, 'The fact that the present form of training is divorced from those who teach in schools diminishes the prestige of teaching and of the profession'. In other words, this particular group of teachers appears to feel a sense of professional resentment or deprivation because specialist institutions are responsible for the training of teachers.

Despite this lingering suspicion of the value of training for graduates, the Secretary of State made it known that those who graduate after 1st January, 1970, will have to train before teaching in primary schools, while those who graduate after 1st January, 1974, will have to train before taking posts in secondary schools. At last the aim of those teachers' associations which have sought to close the profession to any who have not taken a specific course of training in teaching has been achieved.

NOTES

1. N.U.T., *A First Degree in Education*, 1951.
2. Paper entitled 'Emergency Recruitment and Training of Teachers', D.E.S.
3. *The Schoolmaster*, 28th October, 1943, p. 289.
4. Ibid., 28th September, 1944, p. 195.
5. P.R.O., Ed. 401/14, 17th September, 1944.
6. N.U.T. Annual Report, 1945, p. xliii.
7. *Challenge and Response. An Account of the Emergency Training Scheme for the Training of Teachers.* Ministry of Education Pamphlet No. 17, 1950, p. 161.
8. *Teachers and Youth Leaders.* Report of the Committee appointed by the President of the Board of Education to consider the Supply, Recruitment and Training of Teachers and Youth Leaders. 1944, pp. 48–54.
9. *T.E.S.*, 8th December, 1945, p. 582.

10. Ministry of Education, Circular No. 234, 1945.
11. N.A.C.T.S.T., First Report, 1951, pp. 18–19.
12. *The Schoolmaster*, 24th May, 1951, pp. 701–2.
13. *Hansard*, H. of C., 17th December, 1953, cols. 700–8.
14. N.A.C.T.S.T., Fifth Report, 1956, pp. 1–2.
15. *Teachers and Youth Leaders*, 1944, p. 65.
16. N.A.C.T.S.T., Fifth Report, 1956.
17. *The Schoolmaster*, 15th April, 1955, p. 641.
18. *T.E.S.*, 28th September, 1956, p. 1171.
19. *The Schoolmaster*, 14th June, 1957, p. 1141.
20. Ibid., 18th April, 1958, p. 779.
21. *The Economist*, 24th May, 1958, p. 677.
22. *The Schoolmaster*, 20th November, 1959, p. 985.
23. D.E.S. Reports on Education No. 49, Colleges of Education.
24. Ministry of Education, T.C. Letter No. 14/60.
25. *T.E.S.*, 14th October, 1960, p. 485.
26. A.T.C.D.E., News Sheet, No. 30, December, 1960, p. 3.
27. *T.E.S.*, 21st October, 1960, p. 531.
28. Ministry of Education, Education in 1960, 1961, pp. 80–1.
29. *T.E.S.*, 25th May, 1962, p. 1079.
30. *The Economist*, 12th September, 1964, pp. 996–7.
31. *The Teacher*, 30th April, 1965, pp. 4–5.
32. *Education*, 15th April, 1966, p. 795.
33. *The N.U.T. View on Ancillaries and Auxiliaries*, N.U.T., n.d., Appendix.
34. R. A. Manzer, *Teachers and Politics*, 1970, p. 107.
35. Report of the Committee on Higher Education, Cmnd. 2154, 1963, pp. 112–21.
36. *The A.M.A.*, February, 1964, p. 66. The actual institution of the B.Ed. degree by the various universities has led to some disappointment in the N.U.T., which has complaints concerning a lack of uniformity of entry conditions, of the requirements for the degree and of the resulting award with honours available at some universities but not at others. A considerable measure of diversity is of the essence of the university system in this country and a uniform national B.Ed. could only have emerged had some national body—perhaps the C.N.A.A.—been given the task of administering the degree.
37. *Hansard*, H. of C., 12th December, 1963, col. 1338.
38. *Hansard*, H. of C., 11th December, 1964, cols. 1971–3.

39. *The Schoolmaster*, 13th April, 1950, p. 157. Address to N.U.T. Conference.
40. Ibid, 23rd April, 1954, pp. 647–8.
41. *The Teacher*, 14th June, 1968, p. 9.
42. Ministry of Education Circular 30, March, 1945, also contained such a statement.
43. Sir David Eccles, for instance, speaking to the East Midlands branch of the A.T.C.D.E. in 1961, was reported as saying, 'I think we must now run up a warning flag that at a not too distant date we shall expect all newly qualified teachers to have professional training.' *T.E.S.*, 24th March, 1961, p. 592.
44. *The A.M.A.*, February, 1959, pp. 66–7.
45. A.T.C.D.E. News Sheet, No. 31, February, 1961, pp. 33–5.
46. I.A.H.M., Report of the 66th Annual General Meeting, 1958, pp. 41–5.
47. For recent examples see I.A.H.M. Report of the Working Party on the Training of Teachers, 1965, and I.A.H.M. annual meeting reported in the *T.E.S.*, 6th January, 1961, p. 16.
48. Chapter 10.

14
The Administration of the School System

Administration is a subsidiary function whose purpose is to facilitate learning and teaching in the schools, and the best administrative system is that which most facilitates these processes. Teachers' associations have by no means always been agreed on the administrative pattern that would most readily facilitate learning and teaching; the last decade of the 19th century, for instance, witnessed an outbreak of open warfare among them on this very issue. At the same time, since it is through the administrative system that the community makes resources available to the schools, it is here that possible conflicts between the interests of the profession and those of the community are likely to appear. The great majority of teachers are employees of the community, paid to provide a public service. Through the administrative system the central and local authorities will seek to control the service. Teachers, as persons with a professional expertise, may reasonably claim some voice in the administration of the service they perform. When civil servants, or members of local education committees, appear to be lacking in understanding or unsympathetic, teachers may well agree with the view that 'It would be incredible, were it not true, that any body of farmers, shopkeepers and squirearchs should be able to impose their unknowledgeable views as to curriculum and discipline and time-book punctuality, and fitness of school premises, upon people trained and experienced in the performance of their teaching tasks'.[1]

I ESTABLISHING THE BOARD OF EDUCATION

The last years of the 19th century witnessed a movement away from the multiplicity of *ad hoc* boards and authorities which had been established to provide particular local services, in favour of the multi-purpose local authority. It became increasingly clear that the administration of the schools both at the local and at the national level would have to be reorganised, simplified and made more coherent. There was increasingly widespread realisation among teachers that change was likely to produce a sharp clash of views between the N.U.T. and the secondary associations which held strongly contrasting social and educational ideals.

The ultimate ideal cherished by the leaders of the N.U.T. seems to have been of an embracing system of education, extending the large city type of school-board arrangements for elementary schooling to secondary and higher education. The local administration would be in the hands of one *ad hoc* elected local authority under the regulations of one central government department, served by a homogeneous body of trained, certificated teachers who belonged to one professional organisation. 'All educational posts, not only in the public elementary schools, but also in the secondary, technical, and university institutions, were to be thrown open without favouritism to all the members of this united profession. . . . The inspectorate, both local and central, was to be mainly recruited from the more experienced and more able teachers. There were some idealists, indeed, who looked forward to seeing members of the N.U.T. appointed to the Secretariat of the Board of Education, whilst even the post of President of the Board might come normally to be filled by a member of the profession with a talent for politics.'[2] Moreover, there was to be no distinction between the schooling of the manual working-class child and that of the middle-class child, in the quality or salaries of the teaching staff and other amenities, buildings, playing-fields and so forth.[3]

An equally public-spirited and enlightened group of educationalists was sadly disillusioned by what it saw to be the serious deficiencies of the school board system in practice, and by the narrow and ill-educated teachers who taught in the board schools. These idealists, centred largely on the secondary schools, sought a system of education which would offer much more variety and much less rigidity than the system operated by the boards in the large cities, a system offering a higher type of moral and intellectual training than could be hoped to come from any expansion of the board system. Clearly it would not be possible for the country to make this superior system available for every child, but by scholarships it could be opened to the children of manual workers who showed exceptional ability about the age of 11 or 12. The teachers required in such secondary schools ought themselves to be the products of reasonably enlightened education, preferably university graduates, and certainly not certificated elementary school teachers, whose higher education had consisted of little more than the techniques of instructing large classes mechanically in the basic subjects. So far as the administrative arrangements went, different systems would clearly be needed to operate elementary and secondary schools; there was no hope that *ad hoc* elementary boards would be capable of administering this more enlightened system.

The clash between these two conflicting views runs through the evidence offered by representatives of the various teachers' associations to the Royal Commission under Viscount Bryce, whose terms of reference were to consider 'the best methods of establishing a well-organised system of secondary education in England, taking into account existing differences, and having regard to such local sources of revenue from endowment or otherwise as are available'. The Memorandum submitted by the N.U.T. stated that no scheme for secondary education could be regarded as satisfactory which treated secondary schools as a separate class, and the Union expressed strong opposition to the creation of separate authorities for the central or local control of secondary education. On the contrary, it urged 'most strongly' that local control of all forms of education should be vested in one authority and that a single government department should exercise central control over all forms of public education. The Union favoured an *ad hoc* local authority, directly elected for educational purposes only—as the school boards were.[4] The General Secretary, Yoxall, who was a member of the Royal Commission, explained in a note that the unification of educational administration was desirable in order to achieve economy of management, administrative efficiency and the discouragement of unnecessary social prejudice arising from: '(a) Separatism in administration; (b) Non-educational distinction between schools; (c) Want of unity in the teaching profession as a whole.'[5]

The large school board might have provided a model for the N.U.T.'s suggested local administrative pattern, but the small school board was condemned and consigned to the same category as the 'one-man manager' of a voluntary school. Interference with the discretion of teachers in their professional work, the imposition of non-scholastic tasks, and inadequate salaries were all associated with small board and voluntary schools.[6]

Extreme suspicion of any central or local government agency for secondary education was shown by some of the secondary teachers' associations. The representative of the Association of Headmistresses told the Commissioners that her association wished inspection to be in the hands of the universities and that it did not 'desire any State control whatever'.[7] The Headmasters' Conference conceived of a central authority which consisted of a statutory commission composed mainly of persons experienced in educational matters and independent of any other government department. Between this commission and the governing bodies of individual schools, which were to be left as they were, there might be county or provincial educational committees, one-third of whose members should be appointed by the statutory commission, with adequate representation for other educational interests among the rest.[8] The evidence of the I.A.H.M. was on much the same lines as that of the Headmasters' Conference save that the Association suggested that a headmaster should have a 'consultative seat' on the governing body of his school. The extremely cautious attitude of these head teachers' organisations to the question of public authorities controlling secondary schools owed something to what their members had seen of the heavy-handed administration of the elementary schools by the Education Department, with its payment-by-results, its rigidly enforced Code and the annual tests by its inspectors.

The administrative recommendations made by the Bryce Commissioners were much nearer to the advice given by secondary school heads than to the views of the N.U.T. They recommended a separate form of organisation for secondary schools, to be administered at the local level by committees which were to include county council representatives, nominees of the Crown and persons of experience in educational matters. There was to be a Minister of Education who was to be advised on secondary school affairs by a central council of university representatives and Crown nominees. The Headmasters' Conference at its meeting in December, 1895, welcomed the Bryce recommendations as 'an important step towards the establishment of secondary schools in England'. The opening speaker in the discussion claimed that the Royal Commissioners had largely adopted the H.M.C. scheme—which was hardly true—and where they had departed from it had done so for the worse, e.g., in their preference for an Educational Council rather than a statutory commission.[9]

During the seven years that elapsed between the publication of the Bryce Commission's Report and the Education Act of 1902, the different associations engaged in a great deal of lobbying and advocacy of their own favourite administrative pattern. The secondary teachers' associations were stimulated in this by the continued rapid growth of the various forms of higher grade, post-primary, board schools. In a memorial to the Education Department in 1896 the I.A.H.M. complained that these schools, 'supported by rates, and in most cases free of charge to parents, are overlapping secondary schools, and mischief is arising out of a dual system. In populous districts, such as South Lancashire and the West Riding of Yorkshire, large schools have been built, and are being worked at public cost, to the detriment of old foundations, which only require a proper local control and public aid to renew their youth.'[10] In the absence of administrative reform, some of the secondary school heads feared that the large school boards, with the resources of the rates behind them, might move into the secondary field to such an extent as to undermine the position of the endowed schools generally. Although the I.A.H.M. and the Association of Headmasters of Higher Grade Schools agreed on a joint declaration, which they presented to the Education Department in 1898 and which offered a compromise in principle between the two sets of schools,[11] in practice the rivalry continued in many areas and served to sharpen the antagonism between the elementary and secondary interests.

The I.A.H.M., in the scheme for the organisation of secondary education which it adopted, saw as one of the main duties of a new central authority the enforcement of a delimitation of spheres on schools, since no local authority would be strong enough to do this— in other words, no local authority was likely to be strong enough to resist the school boards in the large cities. The headmasters regarded primary schooling as terminating at the age of 12 (elementary standards 1 to 7); higher primary schools would cover standards 6 to 9 while secondary education would begin at the age of 12 and end between 17 and 19. The higher primary schools were to be distinguished from secondary schools in the content and organisation of the curriculum. The secondary schools alone would prepare pupils for the universities, so that there would be two ladders:

primary school — higher primary school—evening classes;

secondary school—$\begin{cases} \text{technical institution} \\ \quad\quad\text{or} \\ \text{university.} \end{cases}$

The local authorities for secondary education would cover the area of a county or county borough and would consist partly of representative members, i.e., councillors, secondly of nominated members who would be drawn from the universities, secondary and primary schools and local industry, and thirdly of co-optative members who would be invited because of their special knowledge and experience.[12]

In an effort to give the government a lead, a Secondary Education Bill was introduced in the Commons in 1898 which had been drafted by the I.A.H.M. and was approved by the executives of the H.M.C., the A.H.M., the Conference of Catholic Schools and by the Hebdomadal Council of the University of Oxford. The cornerstone of this particular measure was the position it took on the delimitation of the primary and secondary areas, and all decisions on this were to be taken by a reconstituted Education Department, the Department being bound to refer all such questions to the proposed Advisory Council, which would represent secondary and higher education. Thus representatives from secondary and higher education would fix the limits of primary education. 'The N.U.T. will be up in arms' warned the *Journal of Education*.[13] It was not only with the elementary schoolteachers that the secondary associations clashed. The co-operation with the technical instruction committee interests, more especially with the Association of Directors and Organising Secretaries, which had been noticeable immediately after the Bryce Report, came to an end when this Bill included a provision that local secondary education authorities (which were not to be county or county borough councils as such) were not themselves to be permitted to provide or manage any secondary schools. The unity of the secondary schoolteachers could only be attained with the co-operation of the public schools, and these hesitated to associate themselves with the technical instruction movement, which tended to obliterate the distinction between secondary and technical education.[14]

H. Macan, the Organising Secretary for Surrey, was chairman of the 1899 Annual General Meeting of the Association of Directors and Organising Secretaries, and in his opening address he referred to the schism that had developed between the Association and 'those with whom they had been in the habit of working'. The Association 'must be careful to see that professional bodies recognised the fact that public education was going to be administered by public authorities and not by bodies appointed under schemes drawn up by a government department, held in tow by a committee of teachers'. It was resolved that no permanent consultative committee should be attached to the Board of Education, and that no such committee should be set up at all before the statutory constitution of the local authorities. This was thought to be essential, since 'the teaching associations wish this bureau to be at work before the local authorities are established, in order principally that it may influence the composition of such authorities and force upon them a representation of those who are practically their own servants'.[15] These differences were not really over the standing of technical education, but over the degree of control of the schools for older children to be exercised by the professionals, the head teachers on the one hand and the representatives of local committees, the local councils and their officials, on the other. This issue was to be one of the most vexing in the period immediately following the Act of 1902, and in a fundamental sense it has remained a latent source of difficulty, flaring into open conflict on occasion.

The passing in 1899 of the Act which created the Board of Education[16] by bringing together the Education Department, the Science and Art Department and the educational work of the Charity Commission was the signal for considerable efforts on the part of secondary school heads that their schools should not be administered or inspected by those administrators and inspectors who had been concerned with either elementary or technical education. An article in *The Times* apparently written by R. P. Scott, a leading member of the I.A.H.M., argued that it would be disastrous if the new organisation for the supervision of secondary education were to be based on the method of administration and actual experience of the Education Department or the Science and Art Department. The activities of the latter had already harmed the tradition of literary training, possibly irreparably, by merely considering only part of the work of a school. If the South Kensington methods of payment for subjects or groups of subjects were to continue, 'it would be preferable that no central authority should be created at all for our secondary schools'.[17] While the Bill was before Parliament the headmasters had vigorously pressed their case upon the Duke of Devonshire, the Lord President. The Committee of the Headmasters' Conference resolved that 'an arrangement by which the three main factors of national education are thus placed on a separate, equal and independent footing is the best method of safeguarding the interests of all three, and of securing their satisfactory development in future'. Dr. Warre, headmaster of Eton, saw Devonshire, and the latter feared trouble in the Commons during the passage of the Bill unless he gave the headmasters the assurances they sought.[18] The assurances were given, but the strong resistance to any change put up by Abney, permanent head of the Science and Art Department, and to a lesser extent by the Charity Commission, led to delay in the effective amalgamation of the various units into an effective Board of Education until Morant became Permanent Secretary, when the new central authority came to be organised under three Permanent Assistant Secretaries, 'for Elementary, Secondary and Technological education'.[19]

The Act which set up the Board of Education set up also not the Educational Council advised by the Bryce Report and sought by many teachers, as a standing body representing teachers and advising the new Minister, but merely a Consultative Committee. In the Act itself this was a very shadowy affair. Gorst told the Commons that the constitution, number of members and the task the Committee was to fulfil were not provided for in the Bill, since it was experimental in nature, and it was thought better to leave these matters to the discretion of the President of the Board of Education, who might make such changes in the constitution of the Committee as experience might show to be desirable.[20] It was quite clear that this body would never be in a position to pose a serious challenge to the Board of Education. When it was first established the Committee in fact had 18 members, of whom about two-thirds represented the universities and other teaching bodies, while the remainder were persons noted for their interest in education, such as Hart-Dyke, Acland and Hobhouse. From the point of view of the N.U.T. the Committee was felt to consist almost entirely of representatives of 'public school' ideals, while the Assistant Masters' Association complained of the omission of assistant teachers from it, 'a number of M.P.s, a certain number of headmasters, but of those who do the practical work of education, not a trace'.[21]

The conflict between the N.U.T. and school board view of the future organisation of education and the view held by the associations of secondary school teachers continued through the period of the Cockerton affair.[22] Both sides continued to press their respective views on the government and to seek public support for them, in an effort to ensure the new administrative pattern which would clearly soon have to be enacted would be to their own liking. The actual settlement secured to the N.U.T. the united educational administration at both central and local levels for which it had campaigned. On the other hand the secondary teachers' associations rejoiced to see the end of the school boards and certain objectionable features of local educational politics, through moving from *ad hoc* elected bodies to multi-purpose local authorities, acting through a committee to which persons of educational experience were to be co-opted. Moreover, the reorganisation of the united central authority—carried through under the terms of the Act of 1899—gave the secondary teachers the separate branch they desired.

It is difficult, if not impossible, to trace any effects of the pressures exerted by either of the groups of teachers on the main lines of the organisational settlement of the Act of 1902. By comparison with the preparation for the Act of 1944, for instance, there was much less consultation with such interested parties as teachers' associations. So far as the administrative arrangements were concerned, the Act of 1902 was much more far-reaching, fundamental, even revolutionary, than that of 1944. Change of this order is seldom achieved by widespread consultation with a view to the emergence of a settlement through a consensus of opinion. In 1902 it seems to have been due as much to the thinking and determination of Morant as to any other factor.[23] The creation of a Secondary Branch at the Board of Education under W. N. Bruce early in 1903 was undertaken as part of a reorganisation of the Board's work on functional lines with three branches, the others being for elementary and technical education, thus creating a logical bureaucratic structure. Had the Duke of Devonshire created such a branch with Sadler or Bruce as its Principal Assistant Secretary three years earlier, his motive would have been simply to appease the headmasters who were still, in fact, maintaining their pressure.[24]

Regarding the local level of administration, the I.A.A.M. executive committee circulated a statement to M.P.s in May 1902 welcoming the Education Bill, 'because it proposes to constitute County and County Borough Councils the paramount local education authorities . . . and because it will compel local authorities to include persons of experience in their education committees'.[25] The N.U.T. regarded it as most important that there should be a single local authority responsible for all forms of education,[26] and this it achieved in most areas under the Bill. The only exceptions were where the government had been forced to concede the establishment of Part III authorities by political pressure from towns of only moderate size. The creation of Part III authorities contravened Morant's own guiding principles, made the correlation of the various levels of education difficult and raised fears among elementary schoolteachers of the continuation in Part III areas of the worst vices of the small school boards.[27]

II TEACHERS, SCHOOLS AND THE LOCAL EDUCATION AUTHORITIES

It seemed very important to teachers' associations that they should secure representation on the new education committees. The N.U.T. had in the past been very active in some cities in getting those candidates elected to school boards who were favourably disposed towards the Union, while the heads of secondary schools had in some areas served as coopted members of technical instruction committees. The Act of 1902 provided for the appointment to education committees of persons of experience in education and acquainted with the needs of the various kinds of schools. In order to enable teachers employed by an authority to be nominated to membership of its education committee, the usual disqualification on those holding an office of profit was not to 'apply to a person by reason only of his holding office in a school or college aided, provided or maintained by the council'.[28] The various associations urged their local branches to bestir themselves to secure the representation on the new committees of 'persons of experience in education'.[29] The Association of Head Mistresses was particularly pleased to see that councils were obliged to make provision for the inclusion of women among the members of education committees.

The N.U.T. issued a pamphlet on the composition of education committees which it distributed to local associations and to local authorities. The executive also issued at intervals a 'Record of Progress in Organisation and Administration under the Education Act, 1902'. This showed the position at the close of 1903 as follows:[30]

Number of schemes (for committees) adopted	313
Number of teachers co-opted on the recommendation of the certificated teachers of the district	123
Co-opted teachers' representatives without nomination	53
Certificated teachers co-opted in addition to the above as persons of experience in education or as representatives of other interests	128
Other members of education committees holding a teacher's certificate	49
Officials similarly qualified	18

Under many schemes the nominating body was the N.U.T. local association, though in some cases the N.U.T. executive had been asked to nominate. The I.A.H.M. in January, 1903, resolved that councils should not only co-opt individual 'persons of experience in education' but should also invite a due proportion of representatives of educational bodies. It was argued that directors and organising secretaries preferred co-option to nomination, but that such co-optees lost some of their independence. The only satisfactory solution was to invite such bodies as the I.A.H.M. to nominate, as had already happened in Essex.[31]

Outside the teachers' associations there were vocal advocates of a system of nomination by the authorities; choice of teacher members by the teachers themselves or their associations was held to be objectionable, by *The Times*, for instance. 'There are obvious objections to giving, say, to the elementary teachers of a given area anything that may hereafter be construed into a permanent right of representation upon the body which will virtually be their employer ... the nomination or recommendation, whichever it were called, of teachers' representatives would tend to fall in the hands of their trade union, which might endeavour for its own purposes to coerce the education committees.'[32] The view of many local authorities was expressed by a leading article in *Education*, which condemned nomination by associations because it was impossible for education committees to deal with nominated members, however difficult they might become. Recommendation by an association was considered acceptable since a person recommended might be rejected by the authority if need be.[33]

Before approving schemes for education committees the Board of Education insisted upon the inclusion of women and persons of experience in education. It felt, however, that 'the precise way in which these objects were to be attained was a matter for the discretion of the different councils and that while some of them might prefer to select all the members of their committees themselves, others might find it convenient to invite outside bodies interested in some form or other of education to nominate representatives'.[34] The outcome of this policy was a great variety of approaches to the way in which non-councillors were appointed to education committees, but the great majority of education committees came to have between a quarter and a third of their members drawn from outside the council itself. With very few exceptions, the balance of membership established in 1903 has survived in most counties and county boroughs, with only minor changes. Teachers' associations have been active from time to time in pressing their claims for additional representation and in the years following the First World War this pressure was widespread—inspired to some extent by the example of the newly formed Whitley Councils in the civil service. In 1919 the N.U.T. executive prepared memoranda on teacher representation on education committees and on the establishment of Whitley committees. These were circulated to local associations, which were urged to renew their efforts to induce L.E.A.s to co-opt teachers if they were not already doing so, and to establish advisory committees. Resolutions urging the direct election of teachers to education committees and the establishment of national and local councils 'on the lines indicated in the Whitley Report' were passed at the Union's annual conferences in 1918 and 1919.[35]

From 1903 advisory or consultative committees consisting of representatives of teachers' associations and the local authority had been set up in some areas. By December of that year the N.U.T. had 159 of its members serving on such bodies. The Union had regarded them as less valuable than teachers on the education committee but it had co-operated with local authorities in establishing them. Other associations shared the same attitude.[36] An increasing number of authorities set up consultative committees in 1919 and 1920, including many of those which had teachers on the education committee itself. The I.A.H.M. in 1919 advocated advisory committees as a means of destroying bureaucratic methods and promoting harmony and unity instead. It felt they could do especially good work in areas where decisions of vital importance to teachers were arrived at without any consultation with them. 'Cast-iron rules are made and entrusted to soul-less officials to enforce.' Under the pressure of demands for Whitley Councils—which would have been standing councils meeting regularly with their own secretariats and not dependent on the L.E.A.s—the Association of Education Committees passed a resolution in June, 1919, favouring the establishment of consultative committees. Many advisory and consultative committees were in fact set up at this time, consisting of teachers and education committee members, usually in equal proportions. Sometimes separate committees were established for elementary and higher education, sometimes there was one committee; in some cases the committees concerned themselves only with strictly educational matters, in others wider matters such as conditions of employment were also discussed.[37]

In the years following 1902 it was the heads of secondary schools among the different groups of teachers who had most difficulty in establishing satisfactory working relationships with the new L.E.A.s. The headmaster of Bristol Grammar School was expressing the view then held by many of his colleagues when he wrote in 1909 that while local authorities endeavoured conscientiously to do their best their understanding of secondary schools was inadequate. 'They still either starve the local grammar school ... by refusing all funds, or take it over and destroy its spirit through ignorance of the fact that a secondary school must educate as well as instruct, and that education is killed when a headmaster is reduced to the level of a second-rate municipal servant, chief shop-walker in a useful knowledge emporium, neither teacher of boys nor leader of men, anxious chiefly to fill his classrooms with pupils and to avoid friction with colleagues, in order that his demonstrated "organising capacity" may be rewarded by appointment to a larger city clerk-factory, or even to a local directorship of education.'[38]

The clash between the secondary heads and the local authorities—particularly the municipal rather than the county authorities—lay in the different sets of traditional concepts which each tried to operate. The municipal tradition of concentrating power at the town hall meant that there was room neither for semi-independent governing bodies, nor for municipal servants armed with the power and authority which heads of endowed secondary schools had enjoyed during the latter part of the nineteenth century. The Schools Inquiry Commission had recommended that the powers of headmasters should be built up so that someone should be clearly responsible for the success or failure of a school. Such matters as the organisation of the school, the appointment and dismissal of assistant teachers, the control of discipline and the choice of teaching methods and books were all to be part of his prerogative.[39] The Endowed Schools Commissioners implemented these recommendations in their schemes for individual schools. The headmaster was responsible to the governing body who appointed and could dismiss him, the governors had financial responsibility for their school and were, in fact, in the position of trustees. The Bryce Commission did not recommend any important change in this position. The Commission did not think that the supervision of the proposed local authorities for secondary education should extend to the details of administration with which governors were concerned; in newly founded secondary schools, governing bodies independent, in their own spheres, of the local authority should be established. It also recommended that every head teacher should be allowed to sit on the governing body of his school, although he should not vote, and should withdraw when, for special reasons, the governors found his presence inexpedient.[40]

Difficulties between heads and authorities arose where endowed schools were aided by local authorities, and where authorities established their own municipal secondary schools under the Act of 1902. The Board of Education's traditional concept of a secondary school made it anxious to preserve the position of the secondary school head, and it became involved in disputes with a number of county boroughs. Some of the county boroughs, and more particularly their directors of education, were much more concerned with establishing a strong local administrative system than with letting schools develop any sort of individuality. The heads believed that each secondary school must have its own strong governing body with adequate powers, to which they would be responsible.[41] The Board of Education upheld this view of governing bodies, and from 1904 its regulations required that a secondary school should have such a body as a qualifying condition for grant. The Reports of the Board in subsequent years contained both encouraging advice to local authorities on the establishment and operation of governing bodies and reproof for those which set up governing bodies which were mere shams. In 1908 the Board explained that what it desired to effect through a well-composed body of governors, responsible for the good management of a school to the L.E.A. which supplied it with funds, was that there should be a small body of persons who could be specially interested in a school (with first-hand knowledge) 'in a way which is quite impossible for the whole body of the local authority or the education committee'.[42] Towards the end of 1908 the Board issued a set of model 'Articles of Government for a Secondary School' and commended their use to local authorities. The Board's policy was strongly resisted by a group of county boroughs which included Manchester, Birmingham, Leeds, Bristol, Norwich and Plymouth.[43] The story of the conflict between the Board and the recalcitrant authorities and directors of education has been described elsewhere.[44]

To the Board and the heads the kernel of the problem lay in the position of local directors of education. They were almost invariably the clerks to governing bodies of municipal secondary schools—in 112 out of 116 cases in county boroughs by 1910[45]—and communications between a headmaster and his governors thus passed through the hands of the local director of education. The latter was liable to be something more than a channel for communications and to use his position to impose his own will and discretion between heads and their governing bodies. The chief of the Secondary Branch at the Board recognised that personal contact between headmasters and their governors was very difficult to achieve through any wording of the Instruments of Government of schools. The Board had fought hard to achieve genuinely independent governing bodies since 1902 because of its desire 'to get general recognition of the view that the headmaster of a secondary school is for the purpose of internal administration not wholly a servant or official of the governing body, but in some degree, as it were, a colleague and indispensable partner. In this respect he differs from other officials of the authority, and must be in a special and immediate relation to the Governors, and not merely one link in a chain of officials.'[46] The outcome of this particular conflict was a withdrawal by the Board of Education at the time of crisis over the Holmes circular, and the transfer of Morant to organise the new National Health Insurance scheme. But a consequence of the Board's pressure over a period of nearly ten years was to establish widely the idea that heads of secondary schools were not merely executive officers of their employers but persons who were themselves possessed of authority by right of their office.

Elementary school teachers had never regarded school managers as defenders of their rights or of the rights of their school in the same way, but among these teachers also there were complaints against the extent to which officials of the local authorities appeared to be getting power into their hands. Towards the end of 1905 concern was expressed at the extent to which officials appeared to have gained influence in London. Since 1903, it was said, the power and authority of the official staff had increased enormously; the control of London's education was passing out of the sphere of public concern 'into one that is purely bureaucratic.' Outside London similar problems were causing concern, and too often the official was supreme.[47] A leading article on the same theme which appeared in *The Schoolmaster* in July 1906 asserted that since 1902 the control of education under large authorities had been 'more or less entirely bureaucratised and the number and power of paid officials have increased enormously'. Although not wishing in any way to return to the pre-1902 management arrangements, the same journal saw some virtue in bodies of managers for non-provided and provided schools. The former had definite legal powers; they should also be established in council schools, for they could be valuable in 'the nursing of that local public opinion which should support the teacher and the school'.[48]

Attacks by secondary and elementary school teachers on the way in which local authority officials appeared to be taking too much upon themselves evoked support from Presidents of the Board of Education drawn from both main parties. It was a theme to which Sir William Anson returned from time to time, and he became increasingly alarmed at the behaviour of some local officials. By 1905 he felt that many authorities had reached a parting of the ways at which they would either promote the education of an area and create an interest in it among persons of good will, 'or else will concentrate all power, not in the hands of the education committee, but in the hands of the organising secretary, who owing to the weariness of the education committee for the mass of formal administrative business, will acquire all the power which the education committee thought ill-advisedly to retain'.[49] Five years later the Liberal President, Runciman, echoed these sentiments when he told the Commons that 'if there is one thing in the organisation of education in the localities which seems a serious danger, it is the over-control of officials'.[50]

In the years between the two world wars and, indeed, down to the present day, complaints have been made from time to time by teachers' associations about the power exercised by officials. But the very vigour of the associations' reactions during the early years of the administrative system established by the Act of 1902 seems to have led to a more circumspect approach on the part of local administrators and a greater respect for the standpoint of the teacher. The teachers' associations have remained vigilant and the I.A.H.M. in particular has been very sensitive to any interference by local officials in those matters which it holds to be part of the prerogative of the headmaster.

An instance where a headmaster's rights appeared to be ignored by the local authority and where the I.A.H.M. did intervene, apparently with some success, occurred at Sheffield, where the King Edward VII School, a municipal secondary school, lost its separate governing body in 1926 and was placed directly under the secondary schools subcommittee of the authority. In 1927 the authority ordered the head to disband the O.T.C. at the school. He protested that this was an invasion of his rights, but was overruled. The headmaster was a member of the H.M.C. and it was made clear that owing to the unsatisfactory nature of the government of the school, no future head would be eligible for membership.[51] In July, 1927, a letter to all heads of Sheffield secondary schools signed by Percival Sharp, Director of Education, stated, 'The Chairman of the Secondary Schools Committee has discussed with me the growing tendency on the part of the heads of secondary schools to address him personally with reference to administrative matters. He asks me to say that all administrative matters should be referred in the first instance to the Chief Administrative Officer of the Committee for decision and such action as he after consultation with the chairman—where such consultation would appear to be necessary or desirable—may deem to be called for.' The heads of secondary schools were horrified. The head of King Edward VII applied for and was appointed to the headship of Whitgift School. In spite of a protest from the secondary school heads, the committee would not formally withdraw the letter, so a notice was inserted in *The Times Educational Supplement* urging intending candidates for the headship of King Edward VII School to communicate with the I.A.H.M. The advertisement was not continued by the I.A.H.M. after it received a letter from Sharp which, when taken in conjunction with the replies given to the Sheffield secondary heads, appeared to render the offending document a dead letter.[52]

The Sheffield affair led to a reassertion by the associations of secondary school heads or their spokesmen of the need for adequate governing bodies if the schools were to operate successfully. The President of the A.H.M. asserted that the individuality and variety of English secondary schools 'could be attributed in great measure to the splendid groups of men and women who have formed their governing bodies'. The Secretary of the I.A.H.M. stated that where there were no governors the individuality of schools, instead of being encouraged, was depressed, since they were treated as items in the supply of secondary education and not as living entities. More power was concentrated in the office of the director of education than ought to be entrusted to paid officials, however excellent.[53] The Headmasters' Conference at its next meeting passed a resolution setting out its belief that every secondary school should have a separate governing body with the largest measure of independence possible.[54] Replies to a questionnaire issued by the I.A.H.M. at this time showed that the great majority of aided and maintained secondary schools had separate governing bodies; the exceptions were nearly all in large county boroughs.[55] In view of the varying experiences of its members in counties and county boroughs, it is perhaps surprising that the I.A.H.M. did not press for local education authorities generally to be responsible for much larger areas. In the bigger counties the administrator might have been 'coldly or uniformly indifferent', but at least he was further away and was much less tempted to interfere with the internal administration of secondary schools. The incorporation of county boroughs into provincial authorities might have solved this problem for the headmasters. The Assistant Masters' Association had proposed the creation of much larger authorities in a memorandum in 1917 which it submitted to Fisher as President of the Board of Education in connection with possible post-war reforms, but the idea had not received the support of the I.A.H.M.[56]

III H.M. INSPECTORS AND THE INSPECTION OF SCHOOLS

Teachers in schools which received grant from either the Education or the Science and Art Departments in the nineteenth century could hardly have regarded the inspectorate as anything other than a part of the administrative system. The inspectors were administrative agents who came round annually to test the work of teachers and pupils and adjust the grants in accordance with their findings. H.M.I.s might have considered themselves as independent of 'the Office' in a technical sense, but such independence meant nothing to the teachers whose schools were being inspected. At the time of the passage through Parliament of the Board of Education Act of 1899, secondary school teachers feared that the inspection of their schools under the aegis of the new Board was to be carried out by the existing inspectors of the Science and Art Department. The Assistant Masters' Association resolved that it was desirable that all inspectors of secondary schools should have at least five years' experience in such schools. The headmasters of public schools were anxious that inspection should not be such as to impose a rigid uniformity of method or system; in order to avoid this they hoped that the President of the Board would take the advice of persons acquainted with the secondary schools.[57] It was partly in order to meet these fears that the possibility of inspection by university organisations was provided for in the Act of 1899. In 1902 the I.A.H.M. called on the Board to make the choice of inspection by a university organisation more effective. According to the High Master of Manchester Grammar School, 'The university inspector should be like the Matinian bee, fertilising school after school by the gentle fanning of his wings and the faint hum of his presence.' To the Science and Art inspector they owed much, and bare justice had been done to him by the profession, but he was rather associated in their minds with the red tape worm.[58]

The inspection of secondary schools by the Board developed only very slowly before Morant became Permanent Secretary. By the Spring of 1901 seven schools had been inspected, while a further 18 inspections had been arranged; by June twenty-seven inspections had been completed. The inspectors had been drawn from the permanent staff taken over from the Science and Art Department and partly appointed on a temporary basis from outside. Two years later the secondary inspectorate was still not fully organised and a large number of temporary inspectors were being employed. In his speech on the education estimates Anson said the Board hoped to recruit more men with literary and linguistic qualifications, 'men of such experience as will command the confidence of the local authorities and the headmasters of the secondary schools'. Later, in 1903, W. C. Fletcher was appointed Chief Inspector of Secondary Schools. As the former headmaster of Liverpool Institute High School he enjoyed the confidence of secondary teachers, as did three inspectors appointed to work under Fletcher, Headlam, Scott and Spencer, who were all experienced in the secondary field.[59] This confidence enabled the new secondary inspectorate to build up good relations with the schools as its numbers increased. By 1911 it was carrying out approximately 200 inspections annually, while some of the independent public schools had invited the Board to inspect them, including Clifton, Dulwich, Harrow, Repton, Sherborne and Wycombe Abbey. The only strong criticism of the secondary inspectorate came from the women's associations. The Association of Headmistresses passed a resolution in 1907 describing as 'most unsatisfactory the limitation of sphere and inferiority of status assigned to women on the Inspectorate of the Board of Education'.[60] They made the same point to the Royal Commission on the Civil Service in 1912.

Relations between the Board's Inspectorate and the N.U.T. were much less encouraging. Not only was there the unfortunate relationship which had grown out of the payment-by-results situation, where the H.M.I.s were the persons who actually came to see that the teachers made enough bricks without using too much straw; there was also the way in which entry to the inspectorate was monopolised by men with public school and older university backgrounds, who had usually never taught—and had probably never even been taught—in an elementary school. The N.U.T. never ceased to complain at the exclusion of elementary teachers.

The Trevelyan Committee of 1853 had recommended that inspectors should be recruited from among young men who had just gained a good honours degree; by entering the inspectorate young they would have the opportunity of undertaking services which would enable them to learn their job while doing it. This system continued to operate and to be criticised into the twentieth century. Inspectors' assistants were recruited from among elementary school head teachers, and Mundella created a class of sub-inspectors in 1881 to which inspectors' assistants might be promoted, but there was little chance of their moving to become inspectors.[61] The tendency to recruit on orthodox lines was strengthened by Gorst when he, as Vice-President, created the grade of Junior Inspector, to which young graduates without teaching experience were recruited before becoming full H.M.I.s of the Education Department—or later of the elementary inspectorate. The N.U.T. regarded this as another device for preventing the opening up of the inspectorate to its members, the certificated elementary school teachers. A leading article in *The Schoolmaster* described the Junior Inspector grade as 'an *annexe* to Oxford and Cambridge'. In 1907 it was reported that 'since 1901, 50 of these Junior Inspectors, youthful, inexperienced, unversed in the work of elementary schools, often tactless, and as a rule unqualified as teachers, have been promoted to the Inspectorate. During that period—i.e. since 1901—two Sub-Inspectors have been similarly promoted'. Promotion was said to depend 'more or less on social rank and less rather than more on natural ability'.[62] One of the first aims of the N.U.E.T. from the beginning had been to open recruitment to the Inspectorate to teachers. The establishment of the Junior Inspector grade and the closing of any further entry to the grade of Sub-Inspector in 1901 appeared to reverse even the slight progress that had been made in enabling teachers to become inspectors.

This apparent reversal of the fortunes of the elementary teachers was not confined to the issue of the inspectorate. During the 1890s the N.U.T. had been consulted with increasing frequency by Vice-Presidents and by G. Kekewich, the Permanent Secretary. Neither Gorst nor Morant took kindly to the influence which the N.U.T. seemed to have acquired. In 1901 Gorst described the Board of Education as being 'notoriously under the influence of the teachers',[63] and during the years when Morant was Permanent Secretary considerably less attention was paid to consulting the N.U.T. or paying heed to its views than had become customary in the late nineteenth century. The policies followed by the Board were diametrically opposed to those often advocated by the Union. Morant's aim of creating a system of publicly supported secondary schools modelled on the traditional grammar school concept was leading to the establishment of a clearly superior system for a minority and an increasingly sharp definition of boundaries between 'elementary' and 'higher' education as defined by the codes. The educational and social ideals embraced by the N.U.T. appeared to be under attack, and the attitude of the Union towards the Board became steadily more critical and eventually hostile; Morant was seen as the embodiment of all the Union was opposed to. Thus the crisis which developed over the 'Holmes-Morant' circular in 1911 was coloured by the Union's reaction to an exclusive inspectorate, but many different social, educational and political issues were involved.

In 1904 and 1905 there were complaints that some inspectors employed by local authorities were re-imposing mechanical methods and testing on teachers in the elementary schools of certain authorities.[64] Most of these local inspectors were ex-elementary school teachers with the limited horizons that the payment-by-results system so often produced. Many of them had been appointed originally by school boards in the larger cities and, in spite of their limitations, their recruitment at least was in line with N.U.T. policy; and the Union contrasted for the benefit of the Bryce Commission their helpful attitude to the schools with the unhelpfulness of H.M.I.s.[65] In 1905 the Chief Inspector for Elementary Schools, E. G. A. Holmes, after a conversation in which Yoxall made complaints about some local inspectors, instructed his inspectors to look into the problem. The results of the inquiries were discussed at a meeting of H.M.I.s and three years later a further questionnaire on the same theme was sent to divisional H.M.I.s. The answers were analysed and circulated to H.M.I.s with a covering note from Holmes on the consequences flowing from the appointment of the wrong sort of people as local authority inspectors. The order to circulate this material to over 100 H.M.I.s was signed by Morant, hence E Memorandum No. 21 has come to be known as the 'Holmes-Morant' circular. This 'strictly confidential' document was issued at the beginning of 1910, but the storm did not burst until March, 1911, when a Parliamentary question set it off.[66]

According to the Memorandum, of 123 local inspectors 104 were ex-elementary school-teachers, and of the remainder 'not more than 2 or 3 have had the antecedents which were usually looked for in candidates for Junior Inspectorships—namely, that they had been educated first at a public school, and then at Oxford and Cambridge. . . .'

'Apart from the fact that elementary teachers are as a rule uncultured and imperfectly educated, and though many, if not most, of them are creatures of tradition and routine, there are special reasons why the bulk of the local inspectors in this country should be unequal to the discharge of their responsible duties. It is in the large towns which had school boards before the appointed day that the majority of local inspectors are to be found. Of those in the 12 largest towns (Liverpool, Leeds, Manchester, Birmingham, etc.), there are no fewer than 75 local inspectors besides a great host of specialists. In these towns the local authorities have inherited from the school board not merely a vicious system of local inspection, but also a large number of vicious local inspectors. . . .

'As compared with the ex-elementary teacher usually engaged in the hopeless task of surveying or trying to survey a wide field of action from a well-worn groove, the inspector of public schools of the 'varsity type has the advantage of being able to look at elementary education from a point of view of complete detachment, and therefore of being able to handle its problems with a freshness and originality.'[67]

The derogatory remarks about 'uncultured' elementary school teachers and the laudatory remarks about the "varsity' type of inspector seemed to the N.U.T. to express in black and white some of the more objectionable prejudices by which the Board of Education under Morant had been guided. As a member of the Commons, Yoxall was able to express the pent-up feelings of the N.U.T. in a debate in July. The Holmes-Morant circular was a symptom of the administration of the Board and not an exception. Education was progressing not because of, but in spite of, the administrative interference by the Board. The spirit of the circular was still uppermost at the Board, 'it has been there all along: but it has grown enormously during the last ten years. There is reason for great dissatisfaction not only by the teachers whose *amour propre* and dignity have been offended, but on the part of the education authorities and all the private persons who are concerned in the work of education.'[68] Yoxall had already suggested that the Holmes circular ought to be called the Morant circular, and that it only constituted one more piece of evidence of an objectionable attitude on the part of high permanent officials of the Board towards the children and the teachers in the people's schools. In the Board of Education reaction and caste feeling had been rampant for years; ever since 1903 permanent officials had been making a determined effort to crush down elementary education into what they considered was its rightful place. Another N.U.T. member of the Commons, Gray, pointed out that the Union had had the privilege of helping former permanent secretaries, but the present incumbent 'was omniscient, knew everything, would not learn from anyone'.[69]

The N.U.T. organised a full political campaign, not simply to achieve the withdrawal of the objectionable private memorandum or to open the inspectorate to certificated elementary teachers, but to bring about fundamental changes in the policy and attitudes of the Board of Education—changes which must involve the departure of Morant. Meetings of protest in different parts of the country, parliamentary questions and debates all served to maintain the pressure until both Runciman, the President, and Morant went. In November, 1911, Morant left the Board, being transferred to the task of organising the government's new National Health Insurance scheme. In a leading article, *The Schoolmaster* claimed that 'It is little more than six months since in this column we warned him (Morant) through Mr. Runciman, that a government department nowadays could not stand long against public opinion organised by the National Union of Teachers. We knew even then that either he or Mr. Runciman would have to go, and we have to thank Mr. Runciman for the most striking vindication of the teachers possible—that they both have had to go.'[70] The victory of the N.U.T. in this affair played its part in the series of events which led to the setting up of the Royal Commission on the Civil Service.

Since 1911 the field of recruitment to the inspectorate has been much enlarged, so that the aim of the N.U.T. of opening entry to teachers has been achieved. Selby-Bigge, Morant's successor as Permanent Secretary, was examined on the background and education of H.M.I.s by the Royal Commission on the Civil Service in 1912. He told the Commission that 21 members of the Elementary Branch inspectorate had been certificated teachers in elementary schools, adding that 'some of our very best inspectors are men who have worked their way up from public elementary schools'. He went on to give details of three of these men; two of them after working in elementary schools went to Oxford, one gaining First Class Honours, the other becoming a Fellow of his college before joining the inspectorate; the third man gave up work in an elementary school to go to Cambridge, subsequently joining the inspectorate.[71] The tone of Selby-Bigge's evidence was conciliatory throughout, stress being laid on the value the Board attached to teaching experience. The Board sought first-rate men and 'a first-rate man, if he has experience of teaching in elementary schools, is more suited for the part of inspector of elementary schools than if he has not had that experience.'[72] At the same time the Permanent Secretary emphasised that inspectorships certainly should never be regarded as the natural prizes of the teaching profession. In the case of a good many first-rate men, two years experience in an elementary school would be ample.[73]

In many ways Selby-Bigge was the ideal man to follow Morant. His principal contribution lay in creating and fostering the partnership of teachers, local authorities and the central government. He quickly won the confidence of the teachers' associations, mainly through making himself readily available to their leaders and being prepared to talk to them. He believed that progress on the main lines of administration was 'quicker and more certain if the concurrence of the teachers is secured'. Concurrence meant understanding, and here personal explanation and discussion were more effective than circulars and memoranda. Such discussion was really only possible through representative bodies; the stronger and more representative associations of teachers were, the better for all concerned. While the associations were naturally much concerned with the professional interests of their members, in the long run professional and educational interests were identical.[74]

The regular consultation with teachers' associations on all major issues such as the Education Act and the Teachers' Superannuation Act of 1918, and the establishment of the Burnham machinery, led to the growth of a real feeling of partnership. An interesting comment on the confidence leaders of the N.U.T. felt in the relationship they built up with the Board under Selby-Bigge may be found in the executive's opposition to a motion at the annual conference of 1926, where it was proposed that the N.U.T. should seek the establishment of a 'real' Board of Education which would include representatives of L.E.A.s, of Parliament and of the teaching profession. The executive opposed this motion on the grounds that the Union should maintain its direct access to the responsible minister, and that they should not hamper themselves by setting up a body intermediate between themselves and the Board. A member of the executive added that Selby-Bigge had given the Union a testimonial the previous year when he said that the N.U.T. went before the Board and stated their views frankly and strongly and that the Board listened to them. This was a position not to be lightly thrown away. The executive won and the motion was defeated.[75]

A further illustration of the change in the official attitude to the participation and involvement of teachers in the control of education may be seen in the representation of teachers on the Secondary Schools Examinations Council set up in 1917. The spokesmen of both the A.H.M. and the I.A.H.M. expressed dissatisfaction over the number of representatives accorded to teachers on a body which concerned their work so vitally, and as a consequence of these protests one more headmaster was added to the Council.[76] But seen in an historical perspective what is notable about this episode is the official recognition that teachers had a part to play. Only 15 years earlier secondary schools were still earning grant by entering their pupils for examinations entirely administered and controlled by the South Kensington establishment of the former Science and Art Department, while teachers in the elementary schools had, of course, never played any part in the administration of the annual Education Department testing of their pupils. The curriculum was also coming to be recognised as an area in which detailed control by officials was inappropriate and which must be left increasingly to teachers.

Since the acceptance of teachers' associations as representative of one of the three partners in education, there have been suggestions from time to time that the inspectorate should cease from 'inspecting' in the traditional sense and become wholly an advisory service or, more simply, that it should just be abolished. Among secondary teachers this feeling gained some currency in the 1920s. Full inspections, taking place under abnormal conditions, seemed to do nothing to increase the efficiency of schools. The greater insistence that the status of a teacher should be that of a member of a learned profession brought with it the feeling that to submit to inspection was to suffer an indignity from which members of the legal and medical professions, for example, were exempt. The style and manner of inspecting also underwent change with the increased professional regard in which teachers were held. A resolution passed by the N.U.T. conference in 1922 drawing the attention of the Board of Education to uneducational conditions still existing, noted 'the sympathy and desire for co-operation with the teachers shown by a large number of H.M. Inspectors'.[77] The change in the concept of inspectors from inquisitors to advisers led the Norwood Committee in 1943 to suggest that they be renamed 'His Majesty's Educational Advisory Service'.[78]

The policy of the N.U.T. during the last two decades has been to urge that a Ministry of Education Advisory Service to Schools should replace the inspectorate. It has also remained a constant feature of the Union's policy to urge that the primary qualification for appointment should be teaching experience of an approved length and character.[79] Recruitment since the Second World War—and to a large extent from the First World War—has been from among those offering good academic and professional qualifications. The appointment of persons without teaching experience has become wholly exceptional.

When the suggestion was made at the time of the hearings of the Select Committee that much of the work undertaken by the H.M.I.s might be taken over by local authority inspectors, both the N.U.T. and the Joint Four were strongly opposed to the idea. The N.U.T. viewed such a development 'with the deepest apprehension'. Over many years there had grown up between H.M. inspectorate and teachers a mutual trust and respect which it would be foolish to jettison. H.M.I.s were more respected than their local authority counterparts, were not the agents of the teachers' employers and were not subject to the same local pressures. The representatives of the Joint Four also greatly valued the independent and wider nature of the central inspectorate: 'they can be much more independent because they are not answerable to the local authorities who are employing the teachers'.[80] The evidence of the teachers' associations to the Select Committee constituted a handsome testimonial to the success of the inspectorate in adjusting its methods and attitudes to the much more professional and much more highly trained teaching body which has developed since the teachers' associations were founded.

IV THE REFORMS OF 1944

The Education Act of 1944 was very largely an agreed measure. It has been remarked that the President of the Board, R. A. Butler, was very good at consulting apparently divergent interests and distilling a common essence which enabled him to proceed on agreed lines. The recognised position of the teachers' associations meant that they were constantly drawn into consultation throughout the period of planning and enacting the measure. They were, above all else, anxious to see a school organisation which would enable all children to have a full secondary education; they were anxious to see the removal of such obstacles to the achievement of this as the Part III authorities and the

1902 dual system still constituted in some areas. They were anxious to see a greater equality of educational provision throughout the country as a whole, which implied having a stronger central government department than the Board had been.

Between the wars the opinion had become widespread among teachers that a full ministry rather than a phantom board would give education a more influential position in the echelons of Whitehall. In 1942 the *Journal of Education* expressed the hopes of many when it looked forward to the creation of 'a real Ministry of Education' to replace 'the present mockery of a Board of Education which never meets and a Consultative Committee which cannot speak unless it is spoken to'.[81] There was a general welcome for a Minister who was given the positive duty 'to promote the education of the people of England and Wales and the progressive development of institutions devoted to that purpose, and to secure the effective execution by local authorities, under his control and direction, of the national policy for providing a varied and comprehensive educational service in every area'.[82]

The proposal that only counties and county boroughs should continue to be local education authorities was welcomed by teachers' associations. While some Part III authorities had been recognised as good employers, in general teachers' associations found most larger authorities easier to work with, and the abolition of these small authorities which dealt only with elementary education met with general agreement. The price which had to be paid for this in political terms was the creation below L.E.A. level of divisional executives and excepted districts, so as to satisfy the very vocal local interests in the Part III authority towns. The new bodies proposed were regarded with considerable suspicion by the N.U.T. and the secondary associations. A deputation to the Board of Education from the N.U.T. made it clear that the Union would have preferred that there should have been no divisional executives at all, but given their existence, the deputation was especially anxious to ensure that the powers delegated to them were strictly limited, especially in any matters concerned with the employment of teachers.[83]

Familiarity with divisional executives and excepted districts has not fundamentally changed the attitude of teachers' associations. In 1950 the I.A.H.M. at its annual meeting passed a resolution asking the Minister to appoint an *ad hoc* committee to review the working of divisional executives, which were described as a waste of time, labour and money. Hostility towards these bodies was particularly noticeable among grammar school teachers in the late 1940s and early 1950s, since the schools recognised as secondary before 1944 had never had contact with any local authority other than at the county (or county borough) level. The interposition of an additional layer of administration between the school and its paymaster—the L.E.A.—produced a good deal of friction and resentment. This was especially true in such areas as Middlesex, where the executives tended to be highly party-political.

The publication in 1957 of the White Paper on the Reorganisation of Local Government, with its proposal to create 55 new excepted districts, caused concern in most teachers' associations. Their views were vigorously expressed in the 'Peter Quince' column of *The Schoolmaster*. 'The history of teachers' struggles towards professional status is, in one respect, the history of their struggle to liberate themselves from being controlled by small local committees. Recognition as a member of a profession does not go hand in hand with subjection to parish pump control. The records of bodies of school managers, local school boards, and small Part III authorities are ample evidence of that. Unfortunately for many teachers, the White Paper proposals are a step backward towards the parish pump.'[85] The experience of teachers' organisations has shown them that the larger the size of a local authority, the more likely it is that their members' affairs are dealt with on their merits and not on personalities. The revival of a similar proposal the next year met with a similar reaction. The N.U.T. was quite explicit in its opposition to the need to negotiate many more local schemes of responsibility allowances, to the possibility of more differences in holidays and attitudes towards sick pay, leave of absence, secondment and all the other items settled locally which do a great deal to make a teaching force contented. The Local Government Act of 1958 made provision for applications for the status of excepted districts. Before issuing a circular in amplification of this, the Ministry circulated the draft in the usual way to teachers' associations for comment. The comments from the associations emphasised particularly that in all matters relating to the appointment and dismissal of teachers and in matters relating to the conditions of employment the final decision should rest with the county authority. The circular as issued stated, 'In view, however, of the practical difficulties that might arise and the danger that the change might in removing some sources of friction create others (the Minister) has decided that the existing arrangements for employment should be maintained in the new excepted districts.'[86]

The Administration of the School System

The principle of co-opting representative teachers to education committees was maintained by the Act of 1944. The attempt to treat the teaching profession as a unity before its members felt sufficient community of interest, which caused friction between the N.U.T. and the secondary associations in the Burnham Committee, also led to some troubles over teacher representation at the local level. The I.A.H.M. wrote to the Minister in 1945 complaining that in some districts the new constitutions for their education committees drawn up by the L.E.A.s laid it down that only one teacher representative should serve on the committee and that he should be nominated by the local association of the N.U.T., to which, in general, few secondary teachers belonged. In his reply the Minister claimed that the policy which was being followed by the Ministry was the one desired, for when draft schemes came in which did not provide for the co-option by education committees of teachers representing the 3 stages of education, this was suggested. He also suggested that the arrangements should provide for the nomination or recommendation of the teacher representatives, either by bodies representing teachers or by the teachers amongst themselves. He added, 'I am sure you will appreciate that it is not easy for me to go further than making these suggestions to the authority. Local circumstances have to be taken into account in each case, and there are some authorities who, on principle object to nomination or recommendation or even, however unfortunate such an attitude may be, to the presence of teachers on the education committee. . . .'[87]

Where teachers were without representation, they continued to press for it and from time to time achieved the conversion of a wayward authority. A decision by Doncaster to grant teachers representation on its education committee marked the success of a five-year campaign by the local association of the N.U.T. In 1955 the Regional Officer of the Union and a deputation had put the case in vain to the education committee. The campaign was conducted by approaching candidates in the local elections and by bringing the matter to the attention of the main political parties.[88] When teachers look at services comparable to the education service itself, such as the health service, they find a much higher proportion of professionals on administrative committees. It is not surprising that their associations are continuing to press for increased representation both on education committees and on sub-committees, including divisional executives. The N.U.T. currently urges that 'a substantial proportion of the members (of these bodies) shall be elected representatives of the teachers with full membership rights'.[89]

The abolition of the official demarcation between the elementary and secondary systems in 1944 and the concept embodied in official regulations thenceforth of primary and secondary schools providing respectively for all children up to or above the age of eleven raised fears among secondary teachers that the degree of administrative initiative which had been either preserved or won for heads and governors at the school level in the distinctive secondary system might be lost. The heads and managers of the reorganised senior schools for pupils over eleven had been operating under the elementary code and had enjoyed nothing like the same degree of initiative. Since the majority of secondary schools would in future be these ex-elementary code schools, the fear of assimilation to the old elementary pattern for future secondary schools was reasonable enough.

Two years before the Act the Joint Four Secondary Associations had issued a memorandum envisaging secondary education for all from the age of eleven, with all schools taking pupils of secondary age administered under a single code. Such a scheme for educational reconstruction would be 'informed by the ideal of equality of educational opportunity'.[90] There was never any doubt that the future expansion advocated in order to achieve equality of opportunity was to be conceived in terms of converting senior schools to the existing secondary pattern. At their annual general meeting in January, 1943, the headmasters resolved that they 'would strongly oppose any measures which would have the effect of limiting freedom in secondary schools both in respect of their government and in their curricula'.[91] In the evidence it submitted to the Fleming Committee on Public Schools, the I.A.H.M. defended the continuation of fees in all secondary schools, arguing that the abolition of fees in state-aided schools and their retention in schools outside the state system would merely lead to an increased demand for admission to the latter. Moreover, the headmasters feared that if the financial deficiencies resulting were to be met by local authorities, 'the latter might claim the right to curtail that freedom of action which has been such a potent factor in the successful development of the secondary schools'. They added that signs were not wanting of a desire to extend to the secondary schools 'those methods of detailed administration which have been characteristic of the local control of elementary education'.[92]

The I.A.H.M. underlined its fears at a meeting with senior officials of the Board. The Board's intention was said to be to give a wide measure of autonomy to governing bodies in the Education Act which would be confined to stating principles. Discussions between governing bodies and local authorities on detailed arrangements would follow later. The Association's representatives felt that the abolition of fees and complete dependence on the local authority would become a *fait accompli* without adequate safeguard for freedom. In these circumstances it would obviously be difficult to negotiate with local authorities on terms of equality, and Canon Leeson (Headmaster of Winchester) wondered whether if the Board were the final authority they would be prepared to oppose the local authorities. The I.A.H.M. followed up this meeting with a letter to the President of the Board embodying its views. While welcoming reform, it objected to any strict and rigid imposition of an agreed syllabus of religious instruction on secondary schools. It maintained its earlier position on fees, but if they were to be abolished in all maintained schools it urged that schools should have the right to apply for admission to the direct grant list. Finally, the financial implications of the proposed reforms led it to fear a levelling down of existing standards of equipment, staffing ratios and salary scales, as local authorities tried to arrive at a common scale between the existing secondary schools and the senior elementary schools. So far as salary scales were concerned, the fears turned out to be entirely justified.[93] The reply from Butler gave away nothing other than reassurances, and he was sure the headmasters need not fear 'a strictly rigid imposition of agreed syllabuses'; he would note their views on fees and he was not apprehensive that there needed to be any lowering of existing standards. He believed that the public generally would look for an improvement of conditions and would not acquiesce in a policy of mediocrity.[94]

When the government issued its White Paper on the principles of government in maintained secondary schools to fill in some of the generalities set out in the Act, it was very carefully examined by the A.H.M. and the I.A.H.M., who made much the same points of substance in the comments they sent to the Minister. Both associations welcomed the main points made by the documents in setting forth the rights and responsibilities of all concerned in the administration of secondary schools within the state system. They hoped that governors would be drawn from a wide background and from outside the membership of the local authority, and that they would be recognised as controlling the caretaking and maintenance staff, would have the right to fix term and holiday dates and so forth. Both organisations made the point that assistant staff should be appointed to particular schools, and opposed any sort of appointment to a staffing pool operated by the local authority.[95] The White Paper admitted that the interests of the teaching staff should be reflected in the composition of a governing body, but added that this could be achieved without giving the staff any right to nominate governors for the purpose. All of the four secondary associations sought to win for the staff the right to nominate at least one governor, not himself being a member of the staff, but with little effect.

In spite of these efforts made by the secondary associations during the planning of the reforms associated with the Act of 1944, the absorption of their own small and hitherto privileged sector in the greater mass of the former elementary sector was bound to lead to a weakening of the position of the schools in which their members served, and a relative worsening of their working arrangements. The much more detailed control of the various aspects of school life hitherto associated with elementary schools came to be applied to them, their terms were lengthened, their holidays and occasional breaks were cut so as to conform to the pattern required by local authorities in all the other schools of the district, and were often fixed now not by the governors or heads but by 'the office'. There is no doubt that the years following the Act of 1944 were years of disillusion and disenchantment for teachers in the older secondary schools.[96] The I.A.A.M. Council in 1946 declared its resolute opposition to all forms of restrictive regulations in the guise of educational reforms and called for 'a vigorous fighting policy against the attacks on the grammar schools and grammar school teachers'.[97]

By the early 1950s the dissatisfaction amounted to something like a campaign against excessive local government bureaucracy. In the evidence it submitted to the Local Government Manpower Committee in 1950 the I.A.H.M. asserted that 'The policy of this Association is based on the belief that the school is the natural unit of educational administration'. Far from recognising this, local authorities had tried to reorganise their schools 'in the spirit of the old Elementary Code'. More and more clerical staff were being employed and there was increasing difficulty in getting anything done. The Association's aim was to secure for each secondary school an effective governing body possessing a measure of financial discretion.[98] At its annual meeting in 1951 the I.A.H.M. resolved that it was 'gravely concerned at the effects of the progressive loss of liberty in maintained schools', and asked its council to bring the matter before the Ministry, the Association of Education Committees and the public, so as to secure a more liberal administration based upon the effective responsibility of governing bodies.[99] The complaints were taken up in the press. *The Times Educational Supplement* suggested in a leading article that it should not require too much imagination on the part of local authorities who were keenly aware of the pressure of central interference, to recognise similar feelings in their schools, particularly in those of them which formerly had a good measure of control over their own affairs. In some areas headmasters, governors and managers had all too much reason to complain of tiresome interference and the arrogation of most substantial responsibilities by the officers of the education committee. 'They no longer decide the appointment of staff, the granting of leave of absence, the purchase of miscellaneous equipment, or the spending of even small sums of money'.[100]

By no means all local authorities sought to impose rigidly bureaucratic patterns upon their schools. One which made a strong and successful effort to give more administrative responsibility to schools was Hertfordshire. Here the county authority put all the internal finances of the school into the hands of its head teacher. At the beginning of the year an assessment of so much a head for each pupil was made and the total sum thus arrived at was paid into an account at a local bank in two amounts, one at the beginning and the other half-way through the year. The head signed cheques and drew on that amount as he thought best suited the interests of his school. The county still dealt directly with wages and salaries, grants, rates and rents, major repairs and buildings along with heating and lighting. This initiative was welcomed by all teachers' associations; the I.A.H.M. annual general meeting saw in it a recognition of the responsibility and freedom of the schools and urged other local authorities to adopt it.[101]

The Act of 1944 certainly failed to establish that there should be any measure of administrative initiative at the school level. It required local education authorities to set up managing and governing bodies for their primary and secondary schools, but gave no power to the Ministry or to anyone else to ensure that these were more than mere shadows, devoid of influence, function and utility. Apart from the voluntary schools, the position after 1944 was effectively what it was before. Some authorities—more especially the counties—have fostered governing and managing bodies, and they play a vital part in giving schools their individuality. Others—particularly some of the county boroughs —operate highly centralised systems, with power in the hands of the local politicians and officers. The headmasters' association continues to claim a wide measure of independence for heads along with effective governing bodies for individual schools;[102] it lies in the discretion of each local authority to give or to withhold this.

V SOME RECENT ADMINISTRATIVE DEVELOPMENTS

The reaction to some of the proposals for changing the system of educational administration since 1944 has shown how strongly teachers' associations are opposed to attempts to weaken the position of any of the three partners of the education service in favour of outsiders. The episode which raised the strongest reactions was the proposal made by the government in 1957 to replace the percentage grants for education and for certain other services by a general or block grant to local authorities. Teachers feared that this change would reduce the pace of educational advance, since in place of about 60 per cent of all expenditure by the L.E.A.s falling on the Treasury, local councils would receive a lump sum to help them meet the total cost of the various services they provided. Any increase in educational expenditure would fall wholly on the rates. Moreover, it was assumed that the position of education committees relative to that of finance committees would be weakened. The shift in financial responsibility must also bring with it a shift in the balance of power, the powers of the Minister would decline and those of the local councils increase. As Sir Ronald Gould told the N.U.T. Conference in 1957, 'fixed block grants must lead us away from the concept of a national system of education locally administered towards 146 separate education systems, each with different standards'.[103] The Joint Four joined the N.U.T. in its fears and in its strong opposition to the block grant proposals; authorities would seek to economise on their greatly increased rate-borne expenditure by imposing economies on those parts of the education service the full development of which could not be secured by prescribing minimum standards or general requirements.[104]

Not only the N.U.T. and the Joint Four but also other teachers' associations such as the N.A.S., the A.T.C.D.E., the A.T.T.I. and the Educational Institute of Scotland joined with the Association of

Education Committees and other educational organisations to mount a nationwide political campaign against the block grant proposals.[105] In spite of this considerable alignment of forces, the government stuck to its proposals. Although leaders of the teachers' associations had fought hard against the Local Government Bill, the mass of their memberships did not feel sufficiently involved to bring strong electoral pressure to bear on the government.

In his report to the N.U.T. conference in 1958, the general secretary forecast that the adoption of general grants would cause three shifts in the distribution of power:

(i) The Ministry of Housing and Local Government, as distributor of the new general grant, would gain power at the expense of the Ministry of Education;
(ii) The Minister of Education would lose power to the local authorities;
(iii) Education committees would lose power to those who received the new grant and controlled the purse-strings, the finance committees and local authorities generally.

The Education Act of 1944 intended that education should be a national service locally administered. If the Local Government Act now made education into a local government service, local authorities would not enjoy their power for long, since there would be an insistent demand either for more national control or to take education out of local government entirely.[106]

The fact that these fears, held by most educationists in 1958, have not proved justified and that the actual change turned out to be no more significant than the administrative change for reasons of convenience that the 1957 White Paper claimed, has shown that the grant system had ceased by then to determine the distribution of power and influence in the way it had done earlier in this century and certainly did in the nineteenth century. The power of the central ministry had come to rest largely on the right to issue directions, to control in detail capital expenditure, to enforce building standards and to supervise staffing and other educational standards through the operations of the inspectorate. Moreover at the local level education is by far the most considerable service administered in terms of cost, and the standing of the education committee relative to others reflected this; the continued advance and development of the education service by local authorities also reflected the extent to which members of the public generally had come to expect from their councils a steady improvement in facilities.

The same anxiety on the part of the N.U.T. to ensure that the status and position of education committees should be fully maintained was shown in a case arising from the reorganisation of London government. One of the newly-created London Boroughs proposed that all appointments of staff should be dealt with by its establishments committee, which would also deal with the conditions of service of teachers. The N.U.T. had always taken the view that it was the function of the education committee to deal with all matters relating to education. The Union's solicitor took the opinion of counsel. This was that an L.E.A. could either exercise education functions itself or it could authorise its education committee to exercise them on the council's behalf, but it could not delegate them to any other committee. The local association of the N.U.T. had a series of meetings with representatives of the authority and eventually the borough decided to revise the constitution of its committees.[107]

A further instance of the anxiety of the teachers' associations to maintain and possibly extend the sphere of education committees became apparent in the controversy over the future of the Youth Employment Service, conducted in some areas by the local education authorities and in others by the Department of Employment and Productivity. After various statements and inquiries the D.E.P. circulated a consultative document at the end of May, 1970, suggesting that the Youth Employment Service should be integrated in a new all-age 'National Manpower Service'. The N.U.T. opposed this integration, and suggested as an alternative that the Youth Employment Service should become 'an education-based service for all young people up to the age of 22' and should be administered everywhere by local education authorities.[108]

It is perhaps not surprising that the National Association of Schoolmasters, which has become so much more influential in recent years, should be showing a different attitude to some of the administrative organs from that displayed by those teachers' associations which have been fully accepted as part of the educational establishment for a much longer period. In its evidence to the Royal Commission on Local Government in England (1966–9) the N.A.S. proposed that education should be administered locally by large single-purpose authorities whose membership should be partly elected and partly nominated by the Secretary of State. The central government would shoulder complete financial responsibility for the training, salaries and superannuation of teachers while the local authorities bore financial liability for school buildings, equipment and maintenance.

NOTES

1. *The Schoolmaster*, 2nd April, 1921, p. 644.
2. Mrs. S. Webb, *New Statesman*, Special Supplement, 'English Teachers and their Professional Organisation', 25th September, 1915, p. 19.
3. Bryce Cssn., 1895, vol. V, pp. 322–4.
4. Ibid.
5. Ibid., pp. 33–4, 'Memorandum on the advantage of having the same central and local authorities for secondary and elementary education', by J. H. Yoxall, M.P.
6. Ibid., p. 330.
7. Ibid., vol. IV, p. 25, evidence of headmistress of Notting Hill High School.
8. Ibid., vol. V, pp. 308–14. Conference of Headmasters, 1894, Draft of Scheme.
9. *Journal of Education*, January, 1896, pp. 67–9.
10. I.A.H.M. Annual Report, 1896, p. 23, 'Memorial of the I.A.H.M. relating to a draft scheme for a bill dealing with secondary education'.
11. 'Joint Memorandum on the relations of primary and secondary schools to each other in a national system of education', printed in I.A.H.M. Annual Report, 1901.
12. I.A.H.M., *The Organisation of Secondary Education*, 1897.
13. *Journal of Education*, July, 1898, p. 391.
14. *The Record*, 16th July, 1898, p. 31.
15. *Journal of Education*, February, 1899, pp. 104 and 107.
16. 62 and 63 Vict., c. 33.
17. *The Times*, 9th October, 1899, 'The New Education Office: Its Tripartite Organisation'.
18. P.R.O. Ed. 24/64, Devonshire to Kekewich, 7th July, 1899.
19. P. H. J. H. Gosden, *The Development of Educational Administration in England and Wales*, 1967, Chapter V, where the issue is discussed in greater detail.
20. *Hansard*, H. of C., 26th June, 1899, col. 616.
21. *Journal of Education*, February, 1901, p. 152.

22. Gosden, op. cit., pp. 172 ff. for the administrative consequences of this case.
23. P.R.O., Ed. 24/14, Memorandum dated 1st August, 1901; Ed. 24/14, 'Points against *Ad Hoc* by R.L.M.; the extent of Morant's responsibility for planning the Act of 1902 is discussed by E. Eaglesham in 'Planning the Education Bill of 1902', *B.J.E.S.*, vol. LX, pp. 3–24.
24. The Headmasters' Conference in December, 1902, resolved that 'it is essential (1) that there should be a Secretary of Secondary Education, independent of the Secretaries of Primary and Technical Education, and at least equal to them in rank; and (2) that his first care should be to redress the balance which now weighs in favour of scientific against literary studies. . . .' *Journal of Education*, January, 1903, pp. 25–6.
25. I.A.A.M. Annual Report, 1902, p. 10.
26. This was the most important theme of J. H. Yoxall's *The Coming Education Bill, The Need for it. The best lines for it.* (N.U.T.), 1901, p. 27.
27. Gosden, op. cit., pp. 179–80; *Journal of Education*, February, 1903, p. 104.
28. 2 Edw. 7, c. 42, S. 17 (3) and (4).
29. E.g. N.U.T. Annual Report, 1904, p. xliii; I.A.A.M. Annual Report, 1902, p. 12.
30. N.U.T. Annual Report, 1909, pp. xliii–xlv.
31. *Journal of Education*, February, 1903, pp. 148–9.
32. *The Times*, 3rd January, 1903, 'The Constitution of Education Committees'.
33. *Education*, 29th January, 1903, pp. 114–15.
34. Report of the Board of Education for 1902–3, p. 7.
35. N.U.T. Annual Report, 1919, p. xxxix; Whitley Councils were so-called after J. M. Whitley, M.P., chairman of the Reconstruction Commission which made recommendations respecting industrial councils.
36. N.U.T. Annual Report, 1904, p. xlv; *Journal of Education*, October, 1903, p. 668.
37. *T.E.S.*, 27th February, 1919, p. 105; ibid., 16th December, 1920, p. 660.
38. C. Norwood and A. H. Hope, *The Higher Education of Boys in England*, 1909, p. 165.
39. S.I.C., 1868, vol. I, pp. 617–19.

40. Bryce Commission, 1895, vol. I, pp. 157, 298–9.
41. *The Times*, 12th January, 1907, I.A.H.M. general meeting had resolved that in the administration of secondary schools by L.E.A.s the utmost care should be taken to avoid weakening the personal responsibility of headmasters, and that any attempt to encroach on the present administration of such schools by their governing bodies and headmasters should be regarded as being prejudicial to the best interests of secondary education.
42. Report of the Board of Education for 1908–9, pp. 127–8.
43. P.R.O., Ed. 12/138, Memorandum dated 14th November, 1910.
44. Royal Commission on Local Government in England, Research Studies 6, School Management and Government, 1968, pp. 23–30.
45. P.R.O. Ed. 12/138, Memorandum by W. N. Bruce, dated 9th November, 1910.
46. Ibid.
47. *The Schoolmaster*, 7th October, 1907, p. 667.
48. Ibid., 2nd November, 1907, pp. 755–6.
49. *Hansard*, H. of C., 1st August, 1905, col. 1203.
50. *Hansard*, H. of C., 13th July, 1910, col. 393.
51. *The Times*, 19th October, 1927, carried a letter from the Chairman of the Committee of the H.M.C. pointing out that the institution of an O.T.C. against the wishes of the Head would have been considered an equally cogent example of the position upon which the H.M.C.'s decision was based.
52. *Journal of Education*, November, 1927, pp. 794–5.
53. *The Times*, 20th October, 1927, letter from L. A. Lowe; *T.E.S.*, 1st October, 1927, p. 440.
54. *The Times*, 24th December, 1927.
55. *T.E.S.*, 28th January, 1928, p. 46.
56. *Journal of Education*, February, 1932, p. 101; *T.E.S.*, 19th July, 1917, p. 282. 'Statement of policy by the Association of Assistant Masters in Secondary Schools'; ibid., p. 281.
57. *Journal of Education*, May, 1899, p. 304; *Hansard*, H. of C., 26th June, 1899, col. 625.
58. *Journal of Education*, February, 1902, pp. 149–50.
59. Report of the Board of Education for 1900–1, pp. 64–5; *Hansard*, H. of C., 9th July, 1903, col. 176; *Journal of Education*, February, 1904, p. 168.
60. *Hansard*, H. of C., 13th July, 1911, col. 505; A.H.M., *Summary*

of the Work of the Association of Headmistresses, 1911, p. 5.
61. Gosden, op. cit., pp. 27–9.
62. The Schoolmaster, 30th November, 1907, pp. 953–4.
63. P.R.O., Ed. 24/16, Gorst to Morant, 23rd June, 1901.
64. N.U.T. Annual Report, 1904, p. xli.
65. Bryce Cssn., 1895, vol. V, p. 328.
66. Tropp, op. cit., pp. 199–203 gives a useful account of the affair; also prints the extracts from the Memorandum read in the Commons on 21st March, 1911 (pp. 271–2).
67. Hansard, H. of C., 21st March, 1911, cols. 277–8. E. Memorandum No. 21 has never been published, the extracts here are from the speech by Samuel Hoare, M.P., in which he read from the copy in his possession.
68. House of Commons, vol. XXVIII, col. 542 (13th July, 1911).
69. The Schoolmaster, 8th April, 1911, p. 706; ibid., 22nd April, 1911, p. 826.
70. Ibid., 2nd December, 1911, p. 945.
71. Royal Commission on the Civil Service, Appendix to Second Report of the Commissioners, Cd. 6535, 1912, QQ. 9086–91.
72. Ibid., Q. 9277.
73. Ibid., QQ. 9282, 9454.
74. L. A. Selby-Bigge, The Board of Education, 1927, p. 276.
75. The Schoolmaster, 16th April, 1926, pp. 690–4.
76. Journal of Education, August, 1917, p. 459; T.E.S., 14th June, 1917, p. 224; 3rd January, 1918, p. 4; 28th February, 1918, p. 96.
77. Journal of Education, August, 1921, pp. 504–5, N.U.T. Annual Report, 1922, p. lxxxvii.
78. Board of Education; Curriculum and Examinations in Secondary Schools, 1943, p. 53.
79. The Schoolmaster, 10th May, 1957, pp. 901–2; Report from the Select Committee on Education and Science, Part I, Her Majesty's Inspectorate, 1968, p. 161.
80. Ibid., pp. 167 and 182.
81. Journal of Education, March, 1942, p. 98; The A.M.A., January, 1944, p. 49, reported a resolution of the I.A.A.M., 'that the Government should set up a Ministry of Education under a responsible Minister of Cabinet rank'.
82. 7 & 8 Geo. 6, c. 31, S. 1; Typical of reaction from teachers' associations was the welcome printed in The A.M.A., March–April 1944, p. 68.

The Administration of the School System 353

83. P.R.O., Ed. 136/588, Note written subsequent to meeting a deputation from the N.U.T. on 23/8/44.
84. *Review of the I.A.H.M.*, March, 1950, p. 56.
85. *The Schoolmaster*, 17th May, 1957, p. 944.
86. *Review of the I.A.H.M.*, December, 1958, p. 92; Ministry of Education Circular 344, 17th December, 1958, para. 21.
87. Ibid., July, 1945, pp. 127–8.
88. *The Schoolmaster*, 17th June, 1960, p. 1565.
89. N.U.T. Conference resolution, 1968; *The A.M.A.*, February, 1969, p. 7, where the President of the I.A.A.M. asked whether the size of teacher representation on committees was as large as it should be since if there were only 2 or 3 teachers' representatives on a big committee, they 'have a great load to carry if the representation is to be adequate'; J. Vaizey, 'Teachers under authority', *T.E.S.*, 9th January, 1959, p. 9, suggested that until teachers are given much wider representation 'they will continue to have employee status and not professional status'.
90. *Review of the I.A.H.M.*, December, 1942, pp. 146–8, Joint Four 'Memorandum on Education after the War'.
91. Ibid., March, 1943, p. 33.
92. Ibid., July, 1943, pp. 131–4.
93. Ibid., December, 1943, pp. 172–9.
94. Ibid., December, 1943, pp. 179–81. Letter from R. A. Butler to the President of the I.A.H.M. dated 10th November, 1943.
95. P.R.O., Ed. 12/510, Memorandum from the A.H.M. on the White Paper on the Principles of Government in maintained Schools; letter from H. L. D. Flecker (President, I.A.H.M.) to the Minister of Education dated 15th August, 1944.
96. *The A.M.A.*, June–July, 1944, p. 126. There were similar complaints from other associations, e.g. *Review of the I.A.H.M.*, April, 1948, pp. 75–8.
97. *The A.M.A.*, January–February, 1946, pp. 48–9.
98. *Review of the I.A.H.M.*, July, 1950, pp. 147–50.
99. Ibid., March, 1951, p. 48.
100. *T.E.S.*, 22nd June, 1951, p. 509.
101. Ibid., 9th January, 1953, p. 16; *Review of the I.A.H.M.*, March, 1953, p. 34.
102. I.A.H.M. Memorandum, 'The Position of a Head Master', 1960, argued the case fully on traditional lines.
103. *The Schoolmaster*, 26th April, 1957, p. 777.

104. *I.A.H.M. Review*, April, 1958, pp. 27–30, for the views of the Joint Four on the Local Government Bill.
105. A.E.C., *The Threat to Education*, 1957, with a Foreword by R. Gould and W. P. Alexander, put the joint case of teachers and local education committees against block grants; the main features of the block grant campaign, 1957–8, are outlined in R. A. Manzer, *Teachers and Politics*, 1970, pp. 73–81, where there is also a useful analysis of the political failure of the educationists.
106. *The Schoolmaster*, 11th April, 1958, pp. 725–7.
107. N.U.T. Annual Report, 1967, p. 99.
108. *The Teacher*, 7th August, 1970, p. 1.

Bibliographical Note

In the preparation of this study the main sources consulted were the reports and publications of teachers' associations, official publications and P.R.O. files, educational periodicals, books and pamphlets. The most directly relevant of these sources are mentioned in the references and no attempt is made here to set out the full bibliography.

It may be helpful, however, to bring together in this note a few of the official reports and other sources useful in studying some of the topics discussed in this book.

I GROWTH AND DEVELOPMENT OF TEACHERS ASSOCIATIONS

Few books have been published on the growth and development of teachers' associations. Among the most useful are:

- D. F. Thompson, *Professional Solidarity among the Teachers of England* (1927).
- A. Tropp, *The School Teachers* (1957).
- W. Roy, *The Teachers' Union* (1968).
- Alicia C. Percival, *The Origins of the Headmasters' Conference* (1969).
- R. A. Manzer, *Teachers and Politics* (1970).

The following articles in periodicals should be noticed:

- Mrs. S. Webb, 'English teachers and their professional organisation', published as special supplements to the *New Statesman*, 25th September and 2nd October, 1915.
- 'The development of professional associations of teachers during the last 25 years', *Journal of Education*, May, 1935, pp. 340–3.

'Guide to the teachers' unions', series of four articles in *Education*.

1. 'The Hamilton House Group', 27th March, 1959, pp. 648–52,
2. 'In Gordon Square', 3rd April, 1959, pp. 709–13,

3. 'From Surbiton to Winchester', 10th April, 1959, pp. 760-1,
4. 'Towards the turning point', 17th April, 1959, pp. 815-17.

A thesis which should be mentioned is that by G. Baron, 'The Secondary Schoolmaster 1895-1915: a study of the qualifications, conditions of employment and professional associations of masters in English secondary schools', Ph.D. London, 1952.

II SALARIES

Official reports

Board of Education, Secondary Education (Accounts and Finance): Statistics relating to annual income and expenditure, especially in relation to salaries of teaching staff, in certain secondary schools in England. Cd. 5951, 1911.

Board of Education, Reports of the Departmental Committee for Enquiring into the principles which should determine the construction of scales of salary for teachers in elementary schools. Cd. 8939, 1918.

Board of Education, Report of the Departmental Committee for Enquiring into the principles which should determine the fixing of salaries for teachers in secondary and technical schools, schools of art, training colleges, and other institutions for higher education, other than university institutes. Cd. 9140, 1918.

Board of Education, Report of the Standing Joint Committee on Standard Scales for Teachers in Public Elementary Schools, 1920.

Reports of the Burnham Committees.

Other sources

Teachers' associations' journals, and particularly *The Schoolmaster* (1872-1963), continued as *The Teacher* (1963-), give very full cover to salary matters.

A. Blades and G. D. Dunkerley, 'Salaries and conditions of service in secondary schools', *The A.M.A.*, September, 1915, pp. 144-7.

P. Sharp, 'The Burnham Committee', *Education*, 16th June, 1944.

The National Federation of Class Teachers and its fight for the Basic Scale (1945).

The Grammar School Master's Salary: A National Problem (1953).

III EQUAL PAY

Official reports

Report of the War Cabinet Committee on Women in Industry, Cmd. 135, 1919.
Report of the Royal Commission on Equal Pay, 1945.

Other sources

E. Phipps, *Equal Pay* (1924).
E. Phipps, *History of the N.U.W.T.* (1928).
H. Meigh, *Schoolmasters' salaries since the beginning of the twentieth century* (1957).
A. Potter, 'The Equal Pay Campaign Committee: a case-study of a pressure group', *Political Studies*, V, 1957.
Arguments for and against equal pay were fully aired in the *Woman Teacher* (1919–60), journal of the N.U.W.T., and *The New Schoolmaster* (1921–), journal of the N.A.S.

IV SUPERANNUATION

Official reports

Report from the Select Committee on Elementary Education (Teachers' Superannuation), 1892.

Board of Education, Departmental Committee on the Superannuation of Teachers, Reports on First and Second References, 1914.

Board of Education, Report of the Departmental Committee on the Superannuation of School Teachers, Cmd. 1962, 1923.

Other sources

W. R. Barker, *The Superannuation of Teachers in England and Wales* (1926).

J. Vaizey, 'Teachers' Superannuation in England and Wales', *B.J.E.S.*, November, 1957.

Family Pension Benefits for Teachers in England and Wales, Department of Education and Science (1965).

V TENURE

There is very little in the way of convenient printed sources.

J. Montgomery, *The Tenure of Assistant Masters in Secondary Schools administered under the schemes of the Charity Commission* (1895).

A. Gray Jones, 'Tenure in Secondary Schools', *Journal of Education*, November, 1934.

A. Sinclair, 'The Problem of Tenure of Assistant Masters in Secondary Schools', M.Ed. thesis, Manchester, 1940.

VI TRAINING

Official reports

Education Department, Report of the Departmental Committee on the Pupil Teacher System, 1898.

Board of Education, General Report on the Instruction and Training of Pupil Teachers, 1903–7, with Historical Introduction, 1907.

Board of Education, The Training of Women Teachers for Secondary Schools, 1912.

Board of Education, Report of the Departmental Committee on the training of Teachers for Public Elementary Schools, 1925.

Board of Education, Teachers and Youth Leaders (McNair Report), 1944.

Reports of the National Advisory Council on the Training and Supply of Teachers.

Other sources

J. G. Fitch, 'The Universities and the Training of Teachers', *Contemporary Review*, December, 1876.

T. E. Heller, 'On the Registration, Certification and Training of Teachers'; Dorothea Beale, 'On the Training of Teachers for High Schools', both papers read to the Education Section, *Transactions of the National Association for the Promotion of Social Science*, 1878.

The Training of Teachers, Memorandum of the Joint Standing Committee of the Training Colleges Association and the Committee of Principals (1937).

Challenge and Response. An account of the Emergency Training Scheme for the training of teachers, Ministry of Education (1950).

A First Degree in Education, N.U.T. (1951).

The N.U.T. View on Ancillaries and Auxiliaries, N.U.T. (n.d.).

M. G. Fitch, 'The History of the Training of Teachers for Secondary Schools in England', M.A. thesis, London, 1931.

A. Shakoor, 'The Training of Teachers in England and Wales, 1900–39', Ph.D. thesis, Leicester, 1964.

VII REGISTRATION

Official reports

Report from the Select Committee on the Teachers' Registration and Organisation Bill, 1891.

Reports of the Teachers' Registration Council.

Board of Education, R. L. Morant, Memorandum on the Registration of Teachers, Cd. 3017, 1906.

Board of Education, Scheme for a new Teachers' Registration Council proposed to the Board of Education by the Representatives of Certain Educational Authorities, Cd. 4185, 1908.

Board of Education, Correspondence concerning Cd. 4185, Cd. 4402, 1908.

Board of Education, Report by the Secretary to the President of the Board in three informal conferences concerning the proposed Teachers' Registration Council . . . with further papers, Cd. 5726, 1911.

Other sources

F. Storr, 'Registration and Training of Secondary Teachers' in L. Magnus (ed.), *National Education*, 1901.

J. L. Paton, 'The Teachers' Register and its possibilities', *Contemporary Review*, August, 1912.

G. Baron, 'The Teachers' Registration Movement', *B.J.E.S.*, May, 1954.

Index

Abbott, Rev. Dr. E., 216
Abney, W., 319
Acland, Arthur, 135, 239, 320
Acting Teachers' Examination, 26
Admiralty, 8
Advisory Service to Schools, 337
Alexander, Sir William, 71, 72
Anson, Sir William, 169, 328, 331
Area Training Organisations, 266, 290–3
Art Teachers' Guild, 137, 252
Association for Promoting Scholastic Registration, 236–7
Association for Science Education, 18
Association of Assistant Mistresses, 82
  foundation and aims, 12–13
  membership, 13–14
  salaries, 42, 48, 77
  Burnham Committee membership, 64
  equal pay, 122, 124
  training of teachers, 224
  registration, 240, 251
Association of Book-keeping Teachers, 253
Association of Directors and Secretaries for Education, 169, 318
Association of Education Committees, 39, 54, 56, 172, 299, 324, 345, 346–7
Association of Headmasters of Higher Grade Schools, 317
Association of Head Mistresses, 14, 17, 82
  foundation and aims, 11–12
  membership, 12–13
  salaries, 48, 77
  Burnham committee membership, 64
  equal pay, 108, 122–3
  training of teachers, 223–4, 230
  registration, 240, 245, 249, 250–6
  government of education, 315–16, 318, 322, 343
  women as H.M.Is., 331
  inspection of schools, 337
Association of Municipal Corporations, 39
Association of Principals of Technical Institutions, 17
Association of Teachers in Colleges and Departments of Education, 17, 284, 293, 296, 300–1, 305, 306, 309, 346
Association of Teachers in Technical Institutions, 35, 82, 137, 149, 187, 293, 346
  formation and membership, 15
  Burnham Committee membership, 64, 83
  closed shop issue, 183–5
  registration of teachers, 251, 254
Association of University Teachers, 18, 292

B.Ed. Degree, 266, 306, 307
Balfour, A. J., 157, 158
Beale, Miss Dorothea, 11, 217
Bell, G. C., 223

Benson, E. W., 7
Berkshire, 158
Birmingham, 45, 292, 326
Birrell, A., 170, 202, 208, 248
Bishop of Hereford, 168
Blackheath High School, 228
Black-listing, 173
Blair, Sir Robert, 106
Board of Education, 120, 285
   teachers' salaries, 25, 31, 37, 42, 49, 50, 51, 52, 61, 63
   mixed elementary schools, 117
   superannuation, 144
   attitude to security of tenure, 158–9, 161, 165, 167–73, 178
   attitude to extraneous duties, 187–9
   training of teachers, 201–12, 229–32, 267, 273–81, 309
   registration of teachers, 245–60
   emergency training scheme, 285–90
   establishment of, 313–21
   schemes for education committees, 323
   governing bodies of secondary schools, 326–8
   inspection, 330–8
   change of name, 339
Board of Education Act, 1899, 244, 247, 330
Board of Trade, 187, 188
Boddington, Dr. N., 198
Boyle, Sir Edward, 198
Bradford Grammar School, 211
Brighton, 218
Brighton School Board, 155
Bristol, 326
Bristol Grammar School, 325
Bristol University, 231, 292
British and Foreign Schools Society, 2, 195
British Association, 281
British Dental Association, 182, 184

British Federation of University Women, 124
British Medical Association, 182, 184, 235
British Society of Teachers, 2, 3
British Teachers Quarterly Association, 2
Brondesbury and Kilburn High School, 223
Browning, Oscar, 219, 220, 221
Bruce, W. N., 167, 168, 321
Bryant, Mrs. Sophie, 228, 249
Bryce Commission, 23, 165, 223, 225–7, 229, 315–16, 325, 333
   teachers' registration, 242–4, 245
Bryce, James, 242
Burnham Committees, 107, 141, 147, 191
   establishment of, 39, 45, 47, 49
   inter-war years, 50–1, 52, 53, 54–6, 62
   since 1939, 62, 63–71, 74–5, 78–80, 83–8
   fusion of elementary and secondary, 63–5, 341
   statutory position of, 63–4
   membership of, 64, 76, 77, 82, 116, 120–1
   relations with Minister, 84
   equal pay, 108–10, 120–2, 125–9
Burnham, Lord, 47, 52, 268
Burnham Reports, 52–3, 73
   of 1948, 1951 and 1954, 71, 74
   of 1956, 78–80, 147
   of 1965 and 1967, 84–5
   of 1969, 85–7
   of 1970, 88
Burnham Technical Committee, membership, 17
Buss, Miss Frances, 10, 11, 12, 13, 218
Butler, R. A., 286, 288, 338, 343
   and Burnham, 64–5, 70, 120, 121
   Chancellor of Exchequer, 126, 127

Buxton, 210

Cambridge, 215
Cambridge Training College for Women, 222
Cambridge University, 8, 70, 216, 218, 219, 221, 222, 239, 292
Canterbury, Archbishop of, 208
Cardiganshire, 51–2
Carmarthenshire, 52
Casey, T. A., 83
Central Advisory Committee for the Certification of Teachers, 275
Chambers, E. K., 273
Charity Commission, 23, 319, 320
and Tenure of Schoolmasters, 164–5, 166
Cheltenham College, 221
Cheltenham Ladies College, 11, 217, 223, 224, 227
Chiswick, 136
Church of England, 198
City of Leeds Training College, 267
City of London School, 216
Civil Service Commission, 8
Classical Association, 18
Closed Shop, 181–5
Clothworkers' Hall Conference, 1909, 254, 255, 256
'Code' pensions, 132–3
Colleges of Education, 307 (see also Training Colleges)
College of Preceptors, 18, 218–19, 227, 235, 238, 239, 240, 244, 245, 249, 251, 259
Collett, Miss, 240
Committee of Council for Education, 3, 132–3, 195
Committee of Vice-Chancellors, 273
Committee on Universities and Training Colleges, 275
Communist Party members in Middlesex, 185

Conference of Catholic Schools, 318
Conservative Parliamentary Party's Education Committee, 146
Consultative Committee (of the Board of Education), 168, 244, 245, 250
Conway, Miss E. R., 107, 109, 273
Corby, 87
Council of Principals of Training Colleges, 268, 269, 273
Council of Women Civil Servants, 124
County Councils Association, 39
Cove, W. G., 112
Cowper Street School, 220
Criminal offences by teachers, 181
Crosland, Mr. Anthony, 303
Cross Commission, 155
pensions for teachers, 132
training of teachers, 196, 197, 198
Crowther Report, 75
Croydon, 52
Croydon High School, 228
Cumin, P., 154, 155, 199

Day, Miss, 224
Day Training Colleges, 199–200
Deferred Annuity Fund, 135–6
Department of Education and Science (earlier Board, then Ministry of Education), 82, 83
relationship to Burnham Committee, 84
registration of teachers, 261
training of teachers, 303–10
Department of Employment and Productivity, 87, 95, 348
Departmental Committee on the Training of Teachers for Elementary Schools, 1923, 267, 270–3
Devonshire,
salaries of teachers in, 22, 25
Devonshire, Duke of, 319, 321

Dinner duties for teachers, 159, 187-9, 190-1
Dismissal of teachers, procedures post-1944, 179-80, 181
Divisional executives, 179, 339-40
Doncaster, 341
Dorking High School, 171
Dorset, 41
Dulwich, Alleyn's School, 167
Dunkerley, G. D., 49
Durham County Council and the closed shop issue, 181-5
Durham Education Authority, 86

East Ham, 104
Easterbrook, James, 254
Eccles, Sir David, 74, 128, 146-8, 306-7
Economist Intelligence Unit, 85
Economy (Miscellaneous Provisions) Act, 1926, 268
Education Acts, 1870, 1, 237
    1902, 10, 12, 14, 21, 24, 158, 166, 168, 197, 205, 208, 228, 266, 316, 321, 322, 326
    1918, 39, 139, 336
    1921, 188
    1944, 63, 65, 70, 72, 182, 187, 189, 301, 321, 347
Education (Administrative Provisions) Bill, 1906, 248-50
Education Bill, 1896, 244
Education Department, 154, 155, 319, 337
    superannuation, 134
    training of teachers, 196, 199
    registration, 240-4
Education (Provision of Meals) Act, 1906, 159
Education (Scotland) Act, 1908, 171
Educational Institute of Scotland, 240
Elementary School Teachers' (Superannuation) Act, 1898, 135, 136

Emergency Training Scheme, 285-90
Emmott, Lord, 141, 143
Emmott Report, 142-3
Endowed Schools Act, 1869, 7, 163, 168, 237
Endowed Schools Commissioners, 154, 164, 219, 325
Endowed Schools (Masters) Act, 1908, 170, 172
Engineers' Guild, 184
Equal Franchise Bill, 115
Equal Pay, 81-2, Chapter 5, *passim*
Equal Pay Campaign Committee, 120, 123-7
Equal Pay Co-ordinating Committee, 114, 125-6
Equal Pay League, 102
Equal Political Rights Campaign Committee, 114
Essex, 41, 52, 323
Eton, 164
Excepted Districts, 339-40
Exeter Girls' School, 232
Extraneous duties, 159, 187-91

Fawcett Society, 124
Federal Council of Secondary School Associations, 14, 249, 254
Federated Superannuation Scheme for Universities, 138, 140
Federation of Teachers in Central Classes, 203
Federation of Women Civil Servants, 115
Finsbury Training College, 220-1
Fisher, H. A. L., 172, 330
    teachers' salaries, 36-40, 111, 116
    teachers' superannuation, 138-9
Fitch, J. G., 225-6, 241
Fleming Committee on Public Schools, 342
Flemming, G. N., 286
Fletcher, W. C., 331

Fletcher-Cooke, C., 128
Forster, W. E., 1, 7, 237
'Forster's Bill No. 2', 237
Froud, Miss E. E., 115
Further Education and Training Scheme, 287

Gateshead, 51, 181
Geddes Committee (Committee on National Expenditure), 50, 53, 55, 140, 171
General Associated Body of Church Schoolmasters in England and Wales, 3
General Medical Council, 235
Giggleswick, 30
Girling, G., 241
Girls' Public Day School Company (later Trust), 11, 13, 165, 218, 219
Girton (College), 219
Gordon Square, 15, 17
Gorst, Sir John, 156, 157, 168, 244, 320, 332
Gould, Sir Ronald, 79, 84, 147, 308, 346
Gow, Dr. James, 251, 254
Graduate Teachers' Association, 76
Graham, Dr. J., 56
Grantham, King's School, 166-7
Gray, Ernest, 134
Grey, Mrs. W., 218, 222

Halifax, 136
Hamilton House, 15
Harrow, 164
Harwich, 52
Haverfordwest Grammar School, 173-4
Headlam, Principal, 207
Headmasters' Conference, 10, 17, 178
  foundation and aims, 6-8
  membership, 6-9

training of teachers, 219-22, 223, 227, 231, 281
registration, 240, 244, 245, 250
government of education, 316, 318-19, 328, 329
Hebdomadal Council of the University of Oxford, 318
Hedley Hill Council School, Durham, 161
Heller, T. E., 200, 238
Herefordshire teachers' strike, 27
Hertfordshire, 345
Historical Assocation, 18
Hoat-Dyke, Sir William, 242, 320
Hobhouse, Henry, 320
Hodgson, C. R., 240
Hodgson, G. E., 231
Holmes, E. G. A., 202, 333
Holmes, Sir Maurice, 113
Holmes-Morant Circular, 1910-11, 202, 217, 255, 333
Home and Colonial Training College, 218
Home Office, 188
Horsburgh, Florence, 74, 144-8
Hughes, Miss E. P., 215, 222
Hughes Hall, 222

Imperial Life Office, 137
Incorporated Association of Assistant Masters, 14, 76, 82, 185
  foundation and aims, 9-10
  membership, 10-11
  salaries pre-1914, 28-33
  salaries 1914-39, 39, 40-1, 42, 47, 51, 55, 57
  salaries since 1939, 66-7, 74, 76-7, 87
  Burnham committee membership, 64
  superannuation, 137, 147
  security of tenure, 165-74
  extraneous duties, 187, 190

Incorporated Association of Assistant Masters—*cont.*
  training of teachers, 224–5, 281, 304, 306, 309
  registration, 240, 246, 249, 251
  government of education, 320, 330
Incorporated Association of Head Masters, 14, 17, 82
  foundation and aims, 8–9
  membership, 8
  salaries, 48–9, 77
  Burnham committee membership, 64
  superannuation, 137
  security of tenure, 165, 167–71
  training of teachers, 227, 281, 293, 309–10
  registration, 240, 244, 245, 247–56
  government of education, 316–19, 323–30, 339, 341–6
  inspection of schools, 330, 337
Incorporated Phonographic Society, 252
Incorporated Society of Musicians, 253
Inspection (of schools), 330–8
Institutes of Education, 292, 306

Jenkins, Mr. Robert, 128
Joint Council of Heads, 17
Joint Four, 14, 35, 55, 142, 146–7, 149, 172, 178, 180
  Burnham committee, 65, 66–70
  the closed shop, 181–5, 186–7
  school meals, 190
  training of teachers, 293, 305
  government of education, 342, 346
Jones, A. Gray, 57

Kay-Shuttleworth, Sir James, 195, 216
Keir, Mrs. Cazalet, 120, 121–2
Kekewich, G., 133, 167, 332

Kempe, Sir John, Treasury committee chairman, 35
  Report of, 37
King, Dr. H., 128
King Edward VII School, Sheffield, 328–9
King's College, London, 3, 207
King's Scholarship Examination, 206
King's School, Canterbury, 7
Kynaston, H., 221

Labour Party, 124, 126, 269
Law Society, 235
L.C.C. General Powers Bill, 1908, 136
L.C.C. Staff Association, 114
Leeds School Board,
  salaries, 22–3
Leeds, teachers' salaries in, 25, 30
Leeson, Canon, 343
Liberal Party, 237
Lindsay, Kenneth, 69
Lingen, R. R. W., 132
Liverpool, 334
Liverpool University, 290, 292
Lloyd George, 137
Local Government Act, 1958, 340, 347
Local Government Manpower Committee, 344
London Association of Art Masters, 252
London County Council, 104–5, 106, 107, 167, 169, 277
London Day Training College, 228
London School Board, 134
London School Board Superannuation Bill, 134
London Schoolmasters' Association, 109, 117
London Teachers' Association, 86, 111
London Teachers' Salaries, 27–8, 31, 33–4

London University, 218, 239
Lowe, Robert, 133
Lowestoft, 51
Lubbock, Sir John, 238
Lumby, Miss, 224
Lunn, Sir George, 54, 108

Macan, H., 318
McKenna, 211
McNair, Sir Arnold, 290
McNair Committee, 290-3
McNair Committee's Report, 1944, 61, 72, 297
MacNamara, T. J., 157, 158
Magnus, Sir Philip, 138, 253
Manchester, 326
Manchester Grammar School, 216-17
Manchester High School, 224
Mander, Sir Frederick, 62, 179
Maria Gray Training College, 222, 223
Marlborough, 223
Mason, J., 122
Mathematics Association, 18
May Committee on National Expenditure, 1931, 53
Mayor, R. G., 275
Meals and Milk—teachers' duties, 159, 187-91
Medical Registration Act, 1858, 236, 239
Medical Registration Act, 1862, 235
Merchant Taylors' School, 167
Mercier, Winifred, 269
Merrick, M., 271
Middlesex County Association (N.U.T.), 185
Middlesex County Council, 169
political tests for teachers, 185-6
Minister of Pensions, 119-20
Ministry of Agriculture, 188
Ministry of Education (earlier Board of Education), 75, 81, 83, 346-7
creation of, 339

security of tenure, 179-81
closed shop issue, 181-5
political tests for teachers, 185-6
registration of teachers, 239
area training organisations, 290-3
training of teachers, 293-302
Ministry of Food, 187, 188
Ministry of Health, 188
Ministry of Housing and Local Government, 347
Ministry of Labour, 184, 188
Ministry of Supply, 188
Mitchinson, J., 7
Morant, Robert, 34, 169, 320, 321, 327
and teacher training, 202, 211, 229
and registration of teachers, 248-60
and inspection of schools, 330-5
Mountain Ash, 104
Mundella, A. J., 332

National Advisory Council on the Training and Supply of Teachers, 74, 261, 293-4, 296, 298, 299-302, 304-5, 306
National Association for the Promotion of Social Science, 200, 238
National Association of Head Teachers, 82, 161
membership, 17
salaries, 68, 79
Burnham Committee, 83, 129
school meals, 190
National Association of Local Government Officers, 119, 124, 125
National Association of Men Teachers, 16, 111, 117
National Association of Schoolmasters,
formation, 15-17
relations with N.U.T., 81-2, 85-9, 112-14, 117-18, 124, 146

National Association of Schoolmasters—cont.
  membership of Burnham Committee, 82, 83, 116, 117–18, 120–1, 128–9
  affiliation to T.U.C., 82
  1969 salary negotiations, 85
  equal pay, 109–10, 112–13, 118, 127
  meals in schools, 190–1
  training of teachers, 295, 300, 302, 304, 309
  block grants, 346
  increasing influence of, 348
National Association of Teachers of the Deaf, 253
National Association of Women Civil Servants, 124
National Council of Women, 124
National Economy Bill, 1931, 54
National Federation of Assistant Teachers, 200
National Federation of Class Teachers, 17, 62, 68, 80, 161, 287
National Federation of Women's Institutes, 124
National Federation of Women Teachers, 16, 102
  the suffrage, 103
  equal pay, 105–6, 109, 110, 112
National Health Insurance, 137, 327, 335
National Manpower Service, 348
National Society, 2, 194, 208
National Society for Art Education, 17
National Training School for Music, 240
National Union for Improving the Education of Women of all Classes, 218
National Union of Bank Employees, 124
National Union of Elementary Teachers (see National Union of Teachers)
National Union of Teachers, 8, 14, 15, 18, 163, 173
  foundation and aims, 1, 4–5
  membership, 6, 16–17
  salaries before 1914, 25, 26–7, 35
  salaries 1914–39, 36, 39, 45–7, 51, 55, 56–7, 62
  salaries since 1939, 64–70, 76, 78–81, 85–9
  superannuation, 50, 133–6, 140–50
  Burnham committee membership, 64
  relations with N.A.S., 81–2, 85–9, 112–14, 117–18, 124, 146
  equal pay before 1920, 102–10
  equal pay 1920–45, 110–23
  equal pay after 1945, 123–9
  relations with N.U.W.T., 114
  tenure of elementary teachers before 1944, 155–62, 174
  closed shop issue, 181–5, 186
  political tests in Middlesex, 185–7
  meals and milk in schools, 185–91
  training of teachers, 196, 200, 202–12, 225, 229, 269–79, 283–90, 293–304
  registration of teachers, 238–9, 245–61
  administration of education, 314–21, 322–4, 339–41, 346–8
  inspection of schools, 331–8
  Act of 1944, 339
National Union of Women Teachers, 287
  formation, 15–16
  equal pay, 113–29
  dissolution, 81, 127–8
  relations with N.U.T., 114
  tactics of, 115–16
  headships of mixed schools, 117

Index

National Union of Women Teachers —cont.
   membership of Burnham Committee, 120-1
National Whitley Council, 124, 125-7
Newcastle, 136
Newcastle Commission, 3
   and pensions for teachers, 133
Newcastle-under-Lyme, 52
Newnham (College), 219
Northamptonshire, 161
North London Collegiate School, 10, 13, 218, 229
North of England Conference, 271
Norwich, 326
Norwood, C., 169
Norwood Committee, 337
Notting Hill High School, 228

Oxford University, 8, 216, 219, 239

Paton, J. L., 257
Part III Education Authorities, 321, 338-40
Pease, J. A., 257, 258
Pelham Committee, 18
Pembroke (borough), 52
Pembrokeshire County Council, 173
Pensions (Increase) Act, 1944, 144
Pensions (Increase) Acts, 1956, 1959, 1963, 1966, 1969, 150
Percy, Lord Eustace, 52, 142-3, 273
Personal Injuries (Emergency Provisions) Act, 119
'Peter Quince', 289, 340
Phipps, Emily, 115
Pickles, A. R., 203-4
Pickthorn, K. W. M., 70
Pierotti, Miss, 127
Playfair, Lyon, 238
Plowden Committee, 304
Plowden Report, 304

Plymouth, 326
Poole, Rev. R. B., 240
Preliminary Certificate Examination of the Board of Education, 25-6
Preparatory Schools' Association, 227, 251
Prices and Incomes Board, 86
Provincial Medical and Surgical Association, 235
Public Schools Act, 1868, 7, 163, 239
Public Schools Commission, Report of, 1864, 163
Public Service Pensions' Council, 150
Pupil-Teacher Centres, 201-5
Pupil-Teacher Regulations of 1903, 201
Pupil-teacher system, 195-200, 201-5, 209

Queen's Scholarships, 195-8
Quick, R. H., 216, 219

Reading University, 258, 292
Redundancy among teachers, 159-61, 171, 174, 180-1
Regulations for the Training of Teachers for Secondary Schools, 1908, 229
Remuneration of Teachers Act, 1965, 84
Revised Code of 1862, 3, 196
Richmond Grammar School Case, 170
Robbins Committee on Higher Education, 305-7
Roscoe, F., 273
Rouse, W. H. D., 23
Roy, Sir William, 278
Royal Academy of Music, 240
Royal College of Music, 240
Royal College of Nursing, 124, 182, 184
Royal College of Organists, 252

Royal Commission on Civil Service, 1912, 331, 335
Royal Commission on Equal Pay, 1945, 113, 114, 122-3
Royal Commission on Local Government, 1966-9, 348
Royal Commission on Secondary Education (*see* Bryce Commission)
Royal Drawing Society, 252
Royal Institute of British Architects, 235
Rugby, 164, 232
Rule, B., 236
Runciman, Walter, 211, 253, 255, 328

Sadler, Michael, 29, 256, 321
St. Helens, 136
St. Paul's School, 216
Salaries, Chapters 2, 3, 4, *passim*
Saunders, V. T., 281
School boards, 314-15, 321
  salaries, 21, 24
Schoolmasters' Defence and Legal Assistance Society, 87
Schools Inquiry Commission, Report of, 163, 325
School Teachers' Superannuation Bill, 1922, 50, 140
Science and Art Department, 319, 330, 331, 337
Science Masters' Association, 18
Scotch Education Commission, 154
Scott, Dr. R. P., 246, 319
Secondary School Regulations of 1906-7, 201, 230
Secondary, Technical and University Teachers Insurance Society, 137
Secretary of State for Scotland, 149
Sedbergh, 30
Selby-Bigge, L. A., 166, 335-6

Select Committee on Education and Science, 1970, 310
Select Committee on London School Board Superannuation Bill, 1891, 134
Select Committee on Teachers' Pensions, 133
Select Committee on the Teachers' Registration and Organisation Bill, 1891, 223
Select Committee on Teachers' Registration, 239, 240-2
Sharp, Sir Percival, 62, 329
Sheffield, 328
Sheffield Corporation, 160
Short, Edward, 260-1, 308
Sidgwick, Henry, 219, 249
Simpson, Miss Helen, 300
Snowden, P., 203
Society of Art Masters, 252
Society of Certificated Teachers of Shorthand, 253
Soulbury, Lord, 70-1
Southampton, 51, 292
Southport, 136
South Shields, 51
Spens Committee's Report, 1938, 61, 72
Standard forms of agreement between teachers and employers, 172
Standing Joint Committee for Salaries in Elementary Schools, 45 (*see also* Burnham Committee)
Standing Joint Committee for Salaries in Secondary Schools, 47 (*see also* Burnham Committee)
Stockton-on-Tees, 184
Strikes (among teachers), 27, 51, 87
Suffragette Fellowship, 124
Sullivan, Sir Arthur, 240
Superannuation, 38, 50, Chapter 6, *passim*, 156

Superannuation Act, 1898, 156
Superannuation Bill, 1925, 142
Surplus of teachers, 174-5
Sustentation Fund of the I.A.A.M., 171
Sykes, J. P., 211

Tate, Mrs. Mavis, 119, 120
Taunton Commission, 236-7
Teacher Training Syndicate (Cambridge), 219, 221
Teachers' General Council, 260-1
Teachers' Guilds, 18, 19
Teachers' Provident Society, 135
Teachers' Registration Bill, 1879, 238
Teachers' Registration Council, 245-8, 254, 257-60, 270
Teachers' (Superannuation) Act, 1918, 38, 139-41, 161, 336
Teachers' (Superannuation) Act, 1937, 148
Teachers' Superannuation (War Service) Act, 1939, 143
Teachers' Training and Registration Society, 222
Technical Instruction Act, 1889, 166
Temple, Dr. Frederick, 3, 7
Temple, Sir Richard, 135, 239
Thomas, A. A., 200
Thomas, G., 295
Thomas, W. Jenkyn, 53
Thring, Edward, 7
Tottenham, 104
Towers, John, case of, 161-2
Trades Disputes Act, 1927, 181
Trades Union Congress, 82
Training College Regulations of 1904, 205
Training Colleges, 198-200, 205-7, 277-9
  local authorities and, 266-8
  emergency, 285-90
Training Colleges Association, 273

Treasury, the, 35, 305, 346
  teachers' superannuation, 134-5, 136, 137, 139, 143, 144, 149
  registration of teachers, 247, 258
  training colleges, 268, 287
Trevelyan Committee, 1853, 331

Unemployment of teachers, 277-9
Union of Graduates in Music Incorporated, 252
Union of Teachers of the Deaf on the Pure Oral System, 253
University Colleges, 199-200
University Departments of Education, 306
University Schools of Education, 291-2, 306
Upjohn, W. M., 52
Uppingham School, 7, 281

Walker, F. W., 216, 217
War Cabinet's Committee on Women in Industry, 1919, 107, 108
War Office, 8
War Savings Organisation, 188
Warre, Dr. E., 228, 319
Webb, Mrs. Sydney, 7
Wellington, 281
Welsh Intermediate Education Act, 1889, 166, 167
West Riding, teachers' salaries, 30, 40
Western Joint Board, 275
Westminster School, 251
Whitelands College, 269
Whitgift School, Croydon, 329
Whitley Councils, 324
Wilkinson, Ellen, 115
Wimbledon, 52
Wiltshire, 41
Withers, Professor, 246
Women's Engineering Society, 124

Women's Freedom League, 124
Women Teachers' Franchise Union, 16
Wood, M. P., 254
Wood, Sir Robert, 285–6

Yorkshire College, Leeds, 198

Yorkshire Training Colleges Examination Board, 292
Young Teacher Conference (N.U.T.), 86
Youth Employment Service, 348
Yoxall, J. H., 134, 156, 208, 211, 253, 315, 334